## THE WELL-DRESSED REVOLUTIONAR

*Ithaka gave you the marvellous journey.
Without her you wouldn't have set out.
She has nothing left to give you now.*

*And if you find her poor, Ithaka won't have fooled you.
Wise as you will have become, so full of experience,
you'll have understood by then what these Ithakas mean.*

**C. P. Cavafy,**
'Ithaka', translated by Edmund Keeley

Resistance Books, London
The International Institute for Education and Research, Amsterdam

# THE WELL-DRESSED
# REVOLUTIONARY

The Odyssey of Michel Pablo in the age of uprisings

**Hall Greenland**

Published 2023 by Resistance Books and the
International Institute for Education and Research

Copyright © 2023 by Hall Greenland

All rights reserved

The moral right of the author has been asserted

No part of this book may be used or reproduced in any manner whatsoever
without written permission from the Publisher and Author
except in the case of brief quotations embodied in critical articles or reviews

Every reasonable effort has been made to trace copyright holders
of material reproduced in this book but if any have been inadvertently
overlooked the publishers would be glad to hear from them

ISBN print 978-0-902869-10-3
ISBN e-book 978-0-902869-07-3

Resistance Books
resistancebooks.org
info@resistancebooks.org

The International Institute for Education and Research
iire.org
iire@iire.org

*The Well-Dressed Revolutionary: the Odyssey of Michel Pablo*
is issue No. 75 of the Notebooks for Study and Research
published by the International Institute for Research and Education.

Typeset in Simoncini Garamond
Cover and text design by Hannah Design

Cover photograph:
a hand-cuffed Pablo escorted into court in Amsterdam,
4 October 1960.
Photographer: Dick Coersen.

Photographs courtesy of ELIA in Athens
and the International Institute of Social History in Amsterdam.

## CONTENTS

|  | Background note: Michel Pablo – The extraordinary life of a utopian realist | VII |
|---|---|---|
|  | Prologue: A death in Athens | 1 |
| 1 | In the beginning was Tolstoy 1911-1936 | 6 |
| 2 | Prison, Elly and exile 1937-1938 | 17 |
| 3 | Dangerous liaisons 1938-1942 | 24 |
| 4 | Pablo's war 1943-1946 | 34 |
| 5 | The revolution will happen (but elsewhere) 1945-1950 | 50 |
| 6 | Mohammed must go to the mountain 1950-1955 | 68 |
| 7 | Vive la révolution algérienne 1954-1962 | 83 |
| 8 | The arms factory in Morocco 1955-1960 | 99 |
| 9 | The trial of Pablo and Santen 1960-1961 | 116 |
| 10 | Prison writings – women, Freud, Cuba, classical Athens and late Marx 1960-1961 | 124 |
| 11 | Joining the Wretched of the Earth 1961-1963 | 139 |
| 12 | Pablo's wager: Athens in Algiers 1962-1965 | 158 |
|  | Illustrations: The Odyssey of Michel Pablo | 181 |
| 13 | Parallel defeats (and Rosa) 1964-1965 | 189 |
| 14 | The Gypsy Years 1965-1968 | 207 |
| 15 | Great expectations: Paris, Prague and Palestine 1968-1969 | 226 |
| 16 | Close escapes and Chile 1970-1973 | 236 |
| 17 | The turn to Europe 1970s | 253 |
| 18 | End of an era 1980s | 269 |
| 19 | The fate of friends and comrades 1980s | 289 |
| 20 | The last battle: how Green is my party? 1988-1989 | 304 |
| 21 | A new era: the final years 1989-1996 | 316 |
|  | Epilogue: A prophet out of time | 336 |
|  | Acknowledgements | 344 |
|  | Endnotes | 347 |
|  | Names index | 368 |
|  | Chapter outlines | 373 |

In memory of Jack, Margaret and Tony

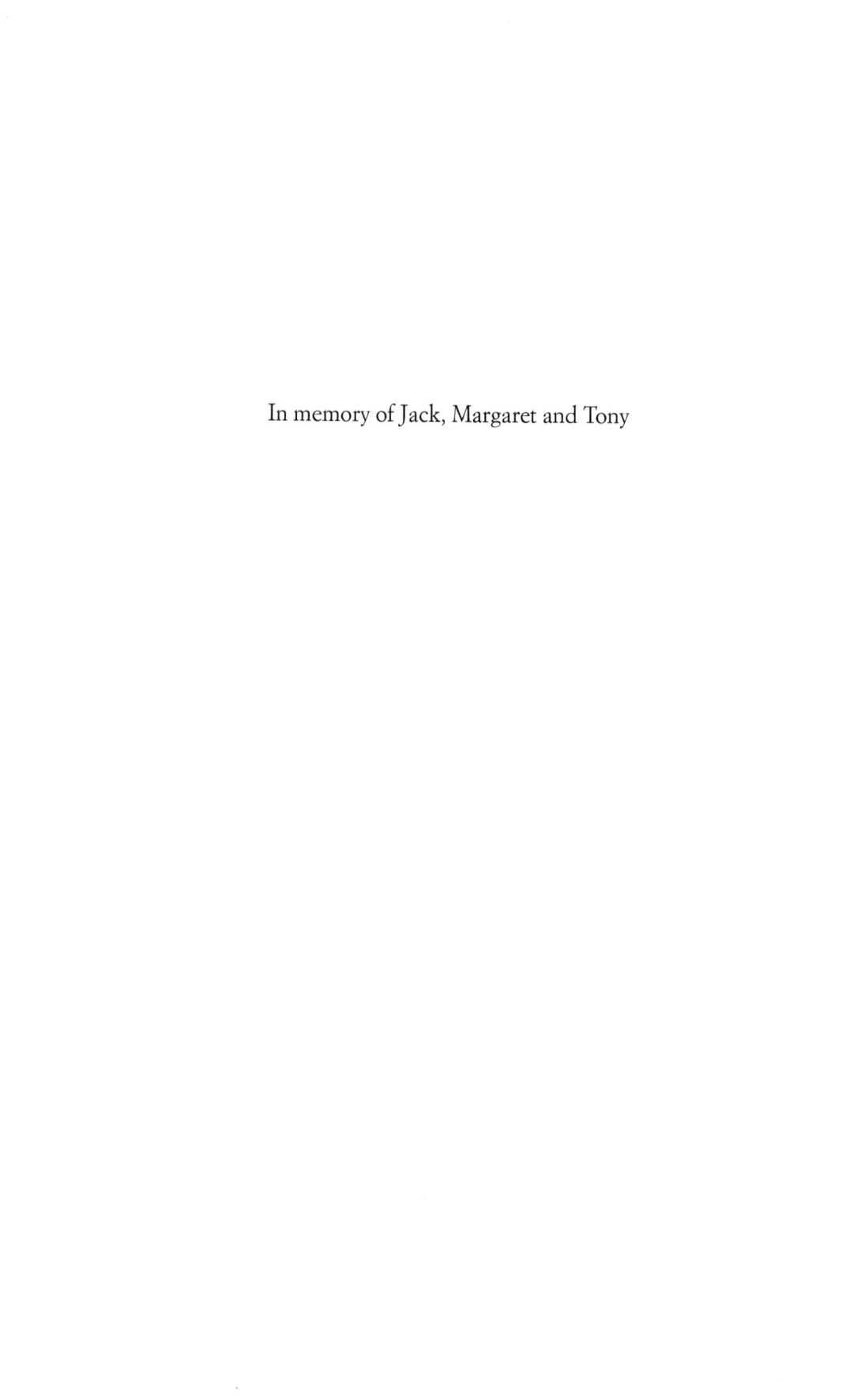

## BACKGROUND NOTE: MICHEL PABLO – THE EXTRAORDINARY LIFE OF A UTOPIAN REALIST

Michael Pablo was a 20th century revolutionary whose life and ideas remain relevant and inspirational in the 21st.

He spent his life engaged in revolutions around the globe – in Greece, France, Algeria, Chile, Palestine and Portugal, to name the most important – everywhere pursuing a genuinely democratic socialism. He was a hands-on participant who advocated and worked for what he called 'generalised self-management or direct democracy' – on a local, regional, national and planetary scale. For Pablo, this was utopian but realisable.

He had a great gift for friendship and was a friend his comrades could always count on – to campaign in your defence when you were in danger or in prison, to help you escape prison, or shelter you when you were on the run.

A life-long egalitarian, he never pretended to be anything else but a relatively privileged cosmopolitan intellectual. He certainly dressed as a bourgeois professional.

In 1960 Pablo wrote a pamphlet anticipating (and celebrating) the prospect of a mass women's liberation movement. In his own life, he was fortunate enough to have in Elly Diovouniotis a fiery, life-long and ever-supportive partner.

In the frequently fractious world of the Left, he was renowned for his tolerance, politeness, patience and generosity, while never resiling from his principles. Nevertheless, his bold and adventurous Marxism earned him enemies and detractors.

Growing up in Cairo and Crete, Michalis Raptis (to give Pablo his real name) began his conscious political life as a Tolstoyan and, while he became a revolutionary Marxist as a student in Athens in the 1930s, he never suppressed the ethical or spiritual influence of Tolstoy and the

Russian's anarcho-communist pacifism. For the famous Greek composer, Mikis Theodorakis, Pablo was something of 'a biblical personage'.

Right into his 80s, he never stopped analysing, writing and campaigning. In all the big demonstrations and pickets in Paris and Athens, the tall, distinguished figure of Michel Pablo could be present – usually wearing a fedora. He was a columnist for not one, but two, Greek daily newspapers and wrote regularly for *Sous le drapeau du socialisme* and *Utopie Critique*.

He had his faults – he was reluctant to admit to error and could be blindly loyal. But his strengths – his insistence on full and direct democracy in all spheres of society, his principled life, his sympathy for the 'wretched of the Earth', an early recognition of the ecological crisis, the need for planetary solutions, the shape of the new revolutionary 'subject', the continued relevance of an open and creative Marxism, the value of an imaginative utopianism – make him vitally relevant in this new century.

PROLOGUE
# A death in Athens

> *'I am a friend of Michel' was one of the best passports all over the world and among the most diverse and sometimes surprising people. Whatever other passport you were traveling with, it opened many doors in the heart of an informal International, among those who remembered and knew what services had been rendered by the man you claimed kinship with.*
>
> David Maurin[1]

THE OLD REVOLUTIONARY knew he was soon to die. Seven months earlier he had given a valedictory interview to Adolfo Gilly, a professor of history and erstwhile revolutionary who had, himself, served six years in a Mexican prison during the 1960s as a result of helping the Guatemalan guerrillas. The interview, conducted on a balcony of a small hotel in the Greek seaside town of Horefto, overlooking the Aegean Sea, had spread over four days, and on a number of occasions Michel Pablo had declared that his death was fast approaching.

The heart attack came without warning as he sat with friends for his morning coffee in the centre of Athens, on the famed Kolonaki Square. The Greek journalist Stavroula Panagiotaki has left us a record of the last walks of Michel Pablo or, to give him his real name, Michalis Raptis, a man she describes as 'the most noble of our revolutionaries'.[2] He was then in his eighty-fifth year, still active, a well-known newspaper columnist and still married to his beloved Elly Diovouniotis:

> … the morning patrons of Kolonaki Square cafes remember the image of that well-dressed couple, of strikingly different heights, coming up the hill from

their small two-room flat on Loukianou Street, towards the busy square to drink their coffee. He was 'Mister Michalis' and she 'Mrs Elly', as they were respectfully addressed by everyone, including their closest friends. Even when serious illness prevented his wife from accompanying him, Michalis Raptis did the morning walk on his own, and returned at the time he estimated Elly would be awake, to prepare her breakfast. Yet, that morning in February he didn't get home from the café in time. His ailing heart beat him to it.

He had been felled by a massive heart attack. It was 16 February 1996. That night in hospital, Panagiotaki relates:

> ... in a momentary breath of life, he uttered his last wish, 'Look after Elly for me,' he whispered to his close friends. 'Don't forget. I'm leaving now.' A few hours later, at dawn the next day, the angel of death fluttered for a moment in the sterile, white room and went out by the window, leaving a line of feathers in its wake.

The loving concern for Elly was a constant in his life. Sixty years previously he had met her in leftist circles in Athens, and two years later had fallen in love with her on a prison island in the far reaches of the Aegean Sea. His loyalty to her was occasionally considered excessive by male comrades, but her love for him had been the indispensable foundation of his life as a revolutionary. She had supported him for much of their life together and, on at least two occasions, she had literally saved his life. In his last years he had gladly accepted the role of chief nurse and aide to her as her condition deteriorated. An old Dutch comrade, Maurice Ferares[3], recalled – with some astonishment – how Pablo even accompanied Elly to the bathroom during a visit to Amsterdam in 1994.[4]

The death of Michel Pablo was headline news in Greece. The main conservative daily, *Kathemerini*, carried the story on its front page with a photograph of him in a dark suit, white shirt and red tie, carrying a newspaper and a trench coat draped over his arm. On his head was a fedora with a jauntily turned-up brim, every inch the 'elegant revolutionary' that David Maurin, an old associate, had once dubbed him. The paper also published a eulogy the following day on page 1, titled 'A citizen of the world'. The liberal dailies in Paris and London, *Le Monde* and *The Guardian*, followed suit with their own obituaries.

His funeral took place in Athens' oldest cemetery on 21 February 1996, with hundreds of people lining up hours before to view the open coffin. 'They came from all walks of life,' recalled Savvas Michael, then a middle-aged doctor who for two decades had been a fierce factional critic but lately mellowed into a friend and comrade. 'There were literary figures, workers, peasants, students, old people and young people. They may not have known all his ideas but they saw him as someone who stood for revolution and was always on the "right" side. Someone who had dedicated his life to human emancipation. He died as a hero of the people.'

As journalists noted, half the Greek cabinet was there, as were various would-be revolutionaries, along with far less reputable figures. Not far from Stelios Papathemelis, a notorious law-and-order PASOK conservative and Public Order Minister, stood Kyriakos Mazokopos, an equally notorious anarchist bank robber.

It wasn't exactly a state funeral, but one nonetheless that the socialist party (or PASOK) government of the day saw fit to pay for. Andreas Papandreou, the former prime minister and PASOK's founder, was too ill to attend but sent a wreath and message of farewell to 'the unforgettable Michalis'. In their youth the two had briefly shared the same political mentor and hero before their paths diverged. They had converged again during the late 60s and early 70s when the military junta ruled Greece, before separating once more. They remained wary friends until the very end.

When the funeral commenced at 3 pm, Papandreou's son and future PASOK prime minister, Georges Papandreou, spoke first, calling Michel Pablo his teacher. ('If that was true, then he was a bad student,' recalled Savvas.) Gilbert Marquis spoke for the wider circle of supporters. He had come from Paris with Simonne Minguet and Pierre Avot-Meyers, former comrades-in-arms from the wartime Resistance and Algerian underground. Hugo Moreno, then a professor in Paris and former Latin American militant, also travelled from France. Spyros Bafaloukos, the cardiologist, and Christos Gogornas, the Montessori school director, spoke for Pablo's Greek comrades. The dean at Ioannina University, Panagiotis Noutsos, paid tribute to Pablo's learning and spoke of the honorary doctorate the university had bestowed on him just months earlier. The old Trotskyist Sotiros Goudelis also made his unscheduled way to the front to speak of the youth he had shared with Pablo in Athens during the 1930s.

Manolis Glezos spoke for the Greek radical left. Glezos had become a national hero in 1941 when, at the age of 18, he'd scaled the Acropolis to tear down the Nazi flag, a crazy brave act that had earned him the title of 'Europe's first partisan' from none other than Charles de Gaulle. Glezos' long journey as a communist had led him to the socialist ideals that were close to Pablo's. During the 1980s Glezos had returned to Apeiranthos, a village on the island of Naxos where he'd then been elected mayor in 1986. He opened up council meetings to all the citizens of the village in a manner reminiscent of the classical Athenian polis.[5] He was, in effect, anticipating the kind of self-managed socialist future that Pablo had championed.

Also in attendance that memorable afternoon were the ambassadors of Iraq, Algeria, Cuba, Libya and Serbia. The Algerian presence was no surprise, given that Pablo had played as large a role as any European in the Algerian Revolution, and in the short-lived experiment with self-managed socialism that followed independence. But the presence of ambassadors from what Pablo had described as 'outlaw' countries was discomforting to some, particularly given Iraqi ambassador Esam Saoud Halil's decision to deliver a eulogy that afternoon.

In the last years of his life, Pablo had organised a campaign – in partnership with Margaret Papandreou (Andreas' former American wife), Algerian revolutionary-turned-president Ahmed Ben Bella, veteran British Labour left-winger Tony Benn and journalist Christopher Hitchens, amongst others – to break the American-imposed blockades on Iraq, Cuba and Libya. In the case of Iraq, Pablo had no time for the country's murderous dictator Saddam Hussein, but he had plenty of time for the Iraqi people who were suffering mightily under the impact of US sanctions. (It is estimated that some half a million Iraqi children had their lives cut short because of these sanctions.) This same logic of solidarity with the victims of imperialism had extended to the Serbs whom he saw as struggling against an American, German and Turkish alliance designed to carve up the Balkans into respective zones of influence. It was a view shared by many Greeks.

The final speaker that day was psychiatrist Marika Karageorgiou, a striking woman who, under the terms of Pablo's will, was there as the executor of his estate and spokesperson for Pablo's "children". 'For those of us who you inspired and educated to pursue the battle for equality, freedom and human solidarity, you will never die,'[6] she told the assembly.

Karageorgiou's presence was entirely congruent with Pablo's own early feminism and enthusiasm for Freud. In his 1960 essay on the liberation of women, he had anticipated the rise of a mass feminist movement and insisted on the moral imperative of revolutionaries living their lives according to egalitarian principles. In his view – and in the view of all those who would seek to emulate him, including this writer – the personal was always political.

With tributes delivered – and to cries of 'immortal' and 'long live the revolution' – the coffin was conveyed to the open grave. As it was lowered, the crowd broke into a rendition of the Internationale with the mourners casting so many red roses and carnations into the grave that one reporter observed there was little room left for the earth to be returned.[7]

Those who had gathered for the funeral in Athens' First Cemetery knew they were farewelling a confirmed revolutionary. For the past 20 years he had laid out his views in regular columns for two Greek newspapers. His 'political autobiography' had also been published in Athens. He appeared not infrequently on television there. But his reach was wider than Greece. As the presence of those ambassadors testified, he had spent his life on numerous continents fighting for his ideals. 'I am an internationalist who loves his country,' he'd said in his last newspaper interview.[8] Michalis Raptis, aka Michel Pablo (the pseudonym he used for most of his revolutionary life), had seen himself as heir to the 5th century Athenian experiment of a participatory democracy and shared commonwealth, one that through a continuous process of revolution and experimentation, he believed could become an actuality for the modern world.[9]

In the 1990s he recognised – how could he not? – that the emancipatory left had returned to ground zero, and while the grand utopia was possible, especially in Europe, there were immediate, pressing and essentially defensive campaigns to be waged against a new barbaric and destructive phase of global capitalism.[10] 'In the march towards a utopia in Europe, the single Europe that is possible and necessary,' he wrote a few years before he died, 'the radical politico-social forces will have to act in the ranks of the real mass movements, taking into account the modest possibilities which we will encounter for a long period.'[11]

**The long odyssey of this Greek revolutionary had begun nearly 85 years earlier in Alexandria.**

CHAPTER 1
# In the beginning was Tolstoy
## 1911-1936

*Clichés such as 'revolutionary' or 'progressive' in themselves mean very little in art. Dostoyevsky, especially in his later writing, is an outspoken reactionary, a religious mystic, bigot and hater of socialists. His depictions of Russian revolutionaries are malicious caricatures. Tolstoy's mystic doctrines reflect revolutionary tendencies, if not more. But the writings of both have, nevertheless, an inspiring and liberating effect on us. And this is because ... they have the warmest love of mankind and the deepest response to social injustice.*

**Rosa Luxemburg**
Preface to the autobiography of V. Korolenko

MICHALIS RAPTIS WAS born on 24 August 1911, in the Egyptian city of Alexandria, the largest city on the Mediterranean coast. His father was a Greek-born civil engineer, son of a military officer from the north of Greece. His mother was the daughter of a couple who had eloped from Crete and settled in Alexandria. According to Raptis, his mother's father was a Cretan who had emigrated from the island, 'stealing away' with a Jewish girl who had converted and married him when they reached Alexandria. Their daughter, Michalis's mother, had been well educated for a woman of her generation, fluent in both French and Arabic.

Soon after his birth the family moved to Cairo and then, when he was six, to Crete where, together with a younger brother and sister, he spent the greater part of his childhood. It left a vivid impression. In the memoir he wrote in his early 70s, he recalled those years. What he remembered of Cairo was the desert that surrounded his neighbourhood, his visits to the Cairo zoo and the 'black servant' who carried him 'on his shoulders as he ran me to school'.[1] For his Cretan years he lovingly summoned up the places he encountered with his father. 'The whole of Crete then had a primitive beauty which sang deeply into my heart,' he wrote. 'I remember the peaceful traditional scenery of the small town – really a village then – of St Nicolas (Agios Nikolaos) with the boats in the harbour, the still waters where I often fished, far from the legendary horror of the nearby island of Spinalonga where lepers were sent to slowly die. Inaccessible to me, that island was the only subject of conversation which dampened the poetic atmosphere in which my childhood passed.'

Michalis attended a village school and, in summer, travelled all over the island with his father, Nicholas, who was supervising the building of roads, bridges and a lighthouse overlooking the Libyan Sea. He had his first encounter, too, with peasants in the mountains of the island and remembered them as independent-spirited, proud of their freedom.

Perhaps because he was living in a relative backwater, there is nothing in his account of his childhood on Crete between 1917 and 1927 about the Exchange of Population that occurred in the early 1920s. The Turkish-Greek war that followed the First World War saw a million Greeks uprooted from Turkey and re-settled in Greece. About 800,000 Muslims were forced from Greece to Turkey. In Crete, about 30,000 Muslims (mostly from the main towns of Iraklion, Chania and Rethymno), were ejected and replaced by an equal number of Turkish Christians.[2] Pablo was only 11 then and a recent history of Crete claims that the resettlement went smoothly on the island in contrast to elsewhere in Greece.[3]

His dreamlike youth on Crete was, however, marred by one signal tragedy: the death of his sister Olga at the age of eight. Pablo could remember lying awake for nights afterwards listening to the sobs of his father and fearing that his 'papa' would also die.

Nicholas had decided that his older son was to be a civil engineer, although his son's interests were increasingly literary. By the time Michalis was a teenager he knew he wanted to be a writer, an ambition he attributed to his mother. With friends he created a number of literary magazines, also a home for his own stories. Three of these stories have survived and, according to the online magazine *Kedrisos*[4], which republished them in 2014, they have merit. One was published in *Avgeniros* in 1926 and the next two were originally published in *Domenikos Theotokopoulos* in 1927. The first, *The "Crazy" Mother*, was written when he was 14 and is a gothic, melodramatic story – to say the least – centred on the final night of a poor, single mother stricken with grief at the death of her baby. The second, *Towards the West*, is a dreamlike and sympathetic account of the last hours of a convict recalling the sweet memories of his lost family life. The third and longer story, *Verger of the Country Chapel*, deals with the life and death of a saintly outcast in a Cretan mountain village in a bygone time.

'The heroes of his stories,' as the editorial introduction by *Kedrisos* points out, 'the mother ..., the convict Larmas ... and Fotinos in *Verger of the country chapel*, are types that "polite" society characterises as strange, outcast, marginal.' The stories were also praised by the editors for their use of the vernacular, their mastery of narrative and suspense, the deployment of the 'penetrating phrase to dissect the character of his protagonists' and the documenting of the social conditions of the time.

Their obvious compassion reflected the teenage author's growing sympathy for 'the wretched of the earth'. Compassion is the gift of the privileged to the less fortunate – and the young Pablo had been born into a comfortable professional middle-class family, a circumstance he could not have been unaware of. Key to a sense of compassion is an awareness of the injustice of the world and of how privilege is a result of birth and luck and is often based on the misery of others. For any Tolstoyan, that understanding inescapably leads to taking moral and revolutionary action, and by his teenage years Pablo had become a Tolstoyan Christian. His first public talk, when he was 16, was an address to the local literary society on the great Russian novelist. This youthful embrace of Tolstoy's philosophy was to accompany Pablo throughout his life. (Admittedly, there is also an element of noblesse oblige in Tolstoyan ideology, and a few future comrades would sometimes detect this in Pablo – and even more in his wife – and be irked by it.)

Fifty years later, in an introduction to Yvon Bourdet's book *Qu'est-ce qui fait courir les militants?* (Paris, 1976), he described his radicalisation in distinctly Tolstoyan terms:

> My own path as a revolutionary militant was marked by an initial period when, still a young child, the church tempted me because of the mixture of the mystical and the pagan which the Greek Orthodox church embodies. For me, it was essentially the aesthetic aspect that predominated: the beauty of the liturgy, the setting, the hymns and the processions. Then, as an adolescent, I was attracted to Tolstoy and his 'social' Christianity, and to classical Russian literature as a whole, which in such an extraordinary human way displays the worth of humble, despised people who are crushed under the development of modern society.

## 1. IN THE BEGINNING WAS TOLSTOY

The Tolstoy of Pablo's youth was renowned not only for the two novels that his fame is associated with today – *War and Peace*, and *Anna Karenina* – but with a third as well, *Resurrection*, the product of his later life and his revolutionary anarchist and pacifist beliefs. It contains pen portraits of the key revolutionists active in the late tsarist period of Russian history. For the most part, Tolstoy's characterisation was positive, although he was no hagiographer. He anticipated the worst type of Stalinist bureaucrat in the person of Novodvorov, the manipulative would-be leader of the exiled revolutionaries. The good revolutionists – to copy Tolstoy's term – shared a commitment to using their education and privilege to help emancipate the peasantry and the working class. To this end they risked their freedom and their lives. It is likely these Tolstoyan portraits helped shape the young Pablo's own self-image and ambitions.

In these years probably lies the origin of the *nom de guerre* he was to assume in occupied France during the Nazi occupation. The precocious Tolstoyan apparently impressed some of his schoolmates in Crete, according to renowned Greek lexicographer and philologist, Emmanuel Kriaras (1906-2014). In his autobiography Kriaras recalls his younger brother often speaking of 'the Tailor', which he later learned was the nickname of his school friend, Michalis Raptis. (Raptis is 'tailor' in Greek, but that nickname might also indicate an early interest in clothes.) Kriaras' brother's first name was Pavlos, which he thinks may have been the origin of Michalis's later *nom de guerre* 'Pablo'. His other theory is that 'Pablo' was taken from the name of a Spanish friend who died in the Spanish Civil War.

In 1928, when the budding author was 17, the family moved to Athens so that he could complete his secondary education. The following year, in obedience to his father's wishes, he enrolled in the Polytechnic as an engineering student, but soon found himself spending more time on the campus of the University of Athens where radical socialist activism was in full cry and students spent much of their time engaged in furious arguments over Marxism and Freudianism. It was here that Pablo graduated to what he described as 'a lucid, quasi-scientific' understanding of social evolution through a reading of Marxism. But that earlier religious impulse never left him. Marxism in his view was not a morally or ethically neutral experimental science, but a methodology in the service of a deeply ethical and humanist vision. As he wrote in that 1976 essay about his early Tolstoyan Christianity:

> It is evident that the revolutionary militant is carried forward by an impetus towards the absolute which is inherent in mankind. But in contrast to mystics and religious people, the revolutionary militant sees 'the absolute' embodied in the infinite future of the social being, of a human society which in fact has no fixed horizon.[5]

In other words, the new Jerusalem on Earth.

Radical talk wasn't limited to the University of Athens. The post-war period in Greece had been the most tumultuous in its history – or for that matter in the history of any nation at that time. The 1920s had seen a disastrous war against Turkey, the defeat and the expulsion of a million of Greeks from Asia Minor, coup and counter-coup in Athens almost yearly as republicans and monarchists, liberals and conservatives, civilians and army officers jostled for power. These struggles at the top reached well down into Greek society, riven by the same conflicts. On top of that came newer, bitter conflicts between capital and the newly emerging labour movement, in which Marxists played a leading role.

Greek governments held down real wages during the 1920s, so when the Great Depression arrived in 1929, economic misery and class conflict intensified. The American diplomat Henry Morgenthau encountered dire living conditions in Salonica in 1929. Malaria and tuberculosis were rife and, in the overcrowded dwellings:

> Cooking is done in little charcoal braziers improvised out of tin cans and bricks. The roofs of these buildings leak with every rain and the walls are full of gaping cracks that let in the cold damp winds of winter. In visiting this settlement, wherever one's eye turns it is greeted by signs of human misery — death, disease, and bodily suffering and semi-starvation.

These were the conditions for the refugee workers, but the situation for non-refugee workers was not appreciably different. Strikes and protests met with police violence authorised by special legislation passed by the Venizelos government in 1929.[6] In the elections of 1932 there was a significant shift to the left; the Communist Party vote was now over 20 per cent in the cities and bigger towns.[7]

The first-year student from the Cretan backwater quickly dived into this political cauldron. For some weeks in 1929, the university students struck against *Idionymon*, the government's legislation curbing civil liberties and increasing police powers. Pablo reputedly recruited 200 students into the Archeio-Marxists, then the biggest organisation on the Greek left.[8]

The Archeio-Marxists originated as a faction in the Greek Communist Party in the early 1920s. Even before the historic split between Stalinists and Trotskyists, the world communist movement was characterised by splits and expulsions. Expelled in 1924, the Archeio-Marxists (or Archive Marxists) had an estimated 2000 members when Pablo joined it – the population of Greece was approximately six million – and its members occupied key positions in the expanding trade union movement. After Trotsky was expelled from the Soviet Union in 1929, the Archeio-Marxists declared their support and the party was briefly the largest organisation in the world supporting Leon Trotsky's International Left Opposition in its battle with Stalin and his supporters.

The party was led by Dimitris Giotopoulos (1901-65) who appears to have been part-oracle, part-high priest or, if you like, straight out of a 19th-century Russian novel. Pablo describes the party as 'primeval, semi-illegal and conspiratorial with an atmosphere that strongly affected the imagination of students but also workers of that time'. That ambience emanated from the leader. Pablo has left an account of his initial meeting, as an 18-year-old acolyte, with Giotopoulos, who had asked to see him. 'One night, accompanied by [the actor] George Vitsoris, the first of my political teachers, I went to a room in a poor working-class home ... Inside a kerosene lamp flickered and seated in a chair I saw Giotopoulos, without being able to fully discern his face. A heavy silence prevailed maybe for a quarter of an hour. Eventually he slowly started to turn until I finally saw his face clearly: impressive, high forehead and two deep-set blue eyes. With his left hand he held his chin partly hiding his mouth. After many minutes of heavy, impenetrable silence he opened with some remarks about the Polytechnic, the syllabus and the theories of Einstein. The monologue lasted a little while, I stammered something, the visit ended with my first impression that the party was directed by a man of few words, serious and with great learning.'

Another (more irreverent) contemporary, Agis Stinas (1900-1987), recalls that when Giotopoulos was confronted by a difficult question he could not readily answer, he would respond by saying that he would consult the party's higher authorities. No such authority existed and it was merely a way of playing for time.[9]

The mystical despotism soon led the young Pablo and his supporters to demand internal democracy and a less sectarian attitude towards Communist Party members. The Archeio-Marxists' policy of physical violence towards members of the Stalinist Greek Communist Party was contrary to Trotsky's position at the time, which was to try to win over the rank-and-file of the Communist Party and form a united front with other elements in the labour movement. In 1931 the dissidents, unhappy with the extreme sectarianism of Giotopoulos, left to form KEO (the Unitary Communist Group).[10] 'The KEO united the most important Archeio-Marxist worker cadres of that organisation – such as Mitsos Soulas, Sakkos, Sklavounos and others – and the most brilliant and militant students who dominated the student movement in the University of Athens at that time,' Pablo recalled.

He would never forget his debt to Mitsos Soulas, a self-educated shoemaker and union organiser who was his chief ally in the Archeio-Marxists and then the KEO. It was Soulas who helped convince him of the sectarian errors of Giotopoulos and introduced him to the working-class world of Athens and Piraeus.[11] Growing up in Crete, Pablo had encountered and been impressed by the peasants' dignity and attachment to freedom; now Soulas introduced him to bakers, printers, dockers, labourers, building tradesmen, tobacco and textile workers. The young Pablo spent most of his student years propagandising and organising in the working-class suburbs of Athens and Piraeus. The material conditions of life were miserable for the workers he met but he found their spirit and courage inspiring. He formed lasting friendships among them.

The workers' conditions he encountered during the Great Depression years were in stark contrast to his own relatively comfortable home life where he was spoilt by his mother. Pablo admits in his autobiography that, before he went into the army to do his national service in 1934, he did not even know how to boil an egg. During his university years when he was a youthful agitator, out to all hours at meetings, his mother would wait up until her eldest son returned safely home. Her anxiety was not misplaced. The Security of the State Act allowed the police wide powers of detention and exile without trial for 'subversives'.[12]

Despite spending his mornings on the campus 'discussing Trotskyism, Stalinism, Freud and Einstein', and his afternoons and nights agitating among bakers, bootmakers, labourers and tailors, he passed his exams to graduate as a civil engineer in 1933. 'I would only study intensely towards the end of each year,' he recalls, 'when my father prepared to die believing that his son would never succeed in becoming a civil engineer.'

University was followed by compulsory national service in the Regiment of Heraklion in Crete in 1934-35. It coincided with the attempted coup by officers in Athens, and Pablo used his influence among his fellow soldiers to resist being shipped to Athens to support the putschists. 'When the battleships arrived at the Heraklion harbour to transport us, there existed in our company an atmosphere of near open mutiny. We were ready to resist. Happily, our transport plan was frustrated at the last minute.'

## 1 . IN THE BEGINNING WAS TOLSTOY

After national service, Pablo returned to Marxist politics in the Trotskyist organisation that had been formed by those who had left the Archeio-Marxists and by dissident Communist Party members, the best known of whom was Agis Stinas. Forty years later, Pablo was to recall two incidents involving Stinas that give a clue to his own hard moral streak. It was a trait he ruefully drew attention to in a 1977 interview, recalling that he was very puritanical at that time. ('J'étais un pur.') It was something that was to persist for decades. In 1963, for instance, it was to cause an irreparable breach with his closest comrade at a time when allies were scarce.

Stinas once told him how he had fancied the attractive wife of a comrade and had arranged for that comrade to be sent out of town on a political mission so Stinas could seduce the wife. (Shades of King David and Bathsheba.) It was a boast Pablo found distasteful as he made clear to Stinas, who conceded he had abused his power in the organisation. The other incident occurred soon after, when Stinas's own wife Eleni fell in love with someone else and announced she was leaving him. Stinas, on Pablo's account, reacted with fury, threatening to kill both himself and her. Pablo felt it necessary to keep vigil in their house in case Stinas carried out his threats.[13] Both incidents lessened his regard for Stinas, although he retained an abiding respect for his commitment and abilities.

Pablo in these years was very much a key lieutenant rather than a leader in his own right. In 1935 he transferred his allegiance from Stinas to Pantelis Pouliopoulos. It was Pouliopoulos who brought Marxism to Greece. The *Communist Manifesto* didn't appear in Greek until 1919 and it wasn't until Pouliopoulos and Georges Doupas translated and published Marx's *Contribution to the Critique of Political Economy* and the first volume of *Capital* and Kautsky's *Economic Theories of Karl Marx* in 1926-27, that it could be said the basics of Marxism were available to those Greeks who didn't have command of another European language.[14] Pouliopoulos was fluent in a number of languages and familiar with Hegel's logic and philosophy, and Pablo believed there were few intellectuals in Europe at that time equal to Pouliopoulos.

Pouliopoulos was an extraordinary figure. Newly graduated as a lawyer, he had volunteered and fought in the disastrous war against the Turks in the early 1920s and been captured. After the war he became leader of the veterans' organisation. By the mid-1920s he was general secretary of the Greek Communist Party (and he served time as a political prisoner on the island of Folegandros). He was removed as secretary in 1927 because of his opposition to the growing and enforced conformity in the world communist movement. By the mid-1930s he had rallied to Trotsky and now led a Trotskyist group called Spartacus that rivalled the Stinas-Pablo outfit. In 1935, Pablo and many of his fellow comrades left the Stinas group to combine with the smaller Spartacus and form the Organisation of Internationalist Communists of Greece (OKDE).[15] In Pouliopoulos, Pablo found a life model. As he wrote in 1989,

> I was irresistibly drawn to that man, whose very high political level and incomparable human qualities I had begun to appreciate. Pantelis Pouliopoulos remains for me one of the most cultivated, fine and heroic figures that I have had the opportunity to know in the course of the revolutionary saga of my long life.[16]

Pouliopoulos' Marxism was for Pablo of an 'international standard', and his courage was to be spectacularly confirmed during the Italian-German occupation during World War II. 'I was quickly influenced as much by the man as his politics,' Pablo recalled. 'In his character I found all that I would intensely wish for myself; he was an example for every revolutionary intellectual, devoted to the labour movement and socialism.'

— ✢ —

Like his inspiration, Pablo would never play at being the proletarian, although he encountered plenty of would-be Trotskyist leaders who did. 'I was and remained not a teacher or a leader, nor a 'proletarianised' person, but an intellectual revolutionary who joined the workers movement with the aim, not to direct them, but to share their struggles and their ideals as they advanced.' Pablo was very much in 'the lineage of Lenin and Trotsky,' writes an historian of the Algerian revolution, 'the same type of revolutionary intellectual, devoted to the cause of the proletariat, long exiled from his country of origin but a tireless organiser, theoretician of unfolding struggles and at the same time engaged in daily combat.'[17]

Pablo's mode of dress confirmed his aversion to any faux proletarian affectations. He dressed as a middle-class professional. There was nothing bohemian about him. His old comrade David Maurin remembered him as 'the dapper revolutionary'. As Pablo himself was aware, this 'bourgeois' appearance grated with some Trotskyist leaders who either affected or remained attached to their working-class origins. He attributed some of the hostility he generated among these comrades to his refusal to change.

In the late-1960s when this author met him in Paris, Pablo's typical outfit was a blazer, grey trousers, white shirt and tie, polished black shoes –

even on the streets of Paris during the days of the barricades in May 1968. It was his long-held style, as distinctive as his unwavering commitment to the cause. Even historian and revolutionary Mohamed Harbi touches on it in his description of first meeting Pablo in the mid-1950s, in the early days of the Algerian revolution or war of independence:

> Tall, dashing, greying at the temples, invariably seen in a blazer and grey pants, Pablo (pseudonym for Michalis Raptis) was a Greek engineer born in Egypt, in Alexandria ... he was the product of an era when idealism, convictions and generosity of spirit forged the destiny of men. He loved adventure and had a horror of only being a spectator, no matter how committed. More than once he had a brush with death and he told me, one day in a vein of confidence, that he had a fear of dying in his bed like a vulgar bourgeois. I knew of no other Marxists who held so sacred a view of the Algerian revolution. 'I need to know,' he said to me at our first interview, 'what you want from us. Our means are limited but we will do all we can.' The aid from Pablo was totally without strings or hidden motives.[18]

— ✢ —

By the time Pablo teamed up with Pouliopoulos, politics in Greece was following the pattern typical of other Mediterranean countries such as Spain and France in the mid-1930s: a revival of working-class insurgency that was then diverted by Communist parties into popular fronts or alliances with the middle class, and eventual failure, followed by right-wing coups. There were some 344 strikes in Greece in the first half of 1936.[19] The most spectacular sign of revived working-class politics in Greece was a general strike and insurrection in May 1936 in Thessaloniki, the second-largest and most working-class city of Greece. 'For a few days, bourgeois power was essentially abolished, to the general surprise of the political establishment and even to the leadership of the Greek Communist Party,' Pablo recalled. The Communists at that stage were campaigning for a popular front government with the Liberals and were not prepared to endanger that aim by encouraging revolutionary acts by workers. Accordingly, the workers of Thessaloniki were 'left isolated and naturally condemned to defeat' after the government rushed in troops to occupy the city. Defeated in that battle the workers may have been, but the government had been forced to concede the eight-hour day, and the labour movement was far from crushed.

The working-class radicalisation continued and prompted the army high command to act. On 4 August 1936, the day before a national general strike was to begin, the caretaker prime minister, General Ioannis

Metaxás, seized power and established his dictatorship. The police immediately began wholesale arrests of leftists. Pablo wouldn't escape their notice.

CHAPTER 2
# Prison, Elly and exile 1937-1938

*He was the product of an era when idealism, convictions and generosity of spirit forged the destiny of men.*

Mohammed Harbi
*Une Vie Debout*

NINETEEN THIRTY-SEVEN was to be the year that determined Pablo's life.

A few months after the coup and as the police continued to comb the city for leftists, Pablo was arrested while waiting for a contact in central Athens. It appears he was picked up at random. It wasn't until his interrogator, Kombocholus, head of Special Security, examined the papers discovered in Pablo's pockets that he realised the prisoner was 'Speros', the leader of a dissident communist group, whose real identity the police had not been aware of.[1]

They found in one of his pockets an envelope from a sympathetic official in the passport office who had suddenly left his job and disappeared. The police proceeded to bash Pablo 'day and night' in an attempt to get information about the man's whereabouts. 'A wasted effort, of course,' says Pablo in his autobiography. The passport official went underground and fought on during the Italian and German occupation. He survived that only to be murdered by Stalinists at the end of the war.

The beatings went on for days until his family intervened. The family mobilised some powerful connections (principally from academic circles, it appears) to put a stop to them, although he was still held prisoner. He was transferred to Folegandros, a rugged and rocky island a long day's ferry journey from Piraeus and the most southern of the Cyclades islands. He made the trip handcuffed to a shoemaker who was a veteran Communist Party member. 'Dsimma came and went into a prison as easily as if into a hotel, calm and neat and at once organising his life in the most logical and dignified manner.' Despite political and social differences the two men bonded – 'he an old worker rebel and me an intellectual and somewhat of a novice at rebellion'.

Meant to serve as some kind of Aegean 'Siberia', the island was even then something of an austere paradise. (Today it is a favoured destination for tourists and Greek holiday-makers.) 'When I reached this far distant island with its wild beauty shining in the unbelievable light of the south-eastern Aegean,' Pablo recalled at the end of his life, 'I did not feel at all that I had been exiled. I found the place full of fighters of the Greek Communist Party, some of our dissident stalwarts, respectful ancients from Macedonia and some gypsies, common criminals, and horse thieves …' The civilian population of Folegandros then was about 1500 and the prisoners numbered 600, among whom there were a few dozen Trotskyists.

Greek prison islands at this stage were still more like the prison camps of tsarist Russia before the war (but with much better weather) rather than Nazi or Soviet concentration camps of that era. Folegandros was then covered with small farms which, along with fishing, made the island largely self-sufficient. There was a police presence, but the exiles were not locked up. They were paid a scant daily allowance and expected to eke out a life on the island, buying or bartering lodgings and food from the locals. The prisoners shared their skills and ran educational classes for locals. The custom was for the prisoners to form communes, buying food in bulk and organising their own cooking and cleaning. Parcels could be sent by family and friends.

Conditions were to deteriorate, however, as the regime continued to round up thousands of leftists. The penal islands became overcrowded and the Metaxas regime was to consciously imitate measures from Nazi Germany.[2] However, in the first year of the dictatorship the old, milder repressive mechanisms still prevailed.[3]

In Pablo's first weeks on the island, the Trotskyists and the Communist Party members cooperated and held political debates – possibly as a consequence of the bond between the old shoemaker and the would-be revolutionary intellectual. However, because the party leaders came off badly in such discussions, they decided to break them up, starting fights and accusing the Trotskyists of being police agents. This was, of course, standard Stalinist practice in those days, and Pablo knew it first-hand, having been beaten up by Stalinists at a May Day rally in 1935. From then on the Trotskyist prisoners led a life apart from the other 'politicals', although Pablo recalls the ordinary party members surreptitiously showed their friendship when they could.

The one regret Pablo had when he arrived on the island was the absence of Elly (Hélène) Diovouniotis, the woman he had met in the spring of 1935 at a study group for young women. 'It was Pantelis' luckiest idea when he sent me to tutor this circle where I first met Elly and felt such overpowering attraction, love and happiness ...' This romance had of course been cut short by his arrest and exile.

But as luck would have it, Pablo was idling by the harbour soon after the break-up of the joint discussions when who should he glimpse – 'as a magical vision', he said in his autobiography – standing in the prow of an arriving boat but Elly. She appears to have been something of a spitfire whose outspoken nature had landed her in prison and now exile. Kombocholus had visited her family home in search of information – the aristocratic Diovouniotis family, prominent in legal circles, could trace their nationalist politics back to the Greek Revolution of the 1820s. The secret policeman had encountered Elly who proceeded to berate him. When she refused to sign a declaration repudiating communist ideas, he had her arrested and exiled. She was also known on the left for her fiery temperament and had already broken with the Communist Party, telling its male leaders in terms which indicated her politics and her social position: 'We bourgeois treat our servants better than you treat your wives', ' she reputedly said to them.[4]

Thrown together on Folegandros, and there Pablo and Elly were to spend something of a summer of love – it was late winter and early spring, in fact – before the colonel in charge decided they were among the chief troublemakers and that he would put an end to what he called their 'dolce vita'. Elly was sent to Kimolos and Pablo to Acronauplia, the prison-fortress in Nafplion in the north-east of the Peloponnese. There he was housed in an overcrowded cell where some of the prisoners were suffering from tuberculosis. While his stint there was brief, it was long enough for him to contract the disease. (Today the prison has been demolished and replaced with a six-star luxury hotel – something of a monument to the persistence of capitalism and survival of its privileged classes.)

The incarceration lasted only a few weeks before he was summarily hauled from the cells one morning, handcuffed and put on a boat to Athens. There he was taken straight to the office of Konstantinos Maniadakis, the minister for internal security, where he was met not just by the minister but also by his father and the head of civil engineering at the Polytechnic, Professor Paraskevopoulos. In Pablo's account, it was the professor who won him his release into exile abroad. He had not gone far into his panegyric about the brilliant young civil engineer and his bright future before Maniadakis interrupted and said all that was required for the prisoner's release was for him to sign a declaration renouncing communism. Pablo immediately refused and had begun to point out that he had not asked for this intervention when Paraskevopoulos interrupted him, 'acting furious and saying, "you see what a blockhead he is, let him go to the devil. Let him go abroad and leave us in peace".' Pablo formed the impression that Maniadakis had already decided to do this favour for Paraskevopoulos, with whom he had had business dealings in the past. Pablo was ordered to wait at home until a passport and travel documents for Switzerland were prepared.

Meanwhile, Pablo secretly met with Pantelis Pouliopoulos, who was living underground, to see if the Trotskyist organisation agreed he should go abroad. On the day, Pouliopoulos was busy translating Shelley and insisted on reading some of the poems to Pablo. On the more urgent matter of exile, Pouliopouls approved, considering it an 'unhoped for opportunity' to make contact with the Trotskyist leadership in Paris.

Before leaving, Pablo sailed to Kimolos to see Elly and, despite a nervous jailer, was allowed to spend a few days with her. In the winter of 1937 Pablo set out for Switzerland on the overnight train from the Larissa Station. It would prove to be a long exile. He would never see his parents again. 'My parents stoically faced the parting from their son on whom they had based so many hopes,' he recalled, 'and then one after the other closed their eyes without seeing him again. Thankfully, through all the difficulties of the war years, the civil war and old age, my brother Kletos supported them so tenderly and exemplarily that he made them forget a little the lost sheep, lost to the histories of the continuing revolution somewhere in the world.'

He was more fortunate with Elly. Soon after he left, she fell ill on Kimolos and was transferred to a hospital in Athens. Her influential family appealed to Metaxas himself to allow her to go abroad. So, at the end of 1937, Pablo and Elly found themselves together again in Geneva, and in the spring of 1938 they left for Paris where they had already made contact with the Trotskyist centre.

They were sailing into dangerous waters. The probability of a new world war was obvious to revolutionaries – Trotsky had been warning of it since Hitler came to power in Germany in 1933. Paris was already a city of the defeated and crowded with refugees. The Popular Front government – a coalition of socialist, communist and radical parties – had entered its final days as its supporters resigned themselves to its inertia and conservatism. In Spain, the revolutionary movement had been suppressed and the Republic was reeling before the relentless fascist offensives supported by Germany and Italy. Hitler had just invaded and annexed Austria, and in the German lands the persecution of Jews, leftists and non-conformists continued unabated.

Added to these looming dangers, Trotskyists faced the more immediate possibility of disappearance and murder at the hands of agents of Stalin's secret police, the GPU. In the Soviet Union itself, Stalin's purges had reached a paroxysm with thousands of old Bolsheviks, Trotskyists and foreign communists the first to be slaughtered. Isaac Deutscher writes that it 'amounted to political genocide: it destroyed the whole species of the anti-Stalinist Bolsheviks'.[5]

Stalin's executioners were already active in Western Europe. Andreu Nin, leader of POUM, an independent Marxist party, had already been 'disappeared' by Stalin's agents in Spain in 1937. Trotsky had made harsh criticisms of Nin and POUM, much to the dismay of some of his followers and supporters such as Victor Serge (1890-1947), Henk Sneevliet (1883-1942) in Holland, and Georges Veereken (1896-1978) in Belgium. Such doctrinal quibbles among anti-Stalinists did not deter Stalin's killers. It was enough that POUM in Spain actively opposed Stalin's line of protecting the private sector and its profits against revolutionary takeovers by workers and peasants.

Erwin Wolf,[6] briefly Trotsky's secretary in his short-lived exile in Norway, had gone to Spain in 1937 to support the revolution. He also disappeared in September 1937, almost certainly killed by the GPU. Likewise Hans David Freund, a 25-year-old German Jewish Trotskyist who travelled to Spain in 1936 to help unify the fractious local Trotskyists and effect united activity with the Durruti anarchists, was murdered in Barcelona in the wake of the suppression of the Barcelona commune in May 1937. A leaflet he wrote and distributed on the barricades in May is referred to in George Orwell's *Homage to Catalonia*.[7]

Ignace Reiss, a key NKVD agent who had defected to the Trotskyists in July 1937, was next, murdered in a roadside ambush in Switzerland in September 1937. Reiss was one of six revolutionary communists who had grown up together in a small town in the Austro-Hungarian empire on the border of Poland, Ukraine and Russia.[8] They had been horrified by the carnage of World War I, by the support for the war among the traditional social democratic parties and were consequently inspired by the Bolshevik Revolution. The six had thrown in their lot with Lenin's Bolsheviks, worked for the Communist International and then become counter-intelligence agents for the Red Army and GPU/NKVD posted in Western Europe. It was not an uncommon trajectory for committed revolutionary Marxists in Europe who came of age during the Great War of 1914-18.

By the mid-1930s Reiss was running the Soviet intelligence network in France. But he was increasingly uneasy about the Moscow Trials which led to the execution of Lenin's old comrades and the fatal disappearance of leading foreign communists who had taken refuge in Moscow, or who like him worked for various secret police agencies. In the summer of 1937, conscious that his friends were now being rounded up, Reiss decided to break with Stalin. He addressed a letter to the Central Committee of the Soviet party protesting the purges, indicting Stalin's counter-revolutionary polices at home and abroad and announcing his rallying to Trotsky and the nascent Fourth International. With his letter, he announced, 'I am returning to you the Order of the Red Banner awarded to me in 1928. To wear it ... would be beneath my dignity.'[9]

This letter, delivered to the Soviet Embassy in Paris, proved to be a death sentence. He'd taken refuge in an isolated village in Switzerland but was betrayed by a trusted friend. His bullet-riddled body was discovered by the roadside on 4 September. The Swiss and French police tracked the assassins back to the Society for the Repatriation of Russian Émigrés, a society sponsored by the Soviet Embassy.[10]

Leon Sedov, Trotsky's son, was in all probability another victim. He had been admitted to a Paris hospital run by emigré Russians for an appendix operation in February 1938. The operation seemed successful, but he died a few days later in suspicious circumstances. He was 32 years old. In all probability he was betrayed by his closest collaborator, Etienne, the *nom de guerre* for Mark Zborowski, who turned out to be an NKVD/GPU agent. It was Etienne who had directed Sedov to that particular hospital. (He later confessed to having immediately informed the GPU of Sedov's whereabouts.) According to Reiss and his fellow agents, White Russians could be found who would happily eliminate communists, sometimes at the behest of other communists.[11]

Trotsky's wrenching anguish at his son's death is evident in the obituary he published for him. It ended:

> His mother, who was closer to him than anyone in the world, and I, as we are living through these terrible hours recall his image feature by feature;

refuse to believe that he is no more and we weep because it is impossible not to believe ... He was part of us, our young part ... together with our boy has died everything that still remained young in us ... Your mother and I never thought, never expected, that fate would lay this task upon us ... that we should have to write your obituary ... But we have not been able to save you.[12]

— ✦ —

Soon after Pablo and Elly arrived in Paris, they struck up a warm friendship with Rudolf Klement, a dissident German communist émigré who was then the main organiser for the soon to be launched Trotskyist Fourth International. Not least among Klement's virtues had been his warnings to Trotsky about the infiltration of the Trotskyist centre in Paris by Stalin's agents, and the danger this posed to his son. In vain he had urged Trotsky to bring Sedov to what he saw as the relative safety of Mexico City. Pablo says he quickly came to agree with Klement about the slack security arrangements among the French Trotskyists in particular, but admits that he harboured no suspicions about Etienne.

In July 1938, Klement himself suddenly vanished. Some weeks later his headless torso washed up in the Seine and then some months later his severed legs. He was thirty years old. It later emerged that a Turkish officer in the GPU had stabbed him to death and dismembered the body. Such were Stalin's police methods.[13]

Before long, however, with France occupied by Nazi Germany, the Gestapo would become the more immediate danger.

In this connection, Pablo and Elly had made a fateful decision after their arrival in Paris. Required to register with the authorities as non-French residents, they resisted advice to register as political refugees and opted to register as overseas students studying at the Sorbonne. This, in fact, happened to be their actual position as Pablo was enrolled in town planning and statistics courses and Elly in literary studies. The choice meant that in the years to come they possessed less incriminating identity papers and fell below the radar of the French police and the Gestapo.

CHAPTER 3

# Dangerous liaisons 1938-1942

*Say to my friends, please, that I have no doubt about the victory of the Fourth International. Go forward!*

**Trotsky's last words**
on his death bed, 21 August 1940

WITHIN SIX MONTHS of his arrival in Paris, Pablo participated in the founding conference of the Fourth International, the would-be revolutionary organisation to which he and Elly were to devote the next 25 years of their lives. The dangerous times meant the conference took place in a secret location in an outer suburb of Paris and was held over just one long day. The 30 delegates from 10 countries were conscious of the risks of a raid either by Stalinists or the French police if proceedings went for any longer. A handful of guards, armed with revolvers, were stationed outside the converted barn where the delegates sat at a single long table. Fifty years later Pablo recalled it was a sombre occasion, tinged by the assassinations and defeats of recent months. Even the normally boisterous and cheerful American James Cannon was subdued. In Pablo's memory, Cannon's legendary flask of whisky stayed in his hip pocket.[1]

The platform that Trotsky had drafted was adopted without amendment. Pablo, who attended as one of two delegates representing Greek Trotskyists, did make two distinctive interventions that day. The first was to argue with much prescience for the recognition of the revolutionary role the peasantry could play in socialist revolutions. This insight, which was to be confirmed most spectacularly in China and Vietnam, did not make it into the manifesto that emerged from the conference. At the time Trotsky

– 'more than any other writer in the 1930s'[2] – noted the revolutionary prospect in China but his conclusion was based on the expectation that the Chinese working class would lead that revolution. On the other hand, Chen Tu-Hsiu, the early leader of the Chinese Communist Party and later sympathiser with Trotsky, tried to convince his fellow Trotskyists of the revolutionary role the peasantry would play in the Chinese revolution. To no avail.

Nor did Pablo's second distinctive contribution (echoing Rosa Luxemburg's post-Russian Revolution 'heresy') make it into the founding document. This was the need to allow party pluralism after the revolution.[3] This commitment to multi-partyism was to evolve into a distinctive part of his model of post-revolutionary or transitional societies. In such societies, he would argue, the aim must be to ensure that the maximum share of real power was in the hands of working people. Competition and contestation between competing socialist parties would be part of that exercise of real power. This was part and parcel of what Pablo was to call 'self-managed socialism'.

The major bone of contention at the conference was whether, indeed, to proceed with founding the Fourth International. For Isaac Deutscher, Trotsky's great biographer and a leader of the pre-war Polish Trotskyists, the founding of the Fourth was premature. The times were just not right. Whatever revolutionary wave had been unleashed by the Russian Revolution of 1917 was now spent. This was starkly clear in the Soviet Union, awash with the blood of people – including Lenin's closest comrades – caught up in the purges. The workers movement in Europe was in retreat everywhere, badly defeated in the space of a few short years in Germany, France and Spain. The disarray within the revolutionary organisations themselves was, if anything, worse.

Deutscher has written sympathetically about the dilemma Trotsky found himself in, caught between the necessity, yet the impossibility, of creating revolutionary organisations in such conditions.[4] He was 'a man out of time', the ground had crumbled under the champion of classical socialist revolution:

> His ideas and methods were those of classical Marxism and were bound up with the prospect of revolution in the 'advanced' capitalist West. His political character had been formed in the atmosphere of revolution from below and proletarian democracy, in which Russian and international Marxism had been nurtured. Yet in the period between the world wars, despite the intense class struggles, international revolution stagnated.

Yet, as Deutscher understood, Trotsky could not stand aside. It was not in his character, and dark as the times were, it was 'an era of worldwide social battles and catastrophes from which a man of Trotsky's record could not stand apart. Nor was he for a moment free to withdraw from his ceaseless and ferocious duel with Stalin.'

These battles, if they were to be won, required an organised revolutionary party. Before 1917, Trotsky and Luxemburg had argued for counting on the spontaneous uprising of the working class to make the socialist revolution. Trotsky saw that as his greatest political error. Lenin had insisted on the need for a revolutionary party if success was to be achieved, and 1917 had proved him right. With social democratic parties, still united in the Second International, forsaking any hint of revolutionary aims or even radical reforms, and the official communist parties of the Third International essentially instruments of Stalin's un-revolutionary foreign policy, an indispensable revolutionary party had to be built from scratch. That was the mission of the Fourth.

The proposal to delay the founding of the Fourth International was put to the conference, by Deutscher's Polish comrades, and rejected by 19 votes to 3. The argument of the majority, of which Pablo was part, was that the social democratic and communist leaderships had failed the working class in one country after another and there were no signs that they had learned the lessons. Trotskyist organisations already operated around the globe; in other words, they already existed as an international political tendency, or organised political current, and the conference was formalising this reality.[5]

Pablo (and the majority), while aware of the current unpropitious circumstances, lived when the Russian Revolution of 1917 and the German Revolution of 1918 were something like contemporary events. They wagered on the outcome of the coming war to unleash a revolutionary wave as had happened in the final years of the First World War. This wave would also sweep away Stalin's regime in the Soviet Union. Trotsky was sure of this; in a speech welcoming the founding in 1938, he predicted: 'During the next ten years the program of the Fourth International will become the guide for millions, and these millions of revolutionaries will be able to move heaven and earth'.[6] In other words, the founding of the Fourth International and its program anticipated developments. The fusion of this party and the workers' movement would come when the revolutionary wave resumed, provoked by the coming world war.

The program adopted at the founding conference was very much a campaigning document. Absent was any deep analysis of the current situation of capitalism and imperialism or what the post-revolutionary (and non-Stalinist) society would entail. It was consciously called 'the transitional program', meaning that it was to provide a bridge from the current circumstances to the opening of a revolutionary situation. Its demands – for a sliding scale of wages (adjusted for inflation), for a shorter working week, workers control and so on – were based on a reading of the prevailing objective conditions and the evolving consciousness of the working class. The fight for the immediate demands in the transitional program would lead to a challenge to the existing order.

This transitional concept was Trotsky's answer to the perennial problem of what socialists do between a normal un-revolutionary situation and the advent of one. The traditional approach was to have a minimum program, compatible with capitalism, and a maximum program which awaited the revolution – with no link between them. Trotsky wanted to build a dynamism into the immediate program.

While the Fourth International was never to attain the mass following the founders hoped for – with the partial exception for two decades in Sri Lanka – Trotskyism did in the 1930s attract a stellar following among intellectuals, mainly writers and critics. The list of 'literary Trotskyists' in the United States, for instance, includes Edmund Wilson, Dwight Macdonald, Mary McCarthy, Sidney Hook, James T. Farrell, Clement Greenberg and Harold Rosenberg. Other writers, such a Norman Mailer and Saul Bellow, had brief brushes with Trotskyism. In Europe there was a similar *trotskisant* ebullition among intellectuals.

It didn't last. By the late 1940s most had retreated or deserted. Deutscher implies that Trotsky asked too much of these followers. 'He demanded of his adherents unshakeable conviction, utter indifference to public opinion, unflagging readiness for sacrifice, and a burning faith in the proletarian revolution, whose breath he constantly felt (and they did not). In a word, he expected them to be made of the stuff of which he himself was made.'[7]

Many baulked at such an all-consuming commitment. And in a short time, uneasy, disillusioned and weary, they seized on the failure of Trotsky's predictions, or errors in analysis, or the extremism of his demands, as reasons to back off. 'Nothing fails like failure,' writes Deutscher. Alan Wald in his landmark study of these *trotskisant* intellectuals lays equal emphasis on the expanding prospects of prosperous careers in academia and publishing, fuelled by a revived post-war capitalism.[8] As important was the survival and expansion of the Stalinist regime in the Soviet Union and the insistence by orthodox Trotskyists that it was to be 'unconditionally' defended, even though it struck some of the early Fourth Internationalists as a greater tyranny than capitalism and imperialism.

Pablo was to have plenty of experience of these retreats by 'exceptional personalities' in Europe. He acknowledged the brilliance of many and believed they generally benefited from their experience in the movement. But in his view they lacked the necessary strength of character and fighting spirit, especially when it dawned on them that revolutionary politics was 'a doubtful battle with no guarantee of success in the short span of one's life'. Nevertheless, he retained an affection and respect for many of these 'retirees' and, equally, many of them retained an appreciation and affection for him. These friendships in the penumbra of the revolutionary movement were to serve him well in difficult situations in the future. If they were not comrades for life, they were often friends willing to help.

— ☩ —

A year after the Fourth International was formally launched, Hitler began the Second World War with a whirlwind attack on Poland, which soon capitulated. With his eastern flank secured, Hitler unleashed his army on France in May 1940, and the French army also quickly succumbed to the German onslaught.

Pablo was later to describe the Second World War as 'the biggest political storm in history' and in this global tempest he was to emerge as an international rather than as a Greek political leader. It largely fell to him to rally and assemble the leadership of the Fourth International out of the scattered and wounded remnants in occupied Europe. Some of his closest wartime comrades, the ones he counted on both in the present and for the future, were to perish at the hands of the Nazis and Stalinists.

Luck and love played a big part in his own survival in occupied France during the dark early days of the war. The first stroke of luck and good management, as noted, was registering not as refugees as so many of the comrades did, but as foreign students enrolled at the Sorbonne. It meant that they were not caught up in police round-ups of political refugees in wartime Paris. The second stroke of fortune, ironically, was Pablo's poor health.

The year that immediately followed the founding of the Fourth International had been dispiriting. Waves of refugees from the lost Spanish Revolution started to arrive in France. The new right-wing government in Paris began to cancel the reforms of the Popular Front years, such as the 40-hour working week. Defeatism was in the air. Britain

## 3 . DANGEROUS LIAISONS 1938-42

and France accepted Hitler's occupation of Czechoslovakia. In August 1939, the world was stunned by the announcement of the Stalin-Hitler non-aggression pact. The communist parties did an abrupt U-turn, repudiating their courtship of the 'democratic' powers which were now characterised as the biggest danger to peace. The Fourth International itself was torn by its first major divisions in the United States and France – principally over how to classify the Soviet Union. To make matters worse, Pablo suffered further attacks of tuberculosis.

When in May 1940 the German armies swept through Belgium and headed for Paris, Pablo and Elly initially hesitated to join the millions who were fleeing south. Once it became clear that there would be no resistance in Paris, they took one of the last trains south towards Orleans.[9]

Leaving the train at Sèvres, they joined the flood on the road. As evening fell, they were stopped by three army officers and, as suspicious foreigners, were about to be escorted to the police station in Rambouillet – a fate that may have dropped them into the hands of the Germans or their French collaborators. It was only when Pablo mentioned he suffered from TB and produced papers showing he was under the care of Dr Rosenthal in Paris that the officers relented and waved them on their way. It transpired that at least one of the officers was Jewish and Rosenthal was a very well-known Jewish doctor.

The flood of refugees, surviving occasional attacks from the air, continued flowing south. After the first run-in with the officers, and given the general suspicion of foreigners in the fleeing crowds, he let Elly do any talking. Her French accent was impeccable whereas his was execrably foreign.

The tightly packed flood of refugees passed right through Orleans where the bridges over the Loire were dynamited to delay the advancing Germans. Eventually they reached the small town of Romorantin where they intended to stop and stay. Simultaneously a regiment of motorised German infantry arrived in the town. The flight had been in vain. To compound their depressed spirits, Pablo had his first serious episode of coughing up blood and fell ill for days with a fever.

Once he recovered, they returned to a Paris bedecked with swastika flags and thundering with the triumphant marches of German troops. They moved into the Latin Quarter in the heart of Paris near the Collège de France to be close to medical treatment. It was there, listening to the radio in late August 1940, that they heard the shattering news of Trotsky's murder. The death was, in its way, inevitable. As Victor Serge wrote:

Beginning with the Moscow Trials, the assassination of Leon Trotsky became both a political and a logical necessity. It is of no use to shoot tens of thousands of men if the loftiest head of the revolutionary generation, the one that it will be impossible to strike out of history, freely survives. And it is obvious that against Trotsky, denounced as the most diabolical character in history, anything is permitted in the eyes of the Russian world poisoned by the frame-up trials.

Trotsky himself expected to die at the hands of Stalin's assassins. After a serious attack on his fortified residence in Mexico City he wrote in a 8 June 1940 article, *Stalin Seeks My Death*:

The accidental failure of the assault so carefully and so ably prepared is a serious blow to Stalin. The GPU must rehabilitate itself with Stalin. Stalin must demonstrate his power. *A repetition of the attempt is inevitable.*

Aware that his means of defence were so small compared to Stalin's vast resources, Trotsky concluded: 'I can therefore say that I live on this earth not in accordance with the rule, but as an exception to the rule.'

The fatal attack – famously, a blow to the head with an ice pick – was carried out by Ramon Mercader, a GPU agent posing as Jacques Mornard, a Belgian sympathiser. Despite rapid treatment by doctors and an extraordinary resistance by the man himself, Leon Trotsky died calmly on 21 August 1940 at 7:25 pm. He was 60. Before he underwent trepanning, he reportedly called the American Trotskyist Joseph Hansen to him and dictated a few words by way of a political testament: *"Say to my friends, please, that I have no doubt about the victory of the Fourth International. Go forward!"*

Even if his death was not completely unexpected, Pablo and Elly were nevertheless devastated, 'aimlessly walking the streets of Paris' unable to reconcile themselves to the fact that 'such an exemplary and outstanding human being, who had enriched and inspired my youthful life with his ideas, his life and his character, had been eclipsed'.

The times made the death even more of a tragedy. From the time of Hitler's accession to power, Trotsky had predicted the outbreak of war between the European powers. In his analysis, the war would be a repeat of the First World War: a clash of imperialisms and ending in revolutions. In these circumstance Lenin's 'revolutionary defeatism' was still relevant. The workers had no interest in siding with their own ruling class and killing their class brothers and sisters from another country, or in saving capitalism which was in their view in its stage of irreversible stagnation, or in preserving the colonies of their own particular imperialist power. When war broke out, it was revolutionary Marxist business as usual: the priorities would be political work among soldiers and encouraging fraternisation, recruiting cadres for the Party, building workers power in workplaces, keeping democracy alive in the labour movement by circulating newspapers and leaflets, and even carrying out acts of sabotage in Nazi Germany, for example. The attack on Soviet Russia, which Trotsky also expected, would complicate matters and call for a more nuanced position on the war, involving support for actions that would help defend the first 'workers state'. But even given that consideration, the best defence of the Soviet Union would always be the extension of the revolution. It would not only relieve the pressure on the Soviet Union but also undermine the siege-like conditions that sustained the Stalinist bureaucracy.[10]

This critical, non-cooperating position was inevitably an isolating one for Trotskyists in the warring powers, as patriotic fever was certain to grip populations in the opening days of war, and this nationalism was sure to deepen in the case of occupied countries. As nationalist movements are typically inter-class affairs, what would be the position of irreconcilable 'class struggle' Bolshevik-Leninists like the Trotskyists?

In those early months of the war, Pablo encountered differing estimates of what the war would involve. France had capitulated relatively quickly before the Nazi invasion of May 1940, and resignation to the German occupation and the establishment of a puppet regime in the south under Marshal Petain was widespread. The French Communist Party was under orders to accept the occupation, as Stalin had signed a non-aggression pact with Hitler in 1939. Into this vacuum of resistance stepped de Gaulle with his rallying broadcast from London in June 1940. He had all the advantages of being first mover, and his leadership of the slowly emerging resistance was cemented by the time the communists joined after Hitler's invasion of the Soviet Union in June 1941.

The already divided and quarrelsome Trotskyists in France were to respond in different ways, deepening their bitter divisions. For some, participation in the Resistance was admissible under certain conditions; for others this was class collaboration, which would help re-establish capitalist rule in France and perpetuate the French empire. A couple of pessimists, resigned to a long period of Nazi rule in Europe, even decided to bury themselves in fascist parties and movements. Given the scale of German victories, this resignation might have seemed realistic but Pablo concluded – by 1942 – that Nazi Germany would lose the war, unable to resist the combined resources of the Soviet Union and the United States.[11]

In this early period the German police and their French fascist allies arrested leftists and would-be resistants 'by the shovelful'. The leftists and resistants had much to learn about clandestine survival. Among the first taken were young Trotskyists – 10 in the 11th arrondissement in Paris, according to one survivor.[12] Even when they had learned the basics of underground activity, informers and infiltrators were always a risk. Lucien Braslawski, Jules Joffé and Henri Souzin were all arrested on 19 March 1942, in Paris, thanks to an informer. On 27 March they were put on the first transport of French Jews out of Paris destined for Buchenwald. They were murdered soon after arrival. Braslawski's fate propelled his fellow student (and fervent admirer) Simonne Minguet into underground activity for one of the Fourth International groups active in Paris.[13] For the next 50 years Minguet was to be a close collaborator of Pablo's.

In the winter of 1940-41, with heating and food in short supply, Pablo's health worsened suddenly. He suffered an attack of pleurisy as well as TB. The ever-resourceful Elly, helped by fellow Greek Trotskyist and actor George Vitsoris, managed to get a place for him on the last passenger train the Germans allowed out of Paris, headed for the south of the country ruled by Marshal Pétain.

Pablo later recalled that he was at death's door. 'When the train departed I had the premonition that I would not survive the winter. The doctors who welcomed me to France's famous Jewish sanatorium, St-Hilaire du Trouvet, on the outskirts of Grenoble, had the same opinion.' They gave him three months to live. The doctors in charge, Daniel Douady and René Cohen, were both Jewish 'with exceptional political consciences and great courage … ready to not only help their patients but every person in danger, whether a member of the Resistance or a Jew'. He hit it off with them both, personally and politically.

Later he was to nominate 'three experiences which quickly taught me the exact and basic parameters of human existence and the deepest social realities'. His time in the army awakened a hatred of the tyranny exercised by officers over ordinary young workers and peasants. Prison opened his eyes to the grim social conditions that society's victims were forced to endure. As for the sanatorium, it 'accustomed me, as nothing else in my life, to the phenomenon of death, which had already puzzled me as a child when I had stood bewildered, hardly breathing, without finding any satisfactory explanation at the premature loss of my sister Olga, who was the most poetic creature in my warm childish fancy'. In the sanatorium, he witnessed 'every day death reaping, left and right around me, young beings some of whom with dramatic determination clung onto life refusing to submit to the inevitable'.

He was more fortunate, not least because of the food Elly was able to procure for him. He spent much of his time – he was at the sanatorium for all of 1941 and most of 1942 – reading Hegel ('for months I stubbornly forced myself to systematically study the logic of Hegel so essential for understanding Marx') and Greek philosophy, and becoming familiar with classical music. He managed to complete his town planning studies, returning briefly to Paris in mid-1942 to take and pass his final exams – and to make contact with scattered Fourth International groups in the capital.

At the end of 1942 he was ready to leave the sanatorium and return permanently to Paris. Before he left, his doctors wanted to operate, but Elly insisted he refuse. The doctors thought this was dangerous 'pigheadedness' – for which Elly was already notorious – but conceded that a quiet life without stress or too much activity might be enough to heal him. When Douady examined him in 1946, after Pablo had spent three years working underground, dodging the Gestapo and cheating death, he pronounced him clear of TB and congratulated him on following instructions. 'When Douady realised what a diametrically different life I had led, for a moment he really lost it, but as a philosopher-doctor he responded that at the end of the day, consumption was a psychosomatic illness. I beat it because of my sort of life, which had fired up my will to live to the utmost.'

As it was, there were challenges aplenty for a Trotskyist in Paris in 1943. In taking up those challenges, Raptis now adopted the pseudonym of Michel Pablo.

CHAPTER 4

# Pablo's war 1943-1946

> *Impregnated with the history of the Russian Revolution ... the militants were convinced that the process of 1917 must necessarily be replayed ... However the growing importance, evident in 1944, of the struggle of the partisans, and the sympathetic echo it found in the population, pushed the [Trotskyist] PCI ... to join the maquis in order to defend a working-class program.*
>
> **Jacqueline Pluet-Despartin**
> Les trotskistes et la guerre 1940-44[1]

A RECOVERED PABLO and Elly returned to Paris in the winter of 1942-43, just as the war was turning against the Nazis. Elly was resuming her literary studies at the Sorbonne, where she recruited couriers among her fellow students to distribute the literature her husband and his comrades were producing. For all the Gestapo's success in rounding up Trotskyists during the occupation of France, they never managed to discover the printery the main Trotskyist group, the Parti Ouvrier Internationaliste, was operating, and Pablo overseeing, in Antony, a southern suburb of Paris. It was a small consolation beside the human losses: 120 comrades arrested and deported and 40 dead either in captivity or in clashes with the occupier and police.[2] These losses – out of a membership of about 300 – were bleaker still in view of the few gains.

The mass Resistance movement that developed in France in 1943 and 1944 was closed to the Trotskyists, even if they had followed Pablo's urging and tried harder to gain entrance. Their activities in those years were nevertheless honourable – they combatted as best they could the

Nazis' murderous antisemitism[3] and the crude chauvinism promoted by the French Stalinists. For Pablo, the cruel irony was that the Greek resistance movement in his homeland was more numerous, more powerful and more revolutionary than in France, even if it was ultimately controlled and betrayed by Stalinists. Pablo's fascination and identification with the Greek Revolution – the rising of the poor of the countryside and the cities in the war years – was never to diminish.

Once settled in a small apartment in Rue Saint-Michel near the Collège de Médecine hospital (for reasons of Pablo's health), Pablo took up the work of establishing contact with the scattered remnants of the Fourth International across occupied Europe, and forging unity among the largest group of Trotskyists, the quarrelsome French comrades.

As an outsider, Pablo had not joined any of the four competing French factions of the Fourth International and was on reasonable terms with all of them – something that would pay dividends in the work he was now undertaking, which was no less than the rebuilding and unifying of all the European Trotskyist groups. His diplomatic skills, together with a steely self-confidence, aided his cause. The first helped in bringing them together, the second to solder them together despite their differences.

Through 1943 and into 1944, Pablo worked on unifying the European and French Trotskyists. The main work was in France and in his memoirs Pablo claims that, despite sharp political differences, there was 'a thirst for unity'. Even so, historians of these years give Pablo most of the credit for bringing the French groups together.[4] On the European scale, a European Secretariat of the Fourth International had in fact already been established in 1942 on the initiative of Marcel Hic, the leading French Trotskyist, but in 1943 Pablo converted this ad hoc body into the 'provisional secretariat' and enlarged its membership. Its declared mission was to organise a conference of delegates from as many countries as possible, as soon as possible, to elect a permanent secretariat and set down policy. It was elementary democracy, but it must have eased any suspicions that the provisional secretariat was a coup by a self-appointed leadership group.

The Nazis' triumphant march through Europe, with only Britain holding out, had left a number of French Trotskyists disoriented and pessimistic, so much so that some comrades in France had turned to joining fascist unions and parties to prepare for better days. Admittedly that detour did not last and only involved a handful.[5] In general, Trotskyists, who preferred the appellation Bolshevik Leninists, sought to live up to that name – but there was disagreement about what that meant faced with this world war.

To understand the ideological cauldron confronting Pablo, it's necessary to make a brief detour into how Trotsky saw the war. From the arrival of Hitler in power in 1933, he had predicted the outbreak of the Second World War and attempted to prepare his followers. In May 1940 there had been an emergency conference of the Fourth International in New York. That gathering had adopted a manifesto on the war that Trotsky had drafted and entitled *La guerre impérialiste et la révolution prolétarienne*. This manifesto conceived the war which began in 1939 as a clash of imperialisms. The Second World War would be a repeat of the First Imperialist World War and Lenin's policy of 'revolutionary defeatism' was still relevant. Revolutionary Marxists could not support sending the workers of one capitalist country to kill the workers of another in the interests of their imperialist ruling class. It wasn't acceptable to support one part of the capitalist world in its war with another when the point was to abolish capitalism entirely. The label of 'democracy' that one side claimed could not be taken at face value when those 'democracies' ruled vast empires of subject peoples and, as was seen in France, their ruling classes would not hesitate to make deals with triumphant fascism. Moreover, if they were really interested in preserving democracy and defeating fascism, why had these 'democracies' abandoned Republican Spain to the fascists? For revolutionary Marxists, their business – if one can use the expression – remained class struggle and revolution.

Trotsky anticipated that the Second World War would be even more catastrophic than the First, and would end in revolutionary situations and possibilities, triggering the overthrow of Stalin's regime in Russia and the revolution in Germany that the Bolsheviks had banked on in 1917. In this world of revolutions, he expected that his followers, organised in the Fourth International, would come into their own as the genuine world party of revolution.

Trotsky did not leave it at that single static reading. Daniel Guérin, who excavated and republished Trotsky's writings in that fateful period, dubbed him 'the Delphi at Coyoacan', the suburb of Mexico City where he had taken up his exile.[6] Trotsky anticipated Stalin's alliance with Hitler but, unlike Stalin, he also predicted that Hitler would turn on Stalin and invade the Soviet Union. He foresaw the Soviet Union making common cause with the 'democratic' powers and he supported the entry of the United States into the war. America's participation would release Stalin from his paralysing fear of Hitler and the economic power of the United

States would determine the outcome of the war. That country would, in his view, emerge from the war as the global imperialist hegemon.

In the months that followed the May 1940 emergency conference, and before his murder in August, Trotsky's views on the war evolved. He had written the May manifesto literally weeks before Hitler's invasion and occupation of France in May-June 1940. As he now wrote in his last article of August 1940, 'A continuation doesn't mean a repetition'.[7] In July he held a series of meetings with American Trotskyists advising them to respond to the Pentagon's recruitment drive by agitating for the union movement to have a say in the new armed forces, especially in the selection (ideally, election) and training of officers. He anticipated that Nazi-occupied Europe would become a 'powder keg', which would mean armed uprisings against the German occupier. Never a pacifist, he saw the future of the world as being determined by armed struggle on a massive scale and that the working class and its vanguard could not and would not stand aside from that reality.

Arguably, Trotsky's final views on how his followers should respond to this clash of arms were evolving and suggestive, rather than finished, clear advice. In all probability, these thoughts from the last weeks of his life were little known to his European followers – a selection of them was only published in the internal bulletin of the European secretariat of the Fourth International in 1945. Nevertheless, Pierre Broué, a French specialist in Trotsky's writings, has emphasised that Trotsky was impatient with political activity that confined itself to explanation and advice – and anybody who considered himself or herself a revolutionary Marxist or Bolshevik Leninist knew that.[8] Revolutionaries could not just be spectators. Lenin and the Bolsheviks, as Trotsky pointed out, did not confine themselves to explaining the imperialist nature of the First World War but intervened in actual events. They became the most powerful party in Russia in 1917 not by exposing the nature of the war, but by their organising and campaigning.

The Resistance had barely emerged in France when in September 1940 Marcel Hic convinced the central committee of the POI – the largest of the French Trotskyist groups – to become involved in it. Not much came of this initiative, although Hic may have made contact with Jean Moulin, General de Gaulle's chief underground resistance organiser in France, over the possible sharing of intel on the Gestapo. Hic's venture into involvement with the emerging Resistance was predicated on pursuing revolutionary Marxist positions[9] but to some it smacked of class collaboration in a Resistance movement whose leaders were very much committed to the restoration of French capitalism and its empire. The other three Trotskyist groups in Paris – the Comité Communiste International, the Groupe Octobre and the Union Communiste – were critical of Hic and the POI majority. For them the official Resistance was a potentially counter-revolutionary force, as were the Allies. These groups pursued a policy of slow recruitment and activity in factories (often employing thousands of workers). Their expectation was that this was where the proletarian uprising would find its base.

What they all agreed on was a policy of 'fraternisation' towards the rank-and-file German troops.[10] This was prompted not just by their internationalism but by their expectation that the war would end with a German revolution which would sweep away the Nazi regime and inspire revolutionary developments across Europe, leading to a Socialist United States of Europe. This, too, was a reprise of the Bolshevik expectation at the end of the First World War. After all, many of the German soldiers were the sons of Social Democrat and Communist fathers and mothers and would be receptive to propaganda encouraging them to overthrow the Nazis and establish a socialist Germany. For all these reasons, they opposed ambushes that targeted ordinary German soldiers. 'The terrorist act creates a barrier between French workers and German soldiers, but no victory is possible without unity between them,' *La Vérité*, the Trotskyist paper, editorialised as early as 15 March 1942. Gestapo, the SS and Nazi officers were legitimate targets but not the men who would be central to the coming German revolution.

This approach gave priority to waging a sophisticated propaganda campaign among the German troops. A German Trotskyist, Martin Monath, who took the pseudonym Paul Widelin, edited and published the newspaper *Arbeiter und Soldat* (Worker and Soldier), to be distributed among occupation soldiers. It focussed on Normandy and Brittany, particularly around Brest where there was a large concentration of Germans.[11] Pablo and Elly enjoyed a close friendship with Monath who often accompanied Elly to concerts in Paris. There were plenty of German officers at those concerts and Monath would joke with Elly, If they only knew who was sitting near them in the audience.[12]

With Martin Monath and local Trotskyists recruiting a group of up to 50 German soldiers, the work was initially successful until one, Private Konrad Leplow, who acted as a liaison between Brest and Paris, was arrested and betrayed them. In September, eleven French supporters in Brittany were arrested and sent to the camps in Germany, except for their leader, the postman Robert Cruau, who was executed along with an unknown number of soldiers. On 13 October 1943, Marcel Hic was arrested at the Paris news agency where he worked. Five other Trotskyists were also picked off in Paris. They were all sent to Buchenwald. From there Hic was transferred to Dora (where he fell foul of the German communists who controlled the camp) and then to Ellrich, which was worse and where he died in December 1944, almost blind and exhausted from starvation and forced labour.

During this disastrous wave of losses Pablo's luck held. He lived in the apartment next door to Hic and just as the Gestapo was raiding Hic's apartment, he was on his way home when he was passed on the street by a complete stranger who muttered a warning about the presence of the Gestapo in his building.[13] He and Elly found refuge with Dimitris Giotopoulos, the former leader of the Archeio-Marxists who was now eking out a living in Paris with his wife making soap. It was another example of Pablo's ability to maintain friendly links with those he'd fallen out with politically.

Monath survived, too, and continued publishing and circulating *Arbeiter und Soldat* until he was arrested six months later after a courier was nabbed with his 'office' address in her handbag. Pablo says that on the fatal night, both he and Elly (and Elly very strongly) pressed him not to return to the room where he stored his papers and copies of *Arbeiter und Soldat* as it was too dangerous, but he had ignored their pleas. He was arrested there in the early morning in July 1944, and taken to the Bois de Vincennes where he was shot and left for dead. A passing policeman discovered him, his body riddled with bullet wounds but still alive, and took him to the Rothschild hospital. Pablo received word of his whereabouts and organised a rescue attempt to be led by Yvan Craipeau. However, the doctors advised a delay until Monath was in better shape. The delay proved fatal. Informed by someone at the hospital, the Gestapo arrived and took him away. This time they did not botch the job.

There was better luck with the Romanian, Nicolas Spoulber, who had been arrested the same day as Monath and was, like Monath, a member of the European secretariat of the Fourth. He managed to escape from police headquarters by jumping from the second floor into a pile of freshly dug soil. He found his way to the nearby flat of Fred Zeller, a Trotskyist sympathiser, and from there Pablo organised his transfer to a safe place.

— ✦ —

In the midst of these devastating losses, the Bolshevik-Leninists, pushed by Pablo, were straightening out their line on the German occupation.

In December 1943, the provisional European secretariat agreed that the partisan movement represented the political activation of the masses and could help the Soviet Union militarily. In other words, that Bolshevik-Leninists should get involved. The resolution of the secretariat recommended to militants to organise their own armed detachments or join the official Resistance (taking care not to leave themselves open to deadly reprisals) and to insist on internal democracy in these armed formations, and that these partisan units act autonomously rather than as mere auxiliaries of the Allied forces. It concluded with a call 'to oppose all policies of assassinating German soldiers ... and to organise propaganda for fraternisation with the occupation troops and to open their ranks to German deserters.'[14]

These exhortations were repeated in the manifesto adopted by the European conference of the Trotskyists in February 1944.

This conference, the fulfilment of a promise Pablo had made to the various groups, was held over six days, bringing together delegates from six European countries. The venue was the stables of a castle belonging to Louis Dalmas, an aristocratic member of the POI. The delegates ate, slept and held discussions day and night for six days in that barn near the Belgian border, guarded by armed members of the local resistance. The delegates present were: Abraham Leon (real name Wajnsztok) and Ernest Mandel (RCP, Belgium); Yvan Craipeau, Nicolas Spoulber, Marcel Gibelin, Alain Le Dem (POI, France); Jacques Grinblat, Rodolphe Prager (CCI, France); Henri Claude-Pouget (October Group, France); Martin Monath (German Group), Michel Raptis, Georges Vitsoris (Greek section); Ernesto Morris, Rafael Font Farran (Spanish Group). It adopted the manifesto drafted by Pablo and the secretariat and united the three French groups into the new Parti Communiste International 'in a wonderful atmosphere of close co-operation', according to Pablo and Rodolphe Prager, a delegate and later the historian of the movement. The conference elected Pablo as its European secretary.

The manifesto, entitled *The Liquidation of War and the Rise of the Revolution*, became the central policy document from which they were not to waiver in the months ahead. It is a very Bolshevik document, taking as its model the evolution of events in 1917 in Russia, but it goes well beyond that. In Italy during 1943, strikes in the big industrial cities had fatally undermined and then led to the fall of the Mussolini regime. At the time of the conference, strikes were continuing to unsettle the German occupation and provide a basis for the Resistance in the north of Italy. The Italian example seemed to confirm the likely scenario of an insurgent working class in France and other countries of occupied Europe being the backbone of any successful resistance.

The conference document recognised that the armed resistance in France had taken on a mass character. As the European secretariat had declared in December 1943:

> Faced with the partly spontaneous character of the partisan movement, and expression of the open and inevitable revolt of broad layers of working people against German imperialism and against the order and the state of the native bourgeoisie, who in their eyes are responsible for their poverty and suffering, the Bolshevik-Leninists are obliged to take into account this will to struggle on the part of the masses and to try, despite the many dangers deriving from the nationalist forms that this struggle assumes, to orient it towards class aims.

The Trotskyists could now participate in the Resistance with their own organised armed detachments and by joining other mixed resistance groups. Simultaneously they were to organise in workplaces to draw all workers – whatever their political attachments – into discussion and action groups. This was to be the basis of a mass, networked movement they called the 'Front Ouvrier' (Workers Front). The immediate policy they were to advocate in this nascent proletarian democracy was openness to all political trends, industrial action to aid the Resistance and disrupt the Nazi war effort, and opposition to illusions about bourgeois democracy.

In this way the working class would be united on both a national and international level. Such a network of workplace groups would lay the basis for the emergence of a soviet democracy in all the occupied countries. After the collapse of the occupation, the 'liquidation of the war and the rise of the Revolution' would continue; the Bolshevik-Leninists were to lead the campaign for the nationalisation under workers' control of large companies, the reorganisation of agriculture and the resumption of food deliveries, and the planning of the economy.

Leaving aside the reaction of American and British army commanders, this hopeful scenario clearly rested on a number of dubious assumptions. Not the least of these assumptions was the emergence of a revolutionary mood in the working class and the consequent loosening of their loyalty to the communist and socialist parties, and the panacea they and the Gaullists were offering of a revived and socially just capitalist democracy. As history was soon to show, these assumptions were never fulfilled. In retrospect,

Pablo was to say of himself and his comrades that they were 'roaring in the desert'. French workers were elsewhere, in another dimension, putting their trust in the traditional workers parties, particularly the Communists who surfed along on the mass admiration of the Red Army, as well as their own role in the Resistance.

There is another school of thought that argues that the lack of success was the fault of the Trotskyists themselves, who were never able to overcome their suspicion of nationalism and their belated and half-hearted embrace of the Resistance movement. This view is spelled out by Gerd Rainer-Horn:[15]

> ... it is significant that the clandestine European conference of the Fourth International, which was held in February 1944 ... had (while condemning "with the greatest vigour" the total refusal of some comrades to take into account "national requirements") reserved the bulk of its criticism to those who "represent a social-patriotic deviation which must once and for all be openly condemned and rejected as incompatible with the general program and ideology of the Fourth International".

According to Rainer-Horn, this meant in practice that little in the way of concrete support was offered to the existing Resistance. Yet straight after the conference, *La Verité* in its 17 February 1944 issue called for 'secours des gars du maquis' and a 'descendre les gens de la milice comme des chiens enragés' ['help for our friends in the resistance' and 'kill the armed collaborators like enraged dogs']. In the 29 April issue the paper called – partially successfully as it turned out – for a general strike on 1 May with a view for preparing to occupy workplaces under workers' control and for the Socialist United States of Europe.[16] Nevertheless there were mixed messages, such as this statement of policy from *La Verité*, June 1944:

> The PCI says to workers: you've had enough of the war; you want to be really liberated; trust no one but your own class. Don't trust Eisenhower. Get organised today in militias, stay grouped in your own factory which is your bastion; don't let yourself be mobilised into the army of liberation; prepare for a new June 1936; you must elect your own committee, your soviet, to free yourself from proletarian slavery.

This was closer to the old position of the CCI rather than to that of the European secretariat (and Pablo). Pablo was to later characterise these mixed messages as a 'delay' in appreciating the mass character of the Resistance and the taking up of opportunities to work in it.[17]

## 4 . PABLO'S WAR 1943-46

As crucial as any confusion, conflict or 'delay' over the attitude towards the mass Resistance, was the lack of numbers and means. At war's end the French Trotskyists numbered in the hundreds – PCI membership peaked at around 800 in 1947-48 – compared with the Communist Party whose membership stood at over 500,000 in January 1945.

As for arms, there are accounts of Trotskyist groups recovering the odd weapon from a downed Allied plane or a small suburban arsenal, but that's all. They did form an underground armed resistance in Val d'Oise, north of Paris, and when Paris did rise and free itself in the third week of August 1944, some Trotskyists led a detachment of 60 armed men in the 14th and 15th arrondissements which helped liberate those neighbourhoods.[18]

During the liberation of Paris, *La Verité* came out regularly, advocating that the insurgent masses should continue to organise themselves in their workplaces and neighbourhoods, federate their organisations, pursue an independent and socialist policy and retain their arms. Individual militants did receive encouraging support in many workplaces around the city. But, as the critical historian Jacqueline Pluet-Despatin points out, the emphasis on organising in the workplaces was misplaced. This was exactly where the Communists proved to be strongest and workplace-based militias and factory occupation committees rarely escaped their control.[19]

To an extent, Rodolphe Prager, who was as close as the Fourth International ever came to having an official historian, confirms the Rainer-Horn critique, concluding that as far as the Resistance was concerned, 'To tell the truth, no important turn in this direction was ever made.' According to Yvan Craipeau, a former leader of the POI, comrade Prager should know, as it was comrades from the former Comité Communiste Internationaliste (of which Prager had been a leader before the Trotskyist groups unified) who frustrated the new policy turn and ensured the PCI remained an isolated sect.[20] In Pablo's account written in 1946, Craipeau overstates the case and Pablo argues that he and others (including Craipeau) were able to wear down and correct the leftist opposition to any involvement with the Resistance.[21] Forty years later Pablo moved closer to Craipeau's position, admitting in a convoluted way that the Fourth International had been slow to recognise the potential of the resistance movements and to get involved with them.[22]

Prager did emphasise the very valid practical difficulty the Bolshevik-Leninists faced in joining the Resistance: 'The problem was complicated by the fact that one had to take care to avoid being identified as a political militant in order to participate in the armed groups at all. The life of anyone discovered to be a Trotskyist would have been in danger.'[23] In danger – and not just from the Gestapo.

This was by no means an exaggerated fear. On the night of 1-2 October 1943, five Trotskyists had taken part in a mass jail break of political prisoners from the Puy-en-Velay prison in Vichy France. The escape had been made possible by Albert Chapelle, a Socialist militant, working as a warder at the prison. One of the five Trotskyists who escaped was Pietro Tresso, a founder of the Italian Communist Party (PCI) who had become a Trotskyist in the 1930s after being expelled from the Italian Party. These Trotskyists were known to the Communist leader of the escaped prisoners and he had wanted to leave them behind, but Chapelle had set the condition: everyone or no one.

One of the five, Albert Demazière (1914-2008), who had been a leader of the Trotskyist underground in the south of France, did not stay in the south but left for Paris where he wrote an enthusiastic account for *La Verité* celebrating the extraordinary escape engineered by the Resistance and extolling the political diversity of the escapees and the climate of cooperation among the freed men.[24] He wrote too soon. By mid-October the remaining four Trotskyists were isolated in the Resistance base and their detention was communicated up the chain of political command. They were executed on the night of 26-27 October. Who gave the order has never been firmly established.[25]

After the war, two truly remarkable women made efforts to establish the truth of these murders. One was Gabrielle Brausch[26] (1910-58), who herself had been imprisoned for four years by the Vichy regime and was the partner of one of the victims, Maurice Ségal, and the other was Barbara Seidenfeld (1901-76), the companion of Pietro and a political organiser in her own right, who had been expelled from the Italian Communist Party along with Tresso. Gabrielle was also the first wife of Jean van Heijenoort, Trotsky's main secretary in the 1930s. They had a young son whom she managed to accompany to Lisbon from Marseilles at the outbreak of the war and put on a boat to join his father, then in New York. Barbara's sister was married to the writer and one-time Trotsky supporter, Ignace Silone. Both women's efforts to find the truth were met by a wall of lies, silence and false trails. Brausch never really recovered from these tragic years and died in 1958, aged 48, of heart disease.

Another victim of the Stalinists was Mathieu Bucholz. All the French Trotskyist groups campaigned against the forced conscription of hundreds of thousands of French workers sent to Germany to work in industry there. They supported all efforts to frustrate this forced labour, from escapes to join the maquis through to strikes. An estimated 50,000 did abscond and join the Resistance in 1943-44. The chief reason Trotskyists opposed the Service du Travail Obligatoire was because it released German workers to fight on the Eastern Front against the Soviet Red Army, but this didn't save Trotskyists from Stalinist reprisals. Mathieu Bucholz was kidnapped in September 1944 by Stalinist partisans and executed.[27] These were the days when Trotskyists were described by communist leaders, taking their cue from Stalin, as agents of the Nazis. The term 'hitléro-trotskistes' was coined for them.[28]

The Stalinist repression was greatest in Greece, with scores of Trotskyists and Archeio-Marxists executed by Stalinist police squads there. After the war Rodolphe Prager's careful investigation of those Greek Trotskyists known to have died during the war accounted for four executed by the Metaxas dictatorship, 15 killed by the German and Italian invaders, and 34 by the Stalinists.[29] Many non-Trotskyist, non-Stalinist leftists were also executed by Stalinist 'police'.

The Nazis and Stalinists weren't alone in murdering Trotskyists, the Italian fascists did their part too. In 1943 Pablo's mentor and comrade, Pantelis Pouliopoulos, was executed in Greece by the Italian occupying forces, along with a group of his comrades. Pouliopoulos' last act was to address the firing squad of rank-and-file Italian soldiers in their own language and persuade them not to fire. Their officers stepped in and shot him. He died shouting 'Long live the International' in Italian.[30]

In June 1944 Abraham Leon (Wajnsztok), was captured and died in the gas chambers at Auschwitz a few months later. He was just 26 and for Pablo this death was 'the most significant loss' of these years. In his memoirs he names Hic, Leon, Spoulber and Ernest Mandel as the comrades he was banking on for the future and who he felt closest to. Only the young Belgian Ernest Mandel, who escaped his imprisonment in Germany, was to continue as a collaborator in the coming decades.

Towards the end of his life Pablo talked of Mandel as having become something of a spiritual son (or nephew) – Mandel was then 20 and Pablo, 33.[31] During the war, Mandel would stay with Pablo and Elly on clandestine visits to Paris to attend secretariat meetings. Despite a spectacular falling-out that would occur in the 1960s, Pablo never completely lost his affection and respect for Mandel's intellectual abilities. Mandel would go on to become a professor of economics and arguably the most authoritative Marxist economist of his generation.[32]

— ✦ —

Remarkably, despite these efforts in rebuilding the Fourth International – wrangling the factions, refining the political line of the organisation, providing the material basis for its operations and writing and publishing its theoretical journal – Pablo did not have exclusivist ambitions for it. As he wrote in the leading article in the first issue of the relaunched *Quatrième Internationale* of August 1943:

> ... in our work for the organisation and development of new parties and the new International, we will march together with all the other revolutionary currents with which we find ourselves in accord ...

To make it clear that these convergences would be mutual rather than a takeover, he added:

> We will exchange our experience with the experience of all the other revolutionary currents, we will abandon, or we will fill out, our political ideas and methods of work which reveal themselves in revolutionary practice to be insufficient.

This absence of organisational fetishism went hand in hand with a critical, even excoriating attitude to the work and attitudes of his comrades. Moreover, his criticism was made in public as *Quatrième Internationale* was not an internal document.

Forty years later, in his memoirs, he could recall this 1943 article with some affection and quoted again the words of Rosa Luxemburg which had inspired him at the time:

> Marxism is a revolutionary conception of the world, called upon to struggle unceasingly to acquire fresh results and which abhors nothing so much as fixed, definitive formulas, and which best tests its living force in the clash of self-criticism and in the storms of History.

He was adamant the Fourth International was falling short of this gold standard. 'Neither the ensemble of our ideas,' he wrote in 1943, 'nor the ensemble of our methods of work are beyond a serious critique.' And he went on more sharply: '... "Trotskyism" [the quote marks are in the original – HG] must proceed to the review of its ideological and organisational weapons and submit them to a profoundly critical examination. It must break resolutely with the petit-bourgeois attitude of certain of our cadres who, isolated from all action of the masses, conceive their political role in the bureaucratic sense of leading – from the height of their grandeur – the masses.'

If the Fourth International's future was open to fusions, that did not absolve it from building a real following in the present. And if any comrades were in doubt as to what he was talking about, he spelled it out:

> Marxists, shut up in a closed world, who elaborate their theory and practice and want to impose it on the proletarian masses from the height of their professional chairs in political science, acting as revolutionary chiefs and guides, forget and mock the essence of our doctrine which teaches us to put our schemas to the test of events and to learn in the practice of the workers movement, by participation in its actual struggles, the art of revolutionary politics.

Trotsky had recognised this need for alliances and convergences in Spain in 1936-37, lavishing support and praise on the Durruti wing of the anarchist movement. The Bolsheviks didn't make the Russian Revolution alone. To win and secure the revolution in October 1917 they formed an alliance with the Left Social Revolutionaries (and there is a strong argument that a more sensible Menshevik party could have been part of that revolutionary coalition to the possible benefit of the socialist cause). Who these other forces were in Europe in 1943 Pablo did not say immediately, but it became clear he (and his comrades) were thinking of members and supporters of the Communist Party. They were banking on large sections of the French Communist Party, for instance, growing unable to stomach the pandering to the Allies and their bourgeoisies by Stalin and the Stalinist leaderships of these parties, and unable to resist the push for revolutionary socialist initiatives coming spontaneously from the working class itself. Stalin had just disbanded the Communist International in 1943 and this renunciation of revolution in Europe could not fail, in the estimation of Pablo and his comrades, to disillusion genuine communist revolutionaries.[33]

That was, as we know, excessively optimistic as far as the revolutionary mood of the working classes and the members of almost all the Communist parties in Europe were concerned. Pablo was not long in recognising that but his faith in the dialectical dance between the spontaneous revolutionary activity of the working class and its allies ('the masses'), on the one hand, and revolutionary or even reformist organisations on the other, was to persist. In his view, its validity would be confirmed in cases such as Yugoslavia, China, Algeria and wartime Greece, where the insurgent masses forced the hand of their organisations. His openness to other revolutionary, or potentially revolutionary, forces would never flag and it would give rise to some tension with comrades of the Fourth

International, of which, for the next 20 years, he was the recognised leader or spokesman.

— ✦ —

As the war wound down, Pablo, Mandel and their comrades still anticipated revolutionary possibilities in Europe. In September 1943, Pablo had noted the potential of the Greek resistance to culminate in a national and social revolution. In the autumn of 1944, as the Germans withdrew from Greece, the Greek resistance forces virtually took power across the country. However, Stalin had agreed with Churchill that Greece was to be in the British sphere of interest, and British troops moved to take control of Athens in December. The Greek communist leaders, in obedience to Stalin, agreed to relinquish control of the capital without a fight.

In January 1945, the European Secretariat (almost certainly Pablo himself) issued a bulletin titled *La Révolution grecque*. It was basically a compilation of American, British and European press reports on the triumph of the Stalinist-led Resistance in the wake of the forced retreat of the German troops, and on the subsequent attack on the Resistance in Athens by a British force in December 1944. Pablo followed up with an article on the subject in *Quatrième Internationale* of January-February 1945. In it he noted the revolutionary mood and actions of the urban working class and poor peasants, the vacillating leadership and betrayals of the Greek Communist leaders, and the mobilisation of the counter-revolutionary forces which had collaborated with the Nazi occupiers. He acknowledged the check the revolution had received from the British intervention but thought it 'wasn't decisive'. He was in no doubt about the revolutionary nature of the Communist-led resistance in Greece: 'Despite itself, despite its nationalist pronouncements, despite its policy of conciliation and class collaboration, the Greek Communist Party grouped around itself the forces which history set in motion and which, in the last analysis, were the forces of the proletarian revolution'.[34]

There were mortal dangers for Trotskyists who might join the Greek Resistance, but Pablo believed that more should have made the attempt, risky as it was. Dimitris Livieratos, who later became a comrade of Pablo's and served in the Resistance, agreed.[35] (Livieratos joined the anti-Nazi resistance in Athens as a student. He was the youngest second lieutenant to graduate from the ELAS Officers' School in Redina, organised by the national liberation movement.) Pablo thought it was entirely possible that pressure from below would force the Communist Party leaders to abandon, or at least relax, their rigid compliance with orders from Moscow and adopt a more radical stance in order to maintain mass support.[36] This was how he read the situation in neighbouring Yugoslavia, where the communist party led by Tito was carrying through a revolution despite the deal between Stalin and Churchill to deny the country such an evolution.

Pablo was in little doubt that there was a 'Tito-ist' or Yugoslav wing of the Greek Resistance which was seriously interested in pursuing a revolution in Greece. Aris Velouchiotis, the most famous Resistance commander, was clearly one such figure. After some hesitation, he refused to accept the surrender and disarmament of the Resistance ordered by the Greek Communist Party leaders and took to the mountains in 1945 to continue the struggle, only to be disowned, betrayed and killed. Andreas Tzimas, arguably the key strategist in the launching of the Resistance struggle in 1941-42, was another. Unlike Velouchiotis, he survived, but he was already sidelined by 1944. Whether a late influx of scores of Greek revolutionary Marxists could have turned the tide against the Stalinist leadership, ultimately obedient to orders from Moscow to lay down their arms and accept the British-installed regime in 1945-46, is doubtful, to say the least.

The Greek events were a foretaste of the suppression, or avoidance, of any revolutionary possibilities at the end of the war. As Churchill frankly relates in his memoirs[37], the division of Europe into capitalist and Moscow communist zones had been agreed at Yalta by the Allied leaders – Stalin, Roosevelt and Churchill – and except in the case of Yugoslavia, the deal was to stick.

CHAPTER 5

# The revolution will happen (but elsewhere) 1945-1950

*It works all very well in practice, but does it work in theory?*

Anon

*All those who seek exact predictions of concrete events should consult the astrologists, Marxist prognosis aids only in orientation.*

Trotsky

*What is actually involved today is the prelude to a lengthy revolutionary period in which the Fourth International will have the greatest possible chances to build its mass parties.*

Resolution of the European Executive Committee
June 1945

FOR PABLO, THE Second World War was 'the greatest storm in history'. But the storm was unpredictable. Pablo, in obedience to the forecasts of the Old Man (as Trotsky was referred to), expected the gales of revolution to blow through Europe at the conclusion of the war – as it had at the conclusion of the First World War.[1] While the hope of a German revolution, a repeat of November-December 1918, was abandoned even before the end of the war, Pablo and his comrades did not give up their expectation of European revolutions. The final roar of the storm was delayed, they conceded, but it was coming.

In retrospect this appears quixotic, and it was as far as the North Atlantic heartlands of capitalism were concerned. However, the green shoots of objective revolutionary situations were indeed emerging if your focus was

## 5 . THE REVOLUTION WILL HAPPEN (BUT ELSEWHERE) 1945-50

wider. A revolutionary partisan movement triumphed in Yugoslavia. A revolution was aborted in Greece but was not extinguished. In Italy only the presence of Allied troops and the role of the Italian Communist Party had prevented a possible revolution. Tens of millions were on the march in China, Indonesia, Algeria and Vietnam. It did appear that Trotsky's prediction of a wave of revolutions at the conclusion of the war was being confirmed, but not in the places and forms he, and his followers, expected.

The liberation of Paris gave Pablo and his co-thinkers their first reality check. The city's residents did rise in response to the call of the Resistance and seized control of the city in the third week of August 1944. Paris was already delivered from Nazi rule by the time the Allied troops arrived. The French Trotskyists were active in the fighting and in organising in the factories in the 'Red belt' west of Paris, but it was soon evident that the communist and socialist parties were in control of the uprising and had no interest in any kind of social revolution.[2] From their eyrie on the Boulevard Saint-Michel opposite the École des Mines, Pablo and Elly witnessed skirmishes between German troops and Resistance fighters. 'The battle for the liberation of Paris became purely patriotic, it even had a chauvinistic character,' he recalled. The battle had 'nothing especially heroic' about it. The German high command had left relatively young and inexperienced troops in the capital to cover the retreat of the main forces to the north-east. When these soldiers surrendered 'some of them were executed on the spot by frenzied crowds and newly recruited Resistance fighters.' In this 'chauvinist hysterical atmosphere', Pablo recalled, without going into detail, that he, Elly and their comrades remained true to their anti-chauvinist wartime work and offered shelter to deserting or surrendering German soldiers.[3]

Soon after the liberation of Paris, hope for the immediate outbreak of revolution in Germany – the holy grail of the Bolshevik-Leninist model for the European revolution – had to be postponed. Pablo was the first – or among the first – of the comrades to realise this. Until the end of 1944 Pablo shared the hope of a German revolution 'which would somehow automatically and unavoidably erupt from the collapse of fascism'. In a resolution he drafted for the European secretariat in January 1945, he recognised this wouldn't be happening. A combination of the Allied bombing, which destroyed the human and material bases for society, let alone revolution, and the extraordinary continuing control of the Nazis, rendered any revolt impossible. The classic novel of these times, *Berlin Finale*, by Heinrich Rein, an intimate portrait of a group of anti-Nazi activists in Berlin during the last months of the war, confirms this analysis. Their homes and workplaces are bombed and destroyed, and the Nazi police, informers and SS killers honeycomb the city, choking off any dissident activity by a terrified population. In fact, the activists spend most of their time evading and hiding from police and SS (and their civilian auxiliaries) until they can surrender to the Red Army who in their turn abuse, rob and rape Berliners of every class.

While acknowledging the non-appearance of the revolution in Germany, its suppression by Allied armies in Italy and Greece, and the anti-revolutionary orientation of the dominant Socialist and Communist Parties, Pablo continued to believe revolution in Europe was only a matter of time.[4] He made this quite clear in that same resolution-report to the European Secretariat in January 1945. The ripening revolutionary situation was structural; it flowed from the congenital incapacity of capitalism to recover and assure prosperity.

This belief that capitalism had exhausted its capacity for growth and prosperity was foundational for Trotsky's followers. It underwrote all their analyses. The revolution would unfold unevenly, there would even be partial defeats and setbacks, but it was inevitable. 'What determines the revolutionary character of the current situation,' Pablo argued in that January 1945 resolution, 'is the fact that the least demand of the masses to rectify the rising cost of living, the famine or unemployment, collides with the possibilities of capitalism and leads to a struggle against the whole regime.' As early as 1943 Pablo had brushed aside any possibility that Keynes or any other liberal economist could succeed in stabilising capitalism and ensuring full employment and prosperity.[5]

Certainly, wherever you looked, any possibility of revolution was being delayed by the actions of the British, American and Soviet armies and their installation of bourgeois regimes (if necessary bolstered by the collaborationist, proto-fascist forces active during the Nazi occupation, as in Greece). It was helped along by the willing agreement of the Communist and Socialist parties who commanded the support of the overwhelming majority of the working class in Europe. The Allies sought – where they safely could – to allow a limited measure of democracy. Nevertheless, the objective situation of famine, inflation and economic ruin, which prevailed throughout Europe after the war, as well as the burdens of the foreign occupation itself, would surely drive the working class into radical and even revolutionary action. Post-war living conditions were grim: in France, for instance, average daily calorie intake had dropped from 2,830 in 1938 to 1,160 in 1946.[6] It wasn't precluded, in this line of thinking,

## 5 . THE REVOLUTION WILL HAPPEN (BUT ELSEWHERE) 1945-50

that the pressure from below would have a radicalising impact on the members and mid-level cadres of communist parties.

In this perspective the small, propagandist Trotskyist groups were to mobilise themselves to help along this revolutionary process. And one of their tasks was to avoid their previous abstention from (and hostile attitude to) the armed Resistance. 'The relentless attacks of the bourgeoisie and foreign imperialism against the people's militias and the armed partisan formations that arose to combat the Nazi occupation, demonstrates that the view of our class enemy was more perceptive than the political intuition of the ultra-Lefts in and outside of our ranks,' Pablo wrote in 1946. 'Instead of ignoring and condemning these formations *en bloc*, supporters of the Fourth International must work to develop their progressive social aims and orient them towards an autonomous political existence in the service of the masses and against the bourgeoisie.' In addition, the Trotskyists should campaign for socialist-communist governments.

Later he would describe these optimistic exhortations as 'roaring in the desert'. In the absence (or rather delay) in Europe, his expectations initially took an even more unreal turn – towards revolutionary developments in the United States. After the war, the Unites States enjoyed boom conditions. However, Pablo viewed this as just the calm before the storm, the boomlet before the recurrence of the Depression. This downturn would lay the groundwork for a revolutionary situation to emerge in the United States. As he admitted in 1958: '… it suffices to say that the prospect of an American economic crisis, counted on in the near future and in a classic form, naturally had as a consequence the over-estimation of the possibilities of revolutionary crisis in the advanced capitalist countries, and especially the United States. This estimate, combined with the importance assigned at that period to American imperialism, caused a premature advancing of the hour of the American revolution.' Premature indeed.

The assumption of a crisis-ridden capitalism was common right across the political spectrum after the war.[7] Eric Hobsbawm cites future Nobel laureate, the American economist Paul Samuelson, as one who predicted a major post-war economic crisis in the USA that would amount to 'the greatest period of unemployment and industrial dislocation any economy has ever faced'. Neither the Trotskyists nor Samuelson were outliers; as Hobsbawm notes: 'Most observers expected a serious post-war economic crisis'. He points to the widely held view, 'absurd in retrospect but natural enough in the aftermath of the Second World War, that the Age of Catastrophe was by no means at an end, that the future of capitalism and liberal society was far from assured'.[8] At war's end Europe did lie in ruins. Harvests were poor in 1946 and there was real hunger, bitter cold and misery in France and Italy in the terrible winter of 1947. Since 1914, capitalism had delivered two world wars, mass murder on an industrial scale and economic failure accompanied by widespread impoverishment. There was a real basis for an overwhelmingly pessimistic view of what capitalism had in store for humanity.

It wasn't as though Pablo wasn't paying attention to the economic news or that his analysis lacked nuance. He paid close attention to the Marshall Plan, the massive package of US economic aid to Europe in the immediate post-war years. He also saw early the boost to the economy from military spending which soared after 1950. As the 1950s wore on he noted the role a vast increase in credit played in boosting the capitalist economy, particularly in housing, automobiles and white goods. But each of these twists in the story of capitalism was conceived as just one more way of putting off the inevitable day of the crisis, the arrival of another of the 'episodic convulsions' that Marx had predicted. It wasn't until the late 1950s that Pablo would accept capitalism's emergence from stagnation and crisis. It hadn't just survived. It was flourishing.

— ✦ —

In preparation of the revolutionary wave he envisaged, Pablo initiated what was billed as an international conference of the Fourth International, held in Paris in March 1946 for representatives from Trotskyist groups in 15 countries. It climaxed in a police raid on the upstairs café where the conference was being held. On the third and scheduled final day of the conference, plain-clothes police stormed up the stairs with revolvers drawn. There was panic in the hall as the delegates initially feared that the raiders were Stalinist thugs. There was some relief when it emerged they were French *flics*. Incriminating documents were quickly scooped up by Pablo and given to the American delegate Sherry Mangan to stuff in his briefcase for safe keeping. Mangan was a journalist for *Time-Life* based in Paris and thought to be protected from any police searches by his status – which turned out to be true. Mangan, who was a Hemingway-esque figure, was also armed but managed to rid himself of the small pistol and its bullets on the way to the lock-up.

The police had been tipped off by a civilian who suspected the gathering might be a clandestine regrouping of European fascists. They were taken to the basement of the Palais de Justice and held overnight while police checked on their status. Pablo reconvened the conference in the basement cells: 'When night came, I moved that we continue the discussion and ignore the group of policemen at the other end of the basement who had settled in to play cards. My proposal was accepted and throughout the night we talked, voted and elected an entirely new international secretariat with me as secretary. When all was completed, it was nearly dawn, we sang with stentorian voices the *Internationale*. Half asleep, our guards looked at us as if we were some sort of cosmopolitan halfwits. In the morning they let us go gradually, with the Spaniards, the Indochinese and me being the last released. Never before in the history of Paris had there been a revolutionary meeting in the basement of the headquarters of French justice.'

Later in 1946, Pablo and Elly set sail from Marseilles for Greece on a 'Lilliputian' yacht. Sherry Mangan was in command and Pablo posed as his secretary. The weather was good and when they reached Greece, Pablo's nostalgia surfaced. 'When we sailed close to the coast of the Peloponnese after so many years and I saw a small, peaceful church standing on the shore, I was overcome with a bout of indescribable shivering. I thought then that some drops of Greek blood still flowed in my cosmopolitan veins.'

The visit to Greece must have been sobering. A right-wing terror prevailed in the country as communist-led resistance fighters, who had surrendered their weapons when the British-backed government had been installed in Athens, were hunted down. Earlier, the security force of these same communists had murdered scores of various non-Stalinist leftists. According to the most complete list published by Marios Emmanouilidis, around fifty Trotskyists, perhaps one in five members of all the Trotskyist groups, and around thirty 'Archeio-Marxists', were murdered. That is more than three times the number killed by the wartime occupying forces.[9] 'I was under no illusions about the danger that awaited the Greek secretary of the Fourth International,' Pablo recalled.

Nevertheless, Mangan booked both of them into the main international hotel in Athens while Elly stayed with her family. Pablo convened and chaired the conference that managed to bring together and unify the various Greek Trotskyist groups. A manifesto was issued calling for the unity of all forces on the Left to resist the right-wing offensive, for the restoration of democratic freedoms, an amnesty for Resistance fighters and fresh and free elections to a constitutional convention. Late in the day, too late in fact, Trotskyists – on Pablo's insistence – were ready to accept that their place was in the reviving Resistance, wherever that was possible.

The following year, Pablo, apparently alone, travelled to New York to meet the leaders of the American Socialist Workers' Party, the largest and richest of the national sections of the Fourth International. He says very little in his memoirs about the trip beyond the fact that it happened and he met James Cannon and other historic leaders of this party. Their continued support for his leadership was important and diplomacy may have been the chief reason for his visit. In the last 18 months of the war and its aftermath, there had been a sharp debate inside the SWP over the strategy that the Fourth International should pursue in Europe. The debate had spilled over into Europe and revolved around relations with the Resistance and whether the emphasis should be on democratic or social demands in their agitation. Pablo and the European secretariat had tried to be even-handed and to treat the debate as a discussion rather than as a fight to the finish over orientation. However, the debate in the SWP became entangled with other conflicts between a majority around Cannon and a minority around Felix Morrow and Trotsky's long-time secretary Jean van Heijenoort. Forced to choose, Pablo and the European secretariat declined to accept the SWP minority's insistent advice.[10]

—⁂—

The backdrop of continuing economic misery in Europe, and its possible political repercussion, was of concern in Washington and Western European capitals, too. Their answer was the Marshall Plan. Initiated in 1947 and essentially comprising boatloads of free American food and dollars for Europeans, the Plan had, Pablo argued, four aims: to revive and consolidate capitalism in Western Europe, to deny Communist parties the economic conditions for their agitation, to provide American capitalism with much needed markets, and to endow the 'American' half of Europe with a prosperity and dynamism that would destabilise the 'Russian' half still sunk in misery and police terror. On this last point he was prescient: 'The United States counts on the power of disintegration and liquidation that would be exerted on the entire Soviet 'buffer-zone' by a bloc of countries revived thanks to American aid.'

There was no denying the rapid and spectacular success of the Marshall Plan in reviving Western Europe and Pablo did not deny it: '… production for the Marshall Plan countries (with the exception of Germany which still lags behind) has surpassed the 1938 level by 13 per cent; in one year productivity rose 9 per cent and the volume of exports 30 per cent. This increase of production must be directly attributed to the aid given by the

Marshall Plan,' he wrote in 1949. But true to the prevailing Trotskyist orthodoxy, this success would only delay the unavoidable crisis. 'The Marshall Plan brings no solution to the fundamental crisis of European capitalism, nor does it change the descending spiral of European economy which began with the First World War,' he believed. 'On the contrary. While eliminating momentarily the catastrophic character that the European economic situation could take without the contribution of vital American imports, the Marshall Plan underscores the enslavement of Europe and the decline of its economy.'

As for plans for the mooted European common market – known as the Schumann Plan – he believed it would be vitiated by the rivalries of national elites and the demands of the United States. Only a socialist united states of Europe – encompassing east and west – could provide the basis for a sustained and balanced economic revival. In its absence, he predicted:

> Now, no one denies the fact any longer that we have already entered the beginning of a crisis which is designated as "depression," "recession," "disinflation," or some other term to soften its effects on the ears of frightened businessmen. Once begun, the crisis will shake from top to bottom the calculations upon which the success of the Marshall Plan was based. Its first effect will be the increased pressure of the United States on the world market to the detriment of all its competitors and the still more acute competition between European capitalists themselves. In the general alarm, the universal watchword will become "every man for himself" ...

As the Marshall plan wound down in 1951, Pablo highlighted the role of the military-industrial complex and arms spending in sustaining capitalism, especially in the United States. 'The insane policy of the bourgeoisie in its historic impasse,' he called it. This course had been adopted before as he observed: world capitalism had partially emerged from the Great Depression in the 1935-38 period thanks to arms spending in the major capitalist economies. 'The Great Depression never came to an end,' John Kenneth Galbraith once observed, 'it merely disappeared in the great mobilisation of the Forties.'[11]

Inflation and diversion of resources from consumption were inevitable consequences of the huge rearmament programs, thereby fuelling working-class resistance and undercutting capitalism's prospects. 'The Western bourgeoisie, by opting for preparation for war and the arms economy,' Pablo wrote in early 1951 as the war in Korea flared and the Cold War set in, 'has for all practical purposes buried all its projects and ideas for restoring its economic and social equilibrium and for meeting the threat of revolution by demonstrating the viability of its economic system.'[12]

As it turned out, it hadn't. Later Pablo would confess to this underestimation of capitalism, although he tempered the mea culpa by blaming the American Trotskyists and Ernest Mandel for keeping him orthodox on this issue. Certainly there were contradictions in his economic analysis of these years. He seemed to be saying, yes the Marshall Plan is reviving European capitalism but it can't last because as an article of faith we don't believe it can.

— ✛ —

The 2nd world congress of the Fourth International was held over nine days in Belgium in April 1948. Delegates from 19 countries confirmed the analyses of the immediate post-war years that it was only a matter of time before capitalism would be in terminal crisis. There was some softening of the overriding catastrophism of the outlook, but it was still apocalyptic. As the main document adopted stated:

> Scarcely three years after the end of the second imperialist war that ravaged the planet and pushed to the pitch of paroxysm all the contradictions of the capitalist regime, mankind finds itself once more before a concatenation of calamities inherent in the nature of this regime as long as it continues to last: the prospect of a new world economic crisis, threats of dictatorship and fascism, the atomic Third World War.
>
> In the absence of a revolutionary outcome, the stepped-up crisis of capitalism threatens to lead once more to fascism and war, which this time would imperil the existence and future of all mankind.

It noted the increased tensions between the US and the Soviet Union but, as in the case of the economic crisis, it believed the coming war between the two was delayed. The United States needed to secure its positions, particularly in Western Europe. It was the onset of a serious recession or depression in the US that would ratchet up the prospect of a war against the Soviet Union, according to the documents of the congress:

> American imperialism, before plunging into war, must feel itself in a real economic impasse and must have stabilised both in Europe and Asia solid support that will permit it to believe that it will be able rapidly and effectively to master the world chaos that would inevitably result [from such a war].

Pablo delivered an optimistic organisational report on the first decade of the Fourth to the conference:

## 5 . THE REVOLUTION WILL HAPPEN (BUT ELSEWHERE) 1945-50

During that period, the forces of the Fourth International, grown more homogeneous politically, were gradually getting rid of sectarian habits and, here and there, of opportunist weaknesses, were becoming conscious of new international and social realities, and were making their way confidently toward their well-thought-out and effective integration in the real mass movement of each country.

That the International had survived the war and the deadly attacks of the fascists and the Stalinists and had grown, was an achievement to be celebrated, and most of the credit must go to Pablo. In organising the congress, he had also tried to enlarge the tent by convincing the Workers Party of Max Shachtman to attend and ensuring the minorities in the American and French parties (represented by CLR James and Cornelius Castoriadis, for instance) were entitled to delegates. However, his report skirted around the bad news: the divisions in the British and French sections, the loss of almost half of the members of the French section following its split in the days before the congress, the short-lived nature of the Greek unification, the split that persisted in the United States (still the largest contingent of Trotskyists in the world) and the isolation of Trotskyists almost everywhere. Certainly, the Fourth International had a wider spread of sections and more members than it had in 1938 when it was founded, but membership was now shrinking, with the exception of Latin America and Ceylon (now Sri Lanka) and possibly India.

The Fourth International that remained may have been more united and homogeneous in its outlook, but arguably that was not an advantage. For example, there was a consensus on the permanent crisis of capitalism, yet the view expounded by some British comrades – that the post-war economic crisis in Europe was not the classical Marxist one of over-production but one of under-production and unmet demand – was more valid. In other words, it was a crisis that could and would be overcome in the short run at least. Homogeneity can often be consensus around an error. Once again the Bolshevik model may be the culprit. It was an article of faith among these latter-day Bolshevik-Leninists that the Russian Revolution had only occurred because Lenin had been able to impose his view – the sought-after homogeneity – on the divided and hesitant Bolsheviks. But even the comforting (and misguided) consensus being celebrated in Pablo's report was soon to be disturbed – by Pablo himself.

— ✛ —

What was beginning to dawn on Pablo was the importance of the colonial revolution. Revolutions were occurring, just not where and in the form revolutionary Marxists had wagered on. The international conference and the second world congress had both declared support for 'the colonial revolution' – particularly in Indochina where a colonial war was raging. Protests had been organised in France against the dispatch of French troops to suppress the national liberation movement in Indochina. However, Pablo later admitted that there was something formal and abstract in these declarations. This was reflected in the proceedings of the second congress when only one of the ten sessions was on the 'colonial revolution' and the final resolution on this issue was shuffled off for more work.[13]

But even this groping recognition met with resistance – especially from Trotskyists in the colonial countries where revolutions were occurring. The victory of the Chinese revolution in 1949 and its adoption of the Soviet model underlined this. Pablo might discern, but the Chinese Trotskyists wouldn't or couldn't, the anti-capitalist nature of the regime Mao and the Chinese communists inaugurated. He had a similar argument to win – against Ernest Mandel among others – about the nature of the regimes emerging in Eastern Europe.[14] Orthodox Trotskyists were misled by what Stalin and Mao said they were intending to do. In China and Eastern Europe, Stalin and his followers declared that socialism was 'an undefined prospect for the future rather than an immediate program' and their aim was 'not to build states on the model of the USSR but mixed economies'.[15] Pablo could see this wasn't the case but there was a lag in acknowledging it among the comrades.

The view of China's Trotskyists was that Mao's victory meant China now had a 'workers and peasants' government which would preside over an economy of small and medium-sized capitalist enterprises. Many months before the final victory of Mao's peasant armies, Pablo had ever so gently attempted to open the eyes of the Chinese comrades to what might actually be happening in China.[16] He conceded that the emergent China was not conforming to the Lenin prescription. Nevertheless, he did strongly suggest that perhaps China's communists were going to do what Tito and the Yugoslav communists had done – come to power on the basis of a victorious peasant insurgency and independently of Moscow, and after that victory banish the local bourgeoisie, implement an egalitarian agrarian reform, nationalise industry and set about constructing a state-owned economy. Furthermore, and about this he was more definite, it was 'very probable' that Mao and his comrades would follow Tito in distancing themselves from Moscow. This mixture of realism and prescience – in their eyes, 'revisionism' – did not endear him to the Chinese comrades.

Similar troubles were in store for Pablo with the Indian Trotskyists and their view of Indian independence.[17] As with their Chinese counterparts, doctrine came first, and if reality did not conform to it, so much the worse for reality. Lenin and Trotsky had decreed that in the age of imperialism, a colonial or semi-colonial country could only achieve real independence via a revolution in the cities, based on the working class which would nationalise industry and implement agrarian reform. Just as the Bolsheviks had done. Accordingly, Indian independence, which definitely didn't conform to this prescription, was fake, or at best semi-independence, as far as the Bolshevik-Leninist Party of India, the Fourth's affiliate on the subcontinent, was concerned. It wasn't until 1950 that they accepted the reality of India's independence.

The health of the Stalinist bureaucracy and its satellite parties in Eastern Europe was equally challenging to the orthodoxy inherited from the 1930s. Stalinism had emerged from the war strengthened, an unexpected outcome from the Trotskyist point of view. Given Stalinism's pre-war record – facilitating Hitler's rise to power, undermining the Spanish revolution, curbing the Popular Front radicalisation in France, mass terror in the Soviet Union and the notorious 1939 pact with Hitler – this was unanticipated. Moreover, Trotsky had expected that the war would lead to the weakening and collapse of Stalin's rule. So the recrudescence of Stalinist power as a result of the war renewed debate among the Fourth International comrades on the nature of the Soviet Union and Stalinism.

The orthodox view inherited from Trotsky was that the Soviet Union was ruled by a transient bureaucratic caste headed by Stalin. It had taken power from the Soviet working class which had emerged exhausted from the First World War, the Revolution and the ensuing civil war. This bureaucracy was concerned to protect and augment its privileges, and was not only conservative but, in international affairs especially, counter-revolutionary. It feared revolution and a resurgent working class as threats to its power and safety. Even before the war, however, while Trotsky was still alive, this characterisation had been challenged in the Trotskyist ranks by a few who saw the Soviet Union as either a form of state capitalism or a new bureaucratic collectivist society.

As these different analyses led to the same conclusion – what was needed was a workers' revolution in the Soviet Union to restore the soviet socialist democracy of 1917 – it might be imagined that the different schools of thought could coexist, however uneasily. Even in the best of times that would have put a big strain on party discipline, but when this issue first arose, in the late 1930s, it was the worst of times. Then, the very existence of the Soviet Union was under threat. Trotsky argued that it was the duty of Marxists to help defend the great accomplishments of the Russian Revolution which were still the very basis of the Soviet Union – public ownership of the means of production and government planning of the economy. These were essentials of socialism even if the other main constituent, a workers' democracy, was clearly, horribly, absent. On the other hand, those who saw the Soviet Union as a bureaucratic collectivist state or state capitalist, felt no special duty to defend it or its appendage parties and satellite governments. In the face of a real situation, the question became more than just an abstract exchange of differing analyses.

The same issue had split the American Trotskyists before Trotsky's murder. In the context of the Cold War which had broken out almost immediately after the end of the Second World War, and as a new world war involving the Soviet Union loomed, the controversy persisted. The debate came to a head at the second world congress of the Fourth International in April 1948 – and seems to have dominated proceedings as two of the ten sessions were on 'the Russian question'. The majority reaffirmed the orthodox position that the Soviet Union was a 'degenerated workers state' that nevertheless must be defended from imperialist attacks. It led to an exodus from the Fourth International of the minorities who thought otherwise. After that congress, Tony Cliff laid the basis for the Socialist Review group in Britain (later International Socialists, then the Socialist Workers Party) which in time attracted such luminaries as Christopher Hitchens, Peter Sedgewick and Paul Foot and were jocularly known as 'the state caps'. In France, Cornelius Castoriadis, Claude Lefort and Jean-François Lyotard left to form Socialisme ou Barbarie, which soon had an energetic presence in Britain as well. SouB, as it was known, envisaged the totalitarian bureaucratic society as a universal threat very much in the same way as Orwell did in *1984*.

Symbolically, the more potent dissent on the Russian question came from Natalia Sedova, Trotsky's widow. For her it was little short of an obscenity to call the Soviet Union under Stalin's regime a 'workers state' in any form, given that workers had considerably fewer rights than under capitalism. She was soon to renounce any association with the Fourth International when they persisted in calling the Soviet Union a 'degenerated workers state' and its Eastern European satellites 'deformed workers states'. At the end of his life Pablo would acknowledge that Sedova was right long before he came to share her view, although he rather

## 5 . THE REVOLUTION WILL HAPPEN (BUT ELSEWHERE) 1945-50

undercut the acknowledgement by putting it down – in a throwaway remark, admittedly – to 'women's intuition'.[18]

He didn't abandon the 'workers state' formula until the early 1970s when he came to the conclusion that the regime of the Party-State controlling a state-owned economy and dominating society, was a barrier to socialism rather than an encumbrance, and it required not a mere political revolution but a thoroughgoing social revolution.[19] As he put it in his memoir:

> I changed my views later when time proved that the structure of the USSR was not a temporary deformity in the leading workers state but the unavoidable result of the manner in which the question of political power was confronted in the USSR in the early years following the October 1917 Revolution.

This was very much the position of Castioradis and the SouB group in 1948.

— ✢ —

On the other hand, in 1948, Pablo was not satisfied with a static and traditional understanding of Stalinism. Its unanticipated post-war expansion depressed many comrades but this expansion, in Pablo's view, would also be the cause of its break-up and weakening. This was the conclusion he drew from the breakdown of Soviet-Yugoslav relations. In 1948 he led the way in analysing the Yugoslav expulsion from Cominform, the international organisation of Stalinist parties that Moscow had recently called into being. This split was indicative of the centrifugal nature of world Stalinism – a consequence of its expansion.[20] In his view, it was no surprise that Yugoslavia should be the first to break the monolithic conformism. Communism in Yugoslavia owed its success not to Stalin and the Red Army, but to its own efforts in leading a mass national and social revolutionary movement. Pablo did not rule out other Stalinist leaderships, even in those countries where they had been installed by the Red Army, running foul of Stalin and Moscow's control. As Pablo wrote in August 1948:

> Stalinist expansion into the "buffer zone" has in fact introduced centrifugal forces and new ferments into the bureaucratic system, which are aggravating all the contradictions within the regime. Although characterised by a set of specific factors, the Yugoslav affair is nonetheless a warning of far more general significance.[21]

Balanced between Moscow and Washington, it was possible that the Yugoslav communists might swing to the right and strike a deal with imperialism. The only way to prevent this was to draw the workers and peasants into the actual government and administration of Yugoslav society: 'To place one's confidence in the Yugoslav and world masses, lean upon them exclusively, install genuine democracy in the party and in the country, break with Stalinism and expose it, call for the real socialist revolution by the masses and for the masses, within the buffer zone, throughout Europe and the world ... And toward that end it is the duty of all the forces of the Fourth International to work.'[22]

A year later[23] Pablo was convinced that the Yugoslav party had gone some way towards this revolutionary approach, spurred on by the Kremlin's economic blockade of Yugoslavia and its labelling of Yugoslavia as a "capitalist fascist state", run by a "clique of spies", which must be crushed at any cost. The proliferation of Stalinist purges and replicas of the Moscow Trials and purges in the satellite countries were more grist to the mill and Pablo was convinced the Yugoslav 'disease' was spreading.

He was full of the possibilities that this revolt could lead to:

> It is not an exaggeration to anticipate, if the Yugoslav affair evolves favourably, if the Tito regime does not compromise with imperialism but on the contrary develops a more consistent revolutionary line, that we may yet witness the debacle of Stalinism in the years to come on a vast scale. For all these reasons, the revolutionary vanguard should be conscious of the immense potentialities of the Yugoslav affair and do the utmost to assist its favourable evolution ... What will happen to the Yugoslav CP and to Yugoslavia depends primarily on the active aid which the international workers movement can give from now on ...

The 'active aid' was not to remain on the pious wish list. In 1950 the Fourth International organised solidarity brigades of hundreds of young people to go to Yugoslavia to work on construction projects. This solidarity was strengthened by the Yugoslavs deciding to launch a program of workers self-management in state-owned enterprises. Pablo would continue to follow this experiment in industrial democracy and his support would mix the critical with the enthusiastic.

The Yugoslav brigades included Gilbert Marquis (1932-2015), a young metal worker, who on returning to France joined the PCI. In time, he was to become Pablo's most loyal lieutenant.

— ✣ —

## 5 . THE REVOLUTION WILL HAPPEN (BUT ELSEWHERE) 1945-50

In June 1950, on the other side of the world, the Korean War broke out. The conflict on this peninsula had been brewing for some time. After the war this former Japanese colony had been divided at the 38th Parallel, with the north under a Stalinist dictatorship and the south occupied by the Americans who installed an anti-communist and counter-revolutionary regime. The northern regime broke this uneasy division by invading the south in June 1950. For Pablo, it was an expression of the colonial revolution which, in a key article he wrote soon after the war's commencement, he repeatedly described as 'the most important revolutionary factor in the world at present'.[24]

In this reading, the war in Korea began as a struggle for unity and independence. It was being fought against an unsavoury police regime serving an indigenous feudal-capitalist ruling class and installed by and reliant on American imperialism. The war had evolved, as such colonial wars did at the time, into a combined civil, socially revolutionary and anti-imperialist war. Pablo brushed aside talk of 'aggression' and 'invasion' by asking how this was possible in what was a single country. He heavily discounted Moscow's hidden hand and insisted that the leftism of the Korean communists, the pressure of the masses and the example of Mao's success in China, were more relevant factors impelling the north Korean leader Kim Il Sung to undertake an attack. It was another example of what had already happened in Yugoslavia and China and was unfolding in Vietnam. It was a war of national and social liberation.

Admittedly the uprising had a distasteful Stalinist leadership, but the key consideration was unconditional solidarity with the insurgent peasantry and their allies. Only if you are in this movement, Pablo suggested, could you hope to struggle successfully against Moscow's exploitation of it. And, as he had already been pointing out, the victory of such movements would lead to the break-up of the Stalinist monolith. Indeed, half of that article was taken up with speculations about the impact of the war on the tensions and conflicts between the American and Soviet blocs. He believed the war justified a revised and downward estimate of the military power of the United States. He noted the impetus the conflict had already given to major rearmament programs in the USA and in Europe and he expected the economic costs of this would weigh on their prosperity.

As for the imminence of a third world war, he continued to downplay the chances. In his view neither the USA nor the USSR was prepared and neither could rationally count on winning such an encounter. Despite the presence of hawks like General MacArthur in ruling circles in the United States, the risks of a war with the USSR were just too great and the American bourgeoisie was not likely to take what could be a suicidal option. The recall of MacArthur from the Korean command a year later, over his proposals to carry the war into China, would confirm the validity of this conclusion, but by then Pablo had convinced himself of the increased dangers of a third world war that combined clashes of conventional armies with revolutionary insurgencies. It was very much the vision of Orwell's *1984,* but with revolutionary characteristics.

This initial analysis of the Korean War was written in August 1950 but, by the time it was published in November, the tide of the war had turned and the American-led troops were driving the Koreans back towards the Chinese border and using their air and naval superiority to obliterate civilisation north of the 38th Parallel. (Napalm was being used extensively.) In the absence of any real aid from either the USSR or China, Pablo now noted, the Korean people faced a bleak future, existing in a devastated graveyard and ruled by a ruthless military dictatorship. However, China did intervene, and in an extraordinary feat of arms, drove the Americans back down the peninsula. The battle front bogged down around the 38th Parallel, although the Americans continued to bomb northern Korea with unparalleled intensity for another two years. If the choices humanity faced were socialism or barbarism, the latter was triumphing in Korea.

— ✢ —

Ernest Mandel's biographer gives Pablo a somewhat back-handed compliment on his quick recognition of what was happening in Eastern Europe and Yugoslavia:

> In the end Mandel was forced to recognise Michel Raptis as his superior in political intuition. Pablo could move more quickly beyond superficial facts and found it easier to distance himself from orthodoxy. He was more of a politician than Mandel, who had difficulty putting aside key Marxist concepts and who held on to his facts with the tenacity of a positivist. Only when it was clear to him that the facts had changed was he prepared to revise his views and follow Pablo.[25]

Michel Pablo looked at the facts too, but also anticipated the changes discernible within the facts. Marxism for him was, as it was for Rosa Luxemburg, an experimental science, its conclusions had to be constantly measured – using all the tools that it made available – against emerging evidence and decisively revised when necessary. Now his conclusions about Eastern Europe, Yugoslavia, Stalinism, Imperialism, the Colonial Revolution and the state of capitalism were about to take a major leap.

CHAPTER 6

# Mohammed must go to the mountain 1950-1955

*Clearly the chief of the Fourth International can no longer accept the sterility of the groupuscules he has brought together. He thinks he has found a way for them to leave their splendid isolation. But he seeks to impose a cultural revolution without any preparation. Like Trotsky, he handles the barge like it's a speedboat ... Implosions are inevitable.*

**Christophe Nick**
Les Trotskistes (Paris 2002)

BY 1950 PABLO'S central concern was to find a way out of 'the desert' for the Fourth Internationalists. He and Elly were now well settled in Paris in their small apartment across from the École des Mines on the Left Bank. The city was then the intellectual capital of the world. Its leading lights were Jean-Paul Sartre, Simone de Beauvoir, Albert Camus and the Existentialists around the magazine *Les Temps Modernes*. Many of the Trotskyists who had left the PCI in 1947-48 in search of an organisation with a larger membership and less demanding politics, had been drawn to Sartre's 'Rally of Revolutionary Democrats', his attempt in 1948 to create a third force between the Gaullists and the Communists. However that party had no sooner been formed than it disappeared. Pablo does not appear to have engaged intellectually with Sartre and the other Existentialists although Ernest Mandel did in some depth. A clue to Pablo's attitude to them comes from his review of de Beauvoir's *The Mandarins* in 1955 when he zeroes in on the resigned, pusillanimous acceptance of Stalinism, misunderstanding of Hegel and political dilettantism of the Parisian intellectuals in the novel.[1]

## 6 . MOHAMMED MUST GO TO THE MOUNTAIN 1950-55

The title of the review – 'The dead souls of a disempowered intelligentsia' – confirms these were not people he would expect inspiration from.

In his search for a way out of the 'desert' of isolation of the International he would be drawn to what were to prove mirages, although they were not entirely illusory. The task of setting the International's course in the new post-war world fell largely to him. No one else seemed willing or able to undertake it. Principally, he was concerned to rally the troops and turn the tide on the pessimism and Stalinophobia among his comrades by emphasising the importance of the growing colonial revolution and the inevitable break-up and fissures in the Stalinist monolith.[2] He said as much in his report to the 3rd Congress of the Fourth International, held in August-September 1951, where he told the delegates his aim was to counter the 'discouragement', 'defeatism' and 'disorientation' in the ranks. His proposals for a new course were endorsed almost unanimously by the sections of the Fourth International but they carried discomforting implications that the majority of the French section would not accept. After a gap of some 12 months, the United States section decided they could not accept them either.

It led to a split in the Fourth International that was remarkable for its verbal and ideological violence. Trotskyists were notorious for their bitter disputes, but in the 1950s they were to plumb new depths, and the legacy of bitterness towards Pablo in particular was to last for the rest of his life, and beyond, right to this day. Pablo, 'pabloite' and 'pabloism' became words that were spat out rather than spoken by 'orthodox' Trotskyists in the decades that followed. Just as the official communist movement had demonised Trotsky, now parts of the Trotskyist world were to demonise Pablo. He rarely responded to the attacks because, he said, he trusted that time, the opening of archives and experience would establish the truth and rule on the divergences. Besides, he had plenty to preoccupy him in the real world without getting mired in 'interminable, sterile and Talmudic polemics with adversaries whose good faith and objectivity' he didn't trust.[3]

We know Marx got stuck – fruitlessly – in the weeds of esoteric and sterile disputes in the world of tiny socialist and revolutionary sects in the 1850s. A century later Pablo tried to avoid that path. Yet he could not entirely escape the consequences of the demonisation. Essentially he was accused of 'liquidationism', or abandonment of the task of building the Fourth International in favour of a 'capitulation to Stalinism'.

Without going into every twist and turn,[4] it's fair to say the crisis evolved from Pablo's apocalyptic, but by no means idiosyncratic, expectation that imperialist countries, led by the United States, were about to unleash the Third World War against an assorted alliance of the Soviet Union and China, the communist parties of the capitalist world and the anti-imperialist movements of the Third World. This war was 'inevitable', it was 'the final crisis' as imperialism saw itself rolled back and hemmed in and consequently struck out against the anti-capitalist tide before it was too late. This war was imminent: in 1952 he postulated the time before its outbreak at two to four years. This new world war would be a war-revolution on an even bigger scale than the Second World War.

The war unleashed by Washington would become an international civil war: 'The civil war character is the consequence of the nature of the war, a war by imperialism against workers states and against the revolution in all its forms, and of the social relationship of forces unfavourable to imperialism (despite the importance of its material, technical and military forces which continue to grow apace).' Pablo was arguing that the clash between the coalitions led by Washington and Moscow would be accompanied by Resistance and revolutionary movements on a much larger scale than in World War II. There would be many, many more Greeces, Yugoslavias, Chinas, Vietnams, Italys and Frances the next time around.

The problem for Trotskyists was that this anticipated anti-imperialist alliance would be largely led by Stalinists. However, for Pablo, the determinant point was the social forces behind the alliance: '… so far as these movements are concerned we make clear our attitude of unconditional support, irrespective of whether their eventual leadership at a given moment is Stalinist or Stalinist-influenced'. This leadership, after all, would only be transient and the point would be to replace it.

Besides, as was already clear, the disintegration of Stalinism had already begun, as shown in the case of the Yugoslavs and the Chinese. As for the communist parties outside the Stalinist bloc, 'they possess the possibilities of projecting a revolutionary orientation, i.e. of seeing themselves obliged to undertake a struggle for power' even if there were limits to this orientation. Pablo argued that those parties and the workers who followed them were 'as a general rule, the best, the most active, the most revolutionary elements in each country'. The looming global war would make them even more revolutionary. It is 'alongside these masses that we will have to carry on the struggle now against the preparation of the imperialist war, and, in case of war, it is on their side that we will have to struggle more directly against the power of imperialism and capitalism'.

## 6 . MOHAMMED MUST GO TO THE MOUNTAIN 1950-55

The challenge for the Trotskyists was 'finding our place in the mass movement as it is ... and to aid it to rise through its own experience to higher levels'. That meant joining the mass movement 'as it exists – often confused, often under treacherous, opportunist, centrist bureaucratic and even bourgeois and petit-bourgeois leaderships ...' For Trotskyists that would mean a struggle in their ranks 'to overcome sectarianism, dogmatism, sterile byzantinism, activism, impressionism, impatience and all the defects inherited from the isolation and petit-bourgeois composition which was an inevitable first stage for many of our leading elements and members'. (That grand list showed a scarcely flattering view of his comrades – or some of them at least.)

It wasn't the catastrophic prognosis about the impending war that aroused opposition. No one in the Fourth International questioned the premise of global conflict. It was very much in sync with the times and plenty of people beyond the Trotskyist ranks shared this fear and expectation of a Third World War. Recall the combustible world mid-century: the Cold War was intensifying, China had fallen to the communist insurgents in 1949, a mini-world-war raged in Korea, the war in Indochina ground on, vicious counter-insurgencies were in progress in Malaysia and Kenya, the colonial revolution was emerging seemingly everywhere and arms budgets were booming.

Instead, it was the organisational conclusions that Pablo drew from this expectation that aroused opposition. He was concerned that the Trotskyists, or the revolutionary Marxists as he preferred to call them, should not isolate themselves from 'the real mass movement', as they had too often in the Second World War. To avoid 'splendid isolation' and be in a position of any influence, they would have to take their place in these mass movements, regardless of their shortcomings. This meant abandoning the quest of building even small mass parties, the focus of most Fourth International sections until then. In any case this had been fruitless, with the exception of Ceylon.

The new course took a three-pronged approach. In countries where there were not already mass working-class parties, then the independent existence would continue and these Trotskyist formations would participate as best they could in any mass movements that arose. In countries where reformist or social-democratic or labour parties commanded the loyalty of the majority of the working class, then the Trotskyists would join these parties while maintaining a skeleton independent organisation. Finally, in countries such as France and Italy where Stalinist communist parties prevailed, the task would also be to join these parties, the unions they dominated and their satellite organisations. While significant independent Trotskyist organisations would be maintained, the 'primary task' would be entry into this Stalinist world.

Aside from any ideological distaste, the mere act of joining these parties would not always be easy. Their internal regimes, particularly within the Stalinist parties, were far from all-embracing, especially if a comrade was open about his or her revolutionary Marxism. Pablo accepted that subterfuge and outright lying might be the necessary price of admission. This 'entrism' would not be a raiding party like the Trotskyist entrist tactic of the 1930s but would be for the long haul. Whether it was the inevitable economic crises or the coming world war-resistance-revolution, the impact of events would radicalise the working class and consequently their parties. The future, more left-wing milieu would be congenial to Marxist politics in these parties. The mass revolutionary party of the future would emerge out of this process.[5]

This whole strategy was given the name *entrism sui generis* – meaning *entrism of its own kind* – and Ian Birchall is surely correct in observing that in using a Latin phrase, Pablo was acknowledging that his audience was essentially intellectuals. He would continue to favour the strategy for decades to come but also recognised it was not a magic key. Burying yourself in the mass party and forgetting why you were there was never advocated by him. That could lead to opportunism and assimilation. A flexible, responsive strategy was necessary. When there was no sign of a 'left centrist' current emerging in the mass working class party, or there were signs of depoliticisation in the working class (which he noted in the late 1950s), then the emphasis should be on building an independent organisation.[6]

At the time it was not Pablo's prediction of the coming Third World War that critics in the International seized upon, but this new entrist strategy. The critics also took umbrage at his clear-eyed view of the long journey to world socialism. This passage from 'On the duration and nature of the period of transition from capitalism to socialism', also written in 1951, caused much offence:

> People who despair of the fate of humanity because Stalinism still endures and even achieves victories, tailor History to their own personal measure. They really desire that the entire process of the transformation of capitalist society into socialism would be accomplished within the span of their brief lives so that they can be rewarded for their efforts on behalf of the Revolution. As for us, we reaffirm what we wrote in the first article devoted to the Yugoslav affair: this transformation will probably take an entire historical period of

several centuries and will in the meantime be filled with forms and regimes transitional between capitalism and socialism and necessarily deviating from "pure" forms and norms.

The course of history has shown itself to be more complicated, more tortuous and drawn-out than the predictions of men who had the legitimate aim of shortening the intervals separating them from their ideals. The best Marxists have not avoided being mistaken, not to be sure on the general line of development, but on its timespans and concrete forms. What is today, in all countries, the possible strategic aim, is the Revolution, the taking of power, the abolition of capitalism. But the taking of power in one country does not settle the entire question. The conditions for a free development toward socialism are still more complicated, and more difficult. The example of the Soviet Union, the "People's Democracies", Yugoslavia and China prove that.

At the time, this long view was characterised as an acceptance of Stalinism. He was, in fact, predicting the break-up of Stalinism in the immediate future, but he was equally convinced that bureaucratic deformations or inequalities would be the inescapable result of economic underdevelopment well into the future. In addition, he meant by socialism a worldwide society of the free and equal, enjoying material abundance and a minimum of necessary labour time, where the differences between mental and physical labour and inequalities between the sexes, between town and country, between nations, had been eliminated.

Meanwhile, the discussions and decisions of the 9th plenum of the International Executive Committee in November 1950, the 3rd World Congress in the summer of 1951 and the 10th plenum held in February 1952, endorsed Pablo's entrist strategy. In the course of these 15 months, however, it became clear that the majority in the French section, the Parti Communiste International, could not and would not implement the decisions taken by the international movement. The French majority alternately temporised, conciliated, negotiated and defied.

In that era, the Fourth International considered itself a 'world party' governed by democratic centralism. In other words, policy would be considered and decisions taken in an atmosphere of the utmost democracy. Once taken, every comrade and every component national section were expected to implement those decisions, while retaining the right to appeal at further world congresses. The rules or statutes setting out this supremacy of the world conferences and the international leadership had been set down at the 2nd World Congress in 1948 and adopted by 29 votes to 1.[7]

For some critics, the almost unanimous endorsement of the entrist line was merely evidence of Pablo's ability to overawe the other leaders at the meetings. There was one crucial incident in January 1952 when there was pushback. Pablo, faced with the refusal of the leaders of the French majority to accept an organisational proposal from the International Secretariat (I.S.), suspended these leaders. Apparently he consulted only a few of the I.S. members before taking this dramatic and punishing step. He asked the full I.S. for endorsement of his action only after the fact and only narrowly received it – five votes to four. It has been cited as an example of his imperious behaviour. However, the following month his decision was reversed and the International Executive Committee lifted the suspensions. It seems the other leaders were far from being his compliant puppets.

The suspension edict did indicate Pablo's anxiety about the delay in implementing the new line. One of his most bitter critics, Michel Lequenne, argues that Pablo 'rushed' the whole business because he was 'afraid' of what would happen if war broke out.[8] Afraid not necessarily for himself but for his comrades certainly. Trotskyists had been picked off and imprisoned, tortured and murdered by fascists and Stalinists during the wars and revolutions of the 1930s and 1940s in Spain, France, Greece, Austria, Indonesia and Vietnam. At the time of this dispute, the Chinese Trotskyists were being round up and imprisoned by Mao. The next time, the Trotskyists needed better cover.

The main motivation, however, appears to have been his desire that the comrades put themselves in touch with the most radical parts of the working class. By rejecting entry into the PCF (Parti Communiste Français – French Communist Party) and the CGT (Confédération Générale du Travail – the main federation of French trade unions), the French majority had, in the view of the I.S. as well as Pablo, separated themselves from the most militant section of the proletariat and 'renounced the opportunity to help these masses to break free from the counter-revolutionary influence of the Soviet bureaucracy'.[9] When looking back on this whole crisis in the Fourth International, Pablo focused not on the erroneous global war-revolution thesis – although he was willing to argue for it when pushed – but on the need to be with the 'real mass movement'. The trouble with the French majority comrades was that their union activity was in Force Ouvrière, the anti-communist federation that had split away in 1948 from the communist-led CGT. The CGT encompassed the most militant workers and was by far the largest of the union federations. Now the French Trotskyists were being urged to leave the 'yellow' FO and join the 'red' CGT as well as the hated Communist Party. Staying with the FO risked reputational damage for the Fourth International in his view.

Pablo's entrist turn wasn't simply predicated by the circumstance of the looming war. The larger implication was that revolutionary Marxists should join the most radical of the mass organisations *regardless of the times* (and he was soon putting the emphasis on that argument).[10] The core of his argument, times and conjuncture aside, was that the Trotskyists had to be in the most radical parts of the mass political movements of their societies. As time went on, he referred to Marx's famous passage from the *Communist Manifesto* that communists had no interests apart from those of the working class. He interpreted this to mean that where the working class, or its most combative and radical sections at least, were, that's where Trotskyists belonged.

A conjunction between themselves and the most revolutionary, or potentially revolutionary, sections of the working class and peasantry was the whole raison d'être of the Trotskyists, or revolutionary Marxists. Those were the social forces that would lead the way to socialism. Yet the link wasn't happening. If the mountain would not come to Mohammed, then Mohammed would have to go to the mountain. The imminence of war only made the shift more pressing.

By mid-1952, with the French PCI's next conference scheduled for July and with the majority clearly in open defiance, members from the French minority raided the party headquarters and commandeered the typewriters and duplicating (or printing) machines. The majority leadership promptly expelled them. Two weeks later both factions held simultaneous party conferences in the same building. For the rest of the decade there were two PCIs in France, both issuing a newspaper under the name *La Verité*. In the national elections held later that year, both parties nominated candidates in the same Paris electorate. It had come to that.

Little wonder a majority of French Trotskyists, already a dwindling number by 1952, gave the game away. The pro-Pablo minority had halved from 50 to 25 by 1955, although it was to increase sixfold by 1958. The majority, which had started with close to 100 members, almost disappeared before recovering in the 1960s.[11] The collapse in membership did rather make 'entrism sui generis' hypothetical, its implementation further hampered when a few years later two key members of the French minority decided to transfer their allegiance to the Stalinist leadership in the PCF and 'out' the handful of entrists.[12] For Pablo, another organisational blow was not long in coming.

— ✦ —

In March 1953, Stalin died. The man who had ruled the Soviet Union for 30 years with unparalleled savagery was finally gone. In the gulag there were wild celebrations among the prisoners, even if their release was still a few years away. Pablo breathed easier, too. He had been convinced during a visit to Cologne in 1949 that he and other delegates to a leadership meeting of the Fourth International had been tracked by GPU agents. 'Some years later,' he recalled in his memoir, 'the German police arrested one of ours who was in effect an agent for the Eastern bloc … and he admitted to informing his masters of our conference in Cologne. The plan was, he said, to kidnap the secretary of the Fourth International and to use him in one of their infamous show trials which they started later against Communist leaders in the Eastern bloc who were accused of being Tito-ists.' Stalin's police-like imagination could not free itself from the crude prototype of a 'centre' directing plots, a trope that he had used in the Moscow trials. 'As long as Stalin lived, I was conscious that every day, every night I could end up like Klement and others who had at some point held important posts in our movement.'

Paranoia, perhaps, as Stalin had bigger fish to fry by then. Nevertheless, a break-in soon after at Pablo's residence in Paris and the theft of his archives fuelled fears the movement was still on the Stalinist watchlist.

Beyond any personal relief was his conviction that Stalin's death would herald the breakdown of the rule of the Stalinist bureaucracy. When Stalin died, 'at that instant I picked up my pen and wrote a small article for *La Vérité* … which ended with the thought that never again would there be another Stalin in the Soviet Union … This did not mean that the bureaucratic system would soon collapse but that the particular form it acquired under Stalin was no longer necessary or acceptable to the bureaucracy.' Pablo developed his thinking about the immediate evolution of the system in the Soviet Union, which was summed up in *The Rise and Fall of Stalinism* 'which Ernest Mandel was prevailed upon to write'. This thinking was anathema to those 'Archeio-Trotskyists', particularly in the Socialist Workers Party in the United States, 'who considered that nothing had changed after the death of Stalin and that we were sowing dangerous illusions'.

In his view the whole Stalinist universe beyond the Soviet Union was also being shattered. 'The Stalinist leaderships have lost their viciousness and their assurance as well as their means to terrorise their organisations,' he told a meeting of the International Executive Committee in the autumn of 1955. 'Fermentation, a critical spirit and even a certain tolerance is developing inside these organisations, making our entrist work both easier and more profitable. Future ideological realignments are maturing in the heart of Stalinist parties ...'[13]

While Khrushchev's report on Stalin's monstrous crimes, delivered to the 20th congress of the Soviet party in February 1956, would confirm much of Pablo's analysis, he was again too optimistic. 'In hindsight,' he wrote in his memoir, 'our forecasts in the period 1953-56 of the instability, ruin and collapse of not only the Stalinist mode of terror but the bureaucratic system in the USSR, were mistaken.' There was no second Stalin but the system persisted for another three decades before its sudden collapse revealed how deeply it had been undermined.

In 1953, this 'revisionist' thinking on Stalinism only added to unease in New York, where a challenge to the majority leadership of the Socialist Workers Party had emerged. Significantly, the dissidents declared they were basing their challenge on the decisions taken at the 3rd World Congress, to join the existing mass movements. The leadership around James Cannon, they said, had failed to implement that orientation. One wing of this American opposition was led by George Clarke, who had been the lead American delegate at the 3rd Congress. The other wing, based on the active trade unionists in the SWP and led by union veteran Bert Cochran, had long wanted closer cooperation with communist party trade union activists to resist union purges and deals by right-wing union leaders. Both these groups of oppositionists – who made common cause – were criticised by Cannon and his supporters for being, like Pablo, 'soft on Stalinism'.

The oppositionists made contact with Pablo, who did not discourage them – in fact, the American majority suspected he went further and urged them on. He didn't, and he hoped the two sides could settle their differences, without splits or expulsions. Theoretically, if members were excluded or expelled from the SWP, the world bodies of the Fourth International could refuse to accept those decisions. Mandel, for one, thought this explained the Cannonites' hostility to Pablo and the elected bodies of the International.

Tensions came to a head in May of that year when Jim Cannon, the grand old man of American Trotskyism and its undisputed leader, launched an attack on 'Paris', a foreign group he felt was attempting to dictate to the American party and had encouraged the dissident minority in its ranks. In his view, the Paris mob had also gone soft on Stalinism. Pablo's response was to deny any interference from 'Paris', to attempt to keep the American majority and the SWP inside the International, and to remind Cannon that what he referred to as 'Paris' was in fact the elected leadership of the previous world congress. If the SWP leadership had issues, then the world congress, due in 12 months, was the place to take them. As for the minority, Pablo counselled them against any attempt to replace the current SWP leadership.[14]

Ironically, Pablo was attempting the role of conciliator in the conflict. He frankly relayed his sympathies for some of the positions of the minority to George Novack, who was part of the SWP majority leadership, but made it clear that he did not think that differences warranted a split and counselled both sides against it. Pablo told the minority it would be dangerous to try to replace the Cannon leadership at such a difficult time (the high tide of McCarthyist anti-communist witch-hunting).[15] Nevertheless, Cannon and the others insisted they saw Pablo's Machiavellian hand at work behind the minority dissent. As the split developed, Pablo grew unhappy with the minority and Livio Maitan claims that Pablo and the minority representative in Paris almost came to blows over Pablo's criticism of what he considered the group's provocative tactics.[16]

As 1953 wound on it became clear that talk of Stalinist parties, in exceptional circumstances, being driven to make anti-capitalist revolution, or the Stalinist bureaucracy in the Soviet Union being forced into permanent concessions to the working class and non-Russian minorities, was anathema to the Cannon supporters. Stalinism was counter-revolutionary full-stop. Besides, rivers of blood separated them from Trotskyists. In recognition of this traditional thinking, Cannon started calling his emerging anti-Pablo faction 'the Orthodox Trotskyists'.

Never one to dally when it came to dealing with oppositions, the Cannon faction expelled their opposition in November 1953. Simultaneously they issued a 'Call to the Trotskyists of the World' to remove Pablo 'and his agents' from control of the Fourth International. 'This faction,' they declared, 'is now working consciously and deliberately to disrupt, split, and break up the historically created cadres of Trotskyism in the various countries and to liquidate the Fourth International.' For good measure they added: 'The lines of cleavage between Pablo's revisionism and orthodox Trotskyism are so deep that no compromise is possible either politically or organisationally.'

Initially, it appeared the orthodox intended to use either the next meeting of the International Executive Committee or the Fourth World Congress, scheduled for 1954, to remove Pablo 'and his spineless lackeys', to borrow Cannon's words. They were confident they had majority support. But such was their paranoia – and their loathing – that they soon decided this would be a trap, that Pablo would use his position to stack these meetings against them; and such was their deep hatred of the man and his works that they could not conceive of staying inside the same organisation.

'The revolutionary task,' Cannon wrote with characteristic aggression, 'is not to "live with" this tendency … but to blow it up. As I visualize the next stage of our strategy, it should proceed from the uncompromising determination to annihilate Pabloism politically and organizationally.' By year's end the American majority, the British followers of Gerry Healy, the former French majority, and the Swiss had formed a 'Committee for the Fourth International' and proclaimed their organisation as the one, true Fourth International. All the offers of Pablo (and others) to facilitate the American presence in the next world congress came to nothing.[17]

— ✧ —

The International not only lost the American comrades but also their dollars. The contributions of these relatively rich Americans had been very helpful in financing past world congresses, and the split put the 4th World Congress in jeopardy. However, Simonne Minguet, one of Pablo's closest supporters, came to the rescue by cashing in an inheritance she had just received and donating the proceeds. The money arrived in time to subsidise delegates' travel and accommodation expenses.

In the manifesto from that world congress, held in the summer of 1954, Pablo recognised that the anticipated general global war-revolution was delayed, although not cancelled.'[18] In 1955, however, in a long rambling report to the International Executive Committee, he went further in acknowledging the pause in the drive towards war, as capitalism enjoyed its continuing boom as yet unthreatened by the advancing revolution.[19]

Pablo never completely resiled from his global war-revolution prognosis, insisting that US Presidents contemplated unleashing war upon the workers states. It is true that Truman mused in public and in his diaries about a nuclear attack on the Soviet Union and China. The United States had already dropped nuclear bombs on two Japanese cities, so that its further use of nuclear weapons was not entirely fanciful. We know that the Joint Military Chiefs in Washington drew up plans for an attack on China, even if General MacArthur was recalled to America, from his command of the US forces in Korea, for publicly advocating such an attack. Underlining these possibilities was the huge increase in US arms spending immediately after the outbreak of the Korean War. We know too from the testimony of the President's brother who was in the room, that during the Cuban missile crisis of 1962, six of President Kennedy's 14-person cabinet favoured an attack on the Soviet Union.

But the analysis and prognosis were wrong. As one of his closest collaborators was to note, Michel was always reluctant to admit mistakes. Within three years he was backing off from the imminent global war-revolution thesis, pointing to the economic boom in the West, the divisions between capitalist governments, the growing public unease about nuclear war and the conciliatory attitude of the Soviet and Chinese bureaucracies as key contributing factors to the reduction in the dangers of world war. Washington enjoyed then, and would continue to enjoy right down to our times, an overwhelming preponderance of economic and military power. Pablo's analysis rested on the assumption of the sudden, mortal threat to the domination of the United States, but no such threat came into being. The only limit to American military power proved to be the reluctance of ordinary Americans to accept casualties. But even when America lost military conflicts, the other side 'won' a dubious victory. As for the loss of markets strangling capitalist economies, capitalism and world trade underwent an enormous expansion right through to current times.

By the mid-1950s it was difficult for Pablo to ignore the quiescence of the working class in the capitalist heartlands. In 1955 he pointed to the 'somewhat euphoric economic climate' in the capitalist half of Europe. Combined with 'the conciliatory policies of the Soviet and Chinese bureaucracies', this had produced 'social peace', 'a climate of softened class struggle in the metropolitan countries' and 'restored to the bourgeoisie a relative confidence and optimism'. This was not the case, however, in the Third World where poverty and injustice fuelled revolt.

The manifesto from the 4th World Congress pointed to this bifurcated reality beyond the pockets of North Atlantic prosperity:

> Never in the history of humanity have we known so many of the exploited and the oppressed fighting on every continent for a better world. Never in the history of the workers movement has the world revolution, the violent struggle of the peoples of the world against war, misery, and exploitation, against capitalist governments, been such a tangible and vast reality as today.

The manifesto went on to 'salute' the risings of the peoples of the Third World – from Korea and Dien Bien Phu to Bolivia and Guatemala by way of Africa and the Middle East, and concluded: 'The colonial revolution today involves a billion and a half human beings who are resolved to put an end to colonial systems, to the subordination of any people, any race, to another.' This colonial revolution would, he hoped, arouse the support and sympathy of the labour movement in the imperial countries.

The same extension of the colonial revolution had ended the isolation of the Soviet regime and, combined with economic progress, undermined the historic basis for the conservative rule of the bureaucracy and laid the basis for the working class to retake political power in the communist bloc. This was already happening, he argued, demonstrated in the workers' uprising in East Berlin in June 1953 and the miners strikes in the Vorkuta region in the Soviet Union. 'These workers for the first time in 20 years have used the class weapon against their bureaucratic masters and have clearly expressed in their demands that they do not desire a return to private ownership of the means of production and bourgeois democracy. On the contrary, their goal has been to move towards socialist democracy which will allow for the unprecedented growth of the planned and socialised economy.'

Such an evolution towards socialist democracy would in his view help inspire the workers of advanced capitalist countries towards such a goal in their own countries. Pablo was concerned in these years to re-establish the classic idea of socialism as being based on the expansion of democracy and freedom for the many.[20]

The two new preoccupations – the colonial revolution and the essential place of participatory democracy in any transition to socialism – were to have liberating consequences for him. In pursuing these goals, in hands-on, practical ways rather than just ideologically, he could escape, at least partially, from the envenomed world of Trotskyism.

In the end, it wasn't all the *sturm und drang* stemming from the 3rd World Congress and the revolt in the French and American sections that had the biggest impact on Pablo's fate. It was something quite different. The 3rd World Congress had a wider representation than any previous meeting – 74 delegates and observers from 25 countries. This was principally because of representatives from Latin America and Asia. These new post-war sections of the Fourth International were welcomed by Pablo as representatives of what he now saw as the main event: the revolution in the colonial and semi-colonial countries. In recognition, the 3rd World Congress set up a Latin American Bureau, based on that continent, which was to coordinate activity there. A similar Far Eastern Bureau was foreshadowed.

For the next decade the Latin Americans, in particular, were to assure him of a majority in the International. In 1952 one of Pablo's closest comrades, the Dutchman Sal Santen, travelled there to help organise the various Latin American sections. All the notional revolutionary elements were present on that continent – a heavy and resented imperialist presence, a weak and compromised bourgeoisie, poor and landless peasantry, a strong working-class presence in urban areas and a critical and disaffected intelligentsia. The main organiser of this tranche of Latin Americans in the International was Homero Cristalli, whose nom de guerre was Juan Posadas. He was later to cut an embarrassing cult figure, entertaining ideas of the value of a nuclear war and the possible visits of extra-terrestrials, but in the 1950s and well into the 1960s he was a capable if flawed organiser of the Latin American Left.

There was no doubt this attention to Latin America underlay the strong support Pablo received from them when the split with the SWP eventuated. The Latin American sections rallied overwhelmingly to Pablo's leadership. Trotskyists in the colonial and semi-colonial countries probably made up the majority of rank-and-file members of the Fourth International at this stage. As far as the Third World Trotskyists were concerned, Pablo recalled in his memoir, 'I easily allied myself to them … maybe because as a Greek and an Alexandrian I was well placed and had the desire to be a sort of bridge between the Europeans and the Third World, a fact which either the one or the other sensed quickly enough – maybe the former were not that happy, certainly the latter were much happier, even enthused.'

It was with these colonial revolutionists that he was to spend the next decade.

CHAPTER 7

# Vive la révolution algérienne
## 1954-1962

*We quickly supplied thousands of Algerian fighters who were victims of an ever-increasing oppression and persecution, not only in their own country but in France too, with identity cards, passports and other documents; we did not hesitate to hide the hunted, to give our house keys to those who needed to hide to avoid arrest and torture; we facilitated their transport to other countries in Europe; we took on the printing of thousands of copies of their illegal propaganda; and we protected from police searches and confiscation the large amounts of cash collected from their members and supporters by the FLN ...*

*A fully fledged, silent underground operation went on for years offering help of all kinds to the Algerian revolutionary struggle ...*

**Michalis Raptis (Pablo)**
*My Political Autobiography*

WHEN THE ALGERIANS began their war of independence against the French on All Saints Day, November 1, in 1954, Pablo was about to turn 43. He was what was then considered middle-aged but at the height of his intellectual powers. He threw himself into support for the Algerians' emancipatory struggle with his usual energy and commitment. Here was the opportunity to be involved in a revolution and he was determined he would not let it pass. In the next decade, his political life was to reach heights it would not approach again. He would be present in other revolutions, but never as such a participant. Robert Alexander, the American academic chronicler of Trotskyism, implies wryly that about the only genuine revolution its adherents ever got close to was the Algerian Revolution, and this was due to Pablo.

The revolution in Algeria was close, just across the Mediterranean. The country had been invaded and occupied by the French in 1830 and by the 1950s there were a million European settlers in the country, living a comparatively privileged life. They were, however, outnumbered by eight million indigenous Algerians who mostly lived lives of severe poverty. Evidence of France's determination to hold Algeria, part of its north African empire, was the fact that the country was officially deemed part of France itself, constituting three departments and sending deputies (elected by the settlers) to the National Assembly in Paris.

There were up to 300,000 Algerians working in France at that time. Pablo vividly recalled these Algerian workers in Paris in the early 1950s, watching their serried ranks, 'compact and combative, dressed in their clean shirts', in the great workers marches marking the anniversary of the Paris Commune, May Day and the fall of the Bastille (the commemoration of which, in 1953, saw seven Algerians killed by police). He had also made contact with Messali Hadj, the historic leader of the Algerian independence movement then in forced exile in France, whom he considered 'the natural leader of the Algerian revolution'. Messali was then a near mythic figure among Algerians. 'I remember his overwhelming meetings in the Mutualité in Paris,' Pablo recalled, 'where in a super-electrified atmosphere the Algerians would rise to their feet and for an hour applaud their Messiah, tall and erect, dressed in traditional flowing robes, with his patriarchal beard – the complete armed prophet.'[1]

Except, when fighting broke out in Algeria, the armed prophet was missing in action. The surprise for Pablo – as well as for the French government and its various intelligence agencies – was that the uprising of November 1 was not initiated or organised in any way by Messali. In the preceding two years the party he founded and led, the Mouvement pour le Triomphe des Libertés Démocratiques (MTLD – Movement for the Triumph of Democratic Freedoms), had split between his faction and the majority on the central committee who wanted more democracy in the movement. Faced with the paralysis of the MTLD, a small group of nationalist militants, many of whom had been active in the 'special organisation' or armed wing of the MTLD in the late 1940s, had decided to pass to action. This small group – they came to be called the 'nine historic chiefs of the revolution' – claimed credit for the scores of November 1st ambushes and skirmishes in the name of the previously unknown Front de Libération Nationale (FLN – National Liberation Front). In the wake

## 7. VIVE LA RÉVOLUTION ALGÉRIENNE 1954-62

of the uprising, Messali eventually formed his own rival armed movement, Mouvement National Algérien (MNA – National Algerian Movement), but it was destined to ignominious failure.

No sooner had the Algerian uprising began than Pablo was rallying the Fourth International and its French section, Parti Communiste International (PCI), to support the rebels. In an internal report to the PCI in that same month of November – 'in an almost prophetic manner', in the words of historian Sylvain Pattieu[2] – Pablo affirmed that 'a new chapter has been opened in the struggle for the emancipation' of the countries of the Maghreb and this emancipation 'could no longer be stopped'. This was indeed a big – and accurate – read of what had been a series of messy attacks in which innocents had died.

The first problem was to make contact with the unknown inspirers of this uprising. Fortuitously the FLN was equally keen for contact with any supportive people in France. They had no confidence in the French Communists and Socialists who had betrayed the Algerians and their independence struggle on a number of occasions. Members of the PCF, its ministers in Paris as well as rank-and-file members on the ground, had been active, for example, in the mass killing of thousands of Algerians in the wake of the uprising in eastern Algeria of May 1945. The Socialists' record was if anything worse. The FLN first approached Yvan Craipeau, an old Trotskyist who had left the International in 1948 but was well connected among independent leftists. This old comrade thought his own networks were unlikely to want to be closely associated with the FLN or able to offer much practical help. He suggested the Fourth International.

At the initial meeting with the FLN during the winter of 1954-55, Pablo represented the International and Simonne Minguet the PCI. (Minguet was one of the rare women among the Trotskyists of that era. She had been won over to Trotskyism by Lucien Braslawski, her first love, when they were students in Paris in the early 1940s. He had been one of the first resistants to be arrested by the Germans. As a revolutionary and a Jew, he was killed by the Nazis. From this 'introduction' into revolutionary politics, Simonne was never to resile.[3]) Later Henri and Clara Benoits, who worked at Renault's sprawling car factory in Billancourt on the outskirts of Paris and who were helping organise Algerian workers at the plant, arranged for Pablo to meet Mohammed Harbi, then an FLN organiser and a rare Marxist intellectual among the rebels. Harbi and Pablo were to become lifelong friends and frequent collaborators.

The 'world party of socialist revolution' was now actually in a revolution. Their rhetorical and ideological support was to be translated into practical aid. This was, in Pablo's view, an historic opportunity:

> If our movement wanted to truly and decisively make contact with the masses, to break out of its isolation, to cease limiting itself to general political propaganda about the 'right' ideas and positions, the opportunity of the Algerian Revolution could not be lost. Not since the creation of the Fourth International had such favourable circumstances arisen for a decisive entry into a great revolution with all the myriad consequences that it would have on our own development.

Pablo was determined that the 'decisive entry' would be more than rhetoric. The initial meetings with the FLN were followed by constant and close collaboration:

> We – and I especially – maintained very close ties with the European-based leaders of the FLN. We were completely aware of the ways in which the revolution was developing, of their needs, weaknesses and mistakes. We tried, without interfering in their internal affairs, to meet whatever needs we could and to convey healthier perspectives to their more politicised cadres with whom we collaborated closely.

For Pablo this unconditional practical aid served as 'the best way to slowly eclipse the justified and centuries-old distrust felt by colonials for the metropolitans, even those wearing the latest revolutionary guise. That is why we never objected to any of their requests. We had decided once and for all that our help towards the Algerian Revolution would be catholic, without conditions, exemplary.'[4] Later other networks were to do similar support work, but the International was first and the most effective.[5]

In 1955 the FLN established the Federation of France of the FLN, which came to be known as the 7th Wilaya – Algeria itself was divided into six wilayas or theatres of operation. Initially it was tough going as Messali enjoyed wide and strong support among the Algerians in France where Messali himself lived in exile. The FLN was as unknown to Algerians as to anyone else. Their organisers had to evade the French police and at the same time win their countrymen from their traditional support of Messali and his MNA.

Initially, the FLN representatives needed propaganda, false identity papers and hideouts. This is what the Trotskyists in France could and did supply. Pablo assembled a small team – it was probably no more than 15 committed activists – to carry out most of the aid that the International was

## 7 . VIVE LA RÉVOLUTION ALGÉRIENNE 1954-62

to give the Algerians. It began with the typing, printing and distribution of *Résistances algériennes*, the FLN's newsletter, which needless to say was illegal. The American writer Sherry Mangan and Pierre Avot-Meyers were the key men in this. Pablo has left this portrait of Mangan at work:

> When we asked him to look after the FLN publications, he took himself off and settled in a village in Normandy, spending much of his days with the villagers who quickly adopted the 'strange American'. At night he typed the FLN's articles, copied them, put them together in a newsletter, which he then put in his suitcase and took to illicit rendezvous in Paris at railway stations and elsewhere where he handed over his dangerous cargo.

It was Pierre Avot-Meyers, later joined by Louis Fontaine after he returned from his stint serving in the French army in Algeria, who secured the various locations for the printing and at intervals moved the machinery – the perambulating printery had to move often to keep one step ahead of the police. They were responsible, too, for the false identity cards. Jacques Grinblat, Simonne Minguet, Michel Fiant, Michel Ravelli and Roger Foirier were among those who ensured the newspapers and documents were delivered to the FLN-supporting cafes and safe houses – Algerians could not drive vans around Paris or other cities without drawing the intervention of the police. Jobs, housing and refuges were provided by Gilbert Marquis and the others as required. Pablo and Elly were among those involved in sheltering fugitives. When a hunted FLN operative needed to be moved to Belgium or West Germany or Switzerland, the Trotskyists supplied a car and driver.

When documents such as passports had to be smuggled in or out of France, the FLN could count on Jakob Moneta, a Trotskyist who worked in the West German embassy in Paris as a labour attaché and could use diplomatic bags. Late in life, Moneta (1914-2012) recalled his own contributions. He hid FLN leaders being hunted by police in his flat in Paris and, under the protection of his diplomatic number plates, smuggled them across borders to relative safety. He remembered also acting as a *porteur des valises* (suitcase carrier):

> On one occasion I took a first-class ticket to Rome with my diplomatic passport. I had two heavy suitcases of money with me and asked the conductor to wake me up at night as soon as we got to Switzerland, because my wife was waiting there for me to go to Rome with her. If she was not there yet, I would have to get off to continue the next morning.
> So I got out in the middle of the night with the heavy suitcases and drove to Geneva the next morning. There Michel Raptis had rented a room for me in

a first-class hotel. He picked up the suitcases and took them to a bank where, in the presence of Raptis, a white-gloved employee counted the many bills donated by Algerian workers and put them into an FLN account without asking a single question – with classic Swiss discretion.[6]

On another occasion he visited a bank in Frankfurt with Pablo to withdraw a large sum of Deutschmarks from an FLN account.

This support was vital in the victory of the FLN in France, where the FLN was battling on two fronts: against the French police and security services as well as the Messalists. The police repression was ferocious and widespread. At the height of the war there were up to 30,000 Algerian political prisoners held in French jails, and hundreds of Algerians (and French police) died in the clashes between the two sides. Even more fell in the internecine war between FLN and Messali-supporting Algerians.

The FLN emerged as the unambiguous victor in this war in the Algerian diaspora. With that victory came the absolutely crucial material support: the taxes the Algerian workers now paid to the FLN, those millions of francs that were stuffed into those famous suitcases and surreptitiously transported by scores of French volunteers to Switzerland to hand over to representatives of the FLN. By 1959 the money delivered by the celebrated *porteurs de valises* funded some 80 per cent of the FLN's diplomatic and military expenses.[7]

There was a dark side to this FLN victory over the Messalist MNA and police in France. It was won with the gun as much as the word. In this fratricidal war – estimates of the casualties went as high as 4,000 dead[8] – it has been argued, the FLN concentrated on the assassination of MNA leaders, while the MNA targeted FLN cafes and meeting places for more indiscriminate killings. Even if this is true, this bloody period in the FLN's history – there were also assassinations and massacres in Algeria itself – revealed the Mafiosi side of the organisation and did not help in winning French support for the Algerian cause. Ben Bella and other FLN leaders, who were in prison at this stage, opposed this fratricidal strategy. As Ian Birchall relates:

> When Ben Bella was informed of the assassination of one of the MNA's most senior trade union activists, Ahmed Bekhat, he commented savagely: 'It's idiotic! There aren't two militants like Bekhat in the FLN!'[9]

Mohammed Harbi, as a member of the central committee of Federation of France of the FLN in 1957, recognised that such bloodletting alienated 'those French people, then a very small minority, who took the risk of supporting our struggle, but did not understand this fratricidal struggle between Messali, the old fighter, and the FLN'. In the federation's central committee, Harbi called for a halt to FLN assassinations; the ensuing vote was tied three-all and the deadlock was broken by the vote of the delegate from the external FLN.[10] The bloodletting continued.

Pablo also regretted such acts.[11] His unease with violence was tested on many occasions as we will see, but he contented himself with suggesting what he termed 'healthier perspectives' to the Algerian leaders. At any rate, it did not deflect his or the International's unconditional support. There was in his eyes a higher morality at work here: priority for the colonials over the metropolitans. Besides, he did not believe there was any alternative to the armed struggle if Algeria were to gain its independence and open up the possibilities of social emancipation. In time, he would come to realise that such armed struggles entail seemingly unavoidable dictatorships. Men (and it is universally true that it's men in charge) who have risked their lives in the revolution are afterwards reluctant to share power with those that have not.[12]

'The practical turn', as Pablo called the new priorities of the International, 'did not happen without internal resistance.' What had to be overcome was the strength of 'practical inaction' – 'the inheritance of many years of our habitual way of acting, our isolation, the social make-up of our organisation, our habits and the culture of our militants and supporters.' This uneven support and the tensions it helped create, or feed, in the ranks of the International is illustrated by the post-box incident.

In April 1956, a parcel of illegal FLN literature addressed to the PCI post-box in central Paris broke open in transit. The customs police alerted the Direction de la Surveillance du Territoire (DST), the domestic French secret police, who promptly arrested the three PCI members who had registered the post office box: Simonne Minguet, Raymond Bouvet and Jeanine Weil. The problem was that Jeanine Weil was no longer a member. Members of the political bureau of the PCI, among whom Pablo's strongest supporters such as Michel Fiant, were prominent, argued that Pierre Frank, as the leader of the PCI, should assume political responsibility for solidarity with the FLN and come forward to absolve Jeanine Weil. Frank was reluctant to do so – the historian Sylvain Pattieu says he didn't want to go to jail, nor risk the PCI being declared illegal. However, Fiant carried the day and the PCI publicly announced that Frank would hand himself over to the investigating magistrate to take full responsibility for the use of the post-box. He was duly arrested on April 12 and Jeanine Weil released. The PCI immediately organised a solidarity campaign with support from Jean-Paul Sartre, Laurent Schwartz, Edgar Morin, Claude Bourdet and other luminaries. On May 9, all three were released without charges.

The incident, according to Pattieu, highlighted the divergences between the 'more prudent' and the more enthusiastic supporters of solidarity with the FLN.[13] In this connection Mohammed Harbi recalls, for instance, that Ernest Mandel's attitude was 'austere'.[14] Trotskyists have a not altogether undeserved reputation for being critics and purists, making them stand-offish about the messy world we live in. They were also many European comrades who believed their continent was the inevitable and permanent centre of the world revolution. As Pablo recalled in more considered terms, 'Despite our theoretical support for the revolutions that were unravelling the great empires of the past, we continued to be first and foremost "Eurocentrists"...'[15]

A clue to Pablo's commitment at this time can be found in an angry 1955 review of *Les Aventures de la Dialectique* by Maurice Merleau-Ponty, in which this ex-comrade of Sartre and de Beauvoir repudiates both existentialism and Marxism and singles out Trotskyism for criticism because of its demand for obsessive activism. Professors such as Merleau-Ponty, Pablo wrote, 'have their work and their leisure, plenty of time in fact to philosophise, they can be onlookers or squarely against the revolution – that depends.' Workers living in the capitalist half of Europe had it tougher but were basking 'in a somewhat euphoric economic climate'. This factor, combined with the pacific policies of the Soviet bureaucracy and their communist parties, had led to 'a climate of softened class struggle in the metropolitan countries that restores to the bourgeoisie a relative confidence and optimism'. By contrast, for Algerians and Moroccans, 'uprooted and dispossessed by imperialism from their lands, from their work and their leisure, driven into the *bidonvilles* (shanty towns) of Algiers and Casablanca, things are different. Their revolt is not the work of professional revolutionaries or philosophers ... their revolution is the fact that men, subject to the conditions of capitalism and imperialism, are going inevitably to reflect on their conditions and are going to act.'[16]

This organic revolutionary motivation was very different to the situation with the European working class who were enjoying 'the euphoria of the capitalist boom'. 'The [European] masses,' as Pablo wrote in 1958, '... have found a substitute for class struggle in earnings from overtime or individual arrangements. The decline in the level of politicisation of the European working class is revealed above all in this passive, if not passively hostile, attitude towards the colonial revolution.' For such words, Pablo is often classified as a 'Third Worldist', someone who substituted the people of the undeveloped world for the proletariat of advanced capitalist countries as the chief motor of revolution. Pablo's response was that he was merely acknowledging the realities of the world situation at that time. Simultaneously he was also expecting that the colonial revolution would radicalise at least part of the youth in Europe – as it did.[17]

Pablo and the International did not neglect more open anti-war agitation, as some critics have charged. As Pablo recalled:

> I made numerous trips to England and Denmark where I tried to set up committees that would offer practical help. Committees for Free Algeria, committees for Algerian refugees, committees for the 30,000 Algerian prisoners in France. Thanks to left Labour MPs we had some success in England, and likewise in Denmark, thanks to survivors of the Scandinavian brigade that had fought in Spain against the fascists in the 1930s.

Rallying support in France itself proved more difficult. For one reason or another – perhaps because media censorship was severe, the traditional workers parties supported the war, and a new level of consumer affluence was now available even to ordinary workers – French public opinion was less disturbed by the Algerian war than the Americans were to be by Vietnam.

Nevertheless, there were stirrings against the war in the initial stages. In the autumn of 1955 and the spring of 1956, the French government called up tens of thousands of young Frenchmen who had completed their compulsory national service military training over the previous two or three years. Most had embarked on careers and marriages and many were reluctant to give it up to go to Algeria. Consequently, there were demonstrations at railway stations, refusals to board trains, interruptions of train journeys by activating alarms, sit-down demonstrations at ports and other acts of sabotage. These acts of resistance and insubordination by draftees were often initially supported by local workers and their unions – and certainly by the scattered Trotskyists. The leaders of the PCF and the Socialists, on the other hand, did their best to limit and break up these acts of resistance and solidarity. This 'strike breaking', plus heavy-handed police and army intervention, managed to bring the situation under control.

While Pablo resigned himself to little solidarity from the 'depoliticised' working class, he still expected that some active solidarity with the FLN would emerge in Europe, especially among students and young workers. 'The aspirations, at least in one wing of the youth, tend to support the colonial revolution – and we must be the organiser of this tendency,' he wrote in an internal bulletin in 1958. The PCI did act on this. Alain Krivine (1941-2022), mentored by Fiant, was an 'entrist' in the UEC (the organisation of communist party students) and set about organising youth support for the Algerians' struggle. In 1960, when fascist supporters of the French in Algeria appeared in central Paris selling their papers and rallying support for the repression in Algeria, Krivine took the lead in organising the flying pickets among the students at the Sorbonne that succeeded in driving the fascists out of the Latin Quarter.[18]

— + —

Pablo's life in the opening phase of the Algerian Revolution wasn't all war and politics. He had his first meeting in 1955 with Natalia Sedova, the widow of Trotsky. Her 'hasty' rejection (as Pablo saw it) of the Fourth International's definition of the Soviet Union and its satellite states as workers states, had led to her publicly breaking with the Fourth International. She could not stomach the International's defence and support of these regimes as progressive. But when she settled in Paris in 1955, she made contact with Pablo and Elly.

'I had rarely met a woman so graceful, lively and calm despite the Shakespearean drama of her stormy, heroic life,' Pablo recalled. She had lost her husband and two sons in Stalin's war against her husband. Along with Pablo and Elly, she visited places in Paris where she had met and fallen in love with Trotsky. As they sat at an outside table at the Café de la Paix in the Place de l'Opéra, Natalia Sedova entertained them with a running commentary on the changes in fashion since the pre-World War I days. She visited their apartment in Paris a number of times and, at her insistence, Pablo prepared his gourmet Greek speciality – a kind of 'artichokes à la polita'. She told them stories of her life with Trotsky. It was a friendship that would stand him in good stead when he came to trial in Amsterdam six years later.

Algeria wasn't the only revolution to inspire him at this time. In Hungary, in October 1956, the workers rose, arming themselves and settling accounts with the police, forming workers councils in their workplaces and sending delegates to a central workers council in the capital, Budapest. For a few short weeks, this 'soviet' power ruled the country before Russian tanks reconquered the country. Pablo declared the uprising as 'the most advanced spontaneous revolutionary activity of the masses since 1917'.[19] In his view it was a welcome antidote to the prevailing line of official communist parties about the peaceful, parliamentary road to socialism, as well as a preview of what the political revolution overthrowing the police regimes in these 'workers states' would look like.

For Pablo, a regime could only be considered socialist, or transitional to socialism, if the new political set-up involved an expansion in the democratic rights and powers of workers compared to that achieved in capitalist democracies. The 'immortal' (his word) form for this was elected councils (or soviets) of the workers. These new ruling institutions would naturally be multi-party and could even include bourgeois democratic parties if these formations accepted the nationalisations and agrarian reforms of the revolution. The expanded political power for the workers would have no meaning if there wasn't pluralism and genuine debate. All this actually came into existence in those few weeks in October and November 1956 in Hungary.

The Hungarian workers went further than the Yugoslav communists or what was being proposed by 'liberal' communists such as the ill-fated Imre Nagy in Hungary and Gomulka in Poland, who also accepted workers councils but only for the administration of workplaces. In Hungary, the workers councils – 'reclaimed from the Museum of History', in Pablo's phrase – exercised political power as well, and this was a crucial difference. 'Instinctively, spontaneously, in the process of their astonishingly rapid political maturation, the Hungarian workers have given the correct political response to the police regime of the Stalinist bureaucracy. They have tried to go beyond rather than return to bourgeois democracy by going forward to genuine proletarian political democracy ... The proletarians and revolutionaries of the entire world can learn from the Hungarian school to draw the lessons from an unequalled revolutionary experience.'

On the face of it, Moscow's brutal suppression of the exemplary Hungarian uprising might have put an end to the idea that the post-Stalin bureaucracy was now less oppressive, more divided or even disintegrating. It was certainly a brutal reminder of its essential nature. But within months it became clear that Khrushchev, the emerging numero uno in the Kremlin, was continuing the course of loosening the centralised regime in order to make the regime more palatable and efficient. Kadar, the new communist ruler imposed in Hungary, was to pursue a variant of this policy, too, as was Gomulka in Poland.

Decades later Pablo could not ignore the obvious conclusion that 'our forecasts in the period 1953-56 about the instability and final collapse of the bureaucratic system – and not just the Stalinist mode of terror – in the USSR was mistaken … It lasted another three decades before just how deeply the regime had been undermined by bureaucratic rule was exposed, beginning with perestroika in 1985, followed by its incredibly quick collapse.' In those three decades he was also to accept that the bureaucracy had calcified into a new ruling class. In other words, Natalia Sedova's 'hasty' conclusion in the late 1940s that the Soviet Union and its satellites were in no way 'workers states', let alone socialist, was indeed correct.

— ÷ —

The 5th World Congress of the Fourth International in 1957 – a gathering which drew 100 delegates from 30 countries according to the organisers[20] – marked the high point in Pablo's influence on the organisation. For all the talk about the colonial revolution being the 'principal driver' of the world revolution, the Fourth International was still very much a Eurocentric organisation as far as its leadership and even its focus were concerned. Nevertheless, the balance inside the organisation was shifting. In themselves the Latin American votes did not give Pablo a majority, but they firmed his hold on the reins. Practical support for the colonial revolution in general and the Algerian struggle in particular was at the heart of the congress' declarations and decisions.

Other notes in the manifesto issued at the end of the congress, and in Pablo's opening remarks at the congress, are worth recalling. The manifesto began with a warning of the threat of nuclear war:

> The structural crisis which for the past 40 years has shaken global capitalism approaches its final phase. Undermined by its economic contradictions, deprived of its former markets by the relentless progress of the colonial revolution, confronted with the growing power of the workers states, capitalism has lost all hope of reconquering the world. Falling back on its last solid positions in the United States and Western Europe, capitalism doesn't intend to abdicate without a last stand against the mounting waves of revolutionary forces. On the contrary, it doesn't cease preparing to go into this last decisive battle, throwing into the balance the enormous technical and military forces of the United States. This is the danger that confronts humanity, a nuclear world war, the consequences of which for humanity's survival are incalculable.[21]

It was in one sense a reprise of Pablo's apocalyptic warning of six years previously of the final showdown between the revolution and imperialism, a conclusion he had been edging away from. However, the fear of nuclear war was now widespread, and a mass Ban-the-Bomb movement had arisen in Britain – and there were the first stirrings of such a movement elsewhere. The manifesto called for Trotskyists to get involved in building that movement on a local and international scale. In an attempt to get the working class involved in what was as yet a middle-class movement, it suggested that nuclear disarmament become the theme for future May Days. The warning about nuclear devastation and the call for genuine disarmament retain their urgency.

The nuclear threat was seen as the dark side of the century's tremendous technical and scientific progress that opened up the possibilities for a 'golden age of abundance' for all humanity – as long as socialism and a culture of planning and sharing were introduced on a global scale. This egalitarian age of material comfort and human flourishing was – for these 1950s techno-optimists – to be powered by nuclear energy and 'even' solar power. This being the age of Sputnik and the Soviet Union's winning edge in intercontinental rocketry, there was also an overestimation both of the Soviet Union's military strength and the speed at which it would catch up and surpass the economic achievements of the United States. That second prediction was admittedly tempered with an acknowledgement of the failures in food and consumer goods production in the Soviet Union, and the significant lag in the productivity of labour compared to the United States. But these failures would be swept away with the overthrow of the bureaucratic dictatorship in the Soviet Union – something that was not far off, according to the manifesto.

In his opening speech Pablo warned that Trotskyists should not get stuck in the rut of being critics and oppositionists. Instead, they should start advancing solutions to the problems that people – particularly post-war youth and women – faced in their lives. He expanded on what this meant for women. It was not just a matter of advocating for equal pay but of addressing fundamental questions

> ... of women's rights and liberties on the sexual plane, on the plane of marriage and children, on the plane of relations with men. These are issues which concerned larger numbers of women than you think and to which the communist movement must provide responses ... not complete answers but the beginning of solutions to these questions.

The Bolsheviks had begun to raise such questions in the wake of the October Revolution. It was time that revolutionary Marxists returned to them. Pablo would again in 1960 when he was languishing in a Dutch prison and wrote an essay on the liberation of women.

This introduction of 'quality of life' or cultural issues into the political discussions reflected his continued rethinking on the economic prospects in advanced capitalist countries. In his opening address at this 5th World Congress, Pablo backed further away from predicting the return of another Great Depression. This was now ruled out, even if he still expected major recessions in the boom-and-bust cycle of advanced capitalism.

The distinctive Pablo stamp on the congress's manifesto was a spirited championing of the Algerian and colonial revolutions in general (which included the recent reawakening of the Black civil rights movement in the United States):

> Of all the manifestations of the colonial revolution since Dien Bien Phu, it is the heroic revolutionary rising of the Algerian people which now represents the greatest danger for world imperialism ... by sapping the economy and finances of France itself, destroying the last hope for 'grandeur' of French imperialism based on the oil of the Sahara, and opening the flank of all black Africa to the spread of the revolution, the Algerian Revolution merits the respect and admiration of all the workers of the world for the spirit of sacrifice and abnegation without parallel of its engaged masses and for the audacity and unbreakable will to victory of its combatants.

The 5th World Congress of 1957 pledged 'not only political support but, as much as possible, material support to the revolutionary struggle that was being fought in Algeria'. Defining how much was 'possible' fell to Pablo as the secretary of the International and as the leader most preoccupied with colonial issues.

After the congress, Pablo set to work on researching and writing his pamphlet, *The Arab Revolution*. It was issued in 1958 as a discussion document rather than an official position, which suggests some hesitation in the leadership to Pablo's thesis. In the opening paragraph he characterised – and this assumption was to be endlessly contested by other Marxists in the decades to come – the colonial revolution as part of the coming of socialism on a world scale:

> The current Arab revolution forms part of the colonial revolution that has been irresistibly developing since the last world war. This revolution, furthermore, is only one aspect of the accelerating and irremediable break-up of the capitalist regime, and consequently forms part of the proletarian revolution by which the end of the capitalist regime will be completed and the new socialist social order will begin.[22]

The colonial revolution was then in full swing across the whole 'Arabised' band of countries from the Atlantic to the Indian Ocean. Morocco and

Tunisia had just achieved their independence. Nasser's Egypt was one of the acknowledged leaders of the Non-Aligned Bloc of newly independent nations. It had emerged from the 1956 Suez war with Britain, France and Israel with its nationalisation of the Suez Canal secured. The pro-Western monarchy had recently been overthrown by leftist army officers in Iraq and Baathists had come to power in neighbouring Syria. There was rebellion led by self-proclaimed Marxists in Yemen. Iran was ruled by the Shah, but strong leftist and Islamist oppositions existed.

Pablo characterised the army officer or 'petty bourgeois' leaderships of these newly independent countries in the Middle East as acting in alliance with, or in the stead of, the nascent industrial or national bourgeoisie, but did not believe they would succeed in achieving real independence and a sustained modernisation (or in Marxist terms, the bourgeois democratic revolution – chiefly land reform, industrialisation and the emancipation of women). That would depend on the emergence of a revolutionary mass party based on the urban working class and the peasant masses.

Algeria was different, or more hopeful, although he did not rule out that it would follow the same path as countries such as Egypt or Tunisia. However, the independence movement was led by what he characterised as 'plebian, petty bourgeois' elements as there was no local indigenous bourgeoisie of any weight, due to the domination of all sectors of the economy by the European settlers. This plebian leadership lacked an emancipatory program that would strengthen its following among peasantry and the indigenous poor of the towns, but there was some hope of a wing of the FLN adopting a more democratic and socially liberating program, and of a revolutionary Marxist current emerging as well. The sources for such developments were Algerian intellectuals who had already embraced or were moving towards revolutionary Marxism, and the immigrant Algerian workers in France. This anticipation was correct, but overestimated its eventual strength and, ironically in the light of future events, completely missed the agricultural workers in Algeria who were to produce the most hopeful socialist experiment of the colonial revolution.

The difficulty for Pablo was that, while there were Trotskyists in most countries of the Americas, Asia and Europe, outside of a handful of settlers in South Africa and Palestine there were none in what Pablo now came to see as the main front in the colonial revolution – the Middle East and Africa. There were none in Algeria and the Left in the FLN was at best marginal.

Nevertheless, what the relative handful of Trotskyist revolutionaries and their Algerian friends accomplished in these years was vital and extraordinary. In the next few years, the International's aid and collaboration, with Pablo at the wheel, was to step up a couple of gears. The personnel weaknesses of the International and the FLN Left would prove to be a recurring disadvantage, and finally fatal. Meanwhile, their finest hours were about to unfold.

CHAPTER 8

# The arms factory in Morocco
## 1955-1960

*Our support for the present Algerian revolution cannot allow itself to be episodic, verbal and incidental, but must on the contrary be constant, practical and one of the essential axes of our activity.*[1]

**Michel Pablo, 1958**

EVENTS MOVED QUICKLY after the 5th Congress of the International in September 1957. A coup, engineered by the most fanatical supporters of continued French rule in Algeria, brought General de Gaulle to power in France in May 1958. Sensing the advent of a more repressive regime in France, the headquarters of the International was moved from Paris to Amsterdam. This brought the Dutch and German members of the International into a more active role in the Algerian solidarity work and made Pablo's contact with the FLN leaders in Europe – essentially the Boudaoud brothers, Omar and Mansour – easier as they were based in neighbouring West Germany, as it was known then.

The move to Amsterdam coincided with dog days for the Algerians. In 1957 they had lost 'the battle of Algiers'. The battle had been fought in the Casbah, the tightly packed Algerian neighbourhood at the centre of the city. It had been an FLN stronghold, but in the Winter and Spring of 1957, the French paratroopers sealed it off and methodically, block by block, rounded up suspects for questioning and torture (and the occasional murder). This process was punctuated by gun battles and house demolitions. Trapped in this redoubt, the FLN members were captured and eliminated. Elsewhere, in the countryside, the FLN were in full retreat before the French offensives. There were now more than 400,000 French troops in Algeria and the French air force had a free hand, bombing, strafing and napalming at will. Two million rural Algerians were uprooted from their villages and herded into concentration camps and shanty towns. The electrified fences and minefields along the borders of Tunisia and Morocco were almost complete, making resupply of the partisans extremely difficult, if not impossible. The French secret service was killing or frightening off the handful of arms dealers willing to supply arms to the Algerians, and any freighters carrying arms were either sunk or intercepted by the French navy. All in all, the Algerian Revolution was in danger of being disarmed, suffocated and snuffed out.

In his meetings with the FLN leaders, Pablo noted 'great concern, even despair', especially concerning the shortage of arms for the guerrillas struggling to fight and survive in the interior. It was a crisis he searched for answers to:

> When I saw before me the possibility of the defeat of the Algerian revolution for which so much blood had been spilt, so many sacrifices made, so many hopes invested in, my imagination began, as often before in my life, to turn to those 'solutions' that seem at first sight to be 'impossible'.

The impossible solutions he had in mind were an international brigade on the model of the Spanish Civil War of 1936-39 and the creation of industrial-scale arms factories in Morocco. The International would do these 'impossible' things. With Elly, he flew to Tunisia in the second half of 1958 to propose these 'solutions' to the Algerian Provisional Government and met with its president Ferhat Abbas. On the way there was another example of Elly's presence of mind and *sang-froid*:

> The plane was above Madrid, and they had just served us a meal, when I noticed that one of the propellers had stopped. I told Elly but she continued eating, even ordering a coffee.

The plane was forced to land in Madrid before continuing to Lisbon and then to Tunis.

The suggestion of an international brigade was rejected, but in 1959 the Algerians agreed to the arms factory. Later, Pablo would reflect, 'Personally, weapons were never my sort of thing ... But it would have been ridiculous to promote my "Christian-Tolstoyan" principles or ethics, towards which an ever-growing education leads ...' For Pablo, Machiavelli had answered such qualms centuries before.

It was a dangerous undertaking. The French secret service specialised in killing arms dealers who supplied the Algerians. Under the cover name of 'La Main Rouge', Service Action, the operational arm of the French secret police, SDECE (Service de Documentation Extérieure et de Contre-Espionnage), carried out attacks and assassinations across Europe and North Africa. Constantin Melnik, the security adviser to then Prime Minister Michel Debré, boasted this killing machine carried out 135 assassinations in 1960 alone. Arms dealers in contact with the FLN were a specific target of their operations. As Thomas Riegler has recently recounted:

> Starting in September 1956, there were at least four attempts against the life of arms manufacturer Otto Schlüter over a period of two years. When the last bomb attack accidentally claimed the life of his mother and wounded his daughter [in June 1957], Schlüter finally retired from business. Another target was the arms dealer Georg Puchert in Frankfurt. He had been contracted in 1958 by the FLN to supply *Wilaya 5*, one of its operations zones situated in West Algeria. Initially, the French used sabotage to deter Puchert: frogmen of the *Action service* scuttled his freighter 'Atlas', which had been loaded with Norwegian dynamite for the FLN, in Hamburg's harbour. Then, in September 1958, Puchert's Swiss associate Marcel Leopold was killed in Geneva by means of a poisoned dart shot into his neck, ejected from a kind of bicycle pump gun. Since all these efforts had failed in discouraging the arms dealer, the Red Hand went in for the killing stroke: on 3 March 1959, Puchert died when a limpet bomb attached under the driver's seat of his Mercedes detonated when triggered by an inertia-based mechanism. Filled with ball bearings, it did relatively little damage to the car, but left Puchert's riddled body slumped over the steering wheel. During the following two years, four more German businessmen with contacts to the FLN were also targeted: one of them was killed outright, another severely wounded; in two cases the attacks failed.[2]

This list is not a complete catalogue. La Main Rouge – the Red Hand – also targeted the strong FLN presence in West Germany: in November 1958 lawyer Aït Ahcene was gunned down in front of the Tunisian embassy in Bad Godesberg. Abd el-Solvalar met a similar fate in front of Saarbrücken's train station in January 1959. It is almost certain the West German police collaborated in these hits, at least to the extent of providing intelligence and turning a blind eye. Belgium, Switzerland and Italy were other places in Europe where La Main Rouge carried out murders of Algerians and their supporters.[3]

All this made Pablo a possible target. He recounts an incident on a visit to Germany, when travelling with the Boudaoud brothers, both

FLN leaders. As they drove out of Cologne, they recognised a colonel [Marcel Mercier] from SDECE following them. 'They took out their guns straight away, suspecting that an assassination attempt would be made,' Pablo recounts, 'and I thought that at any moment one of my mother's prophecies was about to come true: "You, my child," she'd say, "with the crazy ideas you have in your head, will be hung one day".' A high-speed chase ensued – 'Mansour was the most amazing driver I had ever met in my life' – and the French colonel and his companions were left in the Algerians' wake.

Everyone in the car qualified as candidates for assassination by SDECE. The French did kill FLN leaders and representatives. Ben M'Hidi, the FLN top leader in the Algiers, was 'suicided' after his capture in 1957. In May 1959, a car bomb meant for Tayeb Boulahrouf, the FLN representative in Rome, killed a child instead. As for non-Algerian supporters, two solidarity activists in Belgium, Georges Laperches and Pierre Le Gre've, were targeted with letter bombs in March 1960. Laperches was killed when he opened his parcel but Le Gre've was saved by his wife who called the police before the device, possibly defective, could explode.[4] Along with the German arms dealers, Swiss arms dealers Marcel Léopold and Leo Geiser were also assassinated, killed in Geneva in September and November 1957.

Beyond these dangers, there were the practical difficulties of setting up an arms factory. Ideally it would manufacture submachine guns, modelled on the French standard *pistolet mitrailleur* MAT 49. The model was ideal for lightly armed guerrillas, and defectors from the French army in their ranks were familiar with it. Ammunition could be relatively easily sourced by raids and on the black market. The Algerians promised to secure the site for the factory, raise the finance and recruit Algerian workers in France and Algeria itself. The rest fell to Pablo. As he recalled,

> The plan could not be implemented without the help of our movement. First we chose a team of skilled metallurgists, designers and mechanics. We formed a small undercover organisation in Europe capable of supplying the necessary machinery and of sending it safely and speedily to the site of production. Our members and leaders from Argentina, France, Holland and Greece left their jobs, families and countries to go to the secret factories the FLN had established in Morocco.

The best account of the establishment of this factory is from Dimitris Livieratos, the organiser on the spot. Livieratos was Pablo's liaison man.

## 8 . THE ARMS FACTORY IN MOROCCO 1955-60

He shuttled between Casablanca and London for meetings with Pablo and Elly, who was characteristically in the thick of things. London, for possibly the last time, acted as a safe haven for revolutionaries plotting the overthrow of an unwanted regime. Livieratos was involved in all stages of the factory's creation. He got on so well with the Algerians that he was incorporated into the management of their other arms factories producing grenades and mortars. His account is episodic, based on notes and an earlier account he wrote in the mid-1960s but not published until 2001. The original was in Greek, and it was only in 2012 that a French translation appeared. In the intervening decades, there was little talk on the Left about the factory. The title of Livieratos' book, *The Invisible Factory*, could just as well have been *The Unknown Factory*.

Remarkably, the establishment of the factories in Morocco proceeded without interference from the ubiquitous and active French police forces and their allies. Some 30 European and Latin American members and supporters were recruited and made their way to Morocco during 1959 and 1960. They joined with around 400 Algerians to set up and operate half a dozen factories turning out grenades, mortars and submachine guns. The last was the special contribution of Pablo and the international volunteers. They sourced, purchased and shipped the advanced machines needed for their manufacture. One of Pablo's strongest French supporters, Pierre Avot-Meyers, even broke into a barracks in Paris in a bid to steal a machine gun to use as a model. He managed to get into the armoury but found the guns too securely locked away. The gun produced was eventually modelled on designs for a Belgian variation – the Sola Super 9mm – which had never been manufactured.

Not all the internationalist proletarians were members of the Fourth International. One of the non-member volunteers was Albert Oeldrich, whom Livieratos dubs 'the old adventurer'. Oeldrich was a highly skilled engraver by profession, a veteran of the Dutch resistance to the Nazis and a strong independent supporter of Algerian freedom. He played a key role in securing much of the machinery for the factory and the draughtsmen for designing the various parts of the machine gun. However, he could be trouble. Early on in the process, during a visit to Morocco with Livieratos, he attempted to go freelance, making promises to 'Victor', the FLN's boss of supply operations in Algeria, and cutting out Pablo and Sal Santen, the leader of the Dutch Trotskyists. He was recalled to London by Pablo who read him the riot act and pointed out both the dangers of going alone and the difficulty he would have in recruiting collaborators. It didn't end their relationship. In the absence of members with Oeldrich's skills and enterprise, Pablo had little choice but to keep working with him.

There were other dramas. The original factory site had to be abandoned and the machinery shifted overnight, literally, when a high official of the FLN defected to the French in April 1960. To increase security, the FLN's operations were decentralised. The submachine gun manufacturing was moved to an abandoned factory in the middle of an orange orchard in the district of Tamara.

The volunteers were highly political animals, so there were always political crises brewing. There were many long, exhausting meetings and at least two main issues of contention. The first was how the work of the volunteers was to be managed – by workers self-management or by traditional top-down methods. The Argentinians insisted on the first approach, the Pablo model if you like. The Dutch were the champions of the traditional hierarchical model. In the end, a compromise was reached: there would be frequent general meetings of these workers, but day-to-day direction would be in the hands of the three most skilled men. The Algerian workers, for their part, met separately but with the internationalists present, and often invited to speak. Their meetings were in Arabic and occasionally French. Livieratos learned some basic Arabic, enough to follow the gist of their discussions. The Algerians' assemblies were also long and stormy. People could speak freely but the meetings appear to have been more consultative than determinative. Sometimes the leaders put issues to the vote but generally they made the final decisions after hearing from the 'brothers'.

The second point of contention was more narrowly political. Very early on, one of the English volunteers decided he didn't agree with the International's line of priority to the colonial revolution and insisted on being allowed to return home immediately – something Livieratos had to work hard to convince the Algerians to allow. 'Choppy', one of the Jamaican volunteers, agreed with the line but didn't believe that work in this factory was the best way to contribute. Others had a similar view and argued this secret work was not building the International. In a word, it was too selfless.

There was some conflict with the Algerians, too, about the presence of a Frenchman. After much debate the Algerians eventually agreed that Louis Fontaine could join the workforce in Morocco. An active member of the International, Fontaine had served in Algeria with the French army and, on return to France, had devoted himself to aiding the FLN by running the printery the International had created for them. However, the DST (the French police responsible for internal surveillance) had discovered the operation and there was a warrant out for his arrest. Still keen to serve the Algerians, he was an ideal volunteer as his previous civilian job had been in the French weapons design and manufacturing centre.

Ultimately these political arguments did not disrupt the work, but they did add another layer of discontent to a life that was not easy. Because the factory was secret, the workers, internationalists and Algerians alike, were kept indoors, under cover. Virtual industrial prisoners, they worked, ate, slept and met in the same building day after day, week after week, and month after month. The perimeter was patrolled by often officious Algerian soldiers to deter any truancy. The workers were, to use Livieratos' word, virtually 'entombed'. This confinement was relieved by occasional daytrips to the coast, and at one of the factories there was a swimming pool. There was some fraternisation and periodic visits from higher-ups (such as Pablo, wearing suit and tie naturally, and Elly in early 1960). Livieratos does provide a brief glimpse of the workers relaxing:

> Those who weren't required at their posts sat around on their blankets under the trees … We talked of all or nothing, of Brigitte Bardot or dialectical materialism. Day after day we swapped stories from all corners of the globe. Weeks, dates, time itself, lost their importance.[5]

Nevertheless, it was mostly a tough assignment with no promise of glory.

Later, when the factories were up and running and Pablo had finished a prison sentence and found refuge in Morocco, he went to Tamara to celebrate the production of the 5,000th machine gun. 'We had, all of us together, succeeded,' he recalled in his memoir. 'For the first time, a colonial revolution had managed to produce the weapons of its own victory, not in a primitive handicrafts factory but in a streamlined industrial factory. That factory, besides its purely practical significance, also had a huge psychological impact, which the FLN a little later exploited as much as they could.' According to Pablo, the Algerians intended to produce a documentary on the factory, a plan that was shelved after the 1965 coup which made Pablo persona non grata. In one of those ironies of history, the operation of the factory coincided with Moscow's decision to allow its Eastern European allies to ship hundreds of tons of armaments to the Algerians via Tunisia.

The Left's long historical reticence over the factory was mystifying but there are several possible explanations. Any publicity for the effort in France itself could have provoked a backlash, as the guns produced were for killing French soldiers, many of them conscripts. Conceivably too, French fascists, or even the government, could swing into retaliation or prosecutions. Pablo's exclusion from the International soon after the victory of the Algerians would have also dampened any enthusiasm to claim credit for the effort by the organisation itself. But perhaps the main reason for the relative silence was that history moved on and other events now called for attention.

Before leaving this remarkable example of solidarity with a people's emancipatory struggle, it is worth repeating its political justification. Pablo believed the failure of the workers movement in Europe to extend aid and support to the colonial revolution was a failure attributable to social-democratic and Stalinist leaderships and reflected 'the relative decline of the revolutionary character' of the workers movement in Europe. The absence of this support also handicapped the socialist development of the colonial revolution. Practical solidarity from the International would not only aid the emancipatory struggle in the colonial world, he believed, but could heal, or at least narrow, the rupture between the two movements. Moreover, victory for the Algerians would give momentum to the revolution throughout Africa and possibly undermine the Gaullist regime in France itself.

— ✣ —

As Pablo was ramping up the practical aid to the Algerians, sharp political and personal differences were emerging in the leadership of the International.

It was 'a woman problem' – or one woman in particular – that exacerbated conflicts within the leadership in the years that followed the 5th Congress. The International was very much a boys club. So were all political organisations at the time, but if anything, it was even more pronounced in the International. For example, over that decade, there was not a single article by a woman in *Quatrième Internationale*. On the other hand, Pablo and Elly came as a package. They were a tight and devoted couple, and both were political animals. Where Pablo went, so did Elly. That included meetings of the leadership where dissent from Pablo's positions or actions could prompted her to retaliate. We know from Jan Willem Stutje's biography of Mandel that he, Frank and Maitan were particularly annoyed and hurt by her interventions, which apparently sometimes took the form of personal attacks. They were not above replying in kind.

## 8 . THE ARMS FACTORY IN MOROCCO 1955-60

Even Pablo's closest allies took issue with what they saw as Elly's imperious hot-headedness, and their resentment persisted down the years. Gilbert Marquis, arguably Pablo's strongest supporter, was critical of Elly and of Pablo's reluctance or inability to rein her in. He recalls that when he privately objected to her 'right' to be heard at meetings, given she wasn't elected to any position, Pablo excused her on the grounds of her aristocratic background and its apparent accompanying sense of entitlement. He told Marquis that she played with the children of the Greek royal family when she was a child. This cut little ice with Marquis. On the other hand, my own partner of the time, Margaret Eliot, meeting Elly as the women's liberation movement was emerging from inside the chauvinist Left in 1968-69, saw in her the very model of a strong-willed and egalitarian partner. Mohammed Harbi, too, admired her political convictions and forthrightness. He also saw in her a softer side, mentioning her tenderness towards children.[6] (Pablo and Elly had no children, presumably because of their footloose revolutionary life.)

But this difficult presence could get mixed up with and aggravate strictly political differences. For instance, at its 10-11 November 1959 meeting, the members of the International Secretariat wrestled with the question of how bold or accommodating Trotskyists should be as entrists in the communist and socialist parties. Specifically, to what extent should they differentiate themselves from other leftists or 'centrist' currents, when these allies advanced proposals the entrists considered wrong and harmful to the movement.

Mandel came down on the side of moderation, Pablo of a bolder orientation. Mandel felt differentiation risked isolation and exclusion from the parties; it was more prudent to 'accentuate the positive', when these currents agreed with the entrists. Pablo, while also counselling against isolation and reverting to acting like a propaganda sect, argued that the entrists must find ways to make their different approach known when critical policies and actions were at stake. When it came to a vote, there were two votes for Mandel's position (his own plus Maitan's) and two for Pablo's (his plus Santen's). Pierre Frank abstained.

That much is discernible from the minutes. But the meeting was much more explosive. Stutje takes up the story (based on the versions of the clash given by Mandel):

> In November 1959 in Amsterdam, he and Pablo had a blazing row. During a break, Elly disdainfully referred to Mandel as a 'so-called Trotskyist'. Mandel snapped back, 'If you can say that, my response is that you're either stupid

or crazy'. The scene became more grotesque when Pablo ordered him to leave the meeting and Santen, known for his gentleness, threatened him with violence. Mandel felt deeply humiliated. Pierre Frank avoided a break by convincing the Secretariat to refrain from making a choice between Pablo and Mandel.

The clash was part of a wider difference between the pair. Mandel was integrated deep in the Socialist Party in Belgium and edited *La Gauche*, the unofficial organ of the left wing of that party. This was no small accomplishment, but Pablo argued there should also be a 100 per cent Trotskyist presence in Belgium so that the International's particular left-wing politics and its differences with other trends would be clear and public. It would also act as the conscience of the entrists, something to measure their own activity by, inside the Belgian Socialist Party. This independent presence – usually a journal at least – was an essential element of how Pablo now interpreted *entrism sui generis*. According to his biographer, Mandel resented the demand as he was already overloaded with tasks – editing *La Gauche*, membership of the secretariat, teaching, journalism and his research into the evolution of modern capitalism.

Stutje, based on what Maitan told him in 2002, also gives this account on the International Secretariat's move to Amsterdam in 1958:

> Only Pablo had expressed a preference for Amsterdam: the others considered Rome a more suitable location. They had gone along with Pablo to keep him happy. Sal Santen was there: he and Santen were thick as thieves, and Santen was unwilling after his Latin American adventure of 1952-53 to be separated again from his family. Moreover, Pablo needed Santen to back him in the sharp differences of opinion about developments in Europe that were coming to light. In Paris Elly had called Pierre Frank an idiot because he failed to recognise the historic defeat of the working class [in the wake of the coup bringing de Gaulle to power – *HG*]. Frank objected to Elly's presence at leadership meetings and Mandel and Maitan supported him in this. The grumbling trio gave in when Pablo offered them the choice of accepting Amsterdam and Elly or his resignation.

Of course, there were other glaringly good reasons for Amsterdam that Stutje overlooks; the principal one being it was much closer to the FLN's leaders based in Cologne and other West German cities. Rome would have made regular meetings impossible. Amsterdam was more accessible to other IS members, too – Frank in Paris, Mandel in Brussels, Georg Jungclas in Cologne. Adolfo Gilly, who was the new Latin American representative on the IS, was happy to be based in Amsterdam. The significance of this dispute is the trio's discounting of the importance of the liaison with the FLN leaders rather than Pablo wanting to be close to his mates like Sal Santen.

These personal clashes are only skimmed over in the memoirs of Livio Maitan[7], then a member of the secretariat. However, when he does refer to them, it is not Elly but Santen who eggs on Pablo. Where Stutje sees a gentle comrade in Sal Santen, Maitan characterises him as 'naïve and uncouth'. In Maitan's retelling there was little political disagreement, and the division was caused by Pablo's high-handedness and inability to belong to an organisation that he did not dominate. Furthermore, in Maitin's view, Pablo's strengths, particularly his ability to divine political and social developments before others, could also be his weaknesses, leading him to overemphasise the strength of the colonial revolution, the de-Stalinisation in the Soviet Union, the aspiration for self-managed socialism and so on. That 'over-optimism' was a fatal trait he shared, Maitan felt, with Mandel.

The point is, questions over the Algerian aid, the nature of entrist work and Elly's presence were sources of conflict well before a key FLN aid scheme blew up and generated so much more bad blood. Not only that, but the episode would see Pablo end up in prison and, ultimately, driven from the Fourth International.

— ✧ —

No sooner was the arms factory up and running than the FLN approached Pablo for aid for a different project. The leaders of Wilaya 7 (as the Federation of the FLN in France was now known) had decided they needed to make money, literally, and hit upon the idea of a major counterfeiting operation. At the end of 1958 the French government decided to replace the old 10,000 franc note with a new 100 franc note. This struck the FLN leaders in France as an ideal opportunity to replenish their funds by counterfeiting the new notes and hoping they'd pass in the confusion of the changeover. A bonus was that the forged banknotes, being passed by tens of thousands of Algerians working in France (135,000 of them were members of the FLN at this stage) could prove a major disruption to the French economy.[8]

Later, there would be a view that such an operation jumped the boundaries of revolutionary respectability, so it is worth noting that, according to one of the Wilaya 7 leaders, Ali Haroun, the FLN had considered that very question of revolution and 'criminal' acts at the time:

Does it conform to the revolutionary ideals adopted by the FLN? Will the leaders of the FLN be equated with vulgar counterfeiters? How are the rare friends on the Left going to react? Hold on, no sensible person considered the attack on the post office in Oran [in 1949 which netted nearly four million francs for the MTLD – *HG*] as a hold-up by gangsters. Every revolutionary movement considers it their right to look for money where it could be found, principally in the hands of its adversary. Especially if the goal of the action is clearly defined.[9]

They turned to Pablo for technical help. Pablo was also torn and consulted his closest comrades over whether he should help. The help would be to put the FLN in touch with Albertus Oeldrich, the highly skilled printer and engraver who had been involved in setting up the arms factory in Morocco. Sal Santen was definitely supportive. Mohammed Harbi was not. Pablo also asked Ernest Mandel and he agreed that the International could offer support by putting the FLN and Oeldrich in contact.[10] Mandel later fudged this. When the operation collapsed and Pablo and Santen were arrested in Amsterdam and charged with forgery, counterfeiting and arms smuggling, Mandel took no responsibility and used the whole episode (or allowed it to be used by Maitan and Frank) to discredit and undermine Pablo in the International. It was an experience, a betrayal, that wounded Pablo right to the end of his life,[11] and we'll come back to it.

By Pablo's own account, his role in this FLN operation was limited. He knew what the Algerians were planning and he put them in touch with the printer/engraver Albertus Oeldrich. That account is confirmed by Ali Haroun, who was one of the triumvirate of leaders of the FLN in Europe at the time. Haroun is adamant that from beginning to end it was an FLN project, even if the fatal weakness can be traced back to using Oeldrich – on Pablo's recommendation. (On the other hand, its eventual political triumph, as Haroun also makes clear, was all Pablo's work.[12])

In 1958 or thereabouts, Pablo had been introduced by Dutch comrades to Oeldrich, a veteran of the International Brigades in Spain and the anti-Nazi wartime resistance. As noted above, he had played a key role in purchasing and installing equipment for the Moroccan factories. Pablo and Santen had also relied on him for forging identity cards and passports destined for use by the Algerians. He seemed the ideal choice for the counterfeiting project. However, given Livieratos' revelation about his tendency to go off on his own tack, something Pablo was aware of, there was a distinct risk in involving him. If Pablo can be criticised, it is for having too little to do with the counterfeiting operation rather than too

## 8 . THE ARMS FACTORY IN MOROCCO 1955-60

much. He knew the old Dutch 'adventurer' was a risky proposition, according to Liveratos. It was a costly error. But as Livieratos writes:

> He would never confess his error on this subject. He understood it, intelligent man that he was, but never went as far as to admit it. It would have been too humiliating for him.[13]

It all began well enough. Using funds provided by the FLN, Oeldrich bought the specialised offset printing press and the paper stock. Helmut Schneeweiss, another veteran of the wartime underground, was brought in by Oeldrich and he located premises for the operation in Osnabruck in Germany. At some point, Oeldrich decided he needed more specialist help. Without consulting Pablo or Santen, he recruited Hubertus Hompe, a former specialist engraver from the national printery in Amsterdam. Trouble was that Hompe had been sacked from that institution in suspicious circumstances and was a friend or acquaintance of Joop Zwart, a part-time informer for the BVD, the Dutch secret police. It was Zwart who had put Oeldrich and Hompe in contact. So this contact with Zwart was all Oeldrich's doing. In his memoirs, Santen makes it clear that had he known, he would have severed ties with Oeldrich immediately and sounded the alarm.[14]

On 10 June 1960, tipped off by Hompe and Zwart, the German police swooped on Osnabruck arresting Oeldrich, Schneeweiss and Hompe. The raid was well-timed: the printery was primed to begin the counterfeiting. Later, in Cologne, they picked up Abbas who the FLN had detailed to supervise the operation. The same day, some 80 Dutch police swooped on Pablo and Santen, raiding the Raptis apartment in Amsterdam, 'much to the horror of my wife Elly who was celebrating her birthday'. They were charged with forgery and counterfeiting. 'Their charges,' in Pablo's view, 'were a typical police amalgam aimed at covering up the political nature of our arrest and making things as hard as possible for us.'

Under police interrogation Oeldrich cracked, falling for the old ruse of a promise that a confession would result in a lighter sentence. (To his credit, Oeldrich apparently said nothing of the arms factory.) Schneeweiss also admitted certain incriminating facts. Hompe, naturally enough, went free and temporarily disappeared from view. The other three followed different strategies. Abbas denied everything and followed the advice of the FLN leaders to avoid any political motivation. Pablo and Santen, for their part, denied the specific charges but proudly declared their active support for the Algerian cause and accused the secret police of manufacturing the case against them for political reasons.

When the news of the arrests reached the other leaders of the International, they were outraged like respectable petit bourgeois rather than revolutionaries, according to Maurice Ferares, the Dutch comrade who informed them of the arrests.[15] A leader of the Fourth International, the world party of the socialist revolution, arrested for the low crime of counterfeiting! Their reaction disgusted Ferares: 'If that's the vanguard of the revolution ...'

While the top leaders were hesitant, to say the least, to become involved in the case, Pablo's key comrades in Paris had no such qualms. That is, once they realised who this 'Michalis Raptis' arrested in Amsterdam really was. Christophe Nick takes up the story (Gilbert Marquis was one of his principal sources):

> In Paris the PCI sent out a sober communiqué: a member of the Fourth International, Michel Raptis, has been arrested in Amsterdam. Nothing to see here. Some days later Jacques Privas (real name Jacques Grinblat), former Molinierist and ultra-left leader from the war years, puts his head in at the PCI office where he finds Gilbert Marquis and Henri Benoits.
> 'You aren't surprised by what's happened?'
> 'What's happened?'
> 'The Raptis in prison is Pablo!'
> 'What!'
>
> Secrecy has worked too well. As incredible as it appears, few in the PCI knew the true name of the Greek, except for the veterans. Privas quickly brought them up to speed and set the house on fire. 'Imagine if the pope was arrested. You would see the mobilisation in Rome? Well and good, but what happens here? Where's the campaign? The only thing that has been done is the usual procedures. Activities continue as if nothing was going on. What conclusion do you young ones draw from this? Who's fucking with who here? With this allegation about forging money Pablo faces twenty years. If no one starts stirring, that is going to be the outcome.'

With that, Privas, Marquis, Benoits, Minguet, Avot-Meyers and Roger Foirier swung into action. Within days an extraordinary international campaign for Pablo and Santen was under way. In leftist and intellectual circles, all hell broke loose. Christophe Nick continues the story in his usual breathless style:

> A global wave breaks over the Dutch government. In Brazil where they are visiting, Jean-Paul Sartre and Simone de Beauvoir recruit the two most significant local writers, Jorge Amado and José Arthur da Frota Moreira, to co-sign a telegram of support for the 'detainees in Amsterdam who have been

developing an intense campaign in favour of a free Algeria'. The Brazilian parliament also raises the question. The deputies in the state of San Paulo denounce the arrests. In Argentina Posadas mobilises the Buenos Aires bar. The president of the Alliance Française comes out in support, as do academics in the biggest universities. A former minister of the interior sends a telegram of protest. In Chile a delegation of lawyers goes to see the Dutch ambassador. The leader of the Socialist party, Salvador Allende, joins with the major unions and parties of the future Popular Unity alliance to support Pablo. Similar protests in Bolivia, in Peru, in Uruguay. From New Zealand the student and university unions write to the Dutch Minister of Justice. From Sri Lanka the dockers' union sends multiple motions of support, the parliament in Colombo debates the issue, the Prime Minister calls in the Netherlands ambassador. In Japan the left of the Socialist party supports Pablo. The Yugoslavs make a diplomatic approach. In Britain the Trotskyists in the Labour Party convince 30 MPs to send an address to the government in The Netherlands recalling 'the numerous actions in Holland to support the German Jews after the arrival in power of Hitler. No one anticipated that those who struggled against Nazism will be thrown in prison and prosecuted for their activity in support of the independence of Algeria'. The German SPD, the left in Finland, Iceland, Norway, Sweden, Denmark and Ireland, as well as Greece, multiply the flood of appeals. In The Netherlands itself, from unions to deputies, from intellectuals to senators, from journalists to students, from Catholics to Protestants, as well as all the Left, mobilise. In France the free masonry of the extreme Left is aroused by Craipeau, who for the last six years has perfected the technique of committee-petition-meeting-media campaigning. He recruits Claude Bourdet, Maurice Nadeau, Pierre Naville, Jean-Marie Domenach, Michel Leiris, Jean Guéhenno and Laurent Schwartz to lead the charge of support. The Dutch government wilts. They have never experienced anything like this.[16]

The campaign did more than sustain the morale of the prisoners. It raised the public profile of the Algerians' struggle for independence and helped legitimise showing support for it. French intellectuals now found their courage to openly declare their sympathy for the Algerians and their support for French resistance to the war. Three months later, in September, the famous Manifesto of the 121 was issued in Paris, legitimising support for the FLN and opposition to the war in the army itself. Among the 121 signatories were not only Sartre and de Beauvoir but popular cinema figures such as Francois Truffaut and Simone Signoret. Simultaneously, many of the same figures came forward to support members of the Jeanson network who went on trial in September for aiding the FLN. By year's end, anti-war protesters had at last appeared in Paris.

The Amsterdam affair had another silver lining. It allowed the rather isolated Trotskyists – or Pablo's supporters, at least – to reach out to sympathetic figures on the Left and be associated with them in public campaigning. The Fourth International, paradoxically because of its clandestine work, could now appear on the public stage as courageous and principled champions of the colonial revolution – and far-sighted at that, considering that de Gaulle was now being forced to admit that Algeria was destined to be Algerian. However, in Pablo's absence, the remnant leadership failed to take full advantage of that opportunity.

If in the ensuing reckoning, the political benefit became significant, the personal cost of the episode, however, was something else. It was painful, bitter and long-lasting.

In 1995 he talked the whole episode over with Adolfo Gilly. Gilly asked him why he had let himself get mixed up in the day-to-day running of the counterfeiting operation. In the conversation Gilly accepts that Pablo was at arm's length and that Mandel shared responsibility for the decision to offer Oeldrich to the FLN.

> **Gilly:** ... it still upsets me that afterwards he [Mandel] hasn't known how to face the others and tell them, 'I have hidden it from you for such and such a reason, but I did know'.
> **Pablo:** I don't understand it.
> **Gilly:** It is a weakness of character, or something like that.
> **Pablo:** As he is dead now it is difficult to go over this again. In reality, do you understand that he destroyed me in the 4th with what he did? He had provided the basis for an attack on me. It is true that at the time he attacked me I didn't care because I was disinterested. But he committed a terrible thing, unpardonable, for which he was remorseful. It is that which explains ... a letter from him which I haven't kept ... it was when I was in Morocco after my release from prison when they had begun their attacks on me, I was so disgusted that I no longer wanted part of it. Then he sent me a letter saying 'Michel, don't leave, stay, you are the best of us. You have been our guide'... He made a last-minute effort. I believe I replied to him: 'But why have you said that you weren't informed?' I received no reply ... He was ambivalent towards me. I believe that it worked on him all his life that he had split with me in a shameful manner ... It is all very bizarre. I don't think he wanted to make me leave the leadership. But why he did what he did when he saw the others exploit the affair ... It was a very serious business what he has done, don't you think? But I agree with you, let's not talk of it anymore.

In a letter to Mandel in February 1962 after his release from prison[17], Pablo did raise this betrayal directly (possibly in reply to the letter Pablo cites in this interview with Gilly). He asks Mandel, 'why do you allow me to be slandered and misrepresented in Belgium and elsewhere'? Indeed, Pablo's reply is far more emotional and fuller of bravado than he

## 8 . THE ARMS FACTORY IN MOROCCO 1955-60

recalls in the Gilly interview. He apparently received no direct response. The now deeply embittered political conflict between the two old comrades continued.[17]

CHAPTER 9

# The trial of Pablo and Santen
## 1960-1961

*Can you simply close your eyes to these facts and tranquilly
live the quiet, selfish life without involving yourself with
the 'demon of politics'?
I don't think so.
I firmly believe that politics – the science concerned with the
consciousness, the organisation and the control of society – must
occupy a primordial place in the life of all free and critical human
beings in order to avoid further disasters and in order that humanity
can move more rapidly to the abolition of repression and exploitation
and to the most complete possible flourishing of the individual.*

**Michel Pablo to the judges at his trial in Amsterdam**
June 1961

PABLO AND SANTEN were to languish in prison for a year before they were brought to trial. They were kept in separate prisons and only met very briefly at pre-trial hearings. Initially Pablo was kept in isolation and deprived of writing materials and books (other than crime fiction and potboilers). The Dutch authorities found it difficult to admit that Pablo and Santen were political prisoners. Such a category was, by definition, an impossibility in a western parliamentary democracy. Besides, the official legal strategy was to characterise the two revolutionaries as common criminal forgers. But the publicity over the arrests and the outcry from the high-profile protesters – such as Sartre and de Beauvoir, British Labour MPs and a vocal Dutch Socialist senator, George Cammelbeeck – not to mention Pablo's own strong representations and threats of a hunger strike, had good results. He was transferred to a cell shared with a young car thief and provided with the books he needed for his essays on Freud, dialectics in Plato, and the 'liberation of women'. He also read widely on crime and prison experiences – Dostoevsky, Hervé Bazin, André Gide and Oscar Wilde.

His cellmate was cheerful, intelligent and talkative, regaling Pablo with the stories of his car thieving. In time he asked Pablo to explain his politics. 'He listened so attentively that any teacher would be envious. Suddenly he was overcome by a mania for reading ... he studied all day and all night. We would sit on our beds on opposite sides of the cell until the early hours of the morning with him asking for explanations about whatever he did not understand. Before my eyes I saw this man transforming himself, gaining knowledge and talking about the factors that caused him to wage war on society, as he put it. He developed into a sort of raging anarchist.' Along with other prisoners he became a supporter of the Algerians. Unfortunately, when he went to trial 'he gave a furious political speech which cost him the maximum sentence'.

There were inordinate delays in bringing on the trial of the Amsterdam Two. Elly sacked one set of lawyers and hired a more sympathetic team she hoped would hurry matters along. She visited every week, bringing supplies and some news of the outside. Because he was powerless to intervene, she decided to withhold information about the power struggle in the International that had broken out in his absence.

The trial was originally predicted for August; that date passed and then a judge set it down for November. It didn't happen and when the matter returned to court on January, the prosecution, which had been delaying, declared the case would be ready to proceed in a month. After six months in detention and no trial date set, lawyers for Pablo and Santen raised the demand for release on bail. The prosecution opposed the move and blamed their lack of readiness by the delay in the arrival of information from the French police. This went on for weeks, with questions raised in parliament and the Minister for Justice backing the story about the delay from the French police The explanation only fuelled the suspicion that the judiciary, prosecution and police were acting at the behest of the French authorities to keep Pablo and Santen out of circulation. The involvement of BVD – some 40 officers of the Dutch secret police were reported to be involved in the investigation and arrests – also bolstered the theory that the whole case was a joint operation between the French Direction Générale de la Sécurité Extérieure (the French CIA) and their Dutch and West German counterparts.[1]

The trial finally began on 21 June 1961, more than a year after their arrests. The prosecution indictment listed three sets of charges – first on the list was the forging of French identity cards for Algerians, the second was the counterfeiting operation, and the third dealt with two orders to Dutch firms for parts for mortars or artillery. The indictment, provided to the two accused in May 1961, was very detailed, actually naming the Algerians who received or were to receive the forged IDs, gave the estimated number of 100 New Franc notes that were to be printed at Osnabrück – 960,000 – and listing the sums paid to Oeldrich and Schneeweiss for their purchases and wages.[2] (Significantly, none to the informer, Hompe, whom Pablo and Santen denied all knowledge of.)

The defendants insisted on the trial's political nature, and their speeches and declarations were widely reported. Pablo's defence, judging from his various declarations, was essentially to justify his actions in broader terms. He pointed out that the 13-month delay in bringing the accused to trial and the refusal of bail was a favour to the French government. While pleading not guilty to the detailed charges, Pablo and Santen proudly admitted to solidarity actions on behalf of the Algerians. As Pablo told the judges:

> Since the end of the world war and during the rise of the emancipatory movement of the colonial peoples, I have quite naturally and unconditionally taken my place on their side. The right of each subject people to national independence seems to me to be an elementary and democratic right which we defended, using every means available, during the Nazi occupation of Europe, and which Europeans have since tried to deny under any convenient pretext to peoples of colour. For this reason alone, it has been my honour since the beginning of the struggle by the Algerian people for their national liberation to have adopted as a member of the 4th International a position of support for their just cause.

As for supporting armed struggle, he quoted then French president Charles de Gaulle justifying the resort to arms during the war against the Nazi occupation.

As usual he did not hold back on high historical analogies. When the prosecutor complained he had abused Dutch hospitality to undermine the French government, he cited the Dutch printers of the 18th century who had printed the books of Rousseau and Voltaire banned by France's royal government of the day. He cited the cases of Spinoza and Descartes as examples of Dutch toleration and encouragement of critical thinkers. (Isaac Deutscher made similar points in his evidence.)

Naturally he went further than this appeal to the revolutionary democratic traditions of the Dutch, which their bourgeoisie had advanced in previous centuries. He argued that the Algerian struggle was a blow against imperialism, and part of the worldwide revolution opening the way to a socialist future. As such, it was a fight that Dutch workers should support as it was in their interests.

His final line of defence was that the Algerian victory was now inevitable and supported by the majority of the world's governments, that de Gaulle himself acknowledged that reality and was currently involved in negotiations with the FLN over the details of independence. It was therefore pointless to punish men who had acted to bring about this just resolution.

Throughout the week of the trial, a line of distinguished witnesses for the defence – Isaac Deutscher, British Labour MPs Konni Zilliacus and John Baird, the mathematician Laurent Schwartz, editor of *France-Observateur*, Claude Bourdet and writer Michael Leiris – appeared. 'At times their declarations and evidence would leave the judges and the public prosecutor speechless,' Pablo remembered. 'In their bourgeois provincialism these judges were not expecting such famous Europeans to be in such undivided solidarity with every aspect of our movement's actions in support of the Algerian Revolution.' Trotsky's widow Natalia Sedova also addressed a letter to the judges in support for the accused. Little wonder one conservative daily claimed that the shadow of Leon Trotsky hovered over the courtroom. Outside the court, Dutch young people demonstrated in solidarity. In the mornings when Pablo left his cell for court and in the evenings when he returned, the anarchist car thief aroused the other prisoners in shows of support.

The judges obviously gave wide latitude to Pablo to make these speeches in court, but Pablo also tackled the actual case against him.[3] He denied ever knowing the informer Hompe and his handler Zwart were involved. Based on Hompe's statement to the court that he believed he was acting on behalf of BVD, the Dutch secret police, at the instigation of Zwart, Pablo implied that they had acted as provocateurs. He wondered why they had not been charged as they were both deeply involved in the counterfeiting operation.

As to the actual counts against him, he could not recall paying Oeldrich for the forging of the identity cards. He rejected Oeldrich's claim that he recruited him to the counterfeiting operation and that he ever told Oeldrich that the aim was 'to ruin the French economy'. 'I have enough knowledge of political economy to know it was perfectly ridiculous to think we could ruin the French economy,' he told the judges. As for the mortar parts, he admitted to funding what he believed were legal purchases by Oeldrich and wondered why, if it was illegal, the companies supplying these parts had not been summoned to court and why the purchases did not form part of the charges against Oeldrich. He did not, of course, regret in any way helping the Algerians arm themselves. 'Unfortunately,' he told the judges, 'we are at a stage of history where emancipation can only be achieved by force of arms and the balance of forces.'

Much of this was for public consumption, and Pablo on occasion turned and addressed the gallery. He detailed the horrors of the 20th century and claimed a place of honour for those who pursued the politics of liberation. How could you not be political when confronted with the injustices of the world? He finished by paying special tribute to his comrade Sal Santen and to the Algerians whose sacrifices and efforts dwarfed his and Santen's contribution.

How much of it swayed the judges we will never know. What we do know is that the sentence they handed down was on the lenient end of the spectrum. The prosecution asked for three-year prison sentences but the judgment delivered July 16 decided that 15 months was long enough. It was certainly much less than the members of the Jeanson network had received the previous October in their trial in Paris. By contrast, in the other trials, held before that of the Amsterdam 'masterminds', Abbas was sentenced to two years and Oeldrich to two and a half years. Thus, writes Pattieu, 'the failure of a risky operation was transformed into a political success'.

Success has many fathers, as the Chinese saying goes. Even in New York, Joe Hansen published an editorial in the SWP's weekly paper, *The Militant*, entitled 'Victory in Raptis-Santen Case', hailing the success of 'the broad international campaign against the political frame-up' as responsible for the light sentences. The editorial reprinted Pablo's concluding remarks at the trial:

> In prison I was strongly fortified by the powerful voice of solidarity from men not only from free Algeria on the march, but from all of Africa on the march. These men I was certain would not forget us, these men of Africa, whom Europe Christianised and civilised and for centuries ferociously repressed and exploited, selling their children by the millions into slavery, plundering their natural resources and even today massacring the sons of Africa in atrocious colonial wars, such as the war in Algeria and that now flaring forth in Angola ...
>
> The Dutch people can have no interest in showing the least accommodation to the imperialism which is repressing men like ourselves who have struggled

## 9 . THE TRIAL OF PABLO AND SANTEN 1960-61

in modest measure for Africa's liberation. It now appears that our trial is ended and the curtain falls on an episode which is after all insignificant compared to the colossal drama being enacted in the world arena.

Let our conviction, our penalty, serve as an example to the European workers to bestir themselves all the more actively in solidarity with the combat of their colonial brethren. For the interests of all workers are essentially the same and the struggle for socialism is one and indivisible.'[4]

Pablo could have been forgiven a wry smile at such celebrations of his impending release and praise for the 'broad international campaign'. There were yawning factional gaps in that 'broad campaign' and it was difficult not to miss the holes in the solidarity efforts on behalf of the Amsterdam prisoners. Italy was home to the largest Left in Europe, yet little seemed to have been done, although Livio Maitan claimed to have raised considerable donations for the defence. After his release Pablo wrote to one of the Italian comrades who had appealed to him to be less critical of the Mandel-Maitan-Frank trio:

Two of the principal leaders of the International, and among the best known outside the International, including the secretary of the International for the past 15 years, were arrested in June 1960 for their multiform aid to the Algerian Revolution. That represented an opportunity for a vast campaign in favour, ultimately, of the Fourth International. There existed a domain for mass campaigning par excellence, which would allow us to make links with diverse movements and personalities in each country. ... I leave to one side the imperative moral duty for our movement to defend its arrested leaders ...

However, comrade Sirio, I ask you in all sincerity, what have you done in Italy?

Re-read attentively your journal *Bandiera Rosa* from July 1960 to September 1961 and tell me, in those 14 editions, how many speak about our trial, lead a campaign systematically on this issue, how many? Tell me in what issue the formation of a committee is announced, signatures collected or protests lodged?

Unfortunately, scandalously, there is nothing of the sort.

It wasn't only in Maitan's Italy that there was 'nothing'. Mandel's Belgium and Jungclas' Germany were no better:

... And in Germany, and in Belgium, where we dispose of considerable entrist forces, well integrated it appears in the mass movement, with many links to the whole milieu, what systematic mass work have we done? Nothing. Contrast that with the enormous work done in Holland ... which demonstrates the large possibilities which exist even in a country such as arch-conservative Holland ...[5]

This absence was very noticeable in the dossier on the case produced by the Netherlands defence committee[6] on the eve of the trial. It listed messages of support for the accused. There were just two signatories from Italy. None from Belgium.

Such inertia was even more scandalous in light of the general expectation that Pablo and Santen were facing years in prison. In a letter addressed to members of the International a few weeks after his arrest, Pablo himself warned that they would likely be in prison for a long stretch. The sentences of ten years imprisonment handed down by a Paris court to the members of the Jeanson network of FLN supporters seemed to confirm that fear, even if in the end the prosecution in Amsterdam asked for three years.

— ✢ —

In Pablo's absence, the leading comrades of the International had been busy in factional matters. A fight over leadership of the International broke out between the 'Europeans' and the 'Latin Americans' at the 6th World Congress held over the new year, December 1960-January 1961. Juan Posadas, the Argentinian leader of the Latin American section, came to Europe well ahead of the congress to prepare for the battle, telling the Latin American delegate on the International Secretariat, Adolfo Gilly, that a more experienced comrade was needed in Paris at this juncture.[7]

There was little disagreement on political questions at the congress. Juan Posadas and the Latin Americans, however, demanded dramatic organisational changes. Gilly wrote a long and eloquent paper in October advocating an International that was operational rather than only theoretical. If the colonial revolution was the motor of the world revolution at the current time, and Latin America was one of its main theatres, then the International should commit a significant part of its leadership and resources to actually aiding that revolution on the spot and not confine itself to declarations and friendly relations with third-world students and émigrés in Europe. He quoted Trotsky who, in the 1930s, had written that liberal and socialist critiques and condemnations of colonialism and its crimes were all well and good but did not go far enough for Bolsheviks. Their responsibility was to get actively involved in the emancipatory struggles of the colonised peoples.

At the Congress, this translated into a demand that Posadas be made secretary and that the headquarters of the International Secretariat be transferred to Latin America. Pablo's supporters at the congress combined with those of Mandel, Frank and Maitan to defeat this move. The centre remained in Europe and Maitan became virtually acting secretary much to the chagrin, as would soon be evident, of the Latin Americans. The response of Posadas and the Latin Americans was to break away and form their own Fourth International.

According to Christophe Nick, Pablo was distressed when he learned of this new split, and even more unhappy that his European supporters had lined up against the Latin Americans. On his release he let them know he felt it was an appalling misstep. Posadas and the Latin Americans had been his strongest supporters in the past and had done extraordinary work on their continent in organising support for his defence and that of Sal Santen. Yet, according to Livio Maitan, Pablo had been concerned about what appeared to be undemocratic practices in the Latin American Bureau and Posadas's overbearing control. In Maitan's telling, Pablo's attempts to visit the continent were 'constantly obstructed' by Posadas.[8] It was also true that Posadas could at times also be an unreliable ally. In the conflict with Mandel over a bolder entrism back in 1959, Posadas abstained.[9]

There is general agreement that Posadas, at the very least, was a 'talented organiser and charismatic adventurer', to quote Canadian historian Bryan Palmer. The second part of that description has more to do with Posadas's later career in which he became the guru of a cult. Gilly, who was then part of what he insisted was the collective leadership of the Latin American Bureau, testifies that throughout the 1950s Posadas and the Latin Americans were very much disciples of the positions Pablo had developed in that decade. This tie was now cut, to the detriment of everyone involved. Nevertheless, Posadas and his supporters carried through on their advocacy of a more activist approach. Gilly himself was to be arrested and serve six years in a Mexican prison for aid to the guerrillas fighting in Guatemala.

Thirty-five years later, Gilly recalled that Pablo had inadvertently played his part in Posadas' decision to split the International. He related how, before the 6th Congress, Pablo had written to the International Secretariat from prison about organisational arrangements that might be made in view of his expectation of a lengthy prison sentence. The letter was read to a meeting of the International Secretariat and overseas leaders. Pablo mentioned by name a number of younger comrades who might profitably be elevated to the leadership. Posadas's name was not on the list. Gilly saw the look in Posadas's eyes and remembered thinking Pablo would pay for that slight.[10]

CHAPTER 10
# Prison writings – women, Freud, Cuba, classical Athens and late Marx
## 1960-1961

TRUE TO THE traditions of revolutionary political prisoners, Pablo demanded books and writing materials. These were eventually granted to him, and he set to work on a series of essays on the liberation of women, Freud, dialectics in Plato, and crime and punishment. His essay on women's emancipation was something of a premonition of the second-wave feminism that would emerge in the 60s. As we have seen, Pablo hoped that the International would take up this issue of the oppression of women, not only in public campaigns (he was convinced there would be mass support for such initiatives) but in its own ranks and practices. In an early insistence on 'the personal is political', Pablo took the view you can judge the revolutionary communist character of a male militant more by his behaviour towards women and children than by his ideological declarations. Not all his reflections of women and their future were as acceptable but at least he was considering it, and in a bold way. As far as one can tell, this issue wasn't on the horizon for any other male leaders of the Fourth International – or for that matter, afloat in any other current in the Left and labour movement of that time.

The starting point of his analysis was that women's oppression was not just economic. 'The complete liberation of women,' he wrote, 'means, among other things, their fundamental right to a full and free sex life.' He advocated free sexual experiences for young people of both sexes as part of their preparation of finding a compatible partner and forming an enduring couple. The couple, he believed, was the natural unit for men and women, as it brought together the complementary aspects of the human being.

It was the first piece of writing he undertook in prison. He had been intending to write an essay on China, including the role of women in that revolution, but in the enforced 'leisure' of his cell he decided to throw the net wider. The essay on women's oppression was an early sign of a liberation of his own. In a short preface to it, written after his release, he noted the advantages a prison stay could bring to revolutionaries if they could use it to study. In his case, it meant he could roam free intellectually, no longer constrained by day-to-day organisation responsibilities. He read more of Freud and Ernest Jones' three-volume biography of the Viennese genius. He re-read Plato and embraced his theory of knowledge, as well as noting and enjoying Plato's occasional descriptions of the Attic countryside which took him back to his youth. Hegel, Kant and Lenin were also on his reading list. Convinced of the benefits of constant and continued immersion in the philosophic masters, he read Marx's then (and even now) little-known *Grundrisse*, his speculations on the characteristics of a future capitalism.

In a piece of historical prophecy of his own, he conjectured in *Liberation of Women* that 'millions of women' could be drawn to campaigns around sexual freedom and reproductive rights, as well as economic equality. He advocated for these issues to be built into the Transitional Program, the central campaigning concept of Trotskyism. He had raised it at the 5th World Congress in 1957 and now, from prison, championed it again as a priority and major initiative for the International.

In practical terms, it was not enough to verbally support women's demands for comprehensive equality. Comrades must walk the talk, practise what they preached, as far as the liberation of women was concerned:

> The communist nature of the members of the revolutionary party must emerge not only from their political ideas but also from their personal behaviour and their cultural and moral conceptions. The relations between men and women, relations with children, the behaviour of each person within the present-day family, and the education of children – these are more important criteria than the profession of communist ideas for a really communist quality of a member of the revolutionary party.[1]

In the context of acknowledging women's generalised oppression, he broke new ground on the lack of sexual freedom for women, and the legitimate existence of their own sexual desires. Historically, even the best of Marxists writing on the condition of women, 'even Engels', were silent on this particular question, trapped in the repressive conservatism of their times. 'Nobody even dares think about it,' he wrote. This, remember, was well before the sexual revolution of the 1960s. He called for revolutionaries to shine a light on this previously taboo subject:

> Absurd theories have been worked up to justify the myth of woman as, allegedly, organically uninterested in a full and free sex life equal to that sought by man. But one forgets, or pretends to forget, the specifically unfavourable conditions in which women are obliged to work out their sex life. All social pressure – traditions, religion, public opinion – tend to oppress a complete and free sex life on the part of women.
> ... But who could seriously argue that women have less imperative sexual needs than men? On the contrary, there are specifically feminine physiological factors which make women more fit to exercise their sexual functions more frequently and amply than men. But this question has always been put under a taboo to women.[2]

While conscious of the need not to be too far ahead of the working class, he believed millions of women would welcome new freedoms in the matters of sex and reproduction. Moreover, lifting the fear of unwanted pregnancies from women was a 'sacred duty of all really civilised societies'. Aside from access to legal and safe abortions, he foresaw the development of new and better methods to safeguard against unwanted pregnancies: 'Tomorrow no doubt, science will provide us with simpler and harmless means to obtain the same result. We have already made progress in this field.' The contraceptive pill was less than a decade away.

Much of the Marxist reticence on women and sexuality, he felt, could be attributed to a lack of appreciation of Freud and his work. In Pablo's estimation, Freud became more radical, and even revolutionary, the older he became. Much of what Pablo says about a freer sexual life and the early education of children is clearly indebted to his optimistic reading of Freud. In fact, it is useful to read Pablo's *Liberation of Women* essay in conjunction with his essay on Freud written during this same bout in prison.[3] A key lesson he took from Freudianism was how the 'civilisation' created by humanity can positively shape the manifestations of the unconscious and, in turn, our behaviour.

Freud was not the only reference point. Pablo acknowledged the advanced thinkers who, since the 17th century had taken up the question of women and children. There was a nod to the 'daring ideas ... of the pleiad of feminist women, George Sand, Mme de Stael et al.' of the 19th century. Yet there was no mention of more recent feminist writing

– Evelyn Reed and Simone de Beauvoir, for instance – with which he must have been familiar. It may have been merely a matter of space, as the essay is very much, as he points out, a broad-brush effort, 'simple thoughts giving a general guiding line on the question of women, the family and children'. It is 'in no way an exhaustive study'.[4] We know he was uncertain about de Beauvoir. In his review of her 1955 novel, *The Mandarins*, he acknowledged her enormous talent but was undecided about her views on the milieu she was writing about.[5] Even so, failing to acknowledge one of the key contemporary female thinkers on the subject seems an oversight at very least. De Beauvoir's classic *The Second Sex* had appeared in 1949.

Characteristically, Pablo considered the evolution to a truly liberated, non-patriarchal society would take centuries – 'a long period of socialism will be necessary to dissipate the miasmas of a society ruled by men and to give women their full place'. Fortunately, the journey had begun. It is 'already possible to feel the approach of the twilight of the patriarchal family and the gradual transformation of that institution.' He gives as an example: 'It suffices to compare the free unions, and marriages and family of a modern couple – especially of those to be met in revolutionary, intellectual, university and artistic circles – with the traditional bourgeois family'. Even so, these were 'only exceptions' as society was 'still steeped in anti-woman and reactionary prejudices'.

It seemed to him that women sometimes actively collaborated in their own regression, prey to stereotypes and consumer forces. He had in mind the relationship with the fashion industry:

> Present capitalist society ... encourages women to push to their utmost their disguise as mere frivolous and superficial sexual objects. The way modern women blindly follow the extravagant whims of absurd fashions in capitalist countries, is a distressing demonstration of this regression, rather than progression, of women.[6]

Valid as that may be, it is hard not to hear echoes of a Tolstoyan puritanism.

Like all socialists who have written on this subject, he acknowledged the central importance of economic emancipation to women:

> If a woman can earn her living in exactly the same way as a man in terms of working possibilities, vocational qualifications, promotion and remuneration, it means that the age-old chains which harnessed the slave woman of the past to her husband, lover or father – the only possessor of money and exclusive supporter of the family – have been broken.[7]

He was not, however, a believer that 'women can do anything'. He suspected women had specific and different strengths to men, but admitted the jury was still out. 'We do not yet know woman, for conditions are still extremely unfavourable to her development, far more so than men's.'[8]

On the matters of motherhood, the family, children and the couple, his conclusions were more questionable and certainly discomforting for many. His views on motherhood, in particular, were bound to provoke considerable dissent.[9] In his defence, it pays to recall he was writing in the 1950s.

Women, he argued, 'most often' turn to motherhood, especially 'repeated motherhood', as a refuge and consolation from an existence marked by denial of active participation in social life, 'gloomy' domestic drudgery and an unsatisfying sexual life. The better model life for women, he argued, was already suggested by historical examples:

> All women who have distinguished themselves socially, politically and culturally, and have had a relatively full and free sex life, have granted only a limited amount of attention to children and maternity, which represented to them, as they usually do to men, just one aspect among many in their interesting and active life, and not necessarily the principal one ...[10]

At present, he said, it was disappointed women who were in turn entrusted with the education of children in the most formative early years of their lives. That education took place with an institution – the family – marked by egoism, conservatism and antisocial tendencies. Pablo accepted that in the current state of development, the family was both necessary and inescapable. It served an economic function and was a 'haven in a heartless world', to use Christopher Lasch's formulation. Nevertheless, as it stood, its effect on the formation of children, of human beings, was baleful.

Pablo speculated on an alternative which could produce children and human beings imbued with a love of beauty and fellow human beings, with altruism and a cooperative spirit. He nominated two means. The first, controversially, was 'voluntary eugenics', something he spent only three short paragraphs on, but which he characterised as a form of 'family planning'. In a sentence straight out of *A Brave New World*, he writes, 'Besides – who knows? – the reproduction of mankind may at that time be carried out by completely new means'. It echoes Trotsky's idea that humanity will apply science to its own reproduction in a future, truly civilised society, and that a more advanced species will emerge. The singular Shakespeares, Marxes and Einsteins of the past will become more common and 'above them new peaks shall rise'.

The other futuristic measure was the 'social education of children'. He took from Freud the importance of shaping the young child as he or she emerges from the turmoil of their 'inherited' unconscious into the awareness of the world. Ideally, in a future society, children would be educated from an early age in a 'children's world' shaped by specialists, with the aim of producing human beings of a nobler type than the current ones distorted by the family in a class society with all its antagonisms and disappointments. Even so, the bond with parents would (and should) continue. Out of that mix would emerge more socially advanced children enjoying lifelong relations with their parents as friends, comrades and collaborators, but free of any exclusivity.

The essay became in time something that marked him off from other male Marxists and was part of the arsenal of his supporters, particularly in France where it was republished when the women's liberation movement appeared. In the years that followed its writing, Pablo further developed his ideas on *autogestion* (or self-management). It meant he and his fellow-thinkers were more receptive than most leftists to the emergence of the women's liberation movement when it happened.

In France, the female *pablistes* (as his supporters were known in France) helped form the Cercle Élisabeth Dmitrieff in 1970, which initiated the campaign for legal abortion and freely available contraception. These same women openly belonged to the *pabliste* 'Alliance marxiste révolutionnaire' and, despite the women's movement's opposition to organised political groups being involved in the movement, the declared membership and advocacy of these women from the AMR was accepted.[11] They theorised their respect for the movement's autonomy and self-determination in a brochure published at the beginning of 1972, *Pour un féminisme autogestionnaire*. By contrast, other Left political organisations, including the orthodox Trotskyists, were slow to embrace the revitalised feminism of this time or to accept the autonomy and self-direction of the women's movement. The *pablistes* kept a sympathetic eye on the communal childrearing, income and housework sharing experiments of these years, without embracing them.[12] While the Second Wave feminist movement rose and fell rapidly in the 1970s, it left a positive legacy, including the legalisation of abortion (in 1975 in France), legal equality, sexual freedom and a new and more sensitive culture on the question of the oppression of women.

The women's liberation essay and the others he wrote in prison were all published soon after he was released. His 'prison notes' were not and seemed to have been penned for his own benefit. Pablo, very much an active man of the world, assumed that being locked away in a small cell for years would test his personal resources. It would either be an opportunity to know himself and other human beings better, or turn out to be his own private hell. While he was willing to believe that prison could and would increase his compassion, he wondered how much accurate self-knowledge was possible:

> But does one ever really arrive at sincerity in such a confrontation, without witnesses, without judges to condemn or galleries to applaud? Can one ever really know oneself? Doesn't the narcissistic basis of our being always reflect back to us an image of ourselves somewhat embellished in the mirror of ourselves? And in what sense do we know ourselves, when the self, perpetually 'becoming', eternally slipping away, reveals itself as ungraspable as fleeting time, really existing only for an instant, as quickly lost as experienced?

Certainly Freud thought that all biography and autobiography was misleading, that we could never really know ourselves, nor others know us. But Pablo thought it 'wasn't necessary to exaggerate in this matter, for if the essence of being is movement, of perpetual becoming, what is definitive is our comportment in life, the thought that we express, the action we undertake, which objectively outlines, in a rough way, our thinking, and our moral and emotional silhouette.'

The fact that long confinement would make this kind of introspection unavoidable led him to turn, naturally, to memoirs and autobiographies, as well as accounts of prison life – those of Victor Serge, Oscar Wilde, Fyodor Dostoyevsky, Hervé Bazin, and Diderot, among others. He read Plutarch, Seneca, St Augustine, Marcus Aurelius, Samuel Pepys, Montesquieu, Rousseau, Madame d'Épinay as well as the biography of Freud by Ernest Jones and of Rousseau by Guéhenno. The reading and the reflection helped pass the long days, and Pablo savoured any simple joys he could find from that cell: '…the reading of a great book, the effervescence of my own thought, the boundless emotion before the light from a beautiful day which filters in through the bars on the window, the patch of blue glimpsed from time to time …'

He read up as much as he could of prison regimes elsewhere, aware that the reality of prisons was generally well hidden from the public. He saw around him mental illness, recidivism, bitterness and anger rather than treatment, healing, education and rehabilitation. Vengeance and punishment to break the human being was the over-riding objective. 'The prison is a machine that manufactures and reproduces its future prey.' This seemed to be true of penitentiaries the world over, with the possible exceptions of Scandinavian countries and Switzerland.

He was struck by the youth of many fellow prisoners – ' "délinquants", victims of their childhoods and social conditions … these young convicts are for the most part children of poor and broken families in which they have had an unhappy and frustrating childhood. They have grown into adolescence full of rebellion and strong desires in a society in which material luxury is both a temptation and inaccessible, that no other value – heroism, beauty, human fraternity which resonates in the heart of every young person – can compensate. For these men … the prison is as a place of material and emotional privations, of forced, degrading and stupid labour, of incredible indifference to their cultural development, education, and social rehabilitation. It is rather a training school for crime, of coarsening and of revolt, than a place for their rehabilitation.'

He recalled in these notes his 'adolescence, the Tolstoyan education and the writings of Victor Hugo on the torture of each day, of each moment, for one condemned to death, which had led me to oppose the death penalty.' Life imprisonment in the current prisons didn't strike him as any more civilised. 'Even in the case of Rudolf Hess, formerly a high Nazi leader, manifestly unhinged … who for 15 years has goose-stepped up and down his cell singing the Horst Wessel marching song, this is unacceptable.'

At the end of his reflections, he was not optimistic about penal reform in the short run. Humanity was both coarsened and diverted by more pressing catastrophes:

> For a humanity which still hasn't left its animal origins behind, whose history is marked by individual and collective acts of incredible sadism and cruelty, for a society still dominated by relations opposing human against human and of multiple exploitation of man by man, a society which has recently known the horrors of Stalinism and Nazism, of the atomic bomb dropped on Japanese cities and those of colonial wars in Vietnam, in Korea, in Algeria, in Angola, to speak in these conditions of the humanisation of the penal code and the prison system is certainly to preach in the desert and to give one airs of a Don Quixote, in stark opposition to the solid and practical 'realism' of our times. Public opinion, insensitised by war and the current Cold War, by the terrifying prospect of a nuclear holocaust, isn't capable of motivating itself for such 'bagatelles'.

It was a rare moment of pessimism on his part. In the meantime, two things were necessary. Anyone encountering individual cases of inhumanity and sadism was called upon to do their best to stop them. In the second case, revolutionaries needed to renew their commitment to a society that operates on a higher level of human culture where it would be recognised that, 'the true mark of a civilisation is … its manner of treating the weakest and defeated – the sick and the old, the mentally ill, the prisoners.' For him, that meant the struggle for socialism:

> Certainly we will advance by stages, by transitional programs and realisations, according to the material possibilities and the rising cultural level of the people, but without ever losing sight of the final goal: the real liberation of humanity from all prisons.

— ✢ —

In prison, Pablo also wrote the essay *In praise of Trotskyism* (*Eloge du Trotskyisme*)[13]. Much of it is a conventional evaluation of the work and thinking of Trotsky, but within it lay the seeds of his departure from the iron cage of the International and conventional Trotskyism.

He began by paying tribute to the perspicacity and heroism of Trotsky himself, and to the Left Opposition in their struggle against Stalin and his bureaucratic autocracy. There had been no obvious straight line from Lenin to Stalin. Stalin's rule had been built on the ruins of Lenin's ideas and the corpses of his closest comrades. Later Pablo would acknowledge a delay in giving battle, that there had been earlier socialist opponents and that Trotsky and the left opposition had been hampered by their religious attachment to the Party. None of this really detracted from the fact that the Left Opposition's fight had been the most serious opposition. If they had succeeded, the whole disastrous history of the Soviet Union, politically, socially and economically, would have been avoided, along with that of the international communist movement.

The Soviet opposition's perspicacity and valid criticism was possible, in Pablo's view, because they were not in power; they were not identified with any existing state. It meant they had the necessary critical independence. This 'out of office' position allowed them to judge the emerging reality and practice – not to mention the psychopathic brutality – of the Stalinist regime according to the principles of classic Marxism and socialism.

A clear-eyed assessment by revolutionaries was an essential element in any regime emerging from a revolution, particularly in the conditions of the 20th century where anti-imperialist, anti-capitalist regimes in economically and culturally undeveloped countries would be prey to a 'natural' bureaucratisation and compromises in the exercise of power. Pablo came to the startling conclusion that successful revolutionaries should adopt a self-denying ordinance when it came to occupying government positions. They should retire as soon as practicable back into civil society and involve themselves in its activities, building the power of workers, peasants and citizens at the expense of the state. Furthermore, after the experience of single-party regimes, the right to form other parties which accepted the constitution of the new regime had to be embraced, too.

Switching to the then current situation in the Soviet Union, Pablo argued, the ruling Khrushchev wing of the Soviet bureaucracy, under pressure from the Chinese and in order to maintain its influence in the Third World, was now shifting to a revolutionary position, abandoning the previous position of advocating bourgeois alliances.

The Khrushchev faction was, he acknowledged, attempting to rectify and ameliorate the worst features of the Stalinist regime in order to rebalance and recharge the Soviet economy. In relaxing the police oppression, Khrushchev would open the way for the activation of the Soviet working class and intelligentsia. Khrushchev's time was the 'interregnum' between high Stalinism and the next revolution in the Soviet Union. These views ran counter to the more pro-Chinese position of the new leading 'Trio' in the International: Mandel, Frank and Maitan.

There was much more on the revolutionary role of the peasantry, the rightness of the Trotskyist approach to the Second World War and the current and present danger of nuclear war.

In conclusion, he tackled the criticism of Trotskyists that they were right but isolated and powerless as far as the mass movement was concerned. Perhaps, but you couldn't expect critical Marxist thinkers to embrace all the 'huge errors, appalling crimes and distressing nonsense' of Stalinism, or the betrayals of social democracy for that matter, in order to curry favour and boost their popularity. The revolutionary Marxist was a free being attempting to understand as well as possible the world he or she found themselves in. This free, critical power of analysis wasn't confined to capitalism alone, but could be also employed in understanding the workers movement, socialism and the revolution. This refusal to abandon critical thinking and analysis didn't mean that revolutionary Marxists set themselves apart from the labour movement. They advocated the maximum united front in action and didn't welcome their isolation. Where they could, they should organise openly. Where the overwhelming majority of the class was in an existing party or parties, it was necessary to combine a public and separate voice with activity concentrated in the mass party or parties. If there was some subterfuge involved in this latter 'entrism', it was scarcely the fault of Trotskyists. They couldn't be blamed if there were no internal democracy that allowed open advocacy of their politics.

It's easy to picture Pablo deep in thought in his bare cell, free of interruptions, his head full of these ideas, his pen racing across the page. He finished the essay with a peroration that the Trotskyists were 'the most conscious and militant advanced detachment [of the revolutionary movement] and from this fact the most ardent in the combat for the world revolution'.

It is a strangely orthodox piece. It reads almost as a valedictory sign-off. He was never to lose his respect and admiration for Trotsky. He would go on defending and justifying Trotsky's life and work right to the end of his own life. Even so, from that point on, it became obvious that Pablo preferred the term 'revolutionary Marxist' to Trotskyist. For him the 'personalisation' of Marxism as in 'Leninism', 'Trotskyism' or 'Luxemburgism' was an error, as it tended to freeze Marxism into a series of sacred Talmudic texts that could be referred to as infallible guides. One only had to find the right text. But for Pablo, each of those comrades had given Marxism its best and surest expression in the time they were using it to understand the world and its revolutionary possibilities. Times had changed, however, and the challenge was to update the analysis of the world situation by using the tools that revolutionary Marxism and these revolutionaries had bequeathed us. Hand in hand with his emphasis on a constantly renewed revolutionary Marxism was an important realisation about the Fourth International. Yes, it was an international organisation of revolutionary Marxists but not *the* new revolutionary International. It was a component, an important one, but just one.[14]

— ✦ —

In the last days of his imprisonment, Pablo penned open letters to the Cuban and Algerian revolutionaries.[15] The first was to Fidel Castro and his comrades in the July 26 Movement which had marched into Havana nearly three years before. In their determination to free the island from US domination (and invasion), they had found it necessary to carry through nationalisations of US property and turn to the Soviet bloc for protection. The second epistle was to the Algerians, who were on the cusp of victory.

Both letters are infused with an extraordinary optimism and a belief that both revolutions – by their acts of genuine emancipation – could inspire wider revolutionary developments, including in the societies of their former dominant masters: the United States and France. The letter to the Cubans was full of praise and challenges, that to the Algerians more sober but equally daring in its appeals. In the case of both Havana and Algiers, Pablo hoped they would become models or beacons of a socialist future.

If only. Take what he wrote to the Fidelistas:

> You are the pioneers of the Great Pan-American Socialist Revolution, you must be conscious of the grandeur of this historic mission … Countless thousands of proletarians from around the world are ready to die, arms in hand, for the defence of the Cuban Revolution. Thousands of revolutionaries, among whom, in the first line, are members of the Fourth International … are working to make known the achievements and importance of the Cuban revolution, to prepare its defence against reaction and imperialism, and to extend it, by revolution, to their own countries.

He saluted the creative originality of their victory, combining a reliance on the poor peasantry with underground agitation in the towns and cities. Now they faced the enormous challenge of creating a society that could be said to be transitioning to socialism. Avoiding errors of the past was a focus of the letter.

Given that socialism by definition meant the expansion of freedom, any transitional regime had to avoid the bureaucratic, police regimes that had been installed in the "workers' states" to this point. The cause of those deformations had been more than objective, more than understandable responses to outside aggression and internal counterrevolution, and more than the offshoot of the 'natural' hierarchies that flow from marked inequalities in education and technical know-how. Bureaucratic dictatorships had flowed equally from the model of economic and political development adopted by the so-called workers' states.

When it came to economics, Pablo counselled against the Soviet route of heavy industrialisation and autarchy, paid for by crushing exactions on the peasantry. Inevitable peasant resistance to expropriation and exploitation had led to repressive police regimes. The extreme example had been Stalinist Russia, but it had been copied elsewhere by so-called socialist regimes, with similar results. The point was to carry out an agrarian reform that gave peasants the land, encouraged cooperatives and extended technical aid. By raising the productivity and prosperity of the countryside, you could raise the capital necessary for further development.

On the political front, of it was necessary to allow the maximum democracy conceivable in given circumstances. He sketched out the possibility of a new post-revolutionary socialist politics which included Fidel and his comrades stepping aside from state roles. (While he didn't mention this, this was something that Gandhi seems to have envisaged for himself in post-independence India.) The one-party state in the initial phase of a revolutionary transformation may be unavoidable, but it must be accompanied by an acute consciousness of the dangers. The party and the state had a tendency to become one apparatus and the personnel become a new ruling bureaucracy. To avoid this danger, the ruling party must foster the greatest democracy inside its ranks and as soon as possible allow the creation of other socialist parties. The state itself should be based on a federation of local 'councils' and free elections. Inside this new structure, the ruling party should separate itself from the state; its leaders should not also be state leaders. By keeping themselves separate, Fidel and his comrades would retain a moral autonomy and ability to intervene. They would be the revolutionary conscience and inspiration of the continuing revolution.

The active freedom that Pablo counselled would have a cultural front. He was encouraged by the Cubans' efforts to spread education and eradicate illiteracy. As far as culture and scientific research was concerned, he championed its autonomy from state direction. The revolution should happen in the other fields, too – in architecture and town planning, for example, where the basis should be laid for the new cooperative ways of living.

He didn't underestimate the efforts of Washington to smother and defeat the Cuban revolution, but he believed its power to do so was much reduced. The negative effects of the economic embargo could be minimised by links with the Soviet bloc, China and newly independent countries. Cuba had also been fortunate in avoiding the devastation of invasion and civil war that had handicapped other countries undergoing revolutions. As for the military threat, it appeared the Soviets were willing to offer protection. Cuba was, in these ways, the beneficiary of what Pablo saw as a deteriorating balance of forces in the world for US imperialism. Cuba could also benefit from its proximity to the United States by learning from and adapting its technological advances.

In the most optimistic parts of his letter to the Cubans, Pablo noted how their revolution had already aroused strong support not only elsewhere in Latin America, but among the black community, youth and intellectuals in the United States. Indeed, he admitted that his own enthusiasm for the Cuban Revolution was largely based on *Listen Yankee* by C. Wright Mills and the *Cuba: Anatomy of a Revolution* by Paul Sweezy and Leo Huberman. 'I find it significant,' he noted, 'that the best books to date on the Cuban revolution have been written by Yankees.' If Cuba could embark on a more emancipatory path than previous revolutions, it would find an extraordinary resonance in neighbouring societies – advancing revolutionary prospects even in the United States.

All this was standard Pablo, fired by revolutionary optimism, but there was one new element. When counselling the Cubans on ensuring a genuinely democratic regime, he urged them to to emulate the example of nothing less than 4th- and 5th-century Athens. His prison reading of Aristotle and Plato, as he noted in the letter, had reminded him what truly democratic governance entailed and he commended the agora or citizens' assembly and the involvement of 'every' citizen in the actual day-to-day management of the state as actual models for the Cubans to imitate. (He acknowledged that women and slaves were excluded, but these anachronisms did not detract from the demonstration of what was possible.) This Athenian patriotism was the first weak signal that he was returning to his Greek roots.

The letter to the Algerians was written a week later. Entitled *La Révolution Algérienne à l'heure du choix*,[16] it celebrated their imminent victory and honoured their immense sacrifices. He was proud to have played a small part in their victory and hoped he had the right to proffer advice. He considered that the peasants and rural workers, the youth and women, who had made the bulk of the sacrifices, should now be rewarded by a social program that prioritised their needs and aspirations. He urged the FLN to adopt a democratic and socialist program. If it insisted on being the sole ruling party after independence, it should at least adopt a democratic internal regime. Striking messianic notes, Pablo believed that the new Algeria could be the inspiration in both the Middle East and Africa – and even inspire the reawakening of the European working class. He urged it to pursue the goal of a federated, socialist Arab republic and to be the inspirer and principal base for the African drive for complete emancipation from white rule.

He raised the issue of conservative customs and beliefs that had struck deeper roots among Algerians during the national liberation war. It was a way of a people asserting their differences and uniqueness vis-a-vis the occupier and coloniser and it had to be respected, but not reinforced or glorified. There was the counter trend as well. During the war, the young had broken free of clans, village restrictions and gerontocracy and women had broken out of strict confinement to play a role in the struggle. Those realities had to be recognised, too. But his general point was that the masses would not easily abandon their customs and religion in a world of grim underdevelopment. They offered consolation in a hard and heartless world. Such attachments, like the state itself, could only wither away in a world of material and cultural plenty.

In sketching out these possibilities in Cuba and Algeria, it wasn't that he was unaware of the deadening negative factors in each revolution, but he wanted to throw whatever weight he and the International had onto the side of the more radical possibilities. Trouble was, he was betting with reduced forces. He had always exaggerated the International's strength but it was now to be severely weakened – first by the split of the main Latin American sections led by Juan Posadas and then by the conservatism of 'the Europeans'. Even so, these weren't impossible dreams. There were forces present in each revolution that held the potential Pablo sketched out. When he was released from prison after 15 months, he knew where he was headed: to join the revolution in Algeria and encourage those potentialities.

CHAPTER 11

# Joining the Wretched of the Earth
## 1961-1963

*The revolution doesn't need soldiers, it needs revolutionaries.*

**Michel Pablo to Adolfo Gilly**
21 July 1995

LEAVING PRISON TO rejoin the revolution promised to be a messy and possibly dangerous business. In the first place, it was possible the Dutch government would immediately deport him to Greece.[1] It was an unwelcome prospect, but the socialist Senator Cammelbeeck got an assurance from the Dutch Prime Minister that this would not occur. However, the rest of Europe was not welcoming – or safe. La Main Rouge was still murdering supporters of the Algerian struggle.[2] It was distinctly possible Pablo and Santen were on the kill lists of the French state terrorist organisation. Recognising this uncertain environment, the FLN had secured Moroccan passports and visas for Pablo and Elly from the King of Morocco.

The next challenge was to get Pablo safely there. On his release he was met at the prison gates by Elly, a lawyer, Senator Cammelbeeck and two British Labour MPs – John Baird and Anne Kerr – who were to accompany him to London. From there, he and Elly would take a flight to Morocco. All went smoothly until they boarded the Morocco-bound flight at Heathrow.[3]

Pablo believed he had received Home Office assurances that it was a direct flight, but as the plane taxied to its take-off position, the pilot announced the flight would touch down in Madrid en route. Landing in fascist Spain was a risk Pablo was not willing to take. Faking a heart attack, and with Elly's help, he forced the pilot to return to the terminal. For the next two days Pablo, backed by his supporters, refused to board any Morocco-bound flights that did not fly direct – even threatening suicide if forced on to a flight. The London papers duly reported this airport tussle. Eventually Pablo and Elly agreed to join a flight to Morocco via Gibraltar.

All this made for an unsettled return to the world. The political geography had also changed. He now faced a shattered International. The month before his release, Posadas had decided to split the International, followed by the exit of hundreds of the Latin American comrades. In an open letter, Posadas trained his main fire on Pablo, accusing him of pettiness, resentful attitudes and various crimes, including embezzling funds.[4] Posadas' decision to walk out broke Pablo's power in the International. Why did he do it? Gilly, who was then part of Posadas' circle, subsequently gave two reasons.[5] The first was idiocy. At times people do irrational things. The second was traceable to Posadas' offended *amour-propre* or vanity at Pablo's hands. As Gilly tells it:

> After you were arrested you sent a short letter to the International – smuggled out by your lawyer. You sum up the situation as you see it, that you expect to be in prison for a long stretch, and that we must concentrate on the colonial revolution and other things such as that. As to the leadership, the risk, so you wrote and I remember it almost by heart, of a division or split in the Fourth International lay in the rivalry between Mandel and Posadas. You then made some proposals and you emphasised that it was necessary to invest in some young comrades whose development must be helped, and you mentioned as examples Diego and Lucero.
> **Michel Pablo:** I said that?
> **AG:** Yes, you said that.
> **MP:** And I didn't speak of Posadas?
> **AG:** You didn't speak of Posadas. I saw [Posadas'] face at that moment where he said, 'Good, let's read that again'. And we read it again. I knew him very well, and a shadow passed over his face and he said nothing. At that moment I thought: 'That's a huge mistake. He will take his revenge'.

Pablo's reaction to this account was one of bewilderment. 'But Posadas already had an assured position …' – referring to his leadership of the Latin American Bureau. Clearly he found it difficult to fathom the ambitions of comrades. It was a blindness reflected in the cases of both Mandel and Posadas.

Posadas set off on a reckless and bizarre political course – swinging first towards ultra-Maoism on the issue of preventive nuclear war, and

## 11 . JOINING THE WRETCHED OF THE EARTH 1961-63

then entertaining a belief in extra-terrestrial visits to Earth. His Cuban supporters, who had played a minor role in the 1959 revolution, increasingly riled Castro, and it landed them in prison. However, Che Guevara had a certain sympathy for them and is credited with securing their release. Elsewhere in Central and South America in the 1960s, as courageous organisers of workers and landless and poor peasants, the Latin-American Trotskyists were in the front ranks of those who were imprisoned, tortured and murdered by military dictatorships and their death squads. Posadas himself was fortunate to escape with his life. Arrested and imprisoned in Uruguay, he escaped deportation to Argentina and was instead sent to Italy, thanks to his Italian parentage and the [apparent] intervention of the Italian Communist Party. There he set up a commune outside Rome and eventually became the guru of a New Age cult.

The whole extraordinary Posadas story is told in A.M. Gittlitz, *I Want to Believe: Posadism, UFOs and Apocalypse Communism*. While Posadas' name later became synonymous with cultish madness – and for Gittlitz, Pablo understood the reasons for this as well, if not better, than anyone – Posadas also had certain strengths. A self-educated worker intellectual, he had arguably understood the nature of Peronism in Argentina as well as anyone on the Left in Latin America. He was a powerful orator and inspired loyalty, even devotion. His groups contained capable intellectuals such as Adolfo Gilly, Hugo Moreno and Guillermo Almeyra, as well as many active urban workers and students in most of the countries of Latin America. Their courage was redoubtable even if their judgment was awry.

Posada's gratuitous tirades were not the only unwelcome reaction Pablo received on his release. Gilly recalls an International Secretariat meeting soon after the verdict, during which Pierre Frank claimed that the light sentence was the result of a deal Pablo and Santen had made – to hand over archives that implicated the Dutch royal family in collaboration with the Nazi occupiers during World War II. It was more than 30 years later that this accusation was revealed to Pablo and he denied it absolutely. He did ponder whether Santen's wife, who was the daughter by marriage of Henk Sneevliet, might have had such compromising material. Both he and Gilly made the obvious point that if Frank was serious, then he should have demanded an investigation carried out by what in the International was called a 'control commission'. No such investigation took place. Instead, the incident illustrated the hostility of Frank to Pablo. Pablo's earlier decision not to share with Frank details of the Algerian work, understandable as it was on security grounds, may have contributed to this wayward accusation on Frank's part.[6]

Troubling as these developments in the International were, Pablo now had richer possibilities for effective revolutionary practice in Algeria itself. As he told Gilly six months before he died:

> From the moment I got out of prison, I didn't care ... I was disgusted when I got out and understood what had been happening. And on the other hand, there was the Algerian Revolution and I saw that I was much appreciated there and that there were possibilities – even if I saw them in a way that was a little exaggerated ... I was so taken with the importance of what we could do in Algeria that I had no desire for internal struggles. I couldn't mix the two.

But he did care. Either his memory failed him or he chose not to remember. While he was in Casablanca and unable to attend International Secretariat meetings, he waged a paper war with the Mandel-Frank-Maitan trio that now managed the Fourth International. The immediate issue was whether he should be restored to the secretary's position. The Austrian section circulated at least two letters to the sections arguing for this restoration as elementary socialist solidarity. 'Every revolutionary proletarian organisation, which is conscious of its own honour, would, after his return, have restored a well-tried comrade, who has been sentenced to prison because of his help to a current revolution, into his elected function of many years standing,' Franz Modlik, the Austrian delegate to the International Executive Committee, wrote. (The Australian Troskyists, too, unanimously endorsed this position.)

The Austrians also complained about the priority the trio gave to wooing the Americans rather than healing the breach with the Latin American majority who had followed Posadas out of the International in 1961. For the Austrians, this was a choice that showed a preference for First World reconciliation over Third World solidarity, for a 'European/North American' organisation rather than one deeply involved in the colonial revolution of which Latin America – in this era of revolutionary Cuba – was becoming a key arena.

According to Maitan, the new majority on the International Secretariat was willing to re-install Pablo to the secretary's position provided practical details could be sorted out and Pablo undertook to toe the political line of the IS, where he was now in a minority.[7] But differences on political issues were widening and the internal debate sharpening. These differences were not just political but very personal. This is very clear in a letter from Pablo to Mandel in February 1962.

Pablo writes in response to a letter from Mandel which he characterises as part conciliatory, part flattering and part threatening, a mix, he says, that is not a winning formula. It only confirmed the double game Mandel seemed to be playing. If Mandel believed, as he wrote in his letter, that 'no one has ever put in doubt that politically I [Pablo] am by far the most valuable element' in the leadership of the International, then two things should follow: an end to the slanders against him, Pablo, and his incorporation into the leadership. Instead, 'for some years you've pursued a small war, at once devious and tenacious, of a personal nature against me and Sal Santen, in order to undermine our political prestige and that which resulted from our irreproachable revolutionary attitude before and during our arrest and trial'. Pablo adds, 'you are far from having a clear conscience on your attitude towards us'.

Three days before writing this, he had received a report from a Belgian comrade (via Santen) that the decision of her cell, calling for the publication of all Pablo's articles and his restoration as secretary, had elicited a warning from the Belgian leadership. If they persisted, the leadership would reveal the terrible damage Pablo and Santen had allegedly done to the International by their arrest and trial. It is little wonder that Pablo had decided he was no longer willing to refrain from reacting against this 'ignoble and irresponsible dirty war'.

His letter to Mandel goes on to rebut Mandel's charges that Posadas' split is due to Pablo's encouragement of Posadas' attacks on the 'European core' of the organisation; that Pablo was responsible for the 1953-54 split; that he now opposes reunification with the Americans; and that he left the International bankrupt when he was arrested ('the opposite is true, all bills were paid, there was money in the bank and the campaign to raise funds for the trial expenses resulted in a healthy profit'). He finishes by recalling that when he left prison he had fundamental political differences with the two tendencies in the International. That hadn't changed. In a final flourish of bravado, he tells Mandel that if he wants to characterise Pablo's critical stance 'as looking for a fight to wreck everything, that is a game you can play. I have never been afraid of a "fight" in whatever form it takes. I am ready.'[8] Scarcely the response of someone who didn't care.

Pablo had to wage this internal battle by correspondence from Casablanca, mostly via Sal Santen who was a member of the International Secretariat. There are some 140 letters and circulars exchanged between Santen and Pablo dating from 1962 in the Santen archive in Amsterdam. It fell to Sal Santen to argue – in person at the meetings of the International Secretariat – the case for a more resolute commitment to the colonial revolution and a bolder entrist policy in Europe. He found it a disagreeable task. It was clear that he had little affection or respect for the leaders of the Mandel faction, whom he labelled 'les droitiers' or rightists. A decade later in his memoirs, a still bitter Santen even compared Mandel to Karl Kautsky. (In the first two decades of the twentieth century, Kautsky had been acknowledged internationally as the grand theoretician, 'the pope', of Marxism. However, his support for the German imperial war effort, his opposition to Lenin, Trotsky and Luxemburg and hostility to the Russian and German Revolutions, had made his name a byword for turncoat treachery.)

Santen believed that Mandel had supported the opposition to him in the Dutch section. The conflict was over entrism, with the majority taking the same 'quietist' position as Mandel in Belgium and Jungclas in Germany. These careful Dutch entrists had followed the logic of their position to the point of deciding to leave the Fourth International. Santen believed the IS majority (and Mandel in particular) delayed reporting the Dutch departure and then glossed over what had transpired.[9]

In these circumstances, a bitter and suspicious Santen made it clear to Pablo – repeatedly – that he continued to attend IS meetings only because he had promised Michel to do so. In his letters to Pablo in Morocco and then Algeria, it is painfully clear that he entertains no trust in the trio. 'They are absolutely ready to completely break with us if they think it necessary to achieve their unity with [James] Cannon. That is to say, they are ready to deepen the rupture in our international movement, in coalescing with Cannon against us … If they exclude you from the International Secretariat, the moment will have come for me to quit the Secretariat.'[10] Santen even dallied with the idea of setting up a parallel leadership inside the International.[11]

Pablo told his closest supporters that they should prepare to be in a minority for some time but remain at all costs in the International.[12] He assured them that events – the ongoing colonial revolution – would come to their aid. With this hope in mind, there was no way they should contemplate, let alone follow, that 'crazy provocateur' Posadas's example of splitting – whatever the provocations.[13]

For Pablo and Santen these provocations from the new leadership trio abounded. They protested that their letters and documents were not circulated within the International, or given only limited or delayed circulation.[14] They were not informed of some meetings or, if they were, the agenda was kept from them. Minutes were late and doctored.[15] Letters of support for the positions of Pablo and Santen, such as one from the Australian section, sent by the redoubtable Nick Origlass, were not distributed to members of the International Executive Committee.[16] This denial of a level playing field and full internal democracy compounded the bitterness. Pablo proposed a reconstituted IS which might even induce some Latin Americans back into the ranks.[17] Such proposals never flew. Instead, both sides traded accusations of bad faith. The conflict persisted right up to, and then after, the 7th World Congress of the International in July, 1963. That congress saw the return of the American Trotskyists of the SWP.

— ⁘ —

Beyond those internal conflicts, as 1962 unfolded Pablo became increasingly involved in revolutionary Algeria. In the gap between his release in September 1961 and his arrival in newly independent Algeria 11 months later, Pablo prepared himself to play a role in the new Algeria. In March 1962, France and the FLN's Provisional Government had signed the Evian Accords, agreeing to Algerian independence following a referendum on July 1. Even before this agreement, the Provisional Government of the Algerian Republic had commissioned Pablo to write a paper on agrarian reform for newly independent Algeria.

This was going to be a fundamental issue. Algeria was overwhelmingly a poor rural society – some 88 per cent of Algerians lived and worked in the countryside – and access to the land was very unequal. Moreover, it was the peasantry that had fought and suffered for the Revolution over seven long years. They deserved a just settlement of the land question. The result of Pablo's research – *Étude pour une politique agraire en Algérie* – was published in Rabat (Morocco) in April 1962, covering seven chapters. It covered everything from patterns of land ownership to regional soil and climatic variations to the history of agrarian reforms. Above all, he insisted on the absolute necessity of democratic peasant consent and participation in the land reform process (the rural poor, in fact, needed to drive it).

The 73-page pamphlet showered high praise on the land reform undertaken in Yugoslavia – with some 10 pages were devoted to it. The Yugoslav model was a combination of self-managed state farms, cooperatives and small private farms. Thanks to their size and the resources devoted to them, the yields per hectare of the state farms was 150 to 200 per cent higher than for the private farms; that of the cooperatives was also higher. (Or so the Yugoslavs claimed and Pablo took them at their word.) By this practical demonstration of the benefits of medium- to large-scale modern farming, the Yugoslavs hoped to eventually achieve a cooperative regime across the whole of their farm sector.

Pablo felt that model would suit revolutionary Algeria. The new self-managed state farms would be based on the nationalised farms of the colons. This sector accounted for 40 per cent of the cultivated land, and 80 per cent of this land was owned by a few thousand European landowners. It was these large holdings – on some of the best land in the country – that would be the basis of the socialised and democratically managed farms. Under the settlers' or colons' ownership, the yields were approximately half of equivalent farms in France and Pablo believed that the application of modern European and American methods would raise those yields significantly. The balance of the colons' land, combined with the redistribution of the excess of large Algerian landowners and state- and communally-owned land, would be allotted to poorer peasants on the basis of 10-hectare lots. For most peasant households, this would be a huge boon. As far as possible, cooperative farming would be encouraged among these small peasant landholders.

A program such as this, he recommended, should be submitted to democratic local, regional and national assemblies of peasants who would decide on the details of the land reform in revolutionary Algeria. He concluded by emphasising its centrality to a democratic and socialist Algeria:

> ... a socialist leadership cannot have the least chance of success if it does not make a junction with the peasantry. For, in present-day Algeria, it is the only social layer spontaneously presenting a demand that cannot be diverted, which will fundamentally transform the structure of the economy and create a powerful elan among the masses. That is the crucial role of the agrarian reform.

At the time, there were encouraging political developments in the Algerian movement. The Left in the FLN appeared to be in the ascendant – ideologically at least. The 'Tripoli Program', adopted at the FLN congress in Tunis in May 1962, was remarkable both for its radical and secular orientation. Pablo quickly decided this was the document around which the FLN, largely shattered in Algeria itself, should be rebuilt. If that wasn't possible, it should be the basis for assembling a revolutionary Marxist current inside the FLN. He would later be criticised for not recruiting an Algerian section of the Fourth International, but this never appeared to be a goal for him. He had higher ambitions (or fantasies). He imagined building the nucleus, at least, of a mass revolutionary party in Algeria. This nucleus or party would have links with other similar parties

## 11 . JOINING THE WRETCHED OF THE EARTH 1961-63

and movements throughout the Maghreb, Africa and the Middle East. It would form an arm of a global mass revolutionary international.

The Tripoli Program had excoriated the Provisional Government for negotiating an independence deal that left the door open for neo-colonial domination by France. It criticised the FLN for neglecting its social program in the past, and noted that the FLN leaders – imprisoned or refugees abroad – had been cut off from the masses. It celebrated the shattering of semi-feudal practices and prejudices during the struggle for independence (though warning of their possible revival), and insisted that independence was a result of the sacrifices and efforts of the peasantry, the working class, the youth and revolutionary intellectuals. The program further argued that only a socialist economy could guarantee genuine independence and social justice. The basis for such an economy would be an agrarian reform.

This reform, as conceived in the Tripoli Program, echoed Pablo's ideas measure for measure. It also recommended the mobilisation of the rural unemployed into work brigades to undertake reforestation, irrigation works, terracing, and rebuilding villages razed during the war. In other economic prescriptions it also followed Pablo. Industrial development would be decentralised and oriented to servicing the rural market and processing agricultural produce. While the commanding heights of the economy would be nationalised, the takeover of the gas and oil sectors would be a longer-term goal dependent on training workers in the necessary expertise. Beyond these measures, a New Economic Policy on the model of the Soviet one of the 1920s, in other words free markets, would allow the development of a private sector – subject to democratic regulation. Part of that regulation would be independent unions and the right to strike.

The Tripoli Program also anticipated that independence would allow Algeria to rediscover and reanimate its traditional culture. Central was the Arabic language, which would become the new republic's official language. As for Islam, it needed to be stripped of its obscurantist and feudal accretions and become once again a dynamic religion open to incorporating the best of other cultures. Overcoming mass illiteracy was to be the priority in education. Improvements in housing and the creation of a national health service were other prime goals.

The final plank in the social and cultural program was 'The liberation of women'. It is worth quoting in full (and it's not long, as its critics pointed out):

> The participation of Algerian woman in the liberation struggle has created conditions favourable to shattering the yoke that oppresses her and allows her to participate fully and freely in the control of public affairs and in the development of the country. The FLN must suppress all restrictions on the evolution of women and their flourishing, and support the actions of women's organisations. There exists in our society a negative attitude towards the role of women. Under diverse forms, all of them contribute to the idea of her inferiority. Women themselves are frequently captured by this idea.
>
> The FLN cannot go forward without supporting a continuous struggle against social prejudices and retrograde beliefs. In this area the FLN cannot limit itself to simple lip service but should contribute to making this evolution of women irreversible by giving women responsibilities in its own ranks.[18]

That it came last in the priorities list and was so briefly elaborated invited some unease in more radical circles. Still, the fact it was included at all in the Tripoli Program opened what proved to be a brief window of revolutionary hope for the second sex in Algeria.[19]

The final section of the program committed the new Algeria to supporting the colonial revolution in Africa (with particular mention of southern Africa), Latin America and Asia; the eventual unification of the Maghreb, the Arab world and Africa; active membership in the Non Aligned Movement; better relations with the 'socialist' countries; nuclear disarmament and an expanding world economy based on fair trade.

All this was pure 'Pabloism'. His key ally in the FLN, Mohammed Harbi, was one of the main authors, although Ben Bella, recently released from prison by the French, also appears to have played a leading role in its formulation.[20]

One glaring omission, and one that endangered its promise of a democratic socialist future, was any commitment to political democracy or a multi-party politics. It clearly conceived Algeria's future as a one-party state. This was precisely what Franz Fanon had warned against in that classic of colonial revolutionary politics, *The Wretched of the Earth*.

Soon after reaching Casablanca, Pablo read and reviewed Fanon's now fabled book.[21] Fanon, a psychiatrist originally from Martinique, who had trained in France and practised in Algeria before deciding to join the FLN in Tunis, was for Pablo 'the most radical and accomplished theoretician of the FLN to date'. Pablo found himself in general agreement with Fanon on the central role of armed struggle and the peasantry in the colonial revolution. He agreed, too, with Fanon's withering contempt for the traditional European communist and social-democratic parties with their lack of solidarity with the colonial peoples.

## 11 . JOINING THE WRETCHED OF THE EARTH 1961-63

He drew from Fanon two important points he wanted to emphasise. The first was an inference: if national-revolutionary 'Jacobin' parties could initiate and lead armed revolutions in the colonial and semi-colonial countries and initiate radical economic and social development, then there was no reason revolutionary Marxist parties couldn't do the same – while avoiding the dead-ends these other attempts ran into.

The second important theme he drew from Fanon went precisely to these dead-ends. Fanon's book contained a savage and prescient critique of the one-party dictatorships, often ethnically based, being set up in the wake of successful colonial revolutions in Africa. These post-revolutionary regimes transformed the revolutionaries from champions of liberation into the policemen and new rulers of the people. Some of the most stunning passages of *The Wretched of the Earth* concern this trend which Pablo himself noted: 'It is amazing to see on the spot with what fantastic rapidity, within the framework of the extreme material and cultural scarcity which still reigns in the "Third World", particularly in Africa, the revolution "becomes gentrified" or bureaucratised, all the more when its victory over imperialism is confined to the frameworks of tiny states ...'

For Pablo, this critique of neo-colonial or neo-Stalinist regimes arising in the Third World was Fanon's warning to the Algerians and his deathbed plea (he died in December 1961) for them to ensure their revolution was social and democratic as well as national:

> Fanon wrote his book as a political testament intended above all to prevent a "bourguibist" or bureaucratic outcome of the Algerian Revolution which he passionately adopted and served. For him this revolution began and continued as a true enterprise of a whole people, of the "Wretched of the Earth", aspiring to total salvation, "to the land", "to bread", "to freedom and the dignity of the man".

Pablo, of course, was confident that Fanon had not written or died in vain:

> Fanon died before this permanent revolution entered its more particularly social phase, which begins now. And there is no doubt that the authentic Algerian revolutionaries who will come together on the platform of revolutionary and democratic socialism sketched out by Fanon ... will refer to him and his book in order to fully honour the essential message he transmitted to them: not to betray the revolution begun, not to stop it halfway, not to compromise it in "association" with imperialism, but to continue it, deepen it, complete it.

— ✦ —

The Tripoli program wasn't lacking in good ideas. What it lacked was an organisation to drive their implementation (let alone the realisation of Fanon's dream). The FLN had split in Tunis at the very conference where the program was adopted. On the one side were the supporters of the Provisional Government who walked out of the conference before it concluded, and on the other, the emerging alliance between the historic leaders, such as Ben Bella, and the external army command led by Houari Boumediene.

This split in the FLN on the eve of independence added to the chaos that engulfed Algeria at the time. And, indeed, what terrible chaos the vanquished set about creating. In the wake of the Evian Accords, the European settlers reacted with fury. While the Organisation armée secrèt (OAS or the Secret Army Organisation) went on a killing spree, murdering Algerians almost at will, the overwhelming majority of the settlers decided to flee rather than trust the incoming Algerian rule. They wilfully destroyed whatever they could not spirit away in their suitcases – their dwellings, farm and industrial machinery, schools. Scarcely a single tractor in working order was left. Hospitals were not spared the scorched earth policy. Even the library at the University of Algiers, with its tens of thousands of books, was put to the torch – in some accounts by the OAS, in another by the librarian.

This grand-scale sabotage was compounded by the exodus of skills and experience. When Ben Bella, the future president, entered the government building in the western city of Oran, he met just seven employees where 500 had previously worked. In the telephone exchange, there was one worker left where 200 had been employed. Before independence there were 3,000 qualified engineers in Algeria, after independence 30 remained. The French had already systematically crippled the native population in terms of education and expertise. True, the war had prompted the French into some belated educational development but, even so, only 15 per cent of school-aged Algerian children were in school. Even before the orgy of sabotage, the impact of the war was devastating. Pierre Bourdieu estimated that a third of the population – some three million people – had been uprooted and moved into refugee camps and bidonvilles or shanty towns on the edge of the cities. Some 8,000 villages had been razed, along with countless hectares of forest. This had been mainly done to separate the guerrillas from local support, to rob the fish of the sea.

Amid these ravaged and chaotic conditions, the referendum on independence was held on July 1. Algeria's independence was proclaimed days later, on 5 July. Immediately, conflict broke out between supporters of the Provisional Government and the new leadership of the FLN represented by Ben Bella in alliance with the army command. The six Wilayas and their armed forces split equally between the contending parties. However, the Ben Bella-army alliance advanced on the capital, Algiers, from the west with overwhelming firepower. With the people of the towns and cities marching in the streets and interposing themselves when firefights broke out, the Provisional Government and the transitional authority set up by the Evian Accords melted away. Their supporters in the Wilayas came to terms with Ben Bella and the army commander Houari Boumediene, who installed themselves as the new rulers in Algiers.

In the wake of these events, Pablo undertook a 17-day journey through western Algeria – from Morocco to Algiers. It was the same route Ben Bella and Boumediene took on their way to seizing power and showed his orientation at this early stage. In commentary published at the time, under yet another nom-de-guerre – Abdel Al-Krim – he judged the Ben Bella coalition to be the more socialist of the two sides.

Ben Bella had given his first interview after his release from prison in March to the official Cuban news agency. He had spoken of his admiration for the Cuban revolution and how he aimed to make Algeria the Cuba of Africa and the Middle East. As for the army, Pablo saw it not just as the only organised force in the new Algeria, but also as a proto-revolutionary peasant/worker vanguard. To give some context to such a seemingly outlandish claim, according to an American historian 'new evidence from the FLN archives proves that [the army commander] Boumediene was a consistent partisan of revolutionary goals at least from 1959.'[22]

After his tour, Pablo sent his report directly to the leaderships of the sections in the last week of August, 1962. He did so on his own initiative, not in the name of the IS, the usual conduit. (Some of the 'Europeans' had actually supported the Provisional Government faction in the struggle for power in Algeria, further fuelling conflict inside the International.) He concluded his report by calling for the sections to send volunteers to Algeria and to liaise with him and comrades on the spot. A more detailed report followed almost immediately. This was published, along with the Tripoli Program (which had not been previously published in France), by the Parti Communiste International, indicating that his supporters still held sway in the French section of the International. It was later included as a supplement to *Quatrième Internationale* as well.

The September report opened with a devastating account of the ruins of Algerian society and the absolute lack of preparedness of the FLN. While the Tripoli program provided the basis and platform for more detailed policy, that policy work had not even been started. The war and diplomacy had been all the FLN could manage – as well as internal scheming and manoeuvring. Pablo did not hold back on describing the internal chaos and infighting which riddled the FLN. It was not so much an organisation as a conglomeration of dogfights.

On the organisational level the one bright spot was the ANL, the Algerian army. Pablo viewed it as the disciplined incarnation of a junction between revolutionary students, in their role as politically radical commissars, and the peasantry. This hardened and seasoned force was alert to the dangers of neo-colonialism and opportunist nationalists 'of the last hour'. It was committed to rebuilding the party and the state on the basis of the Tripoli Program. Pablo's initial idealisation of the army included his estimation of the army leader, Houari Boumediene:

> The personal magnetism of Houari Boumediene simultaneously charms and unsettles. What are the omens: Savonarola, Cromwell, Bonaparte, Boulanger, Nasser or Castro? I am for my part inclined to believe that this man from whom emerges a sincere faith in the people and, I will add, the mystique of the revolution, isn't simply a 'Nasserite socialist' willing to settle for re-establishing a copy of the colonial state. He will struggle alongside his political commissars and officers, as the incarnation of the revolutionary will of the ALN, "the iron lance" of the Revolution, for the profound restructuring of the country.[23]

The colonel, of course, would turn out to be the very thing Pablo acquitted him of. It was not the last time Pablo would be tempted to place some hope in army officers, even if he would also maintain that such hope was only ever transient and that standing armies would always and ultimately remain a danger to democracy and socialism.[24]

At this point, the trade unions were basically organisational shells of leaders without members, but nevertheless Pablo nominated the small but strategically located working class for the central role in the future of Algeria. 'If it is true that the armed struggle began with the junction of a limited cadre of leaders with the revolutionary landless peasantry and has been able to be continued until independence, thanks to the efforts and sacrifices of this peasantry, there is no doubt that the Revolution's fate will be decided principally in the towns.' While he considered the union leaderships too pragmatic, noting they were yet to endorse the Tripoli program, in their favour was the fact they, like the army, officially supported the spontaneous occupation and management by their workers of farms and enterprises abandoned by their European owners.

## 11 . JOINING THE WRETCHED OF THE EARTH 1961-63

Pablo was more favourable to the staff at the FLN daily *El Moudjahid*. The paper was staffed by 'brilliant young intellectuals' of independent mind, eager to rebuild Algeria on a socialist and democratic basis and who warned not only of the danger of a neo-colonial outcome but – with prescience – of rule by a 'masonic coalition of disparate feudal clans' enunciating a 'doctrine of obscurantist religio-socialism'.[25]

Even more glowing was his evaluation of Ahmed Ben Bella, then emerging as the paramount leader and soon to be elected the first president. The two met, it seems, for the first time in Algiers at the end of Pablo's trip. It was an article of faith for Trotskyists that revolutionary leadership is a key necessity for a victorious revolution. Without Lenin, Trotsky had argued in his *History of the Russian Revolution*, there would have been no victorious Russian Revolution. Pablo realised that Ben Bella was, unlike Lenin, an arbiter of the demands and pressures of powerful factions and different forces, not the leader of a disciplined party. Nevertheless, 'if Ben Bella continues to incarnate the revolutionary aspirations and will of the Algerian masses, and to show intelligence and character, firmness and audacity, he will have succeeded to this role in History'. (Big 'ifs', as it turned out.)

Behind this extravagant hope was a meeting of minds. Ben Bella agreed with him on the immediate social measures to be taken – the annulling of debts and back taxes owed by the peasants, and the takeover and management of the abandoned farms and workplaces by the workers themselves. Pablo also secured a commitment from Ben Bella for the establishment of democratic village assemblies and councils – a kind of Athenian democracy – as promised in the FLN's original platform, adopted at the congress of the Valley of Soummam in 1956. Ben Bella preferred to see such local democratic assemblies as the re-establishment of traditional djemaas or village councils which had long fallen into disuse.

Pablo's September report finished by re-capping the priorities for Algeria: a simplified state structure based on local assemblies and elected committees of peasants, workers and soldiers; the election of a constituent assembly to form a government and write a constitution; a rebuilt FLN with the Tripoli Program as its basis and the organisation within it of a revolutionary Marxist wing. Other priorities, besides the cancellation of the tax, loan and rent debts of the peasantry, were a literacy drive and schooling program; formation of commissions to draw up plans for agrarian reform, education and training, and indicative economic plans (which should include tourism for the newly prosperous European working class!).

Its final peroration was pure Pablo, very much what he would be advocating in the next three years:

> The factor which can imperceptibly swing Algeria onto the irreversible way of anti-capitalist measures and the application in deeds of the Tripoli Program ... [is] the revolutionary people, hardened by experience, free of fear, the majority of whom are young and who demand radical solutions.
>
> This is not to say that it is not absolutely necessary to rebuild the revolutionary FLN, nor to organise within it a revolutionary Marxist wing on which the fate of the revolution will definitively depend. Nor that it is necessary to minimise the neo-colonialist activity of opportunists and businessmen, proliferating with extraordinary rapidity (as in the rest of Africa) ... with these elements already infiltrating into the administration of the state and economy and the Party itself.
>
> It is possible that the Algerian Revolution will traverse a still long period, a development marked by crises, pauses and setbacks before the considerable, but scattered, revolutionary forces regroup for a final assault against the vestiges of the past and the neo-colonial elements presently developing.

The report again called for the maximisation of aid. 'A socialist victory in Algeria will have historic repercussions on all of Africa, the Mediterranean and even on Europe – from Portugal to France.' He announced that the African Commission of the Fourth International would now be based in Algeria – he would soon argue that the leadership of the International should transfer there, too, to what was to be dubbed "the Mecca of Revolution". For the time being, the report appealed for doctors, nurses, technicians, and teachers to come to Algeria for at least six months – preferably these volunteers should be supporters of anti-colonialism and socialism. Wages would be modest and accommodation basic. Ultimately, the task was to 'consolidate the socialist perspective of the Revolution' and it was time for Left forces to sign up. He finished by giving a contact address in Algiers for these reddest of what came to be dubbed the 'pieds-rouges' in contradistinction to the settlers, the 'pieds-noirs'.

— ✦ —

All this exploratory research and writing was preparation for a permanent move to Algeria. He and Elly took up residence in Algiers in October 1962, in an abandoned villa on the heights overlooking the city. Pablo accepted the position as economic counsellor to the new president. It seems it was his first paid employment. He was 51.

His critics were quick to mount arguments against his continuing Algerian engagement. The overriding one was that a neo-colonial or bureaucratic dictatorship in Algeria was inevitable and Marxists were wasting their time imagining, let alone working, for anything else. Jean-François Lyotard, writing in the magazine *Socialisme ou Barbarie*, developed a sophisticated version of this fatalism. He was himself Algerian-born and, in a series of articles during the war and immediately after, he celebrated its revolutionary impact on the youth of the towns and on women. However, by 1963 he considered that civil society was too shattered and the rural and urban working class too weak to form the basis of the radical social democracy Pablo aimed for.

Such fatalism was not in Pablo's nature. Besides, Marxists worked with history as it presented itself, as Marx's much quoted paragraph from *The Eighteenth Brumaire of Louis Napoleon* has it. History had presented an opening to a democratic, socialised economy in Algeria with workers spontaneously taking over and running abandoned farms and factories in the summer of 1962, and Pablo was not going to miss this opportunity, no matter how mixed the possibilities were. It wasn't naivety. It was a commitment to action, a commitment to hope.

As 1962 drew to a close, he responded to criticisms from the Left and defended his involvement there:

> I am personally taken to task for my "benbellism". We are here in Algeria a handful of European revolutionaries, communists of all persuasions who, fully conscious of the facts, have preferred active participation in the places where the socialist future of the Algerian Revolution is being forged and its immediate fate being decided, rather than sit back at home and deliver from afar denunciations, so easy, but how equally sterile, of the several shortcomings and obvious dangers.
>
> That our participation doesn't suffice to alter, even a little, the "class character" of a government, we know perfectly well. It would be even grotesque to dare to pretend that it did.
>
> But whoever pretends ... that the game is already decided in Algeria, ignores the embryo of a new social order which continues to push forward in this land, and accords no positive value to resolute, efficacious work which inserts itself in this framework. [Such critics] are incurably sectarian, or unthinking, chattering representatives of a certain frustrated, demoralised, incapable European "Left" that we push back against from the innermost depths of our being.[26]

Whether Pablo was in 'full knowledge of the facts' and was as aware of the 'several shortcoming and obvious dangers' as he claimed, is something his chief ally in the FLN Left, Mohammed Harbi, now disputes. But these were heady times, as recorded in the classic Algerian novel of these years: *Children of the New World* by Assia Djebar. Djebar has commented on 'the exuberant feelings of those first few years of the newly independent republic, when everyone felt young and everything seemed possible, including a full measure of female agency and equal civil and political rights for all.'[27]

The justice of the charge of 'benbellism' was already obvious. As we shall see, his affection for Ben Bella persisted despite the latter's unreliability and weaknesses. His comrade Harbi certainly could never be accused of such 'benbellism', but for a time he also accepted the role of counsellor to the new president, although he was never as close to Ben Bella as Pablo. In Pablo's defence, it is worth recalling that this was the epoch of 'big men' or historic leaders, incarnating the will of an insurgent people and shaping the destiny of their countries – men like Nehru, Kenyatta, Mao, Ho Chi Minh, Nkrumah, Soekarno and Fidel Castro. Pablo's bet was that Ben Bella might be of this type, but benevolent and committed to a truly democratic socialist path.

— ✢ —

When he called for international volunteers to work in the new revolutionary Mecca and celebrated the presence of 'communists of all persuasions', there was one notable absence: his old and dearest comrade in arms, Sal Santen.

Santen never made it to Algeria. Between the pair's release from prison, in September 1961, and early 1963, the partnership between Pablo and Santen flourished. Their correspondence – as noted, Santen's archive contains 140 letters from and to Pablo over the 15 months – is full of warmth and it included Elly, who exchanged domestic and political news with Santen. There can be little doubt that Santen became the indispensable comrade for Pablo. It was a role he freely adopted, writing to Pablo on 21 January 1962, for instance: 'I repeat what I have written several times, you can count on me and in whatever role you think most useful.' It was Santen who arranged printing of pamphlets, who liaised with lawyers pursuing Pablo's libel cases against the Communist Party newspapers in Holland and France, who organised translations and distribution of Pablo's articles, who maintained contact with their Austrian and Belgian supporters and tried to rustle up volunteers for Algeria, as well as carrying on the fight at meetings of the International. He did all this while working fulltime to support his family, suffering from poor health and providing leadership to the Dutch Trotskyists.

We cannot be sure what split the partnership. The version from the lifelong Trotskyist and *pabliste*, Maurice Ferares, another Dutch comrade, is that Santen established a close relationship with a Belgian comrade after he left prison – 'Suzanne' is the name used in the Santen-Pablo correspondence. According to Ferares, Santen wanted to come to Algeria with Suzanne – which would have meant leaving his wife and family – but this was vetoed by Pablo and Elly. This version is corroborated in a letter Pablo sent to Santen 20 years later, after a filmmaker attempted to set up a meeting in Paris between the old comrades. Santen backed out at the last moment and Pablo wrote to his old friend complaining about his treatment by the filmmaker. He added this P.S:

> As time runs out and Hellie [Elly] and I prepare for the 'grand depart', I would add this: by common agreement, Hellie and I decided not to support your arrival and installation in Algeria, fearing that you [Pablo uses the intimate 'tu' in this letter – *HG*] were about to commit an act in your private life that you would regret very quickly. You know well of what I speak. *A posteriori* you must be a little grateful to us.[28]

Given that Pablo was to later confess to a certain puritanism in his judgments, the Ferares explanation for the end of the friendship, based on the rejection of the arrival of Santen and his lover, does seem probable. Pablo's care to include Elly in the decision seems to indicate she played a big role in this too. Decades on, Santen, who became a successful writer, told Elspeth Etty[29] that he had remained a Trotskyist (very much in the Pablo version) and that his greatest achievement in life was his family. The Nazis had murdered his entire family of birth in World War II but he had managed to rebuild one, at least in part. If the Ferares version of events is accurate, as it appears to be, Santen owed a lot to his old comrades Pablo and Elly. As it turned out, in saving him from an impulsive move, they sacrificed their friendship with him and gave him a chance to be (in his own view) his better self. And Santen didn't take it badly. While he dropped out of left-wing politics soon after – his health was bad too – he fired off protests at the sanctions the majority in the International imposed on Pablo in the next few years. Finally, in his memoirs he pronounced himself still a *pabliste*.

CHAPTER 12

# Pablo's wager: Athens in Algiers
## 1962-1965

*World history would indeed be very easy to make if the struggle were taken up only on condition of infallibly favourable chances.*

**Karl Marx to Ludwig Kugelmann**
17 April, 1871

IN THE WAKE of the March 1962 Evian Accords that ended the war in Algeria, the European settlers began to leave in droves. From villas, apartments, factories, stores and farms, the great exodus began. Nearly a million people departed. The property they left behind – the *biens vacants* – fell into an array of hands. In some places it was the big men with money and guns seizing the property or cutting deals with the departing owners. Elsewhere, the local guerrillas or army units took over.

Mohammed Harbi returned to his home town of Skikda (Phillippeville under the French) in 1963 to find the local mafia presiding over the choicest farms and businesses. They threatened to shoot anyone who challenged their control (including Harbi himself).[1] If Algeria faced three alternatives – neocolonial capitalism, bureaucratic 'socialism', or a transition to democratic socialism – then this 'Wild West' appropriation favoured the first. Left to flourish, it would mean, in Ben Bella's words, 'replacing French colonialism with Algerian colonialism', something he was determined to thwart.[2]

Fortuitously, in many places the workers themselves blocked the gangsterism, taking over and managing the farms and firms. This 'socialism

## 12 . PABLO'S WAGER: ATHENS IN ALGIERS 1962-65

from below' was born of necessity rather than of political aspiration.[3] It was full of possibilities, if not intentions.

This initiative from below was what Pablo was counting on to forge a new alternative to capitalist or bureaucratic, Soviet-style development models still dominant in the newly independent nations of the Third World. Late in his life, considering the future of then Tsarist Russia, Marx had toyed with the possibility of a non-capitalist, cooperative development path. Pablo's third way would have at its heart an expanding democracy. As Pablo told Gilly thirty years later (and this was no post-facto rationale as we shall see):

> In a whole series of examples, there doesn't exist a single example where, after victory, the concern for democracy has dominated. This concern for democracy must be the goal of the revolution ... We don't make the revolution in order to set up a revolutionary dictatorship. We undertake a revolution in order to truly allow the masses to govern themselves, for society to rule itself.[4]

The first test of the new Ben Bella government, formed in September, was to prevent the big steal and instead to recognise the 'self-management' tendency that had been spontaneously unleashed across the country by tens of thousands of workers taking over and managing the abandoned farms and firms themselves. It was these workers, constituting and working under committees of management, who managed to sow and bring in the good harvest of 1962 in the absence of their former European masters.

Pablo's initial faith in Ben Bella, now official leader of the new Democratic and Popular Republic of Algeria, was not misplaced. In a series of decrees in October and November, Ben Bella annulled all real estate transactions since July 1 and promised a review of those that had taken place between the Evian Accords and independence. He also mandated that vacant farms and enterprises be run by management committees of the workers.

Ben Bella tasked Pablo with drawing up the plans for how the abandoned farms and factories would be managed democratically. As Pablo put it 30 years later:

> I appreciated, from the moment I first knew him, his truly revolutionary disposition, his generosity, his courage, and his willingness to open up to revolutionary developments, including in the social field in Algeria. For example, he immediately agreed that with regard to the properties left vacant by the colonists ... that they should not be state-owned and run, or distributed to private individuals, but that they would be turned over to a

self-management regime. He immediately accepted this idea, and in part he entrusted me with making this idea come true, and it was thanks to him, with his agreement, of course, that we were able to do this ... For this experience, Ben Bella's agreement and support was essential.

One of the first acts of the new Ben Bella government was the creation of the *Bureau National* à *la Protection et* à *la Gestion des Biens Vacants* (BNBV). Pablo was at the heart of this bureau. It included, as Harbi has pointed out, a corps of Arab socialists released from detention in Egypt by Nasser on the request of Ben Bella.[5]

As we've seen, committees had already appeared spontaneously in many places to take over the running of abandoned farms and enterprises. The October decree formalised what was happening already and encouraged its extension. However, Pablo and his colleagues in the BNBV soon noted that its implementation was being sabotaged and frustrated in many parts of the country. In an urgent report to Ben Bella and his cabinet in December[6], the BNBV spelt out these 'anti-national' actions:

> The vacant properties have become the object of a frenetic speculation whose beneficiaries were the least in need, such as certain leading figures in the party, the administration and the army, as well as large landowners and local leading businessmen. Profiting from the general confusion, some of them have made, or have tried to make, large profits at the expense of the national treasury.

There was also subterfuge:

> Elsewhere, phoney management committees substituted themselves for the former owners, sometimes with the latter's consent or following sham legal transactions ... Every day abandoned industrial enterprises, commercial firms and apartments are illegally occupied or sold or leased as favours despite the law forbidding such transactions.

In the power vacuum of the times, there were also alternative 'nationalisations', with the Army and Ministry of Agriculture taking over farms and converting them into 'state farms' on the Russian model, in direct opposition to the cooperative or socialised self-managed model that had been adopted by Ben Bella's cabinet. In the absence of detailed legislation, local bureaucrats in some districts were also creaming off profits from the abandoned farms.

To counter these infractions, BNBV demanded a significant media campaign and the creation of a corps of inspectors to promote the new self-managed socialist sector of the economy and the rights of the producers. At the end of December, the government acceded to these demands.

Simultaneously, Pablo was given the task of drafting more detailed laws governing self-management. They covered the new management structure, setting out the precise powers of the general assembly, introducing workers councils in the larger enterprises which would meet more frequently than the assemblies and act as a check on the management committees. The legislation also detailed the financial regulations for the new management bodies, and the rules for the appointment of managers who would be technically competent and charged with the daily administration of the farms and firms. The managers or directors would be appointed, in order to represent the general interest, by local or national government. These laws became the three March Decrees of 1963. In a nationwide radio and television broadcast on 29 March Ben Bella announced 'henceforth we will no longer talk of "abandoned properties" but of enterprises under self-management'.

The decrees, short and concise, were launched with great fanfare. Ben Bella toured the country extolling the 'democratic socialist opening' that the Revolution had now taken. This was a reward for the long struggle of the Algerian people, but Ben Bella also emphasised that the sector – the most developed and profitable in the country – was to be subject to progressive taxation so that it could play its role in aiding the development of less developed and poorer parts of the country. Symbolically, he officiated at the election of the first workers council at the farm formerly owned by the Borgeaud family, the largest and most notorious of the colonial landowners.

BNBV was now renamed *Bureau national d'animation du secteur socialiste* (BNASS) (National Office for the Animation of the Socialist Sector) and given the task of ensuring the new structures were put in place everywhere. This was far from ideal. 'For self-management to function according to the letter and particularly the spirit of the March Decrees,' Pablo later said, 'it would have needed the existence of committed organisers, technical supports and a state, a party and unions acting in a conscious and coordinated manner towards this goal. However, even in the best of circumstances, it would have required time.' And time was never on their side. An initial setback occurred early in Ben Bella's national self-management tour when his foreign minister, Mohamed Khemisti, was assassinated (it appeared to be a crime of passion by an aggrieved husband rather than political) and the president dropped the tour to return to Algiers for the funeral in early May.

Pablo hoped that the March Decrees would be followed by more detailed legislation on how workers would be remunerated (as producers rather than wage-earners) and by economic planning. He saw this as imperative in order to prevent the enterprises becoming as decentralised, competitive and 'egotistical' as those they replaced. In other words, they were required to play their part in the cooperative development of the country, in return for which the government would facilitate technical, financial and marketing aid to these enterprises. 'Unfortunately,' Pablo later noted, 'the decrees only had political exploitation and little attention was given to their further technical and economic elaboration and application.'[7] Harbi and others make the same point but sheet responsibility home to Ben Bella for taking all the political credit and popularity that came with proclaiming 'self-managed' socialism, while having little or no interest in the details of how it would operate and flourish.

Equally unfortunate was the almost simultaneous creation of the Organisation nationale de la réforme agraire (ONRA) (National Organisation for Agrarian Reform). Answerable to the Minister for Agriculture, it was responsible for liaising with directors and presidents of management committees and for financing, technical aid and marketing for the self-managed enterprises. It was even empowered to amalgamate and reorganise self-managed farms. ONRA also controlled the formation of local communal councils of self-management which appointed directors. Not surprisingly, it spawned a new set of bureaucrats. Internally the committees of management and their presidents, frequently the best educated and skilled workers in the enterprise, tended to become the new rulers of the enterprise. They were encouraged by ONRA which also used its own leverage to 'guide' the self-managed enterprises.

ONRA argued that their intervention increased efficiency. Pablo strongly contested that claim, pointing out that the technical and educational level of the bureaucrats in the ministries was low and that their intervention discouraged the creativity and enthusiasm of the workers. He cited the example of the Soviet Union where the centralised and authoritarian management of the economy led to a proliferation of bureaucrats and stagnant labour productivity. Harbi later confirmed that ONRA, and the generally bloated bureaucracy, was a source of much corruption.[8]

The advance of this bureaucratic tutelage was helped along by the abolition, in the autumn of 1963, of BNASS and the cancellation of its radio program 'Voice of Socialist Algeria', for which Pablo wrote many of the scripts. Ben Bella sanctioned the step under pressure from the Minister of Agriculture, Amar Ouzegane, a comrade he'd shared prison with during the war. Ouzegane was no friend of self-management, unlike the director of BNASS, Abdelkader Maachou, who was a firm friend and ally of Pablo's. There was a similar 'capture' of the much smaller self-managed industrial sector by the ministry for the national economy.

This apparent victory for the bureaucrats during the autumn of 1963 was compounded when Ben Bella failed to approve a project from his advisors, of which Pablo was chief, for the creation of an economic coordinating body for the socialist sector of the economy. This body would have been responsible for some indicative planning and setting criteria and priorities for public investment in agriculture, industry, marketing, housing and tourism.[9] Theoretically this planning body would work with local democratic communal councils, which would bring together local citizens and workers to prepare local plans. These local councils were yet to be formed. It was another project Pablo was urging Ben Bella to adopt. All this was clearly aimed at bypassing the various ministries and ministers and putting power more securely into the hands of workers and peasants.

In August 1963 Pablo wrote a long memorandum to Ben Bella in an attempt to arouse him to reverse the bureaucratic trend.[10] He reminded the President of the political importance of a self-managed socialism, its universal appeal, and how he had championed it by issuing the March Decrees. He pointed out how the workers themselves had saved the country by taking over the abandoned farms and by ensuring a good harvest in 1962 and 1963, and how the enthusiasm and creativity of the workers was the strongest factor in the economy, given the shortage of all kinds of experts and expertise. If workers were not free to administer their enterprises, then the country would be in trouble.

Pablo didn't stop there. He then detailed the ways in which ONRA and its fellow agencies were gutting self-management. They had falsified or overturned elections; made deals with presidents without reference to the wider elected bodies. They had taken possession of tractors and other machinery and were renting them back at inflated prices; they had overruled decisions about what crops the farms would plant, despite the local expertise of farmers. They were monopolising the selling of the harvests. The list went on. On top of all that, they were also withholding income and paying workers as though they were merely state employees.

All this Pablo put in the larger picture of what happens during revolutions:

> It is in the nature of socialist revolutions that, as they develop, ideological differentiations emerge. There aren't only declared enemies of the revolution

who place themselves deliberately and openly outside the revolution; there is inside the revolution an inevitable differentiation between the democratic left of the revolution which places its confidence in the masses, which does not conceive of the revolution without the conscious and willing participation of the masses in the management of the economy and the state, and the bureaucratic wing of the revolution with its feudal and authoritarian mentality. [This wing] has the tendency to substitute itself for the masses and reduce them to employees of the state and to simple executants of its decisions. It is my firm conviction that this danger has arisen in our revolution, around the question of self-management in particular, and it is highly desirable that you intervene energetically – and in time.

By the beginning of the second year of the Algerian Revolution, Pablo saw the future of the Algerian socialism as being a contest between its democratic and bureaucratic variants, as he noted in report to the International dated 27 August 1963.[11]

He admitted that this essential conflict could be difficult to discern, as Algeria 'advances along the revolutionary road empirically, under the distinctive impulsion of social forces which clash in great ideological confusion'. He warned against judging the revolution on the basis of the state of the superstructure – the form of the constitution, the position of women, the pervasiveness of religion and so on. Those indicators could suggest the counter-revolution had already been successful. While admitting that all kinds of reactionary and conservative political phenomena still existed – 'these recent political manifestations certainly do not fit in with a political socialist democracy' – he argued that for a Marxist, the key consideration was the structural transformation of the country. That was happening and he remained optimistic:

> ... we were from the outset conscious of the inevitable limitations of the regime in terms of political democracy, without concluding that the advance of the Revolution would thereby necessarily find itself blocked.

He was still banking on Ben Bella to favour the democratic socialist option by setting up democratic local or 'commune' administrations and by opposing 'the attempts by the bureaucratic wing of the Revolution to adulterate self-management in the interest of a state-controlled economy administered from above in an authoritarian way'. Significantly, the earlier characterisation from a year before, of the Army as the revolutionary peasant and worker vanguard, has disappeared.

This wish that Ben Bella intervene 'energetically' on the side of the democratic wing was to prove a vain hope. At the same time, Pablo would never share the critical attitude to Ben Bella held by leaders of the Algerian Left such as Mohammed Harbi. Harbi certainly did not have Pablo's 'indulgent' view of Ben Bella – or any illusions about the army leaders. For Pablo, Ben Bella was at worst a Bonapartist figure juggling competing factions. For Harbi, Ben Bella was an opportunist, improvising and scrambling to keep up with events. 'He went to the right, then to the left, proceeding all the time through personal relations and contacts; there was no organisation to base himself on. He had no strategic vision.'[12]

On the other hand, Harbi recognised the benefits to Ben Bella of Pablo's friendship – 'for him the discussions with Michel were very interesting, an apprenticeship ...' When Pablo asked Harbi to join in the team working with Ben Bella, he initially rebuffed him. 'I told him, "I don't think Ben Bella is capable of going where you believe he can. Algerian nationalism has a history that you're not aware of. There's a strong streak of conservatism and the Algerian army isn't like the bearded revolutionaries in Cuba ..."'[13]

The suspicion was mutual. Ben Bella took his distance from Harbi after being told he was a communist. Nevertheless, he approached Harbi for advice from time to time, but he gave the Left no position of real power in the regime. The Left were good for advice and technical help – 'all the ideas and text of the March Decrees came from Michel,' says Harbi – but little else. 'He gave us the press, but that's all.' Also, most of the Pablo team were not Algerians. As early as the summer of 1963, the conservative opposition was making great play of this. The army newspaper, *El Djeich*, published a letter that railed against 'the cosmopolitan fauna that regularly lands on our soil, these beards and intellectuals in turtlenecks, socialism's Saint Bernards'.[14]

Harbi didn't see eye to eye with Ben Bella on the question of religion or his continued friendships with people hostile to self-management and democratic reform. Harbi felt that Pablo refused to accept the importance of religion in the Algerian context – he saw it as an old mistake of historical materialists to underestimate the superstructure in favour of the economic base. In the three years of the Ben Bella regime, as the Ottaways have pointed out, Algerians financed the building and renovation of some 400 mosques.[15] Conservatives in the army and the FLN regularly drew attention to the foreign and communist unbelievers in the heart of Ben Bella's regime. Harbi warned Pablo that he was underestimating the hold of religion and chauvinism, but to no avail.

Harbi had fought, and lost, battles on the issue of Islam. As an organiser of Algerian students in France during the 1950s he had supported the creation of an all-embracing 'Association of Algerian Students', but lost out to the religious communitarians who wanted the exclusivist 'Association of Muslim Algerian Students'. Ben Bella would have had no problem with that. He told Harbi, 'For me, my religion is essential.' According to Harbi, Ben Bella wanted the GPRA (Provisional Government of the Republic of Algeria) to carry the extra letter M for Muslim. It was Nasser himself who dissuaded Ben Bella, telling him, 'While I'm engaged in a battle against the Muslim Brotherhood you want to hurl this rock at me ...'[16]

In light of all that, why did Pablo persist in his hopeful commitment to Ben Bella? The answer lies partly in the personal affection and friendship he had for Ben Bella, but also in his realisation of the role the popular president could play in the absence of a strong revolutionary organisation. Ben Bella strongly supported the colonial revolutions in Africa and Latin America. He might be a laggard and unreliable at home, but he was constant in his support of revolutionary and anti-imperialist initiatives abroad. He turned Algiers into the second Havana, a second revolutionary capital, the 'Mecca of Revolution', to use the title of Jeffrey James Byrne's magisterial account of the revolutionary diplomacy of the Algeria of the Ben Bella years.[17] Pablo forged friendships with many of the revolutionary pilgrims to Algiers in these years, particularly those from Portugal, Angola and Mozambique.

The celebration of Algeria's independence in July 1962 had drawn many of the leaders of colonial revolutionary movements to Algiers. Leaders of the African National Congress rubbed shoulders with those from the Portuguese anti-Salazar or anti-fascist resistance. In the following years, Algiers hosted major offices for the world's revolutionary movements, extended them financial aid and trained and armed their fighters. Algeria's few freighters were used to transport arms to Latin American guerrillas. Its planes shipped arms to the African bases of the independence movements in Southern Africa.

Ben Bella's first trip abroad was to the meeting of the UN General Assembly in October 1962. In his speech, he paid particular homage to revolutionary Cuba. This was despite the importance to Algeria of aid from Washington and the personal support the American president John F. Kennedy had given the Algerian struggle, as a senator from Massachusetts. On his return journey from New York, Ben Bella stopped off in Cuba where he was welcomed by cheering crowds as he toured the island with Fidel Castro. He brought with him, according to Pablo and Adolfo Gilly, a consignment of foreign exchange to help Cuba deal with the already crippling American blockade.[18]

This visit was the first step in establishing a special relationship between the two revolutionary capitals – and, for a time, the two revolutionary leaders. The most significant manifestation of that relationship was the help that Algeria extended to Che Guevara when he attempted to restart the revolution in the Congo. Che and a handful of Cuban fighters travelled to the eastern Congo via Algiers in 1964. Arms were also shipped to them from Algiers. Pablo was a key intermediary in this support. The Czech arms destined for Che were to be delivered via a back channel and Pablo was the intermediary. This, of course, was not without its ironies. A Trotskyist facilitating aid from a still Stalinist regime to a revolutionary force.

The quintessential revolutionary of this period, Che Guevara, visited Algeria in the summer of 1963. Pablo, the Greek-born revolutionary Trotskyist, spent one memorable night in discussion with Che, the Argentine-born Marxist revolutionary legend, in the garden of the Cuban embassy. At the time, Pablo was neither aware of Che's falling out with Fidel over the Cuban leader's cosying up to the Soviet Union, nor did he know of Che's intervention to release the Cuban Trotskyists from prison. He was aware of Che's irreproachable revolutionary integrity, and of his anxiety to relieve the pressure on the Vietnamese by spreading revolutionary war to more and more theatres. He found him impressive, if reticent and watchful. In the long discussion that night in Algiers, they exchanged their different views on the economic policy best suited to transitioning post-colonial countries to socialism. Che Guevara was very much the advocate of heavy industry, centralised top-down control and moral incentives, while Pablo emphasised self-management, light industry and a role for material incentives. Neither shifted position. In his memoir Pablo says the night was memorable for him because he caught in Che's eyes a certain fatalism about his future. Che's demeanour recalled for him the lines from Swinburne's poem 'Atalanta of Calydon':

*In his heart is a blind desire,*
*In his eyes foreknowledge of death*

It was not a complete surprise to him that Che was to die just three years later in Bolivia in what Pablo saw as a tragic, ill-prepared and 'suicidal', mission.[19]

— ✦ —

At the beginning of 1964, Pablo again spelled out his anxieties about the Algerian Revolution, in an editorial in *Sous le drapeau du socialisme*

(Under the Flag of Socialism), published in Algiers as the journal of the African Commission of the Fourth International. The title of the editorial indicated his view: 'The necessary relaunch'.[20] He recognised that Algeria was wallowing in economic difficulties and stagnation, and a series of catalytic measures were needed. He outlined these in some detail: spreading cooperatives in agriculture and marketing; mobilising the unemployed and underemployed in public works such as reafforestation, irrigation repair and building public facilities; diversifying export markets; cracking down on corruption and privileges; formulating a short-term economic plan with precise goals and establishing specialised agricultural and industrial banks. It was time, too, for the democratisation of the administration, the FLN and the unions and egalitarian incomes and taxation measures. He summed it up as a relaunch 'by the masses for the masses and against the networks and clans which shelter and breed anti-socialist, traditionalist forces'.

The left of the FLN took up these ideas. In April 1964 the FLN held its first post-independence congress and adopted the *Charter of Algiers*, committing Algeria to the goal of a self-managed socialism. Harbi was the principal author but he discussed his drafts with Pablo. The one suggestion from Pablo that Harbi rejected was support for multiparty democracy. This was an essential element in any socialist democracy in Pablo's view. It was something Rosa Luxemburg had insisted on in her debates with the Bolsheviks after the Russian Revolution and which Trotsky later accepted. While Harbi held a similar view, he thought an attempt to include it in the Charter would imperil the acceptance of the whole document. It would be asking the sole ruling party to give up its monopoly. Both he and Pablo were aware that their influence exceeded the real forces they commanded in the country, but Pablo thought it was worth raising the multiparty issue. However, he accepted Harbi's call. After all, 'Harbi knew the FLN better than me'.[21]

The Charter held out the hope that self-management would move beyond the purely economic realm and that its current form was the first step in a more general and ambitious reform agenda. The Charter went further, in fact, and argued that self-management or direct democracy in one realm would inevitably raise the question of its extension elsewhere.[22] It might, but the spread or contagion was far from automatic.

At the congress, the army controlled the subsequent elections to the executive positions in the party. Ben Bella did nothing to interfere with this. Harbi recounts a telling incident. He was sitting next to Ben Bella and Boumediene when they were reading through the list of nominees for the central committee. In Harbi's account, Boumediene put a line through two names, one of whom was army captain Abderrazak Bouhara, 'very favourable to *autogestion*' (self-management), and replaced them with the names of police chiefs Bensalem and Ahmed Draya, both protégés of Boumediene. When Harbi objected, Boumediene turned on him, 'Mohammed, don't interfere in the affairs of the grown-ups.'[23] The left might have carried the day ideologically but the actual organisation, the FLN, remained more firmly in the hands of the bureaucracy and its army champions like Boumediene. Pablo's hopes that, as a result of the adoption of the Charter, the FLN – or its left wing – would emerge as the transmission link between a bolder Ben Bella and the insurgent peasants and workers were proving flimsy.

By now Pablo realised that Harbi was correct about the army. 'They weren't like the bearded ones in Cuba', even if Pablo still had lingering hopes for the 'radical forces' within the army.[24] In Harbi's view it was the army – and particularly its intelligence service – that was behind the continued warnings in the media about 'foreigners' (such as Pablo) and who also used racism against Ben Bella for his welcome to African liberation movements, many of which opened offices in Algiers.

Pablo's Algerian experience would show him the limited role any army could, or should, play – even one professing to be revolutionary. 'The revolution doesn't need soldiers,' he told Gilly thirty years later, 'It needs revolutionaries, that is, self-developed beings, deeply convinced of why it is necessary to make the revolution, men and women who have very consciously agreed to make the ultimate sacrifices, if necessary.' As he recognised at the time, soldiers may help in the overthrow of the regime, but when it came to the encouragement of a wider and participatory democracy, they were not to be counted upon.[25]

In that last interview, Gilly would not let him escape the difficulty of his position.

> **AG:** But when it comes to armed struggle, the revolutionary movement has to build an army, even underground, and it needs discipline and soldiers. How do we put the two things together?

And Pablo answers:

> **MP:** I am absolutely in favour of the absolute necessity for the revolution to use revolutionary violence against the enemy. I'm not for being sentimental. The class struggle and the revolution are very hard, and ferocious struggles take place in a world which is, on the whole, prehistoric and barbaric. But

if you do not use these means to fight against the barbarism of others, you betray the victims of this barbarism.

It was a conundrum he believed could be solved by the widest practice of democracy – even in the midst of armed struggle. It would always be a matter of weighing up the pros and cons of more civilised behaviour, in any conflict. He cited examples from the Greek wartime resistance where whole battalions and even villages debated and voted on whether to kill German prisoners in retaliation for German atrocities. There were instances where such general assemblies restrained the party leaders who had ordered such reprisals.

He recounted the wartime incident in the town of Zagora, in the mountain above the coastal village of Horefto (where the interview with Gilly was taking place). The Italians who were occupying Horefto appealed to Zagora, held by the Resistance, to send their doctor to treat an Italian who was dying. The Resistance called a meeting of the village to discuss whether to send the doctor (who was the father of Marika, later a close comrade of Pablo's). The discussion was veering towards a refusal when the doctor rose in the meeting and announced that, because of his ethical commitment to save life, he was going to mount his mule and go through the snow to Horefto. The village could either try to stop him or punish him when he returned. The villagers and the partisans were astonished, but accepted the doctor's decision. 'It is an example of revolutionary fraternisation. Very good.'[26] Pablo added that it was also an example of successful defiance of the Stalinist chiefs, who were in general very severe and brutal.

— ✦ —

At the FLN conference in April, 1964, Ben Bella had echoed and endorsed the clarion call to move forward towards a more genuine transition to self-managed socialism. However, it proved to be rhetoric, as Pablo realised, the mollifying act of a man under pressure.[27]

In the wake of the FLN congress, Ben Bella continued to distance himself from Pablo and the FLN Left. It was, Pablo noted, a strategy of self-preservation:

> He did it because he saw that he was threatened, because there were very strong reactions in his entourage against the 'pieds-rouges' – I was a *pied-rouge* – those foreign atheists, who in reality did not bother him, and they opposed us not because we were Reds and atheists, but because we were for

self-management ... which they saw as the most potent enemy of their own state power. It was on the question of self-management that the opposition between them and us crystallised.

Ben Bella didn't break completely and was, Pablo felt, a little embarrassed at the new coolness he practised towards his Greek friend who had done so much to help Algeria. Given Ben Bella's own deep attachment to Islam and his Arab identity, it was not surprising that he was susceptible to the reactionary pressures coming from the army and the religious establishment. Besides, some of his oldest comrades were conservative believers. Ahmed Mahsas, whom he appointed Minister for Agriculture in 1963 and who had been imprisoned with him in the early 1950s, was one example. Then there was Safi Boudissa, who had helped Ben Bella and Mahsas escape prison in 1952. Neither was a supporter of self-management, and both supported the coup when it came.

Throughout 1964 Pablo himself recognised the strength both of conservative culture and the corruption that comes with power. It didn't jeopardise the 'socialist opening' because – in his view – the publicly owned sectors of the economy were already predominant and expanding. If this course continued, then the potent social conservatism would wither away:

> ... the superstructure – religion, education, the condition of women and the family etc, culture – still remains greatly influenced by the Arab-Islamic past of traditional society. The radical changes in these domains will only emerge from the economic and cultural development of the country, which itself will flow from a serious commitment to a socialised and planned economy.[28]

But these superstructural factors did determine the nature of the political regime in the immediate and medium terms – especially in the absence of that 'serious commitment'.

By year's end it was apparent there was a political revival at the grassroots. This was abundantly clear at the second congress of agricultural workers held in Algiers on 25, 26 and 28 December 1964. It was the largest national gathering of workers since Algeria had gained its independence. The conference opened in uproar over the attempt by the Ministry of Agriculture to stack the congress with its hand-picked delegates. For three hours the elected delegates refused to take their seats and allow the congress to begin. Things only settled down with the arrival of Ben Bella. He was cheered into the auditorium to chants of 'Victory to the truth' and 'May God protect you'.

Typically, Ben Bella began his speech by equivocating, 'I am on the side of neither the Ministry of Agriculture nor the UGTA [the trade union federation] but I will say something sincerely.' And he then indicated his sympathy for the militants. 'This congress is the realisation of one of our dreams, to see the organisation of a federation of workers of the land. You took decisions at your first congress. The majority of those decisions have not been implemented and I come here to speak sincerely to you of our shortcomings.'

The 'old' Ben Bella was emerging. He wondered aloud, 'Has self-management been implemented?' and answered, 'No, the workers still don't play their rightful role. The general assemblies of the workers, the committees of management, the workers' councils still don't fulfil the role that was laid down in the March Decrees and the Charter of Algiers.' Given the green light, the elected delegates now took control of the congress, challenging and criticising the ministry and party officials for their privileges, interference, appropriation of profits and lack of useful aid to the self-managed farms.[29] The clamouring, insurgent spirit of self-management was very much alive and well among these delegates.

This was clear in the report for the major (and conservative) French daily *Le Figaro* by David Rousset, the old Trotskyist, survivor of the Nazi camps and now prominent Gaullist.[30] He was struck by the appearance of the crowd in the auditorium. 'The government officials, administrators, officials and leaders of the FLN dispersed throughout the hall were submerged by the fellahs [agricultural workers]. They stood out, dressed in their town suits in the midst of a sea of turbans and country robes.' When the conference began, the delegates insisted Arabic be spoken. Any reports delivered in French were spontaneously translated by delegates for fellow delegates.

When it came to speaking, these country men quickly overcame any reticence. As Rousset's account continued:

> Certainly in approaching the high table of officials, many hesitate. Some make a military salute, others a more traditional acknowledgement. And then quite simply they shake the hands of the ministers and party officials who sit quite stiffly at the table. But on taking the mic they are at home. Three thousand delegates, men like themselves, applaud them and fix their gaze on them, expectantly. Then they do speak. Fired up, they mix the cadences of the Koranic school with warm Mediterranean gestures and the truculence of the village and the occasional sudden laugh ... One delegate says they will not accept being dictated to by anyone and the room rises to its feet in a tumult of applause. They speak before the president, before ministers, before

the nation, without worrying about formalities, like they think, in a direct manner, in a flood of words.

In their comportment the delegates seemed to remind Rousset of the heady days in revolutionary Barcelona in 1936-37 that were captured so lyrically in George Orwell's *Homage to Catalonia*. Rousset continued:

> In their speeches there is a certain pride. They have ensured production was maintained despite the desertion and sabotage of the former owners and managers. They don't hold back on the obstacles and problems they face. For the first time they don't require anyone to speak for them. This is the central fact of things, and it is going to weigh heavily on the future of the Algerian revolution. In breaking the silence, the Algerian farm workers have destroyed an ancestral fear stemming from their age-old humiliation which had still paralysed them these last few months. They are now completing the social emancipation that the seizing of the land had only prepared. They have said what they think in the most vivid terms, without circumlocutions, without their traditional prudence, and they have said it directly to Mahsas, their minister, to the central authorities of the FLN, to the State itself ...

The delegates echoed the critiques that the proponents of self-management had been making. Essentially their demands and resolutions fell into two groups. The first was respect for the autonomy and freedom of the self-managed enterprises. The fellahs demanded that requisitioned machinery be returned to the farms, control of marketing and provisioning be in their hands, bank accounts put under their control, and steps taken to set up a supportive agricultural bank. The second preoccupation was with pay and social security. They wanted a national pay scale agreed to, social security and workers injury insurance extended to agricultural workers, a natural disasters fund created, and further discussions on how the surplus, or profit after tax and insurance outgoings, was to be distributed.

Ben Bella gave the closing address and promised that the March Decrees would be implemented along with the resolutions of the congress. But it was the spirit of the delegates that struck observers; Rousset wasn't alone in that. Pablo saw the possibilities of such a gathering:

> At this congress they could become conscious of their social power, share experiences, clarify the problems of self-management and its relations with the state administration and get a better idea of the government that now presided over the destinies of liberated Algeria.[31]

The conference of the workers in the self-managed industrial sector which followed in March 1965 displayed the same discontent with the non-application of the March decrees. Pablo noted, however, an emphasis on compromise with more 'state control' and a greater concern for increased wages among the town workers.

Pablo was a strong advocate of the so-called 'material' incentives position although he did not accept that this was necessarily in opposition to 'moral' incentives. A revolutionary regime would always appeal to the conscience and idealism of the people. The vital issue was what would happen to 'the remainder', that part of the earnings of a firm or farm that was left after all taxes, depreciation allowances and levies had been paid. For him it was a crucial principle:

> It was a question of whether the workers, the direct producers of the country's wealth, would have the right to improve their standard of living in so far as they raised the productivity of their labour. In terms of the March Decrees, this right was theirs. It was founded on the general consideration that the productivity of the workers is stimulated and conditioned by the constant improvement of their standard of living. We are dealing with an economic and not moral factor of universal application.
>
> But, as well, in the framework of a regime aiming towards socialism, the tendency in the remuneration of workers must be that which abolishes the fact of wage-earning by moving towards remuneration according to labour furnished in quantity and quality. Thus, when we speak of 'material stimulants', against which mistakenly in our opinion opponents want to pit the primacy of 'moral', 'political' or 'ideological' incentives, we want to simply respond that it is necessary to begin to distribute income to workers according to their work, which is the most moral mode of remuneration according to orthodox socialist doctrine.[32]

Despite the encouraging congresses, the bureaucratisation continued.[33] After the abolition of BNASS in the autumn of 1963, no other body was formed to elaborate the legislation necessary to strengthen self-management and regulate its problems. This led to discouragement and ultimately the failures of self-management. Production levels were maintained but once products left the farm there was wastage and corruption.[34]

Pablo never believed that self-management at the enterprise level would be enough. He had two wider priority targets as well: agrarian reform and self-governing communes. The first would be based on equalising land holdings and encouraging cooperatives. The second would depend on the creation of administrative communes whose boundaries would be decided by economic and clan or tribal factors. Freely elected councils encouraging the widest possible participation (Athenian democracy essentially) would govern these communes and provide the democratic basis of the regime. Again he would be disappointed: 'These two reforms, widely anticipated, once realised, would have delivered enormous impetus to self-management and the general elan of the revolution.'[35]

The self-managed agricultural sector did not involve the bulk of the Algerian rural workforce. Covering the best land on the coastal plains, it produced more than half the food and the bulk of Algeria's agricultural exports, but employed only about 200,000 full-time workers and approximately 400,000 seasonal workers. It occupied nearly two million hectares. It was potentially the very profitable sector whose earnings would help drive investment in the rest of agriculture.

The remaining seven million hectares of cultivated land were in private hands. The bulk of it was held in very small, uneconomical lots. Algeria's peasants mostly eked out a bare survival on half a hectare. Unable to survive on this mote, the men gravitated to the cities and the more adventurous went to factories in France. However, about 8,500 Algerians owned more than 100 hectares and another 15,000 owners had holdings of 50-100 hectares. This amounted to more than 2.5 million hectares. These lands, in Pablo's view, needed to be nationalised, the owners compensated with interest-bearing government bonds and the land shared among landless and poor peasants. Peasants should have title to 10 hectares (or its equivalent in poorer soil areas) and would be encouraged to join farming cooperatives and to form cooperatives for marketing and purchasing. Such cooperatives should be given priority in government technical and financial aid. None of this cooperative push should be compulsory. Peasants should be able to decide to continue farming individually or to commit only part of their land and labour to the cooperatives.

These agrarian reform proposals had been included in the detailed study that Pablo had prepared for the Provisional Government prior to independence. In August 1963, he repeated them in the memo to Ben Bella. He pointed to the many political virtues of such a reform – boosting the popularity of the government, rewarding a peasantry that had borne the brunt of the liberation war, bringing peasants into the economy and developing an internal market to spur development. In January 1964, in response to an explicit request from Ben Bella, he had drafted the outline of an agrarian reform law.[36] The FLN congress in April 1964 declared in favour of a radical agrarian reform. At the congress Ben Bella spoke in favour of nationalising and redistributing the land of bigger landowners.

> 'These 23,000 holdings cover two and half million hectares while the remaining 4 million hectares are divided into more than 600,000 lots. Two

million 'fellahs' are unemployed, while most of the big landowners only visit their properties to check the harvest or to collect their rents.'[37]

But there was no follow-up. In June the FLN central committee postponed the reform to the following year and decided to target only the largest of the landholdings. The only step taken by the government was in October 1964, when the land of wartime traitors was nationalised.

Equally important for Pablo had been the creation of communal councils, made up of representatives from the self-managed enterprises and cooperatives as well as directly elected citizen representatives. These councils would be responsible for writing local plans and contributing to the elaboration of a national plan. They would also manage public works projects and the mobilising of the local population, many of whom were unemployed or underemployed, to carry through these projects. The decisions about local priorities would be made through open decision-making processes involving as many residents and workers as possible. Pablo envisaged committees and commissions made up of elected representatives and ordinary citizens. Large citizen assemblies and referendums would also be part of the means encouraging the widest possible participation.

In August and December 1964, he wrote papers for Ben Bella outlining their basic, democratic structures and arguing the case for them. Again, nothing happened. Algeria went on being administered along the old colonial lines, run by prefects and officials belonging to the one single party, the FLN.[38] As Harbi has noted, many of these prefects interfered with the self-managed farms, often 'solving' unemployment problems by stacking the self-managed farms with these surplus workers. As a result, the workforce was sometimes four or five times as large as pre-independence.[39]

In the first months of 1965 there were still signs of the 'old' Ben Bella reappearing as he responded more positively to initiatives from below, and signs of the strengthening of the more radical elements in society. He stopped interfering in the unions and allowed them to elect their own leaders (who, however, remained suspicious of the president).[40]

By May 1965, it looked for all intents and purposes that Ben Bella had decided to strengthen his own position vis-à-vis Boumediene. His initiative in forming a people's militia to counterbalance the regular army had been stymied by Boumediene, but Ben Bella further tested the defence minister by making clear his intention to replace the foreign minister Abdelaziz Bouteflika, a close ally of Boumediene. Ben Bella must have imagined he had the strength and popularity to carry off such a move. According to the American historian Jeffrey Byrne, if Ben Bella did not yet have that strength, he was on the threshold of acquiring it. At the end of June he was to host Bandung II, the meeting of the global Non-Aligned Movement, which would have brought together the Third World heads of state in Algiers. In this role, Ben Bella would arguably be more impregnable than ever as Algeria's paramount leader. He would be at the centre of a phalanx of anti-imperialist leaders including Tito, Zhou Enlai, Fidel Castro, Nasser, Ho Chi Minh, Soekarno, Nkrumah, Sihanouk, and Jomo Kenyatta.

It was the heyday of such 'heroes' and it was this looming prospect, Byrne believes, that prompted the plotters to move. It was now or never. On June 19, the army faction staged a coup that deposed Ben Bella. Pablo would later agree it was a pre-emptive strike by Boumediene, but also a way to block a further shift to the left by Ben Bella. At the central committee meeting of the FLN on 14-16 June, 1965, a series of decisions had been taken to strengthen self-management, nationalise the larger landholdings of rich Algerians, proceed with local government reform and set up a government agency to manage exports.[41]

By the spring of that year, it had become clear Algerian society was polarising. In March there had been a huge and unprecedented International Women's Day march in Algiers. Photographs from the march make it abundantly clear that it was very far from being an affair of elite women. Assia Djebar's novel *Children of the Future* reveals how much the war reached deep into conservative Algerian society. Algerian women broke many traditional taboos and restrictions, venturing out of their homes to carry support to their husbands, brothers and sons. There was, of course, a stern reaction to this from traditional Algerian men, some of whom were those very bureaucrats that Pablo saw as the main enemy of *autogestion*. Henri Alleg, the editor of *Alger Républicain*, the communist party newspaper and the biggest circulation daily in the country, has left this description of that women's march on 8 March 1965:

> ... tens of thousands of women ... women of all ages, some wearing the veil, others not, took to the streets of Algiers, carrying banners in support of the revolution that would give the same rights and same possibilities to men and women alike. The newspaper staff momentarily left their stations to stand on the balcony and watch the immense procession of women marching down Boulevard Amirouche. Mothers, sisters, wives and other relatives ululated to them as they passed by. In return joyful, fraternal greetings rang out from the balcony ... Those who marched and those who watched from their windows

knew they were witnessing something new and extremely important.

On the other side of the boulevard, opposite the newspaper [offices], was the Ministry of Agriculture. The people who worked there had also stopped working to watch the procession from their balconies. Their reaction stood in contrast to the noisy enthusiasm of the staff of *Alger Républicain*. They stood there silently, not responding to any calls, with a look that could not have been more solemn had they been watching a funeral procession pass by. Clearly they did not approve – to say the least – of the march even though the radio broadcasts and official newspapers the following day unanimously praised the event.[42]

Boumediene's coup was made on behalf of those men and those bureaucrats. It was immaculately planned. Ben Bella was arrested in his flat in the early hours of the morning of 19 June by the presidential guard. Armoured units occupied the main cities in the pre-dawn hours. Radio and television stations were commandeered to broadcast the statement of the coup leaders. Students hurriedly organised protest demonstrations in the capital but were dispersed by troops firing live ammunition. 'Women took to their balconies hammering pots to the cry of 'Ya-hiia Ben Bella' – Long live Ben Bella – but street protests were timid and died down quickly,' according to Henri Alleg. In Oran there were reports of up to 50 students shot down in the street. Harbi notes that there were determined protests in Annaba, organised by self-management supporters. Pablo, then in hiding, watched the brave but small student protests in Algiers from a window and noted the closed and unresponsive faces of the 'conservative and frightened' Algerian men on the sidewalks.

Pablo was tipped off about the coup by a neighbour – the Reuters reporter in Algiers – who had woken him and asked to talk to him in the garden. In the early morning light Pablo, from his house on the heights, could see tanks and armoured cars making their way into the centre of Algiers below. Pablo immediately packed a suitcase and went into hiding. (Once again his personal archives were lost when the police raided his apartment.) Elly, by chance, was in Geneva when the coup occurred.

Michel Pablo was a marked man. Without naming him, Boumediene's speech justifying the coup had singled out the atheistic, anti-Islamic, communist foreigner advising Ben Bella. Later in 1965 he did name him and accused him of personally profiting from his role as Ben Bella's advisor. According to Boumediene, this so-called socialist was paid one million old francs a month when the average Algerian worker received less than a thousand. (Pablo said he was paid 2,300 and 600 of this went in tax and another 200 in rent – and his bank and the government records would prove it.[43])

In the immediate wake of the coup, he drafted an appeal urging the formation of an organisation of resistance to the military dictatorship. Following a meeting with Harbi, he decided to flee the country. A clandestine existence for this tall European would be impossible. Roger Foirier arrived from France with a false passport that required a photo of a disguised Pablo sporting a false moustache. Pablo initially decided to try leaving by the port city of Oran, in the west, where police checks were thought to be laxer. But on arriving in Oran, he came to the conclusion the disguise might not work, and the humiliation of his arrest in such a disguise was not worth the risk. He promptly returned to Algiers and the next day went boldly to the airport, selected the most sympathetic-looking airline employee at the counter and bought a ticket to Switzerland, saying he was going on holidays. After a tense half-hour wait, he was waved through customs and flew to Geneva where Elly had been visiting.

Years later, a cabinet minister claimed that Boumediene was incandescent with rage when he learned the chief of the *pieds-rouges* had slipped away.[44] Most of the other *pabliste pieds-rouges* also managed to get away, although some were arrested and roughed up before being expelled. The leaders of the FLN Left, Harbi, Bachir Hadj Ali and Hocine Zahouane, managed only a few months underground before they were caught and imprisoned.

And so the experiment in self-managed socialism effectively ended, in Algeria at any rate, although the regime continued to proclaim itself 'socialist' and even to maintain the façade of self-management. Twenty years later, in his autobiography, Pablo acknowledged that the experiment had been 'premature and did not correspond to the subjective and objective circumstances'– by which he meant the weakness of the left wing of the FLN and the paucity of his own followers, as well as the political consciousness and experience of the Algerian workers themselves. Nevertheless, for him 'the future is foretold by the exemplary exploitation of revolutionary possibilities when they exist and for as long as they exist'. The Algerian Commune had lived and breathed and that very fact was important. Lessons could be drawn by future revolutionaries. One surprise for Pablo was how quickly the bureaucratisation of power had occurred. Nevertheless 'it helped me to understand more deeply the basic phenomenon of the qualitative change in the revolutionary party once it gains state power – regardless of whether it is Marxist or nationalist or populist'. In other words, power corrupts – and very quickly. As he recalled from those Algiers days: 'I saw the animal-like struggles between members of the FLN over who would have the biggest office.'[45]

Mohammed Harbi adds a personal factor to the 'failure' in Algeria. After characteristically paying tribute to Pablo as a human being – 'He wasn't a Greek from Greece but a Greek from Egypt, he was an oriental, spontaneous, warm but also thoughtful and receptive to what you would say to him … In personal relations you could say he was "tops".' However, 'his strengths – his political experience and convictions – were also his weaknesses. It led to a tendency not to hear, yet he really didn't know Algerian society and he misjudged Ben Bella whose real convictions lay elsewhere.'

This may be too harsh a verdict. Pablo did bank on possibilities rather than probabilities. He always made it clear that it was a wager. Any reliance on Ben Bella was not so much a weakness in itself as a reflection of the general weakness of the revolutionaries' position. There was no corps of revolutionary democrats, the FLN Left were weak and the workers and peasants were relatively disorganised or unorganised. Their views were unmistakable when they came together at the occasional conferences, but then they scattered back to their localities. There is no better testimony to all this than from Harbi himself.[46] On the other hand, the army and the administration were organised and concentrated in the centres of power. They were infused with a practical, hard-nosed realism and bolstered by the age-old belief that the division between the governors and governed was natural. Faced with a challenge to their power, they acted decisively. They have evolved, as Pablo anticipated, into a new ruling capitalist class.[47]

The people of Algeria are still shut out of real power. In the late 1980s, and again in the late 2010s, they rose to lay claim to a genuine democracy, so far without success. Rather than be overwhelmed by pessimism at these failures, however, it may well be that in the long view of history, it is entirely possible that the victors of today will be the vanquished of tomorrow and the defeated of today the ultimate victors.

*The Raptis family, probably soon after their arrival in Crete c. 1917. Pablo is bottom right.*

*Pablo as a schoolboy.*

*Pablo as a student with his mother in Athens, 1929.*

*Political prisoners arrive on Folegandros in 1937. Pablo is pictured in the centre of the photograph.*

*Pablo and Elly Diovouniotis in Paris c. 1938.*

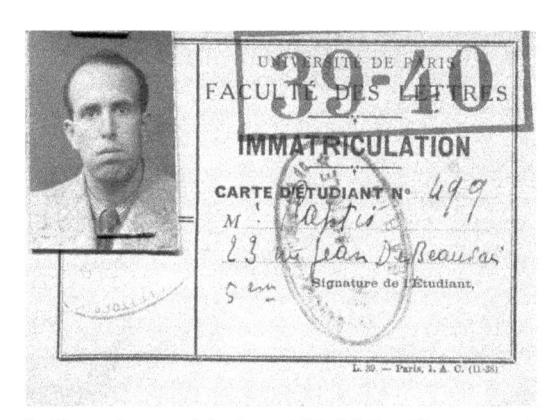

*Pablo on the eve of the Second World War. The wartime Sorbonne student card.*

*Pablo's brother Kletos, with Pablo's parents c.1938.*

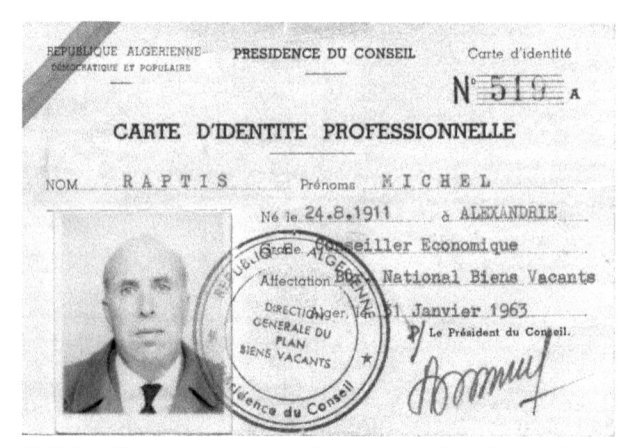

*Pablo's staff card when working for President Ahmed Ben Bella.*

*Pablo with his brother Kletos, probably in Paris in the 1960s.*

*Pablo (left) and Elly (third from left) at dinner with David Rousset, former Trotskyist, survivor of Buchenwald concentration camp and latter Gaullist MP, late 1960s.*

*Otelo de Carvahlo is introduced to the media by Pablo (right), Athens 1990.*

*A Protagoras Circle meeting in Athens in the 1980s. Elly is second from the left in the front row, Pablo fourth from left.*

*Pablo, Marika and Otelo at dinner, Athens 1990*

*Adolfo Gilly (right) and Pablo in Horefto, July 1995.*

CHAPTER 13

# Parallel defeats (and Rosa)
## 1964-1965

*Comrade Pablo totally forgets that the position of our International on the Sino-Soviet conflict had been set at the World Congress ... This position is law for our movement.*

**United Secretariat majority**
29 September 1963

PABLO'S VIRTUAL EXPULSION from Algeria was the first of two that year. He had been living two lives, two struggles: one in Algeria and the other inside the Fourth International based in Paris. Both ended in defeats. By the end of the year, he and his supporters had been expelled or, to use the euphemism of the majority, 'excluded' from the Fourth International for 'indiscipline'. In neither this case, nor the Algerian, did he consider the defeats definitive. The struggle for a libertarian, ultra-democratic, classically Athenian, socialist democracy would continue – as would the attempt to forge an international organisation suitable for the task. He firmly believed that the conditions for such a political and social system were emerging on a much wider scale than at any other time in history.

The differences with the new majority leadership of the International had emerged during the lead-up to the 7th and Reunification World Congresses of the International, in the summer of 1963. Pablo had been in Algeria almost a year by then. The differences persisted through those meetings and into the months that followed. Much of the division boiled down to four or five issues: whether to accord 'critical support' to the Chinese communists in their bitter disputes with the Soviet leadership;

the importance of de-Stalinisation; whether to base a part, at least, of the leadership of the International in Algeria; whether or not to support Holden Roberto and his FNLA or Agostinho Neto and the MPLA in Angola; and whether *Sous le drapeau du socialisme* (*SDS*), the journal published by the African Commission of the International and edited by Pablo, should always strictly toe the line set down by the majority in the International leadership.[1]

But beyond these discrete issues was Pablo's search for the revolution and his readiness to go where he found it. He was still convinced that revolutionary prospects and developments were to be found in the Third World and in the evolution of the Soviet bloc rather than in the advanced capitalist countries where a mood of economic euphoria prevailed and the labour movement was relatively quiescent. He didn't rule out the occasional outbreak of a revolutionary situation in western Europe, but thought it would partly be the result of the impact of the colonial revolution and de-Stalinisation in Eastern Europe.

It followed, then, that his mission was to make the International more international and less centred on western Europe and the United States. The particular disputes that dominated the period 1962-65 in the International were elements in this larger project of rebalancing the focus – that is, 'de-Europeanising' and 'de-North Americanising' the organisation.[2]

What he meant by these awkward neologisms was that some men and women from the north Atlantic bases of the Fourth International should be prepared to go to Africa, Latin America, the Middle East and Asia, where the action was. It was a discomforting demand and led to some unease among those Europeans and Americans. In a private letter, Livio Maitan 'blamed' Pablo for getting involved in disputes between African revolutionaries (apparently the Angolans) that a 'foreigner, especially a white man, should avoid to be mixed in'.[3] This was rather gratuitous advice – as we have seen in the case of the Algerians, Pablo was aware of the sensitivities of 'colonials'. Maitan and his comrades also argued that they could be more help in building solidarity movements in their own countries and offering material and technical aid, from the relative safety and comfort of their capitalist homelands. For Pablo it wasn't either/or. He thought it quite natural for revolutionaries to cross borders and throw themselves into emancipatory struggles wherever they occurred – as citizens, or comrades, of the world.

There was a long revolutionary tradition of men and women doing exactly this. Tom Paine and others in the American and French

Revolutions. Byron (and he was far from being alone as an international volunteer) in the Greek Revolution. Garibaldi in Latin America. Annie Besant in India. Rosa Luxemburg, a Pole, a Jew, and a woman, yet the founder of the revolutionary wing of the German Social Democratic Party. Leo Jogiches, Rosa's long-time companion and also a Pole. Victor Serge, Felix Dzerzhinsky and Karl Radek in the Russian Revolution. Henk Sneevliet (Sal Santen's father-in-law) a founder of the Indonesian national liberation movement. The Armenian Missak Manouchian and the refugees who formed the early heroic detachment of the French Resistance. The men and women who came in their tens of thousands from many continents to defend democratic and revolutionary Spain in the 1930s. Franz Fanon, from Martinique, and many others from France, Greece, The Netherlands and Argentina in the Algerian revolution. And, of course, Che Guevara. For Pablo, this kind of internationalism had its place in the Fourth International, which is why he believed there were openings for real participation in the revolutionary parties of the colonial revolution if the Fourth International invested cadres and resources. Algeria had struck him as a prime candidate.[4]

Algiers, after all, was the refuge and base for almost all the revolutionary anti-imperialist organisations of Africa and even the Middle East and Latin America. Algeria was much more the international school for revolutionaries than Spain ever was.[5] Amilcar Cabral rightly dubbed Algiers 'the Mecca for revolutionaries'. Even before independence, the Algerians were training revolutionaries and guerrillas from other lands – Nelson Mandela, for instance, though it seems he wasn't a great student. While Ben Bella's Algeria was always deferential to Egypt when it came to Arab affairs, it took the lead in training and encouraging the first batch of 200 Fatah fighters from Palestine. The National Liberation Front for South Vietnam, the legendary 'Viet Cong', had a mission in Algiers. Algeria offered not only military training but political debate and education. In other words, Ben Bella's Algeria was for a few short years the melting pot for the colonial revolution. A larger Fourth International presence made sense.

Looking at these disagreements and conflicts, what is striking is how furious the dissidence of Pablo and his supporters made the majority. Rereading Pablo's 'offending' texts – even taking into account that they were made in the public arena – it is hard to credit them as the sole source of the crushing sanctions brought down on him. He was, after all, careful not to publicly criticise the majority. The most obvious conclusion was that the new Western European-American majority was keen to get rid of Pablo altogether. Aside from his ideas, there was a certain hauteur in his manner which did not always endear him to some comrades. When he wrote his own account of his ousting a few years later, he entitled it *Trotsky et ses épigones*. The inferior imitators he had in mind were the new leaders of the Fourth International.

The whole affair serves as a reminder that simmering away inside every political formation is interpersonal drama, often bitter or driven by resentment. It shapes outcomes as much, if not more, than the declared positions and avowed high-minded motives of the participants. In these years Mandel, Maitan and Frank developed a story that they were just trying to restore a collective leadership for the International, something that had been disrupted by the uncontrollable Pablo in the late 1950s. That disruption had not been caused, in this trope, by Pablo's insistence on more committed support for the Algerians, or for combining entrism with independent activity, or by his loyalty to Elly and Sal, but by his outsized ego and inability to work in a team. Mandel had first laid out this theory in 1962 in a letter addressed to all the sections of the International:

> The origin of the break-up of the team, which in fact has led the International during ten years, lies precisely in the ever-increasing difficulty which comrade Pablo manifested to collaborate on equal footing with other cadres of the movement inside a team, [and] lies in his increasing pretention of being the 'natural and legitimate secretary' (Santen dixit) surrounded by faithful executants to which he dictates 'the line'.[6]

Yet, as we will see, in the wake of the 1963 congresses it wasn't Pablo who wouldn't work as a team. He was frozen out of decisions and not consulted over the Sino-Soviet issue. Later, when the criticism was that he was acting unilaterally in Algeria, he suggested he work with a team from the majority leadership posted to Algiers. That suggestion was rebuffed. When it came to organising the next world congress, Pablo and the minority's requests that they be involved in its preparation were ignored.

In the same letter, Mandel laid out the case for a collective leadership:

> In the extremely complex and constantly changing international situation in which we live today, we would court disaster if we were to abandon the leadership of the International to a single 'thinker', surrounded by a few 'dynamic' elements, satisfied with executing his orders. The only political leadership possible for the International, which limits to the utmost the risk of grave political errors, is a leadership composed by a team of leading comrades from the main centres, who dispose of the necessary political maturity, experience and knowledge to correct their mutual mistakes. Only the *praxis*

## 13 . PARALLEL DEFEATS (AND ROSA) 1964-65

of thirty, forty Trotskyist organisations all over the world, albeit small ones, enables us today to embrace really the evolution of the world situation.

This is a nicely put case for collective, democratic leadership. In the abstract it is difficult to object to. But the reality of 1963-65 didn't appear to reflect these lofty aims. Was the majority taking account of all 'the political maturity, experience and knowledge' available to correct 'mutual mistakes', like the 'critical support' for the Chinese Stalinists in the Sino-Soviet conflict? Even if the majority found it impossible to share Pablo's enthusiastic analysis of de-Stalinisation in the Soviet bloc, wasn't the position he and his supporters advocated at the world congress – of keeping an equal distance from both sides in the Sino-Soviet dispute – the better option? On the Angolan issue, the question is even sharper. Pablo in Algiers was much closer to African revolutionary politics and better informed than the men in Paris, and yet his 'political maturity, experience and knowledge' counted for nothing.

Were Mandel and his majority comrades really interested in building a 'team', or rather a faction intent on freezing out Pablo and his 'dynamic executants'? It is difficult to avoid the second conclusion. (Equally, as Mandel did point out, Pablo might have been saved from his overestimation of the economic prospects of the USSR compared to the United States if there had been a team of comrades working on the analysis.[7])

Two years later, Mandel would tweak the criticism to say that Pablo's sin was to reject 'the team' or the 'collective leadership': '… he has in fact ceased to consider the cadres assembled in the Fourth International as essentially the forces necessary to insure the triumph of revolutionary Marxism in the world workers' movement …'[8] This faith, in so far as Pablo ever had it, had been fatally undermined by the response to the arrest and jailing of himself and Santen. This breakdown in trust is illustrated in the response of Pablo-supporter Maurice Ferares to Pierre Frank's call for him and the Dutch comrades to respect the majority line. Ferares recalled the recent past: 'During the years that we organised the defence of comrades Michel and Sal, Holland was terra incognito for you. You weren't even capable of extending the most elementary proletarian solidarity …'[9]

Nothing had happened since to restore any affection or respect Pablo (and his partisans) might have for the majority leaders and their followers. Pablo was by then emphasising that the Fourth International was one ideological current, even the most important, but that the mass revolutionary International of tomorrow would involve other currents, and this International would need a different framework. He scandalised some of the majority at the world congress by declaring that he refused to make a fetish out of the Fourth International.[10] But even so, he did not leave it. Instead, he was excluded, or to use the bizarre formula preferred by his opponents, he 'excluded himself'.[11]

The other unsurprising feature of the conflict was the extent to which the contenders talked past each other. Pablo did acknowledge the favour the Chinese had performed for international communist movements in raising the necessity of armed struggle and revolutionary strategy in the struggle for power, but for Pablo the principal problem for revolutionaries was bureaucracy. Bureaucratic dictatorship, or the emergence of a new ruling caste or class, had plagued 20th century revolutions. Understanding and combatting the causes of this deformation – which resulted in 'socialist' societies in stark contradiction to what classical Marxists considered socialism to be – was the major challenge to revolutionaries as far as Pablo was concerned. He was up to his neck in grappling with this problem and challenge in his day-to-day activity in Algeria. He left the 1963 world congress three days before it finished because of the pressure of work in Algiers. Little wonder he tended to see all issues through this lens.

For Pablo, the key criterion in judging workers states was the extent to which the power of these bureaucratic dictatorships had been eroded. In the Soviet case economic, social and cultural development had forced the Khrushchev wing to expose Stalin and his crimes and to make concessions which opened the way for the working class and the intelligentsia to become politically active. The spread of the colonial revolution had also liberated it from the timidity of the Stalin years when Moscow had curbed or betrayed revolutions that threatened its diplomatic interests and safety. Its defence of revolutionary Cuba, on Washington's very doorstep, was proof of this. In the Chinese case, the very economic backwardness of the country was the condition that explained the overweaning power of that bureaucracy and its attachment to Stalin and Stalinism.[12] Any Khrushchev-like liberalisation would be a mortal danger to them.

This was the time of the 'thaw' in the Soviet Union. The gulags had been emptied of political prisoners, Stalin and his crimes condemned, and censorship relaxed to the extent that Solzhenitsyn's *One Day in the Life of Ivan Denisovich*, about life in Stalin's gulag, was published. Battles between liberal and conservative factions in the ruling parties were a feature of these years in the Soviet bloc. The process would culminate in the emergence of Dubcek in Czechoslovakia and the Prague Spring in 1968 with its aim of 'socialism with a human face'. For Pablo, intra-

## 13 . PARALLEL DEFEATS (AND ROSA) 1964-65

bureaucratic conflicts and the easing of the police regimes that was taking place would 'ineluctably' open the way for the working class to become politically active and lead to the overthrow of the bureaucratic regimes. That process had begun and it was also having an impact on the mass communist parties in Italy and France. Rather than trying for coalitions and unity with pro-Chinese communists (which was the majority's aim), Pablo argued it would be better to intervene and support the de-Stalinisation process in the pro-Moscow parties, some of whom at least were adopting more Marxist positions on armed struggle and the problems of bureaucracy and democracy.

As we know, the de-Stalinisation champions proved to be weaker than Pablo anticipated. Khrushchev was deposed as First Secretary of the Communist Party in October 1964 and the Soviet Union, and its satellite states, stagnated and suffered under the conservative wing of the bureaucracy for the next 20 years. The highpoint in de-Stalinisation, the Prague Spring in Czechoslovakia, was snuffed out by a Soviet-led invasion. By 1965 Pablo admitted overestimating the strength of the pressures for de-Stalinisation and the retreat of the bureaucracy. Marxism, after all, was not a failsafe method of analysis and divining the future. All the great Marxist thinkers had made mistakes. The point was to acknowledge errors as quickly as possible and readjust. But admitting an overestimation of the pace and strength of de-Stalinisation, or the colonial revolution, was not a denial of their relative revolutionary importance vis-à-vis the advanced capitalist countries.[13]

— + —

When the 7th World Congress of the Fourth International met in that summer of 1963, it agreed unanimously to heal the split with the American Socialist Workers Party. It adjourned and reconvened as a Reunification Congress, with the participation of the SWP delegates. In the elections and other policy votes at these congresses, Pablo and his supporters were very much in the minority. The only *pabliste* victory was the belated acceptance that wherever entrism was being practised, there needed to be a 100 per cent Trotskyist group publishing a journal and recruiting, particularly among the youth and dissident communists.

Much was made of this minority status at the time and later. Pablo had the support of only 15 per cent of delegates to the 7th Congress and an even smaller percentage at the Reunification Congress after the Americans were added. The leaders of this new majority would continually emphasise what a small group the *pablistes* were. Of course, that raised the question of why, if that were the case, so much energy was devoted to marginalising and attacking them. The answer is partly that the actual voting strength underestimated Pablo's support; for instance, the French section, still the major group in Europe, was at least evenly divided between Pablo and majority supporters right up until 1965. Still, he had resigned himself to this minority position for some time and the congress result came as no surprise. Even before the congresses, the desertion of Posadas and the Latin Americans had left the Mandel trio in charge and in his view, they had not scrupled to use that position to strengthen their control.[14] In the United Secretariat, the day-to-day leadership newly elected at the 1963 congresses, he and Sal Santen, and later he and Gilbert Marquis, were outnumbered by ten supporters of the new majority. In the larger International Executive Committee which met irregularly, Pablo's support amounted to four or five out of 20 or more delegates.

How this would play out very soon became clear. Three weeks after the congress ended, the United Secretariat majority issued a public statement on 'The new rift in the Sino-Soviet Conflict' but without showing the text beforehand to either Pablo or Sal Santen, the minority members. Next they published an issue of *Quatrième Internationale* containing the congress documents: 67 pages were devoted to the majority's and just 5 to the minority. In September Pablo submitted an article for publication on the Sino-Soviet conflict entitled 'It's time to see clearly now' which was rejected. In October, the majority issued a statement on the Nuclear Test Ban Treaty, criticising it as aimed against China and its acquisition of atomic weapons. In each of these cases Pablo protested about not being consulted. The majority repeated that they were now the majority, policy had been decided by the congress in July and the 'No.1 necessity' was to bed down the unification, which meant not stirring up debates about 'critical support for the Chinese' and de-Stalinisation. They spelled out this position in a 5,000-word response to Pablo's rejected article and protest letter of 8 October circulated to all the sections.[15]

Brushed aside was Pablo's argument that the Bolshevik party under Lenin had allowed the public airing of different points of view on important questions, presumably on the grounds that the working class, of which the Bolsheviks were the self-proclaimed vanguard, had every right to know what those leaders were thinking. That kind of free discussion was all the more vital, in Pablo's view, because the 'critical support for the Chinese' had not been fully canvassed before the congresses and was, in his view, a growing embarrassment.[16]

By December, in the face of more strident defences of Stalin coming out of China and highlighted by Pablo, some sections – notably the Australian and the French – called for renewed discussion on the Sino-Soviet issue and the International's position. Pablo, however, was not willing to wait for the doubtful green light from the majority. It was not in his nature to accept a rebuff on as vital a question for Marxists as the Sino-Soviet dispute – and he didn't. Instead, he found a way not to be silenced.

A highlight of the 7th congress, according to Livio Maitan, had been Pablo's report on progress in Algeria. As a result, the congress had authorised an African Commission to coordinate the International's activities on that continent. It was convened by Pablo, and its members were his supporters in Algiers – this composition was not surprising since these were the Fourth Internationalists working in this sphere. (Later the majority would make much of the absence of Africans on this body. In fact, it was the 7th congress who had authorised its composition.) In January 1964, the African Commission published the first issue of *Sous le drapeau du socialisme* (*SDS*). It carried a mildly heretical article on the Sino-Soviet conflict.

It was not strictly forbidden for sections or bureaux of the International to publish their own journals or newsletters. Indeed, it was common, even obligatory. The trouble with *SDS* was that kicked off with that article – 'China, the USSR and the Colonial revolution' – which didn't reflect the majority's position of critical support for the Chinese. It didn't explicitly cite or oppose the International's policy and Pablo set out his analysis in a mild, even bloodless, manner. It was calm and straightforward. Like the majority, Pablo endorsed the Chinese criticisms of the Soviet Union in its policy towards the colonial revolution, but noted the gap between the Chinese rhetoric and its actual foreign policy. The origins of both sides' shortcomings lay in the fact that each was ruled by a bureaucracy that pursued its own opportunistic interests. Only by acknowledging and tackling this bureaucratisation that followed the revolutions – which had taken an extreme form under Stalin – could genuine Chinese and Soviet communists understand and correct their current positions. The Chinese leaders had, however, set themselves against any de-Stalinisation and actually celebrated, as well as defended, Stalin. Only the Yugoslavs – despite all their own limitations – had broached this question of the emergence of bureaucratic dictatorships in economically undeveloped countries.

The article, mild as it was, caused a furore. The reaction of the majority on the United Secretariat was immediate and brutal – it issued a public repudiation of *Sous le drapeau du socialisme* and disowned it.[17] To make matters worse, in the same issue of *Quatrième Internationale* that carried the disavowal, there was a note about the revolution in Angola, *Sur la Révolution Angolaise*, which called for support for the FNLA led by Holden Roberto and wrote off the MPLA (Movimento Popular de Libertação de Angola).

It flew in the face of Pablo's position on Angola. Pablo had already written on the Angolan independence struggle, as early as February 1962 – in the very same journal, *Quatrième Internationale*.[18] A rising in the capital, Luanda, in February the previous year had involved an attack on the main Portuguese military barracks and the city jails in an attempt to release jailed nationalists It had been beaten back and in the reprisals that followed, thousands of Angolans were killed. The uprisings, however, had spread to the countryside. In the north, on the border with the Congo, there was already an armed resistance to the Portuguese. The independence movement was divided between the MPLA, which led the Luanda uprising, and the FNLA of Holden Roberto, which was responsible for the northern revolt.

The MPLA was definitely the more cosmopolitan of the two, encompassing indigenous Angolans, 'assimilados' and even Portuguese. In that 1962 article, after sketching out the history of Angola, the nature of Portuguese colonialism and the evolution of nationalist politics, Pablo noted there was little or no difference in the platforms of the two contending nationalist parties. In their favour, the MPLA had proposed a united front, which had been rebuffed by Holden Roberto. However, the final judgment on the rivals would be determined by which of the movements deepened their program to include social liberation and the attitude each of them took to Washington, which was consolidating its power and role in southern Africa.

With some prescience, Pablo anticipated that the struggle in Angola would face particular geo-political obstacles. The country shared borders with South Africa and Rhodesia whose white regimes, along with the Americans, would intervene to prevent any dangerous revolutionary victory nearby. (This is what happened.) It was why Pablo emphasised the vital importance of spreading the struggle south of Angola, and cementing alliances with the liberation movements in South Africa and Rhodesia/Zimbabwe. The revolutionary panorama he sketched out also predicted that the Angolan struggle would hasten the end of the fascist regime in Lisbon. (This, too, occurred.)

Typically, he called for the formation of solidarity committees in Europe. Once he was established in Algiers and met the MPLA leaders and Portuguese exiles, his implicit support for the MPLA evolved into full solidarity, although he continued to call for a united front of the two organisations. Holden Roberto was becoming an increasingly dubious figure. During 1964-65, Roberto's close links with the Congolese dictatorship in Leopoldville (now Kinshasa) and the Americans became clearer. Credible reports circulated that Congolese and FNLA troops, strongly entrenched along the northern Angolan border, ambushed and hindered MPLA fighters attempting to cross into Angola. In addition, the MPLA became stronger inside Angola itself and widely recognised in Africa, and by the Portuguese Left, as the more anti-imperialist and effective of the two organisations.[19]

Nevertheless, the majority ignored Pablo's counsel and continued to support Holden Roberto's FNLA as 'the principal force struggling in Angola'.[20] It was probably not irrelevant that the Chinese supported the FNLA while the MPLA had the support of Moscow. The majority's stand, and their insistence that Pablo embrace it as a matter of discipline, infuriated him. He saw it as purely factional and wilful 'European' ignorance that helped to discredit the Fourth International and make it irrelevant among Africans fighting for national and social liberation. It confirmed what he saw as their refusal to become involved in the 'African revolution', which had been demonstrated by the rejection of the proposal to base at least part of the United Secretariat in Algiers, then the headquarters of most African liberation movements:

> I had said to them on several occasions: "The heart of the anti-colonial revolution, at least in Africa and for larger regions, even in relation to Latin America, is to be found in Algiers. We must send a delegation of the Unified Secretariat to Algiers, not all of the United Secretariat, but there should be a very important level [there], because here, in Algiers, very important things are happening … Come here." But they were against it, and it was for little factional reasons: "What are we going to do there? He's the one who has the prestige … "[21]

Mandel actually wrote that Pablo's criticism of the Chinese and sympathy for the Khrushchev faction in Moscow 'stands in the way of working with the left currents of the colonial countries, since these currents are generally pro-Chinese'.[22] They weren't. If there had been a serious attempt at a collective leadership that lived up to Mandel's claims (which surely included incorporating Pablo's views), this could have put Mandel and the majority cadres right about Angola and elsewhere in Africa.

With the differences over support for China and Holden Roberto now out in the open, the majority demanded that Pablo stop publishing articles at odds with the majority party line. Pablo stood his ground. *SDS* kept on appearing each month as regular as clockwork and, while news and analysis of developments in Africa predominated in its columns, more general articles continued to include analysis of what was happening in the Sino-Soviet dispute. The journal quoted recent analyses of Isaac Deutscher, Paul Baran and Georg Lukacs – all highly respected Marxists – in support of its position.[23]

The situation grew more heated. In May the International Executive Committee met to consider the suspension of Pablo and Marquis from the United Secretariat and the fatwah against *Sous le drapeau du socialisme*. Pablo mounted a spirited defence, but without giving an inch on his estimation of the possibilities that would flow from actual participation in the colonial revolution and de-Stalinisation, if only the majority would forsake its 'conservatism', 'sectarianism', and 'routinism'. Without false modesty, he reminded them of all the times he had to shake them out of their rigid conservatism in the past. He recalled how the Americans, now part of the majority, had refused to face the new realities of the post-war world. He confronted the majority with their choices. Did they want to stagnate forever in boutique organisations with 50-100 members or did they want to actually get involved in the genuinely emancipatory flow of history? Did they want to waste their time running after neo-Stalinist, pro-Chinese communists, or make contact with the communists now rethinking their whole Stalinist past? These were the pressing questions he posed. The dead, dogmatic past, or the living historical moment as grasped by genuine revolutionary Marxism? If the latter, then they should lift the sanctions against him and his comrades and reinforce the work being done in Algeria, as well as make contact with the best elements in the communist parties. He also challenged, again, the majority's stubborn grip on the idea of imminent socialist revolution in advanced capitalist countries. Not only was this exclusive focus misplaced in the current historical circumstances, it was a failure to understand the evolution of capitalism and the new needs and aspirations of the modern working class. All in all, it was an address that gave no quarter. It demanded full freedom for Pablo and his comrades to pursue their goals. It urged the majority to abandon their short-sighted and repressive approach in favour of collaboration and working out a modus vivendi.[24]

It fell on deaf ears. Perhaps there was already too much bitterness in the air for it to have had the smallest chance of swaying his opponents.

Instead, the majority of the International Executive Committee suspended Pablo, Marquis, Minguet, Michel Fiant and the Australian Denis Freney from their positions on the United Secretariat and the IEC itself. The old African Commission was dissolved and a new one appointed. (The make-up of the IEC majority at this session was the epitome of what Pablo was seeking to change: 3 Belgians, 3 Italians, 4 Americans, 1 Canadian, 1 Austrian, 1 French and 1 Chinese.) It was a complete repudiation of the *pablistes*. Clearly there was no appetite for compromise. The new membership of the African Commission was three majority comrades and two minority (including Pablo). The chair and controlling vote was Livio Maitan who planned to steer the new African Commission remotely from Europe. His first communication to Pablo was to ask for the proofs of the next issue of *SDS* to be posted to him in Rome.

In the months that followed, Pablo tried again to get through the resistance. He offered various proposals for a modus vivendi that would allow him and his supporters some freedom while observing the majority's stricter version of democratic centralism.[25] For the latter, however, it was an open-and-shut case: the majority had decided where the International stood on supporting the Chinese and Holden Roberto, and the minority was required to toe the line. Anything else was flagrant indiscipline.[26] Pablo's response was that the situation in the international Left was fluid and debates were raging. This was not the time for the International to become monolithic and to shut down or hide debate. Everything should be on the table and the next world congress brought forward to the summer of 1965. For those who reminded him of his own insistence on strict democratic centralism in 1952, his answer was that the context was very different. Besides, the statutes did authorise 'a free international discussion ... each time that historic events of exceptional importance required special discussions'.[27]

By now, clearly, he had begun to prefigure a different model of the revolutionary organisation. Members, being critical thinkers, should have the ultimate right to refuse to embrace policies that conflicted with deeply held convictions, without endangering their membership. As he explained to Gilly[28]:

> This is different from organisations in perpetual discussion, without serious discipline. That I am absolutely against ... when a matter is not of paramount importance, even if you consider that the decision made by others is wrong, you follow it. But when the question is very important, you say to them: "Comrades, give me the opportunity to say, and this will not lead to a catastrophe, that I do not agree with what you have decided".

Unbowed by his suspension, he pursued this position, which he claimed allowed dissidents 'to keep their revolutionary dignity', in the debates that raged around China, Angola, the location of the International and the right to publish *SDS*. While this critical view of Mao's China did not translate into critical support for the Soviet Union in the Sino-Soviet conflict, Pablo had some sympathy for Khrushchev's faction in their battles with more conservative factions in the Kremlin, because of their de-Stalinisation efforts.[29] The coup that removed Khrushchev in October 1964 was for him a setback for the political and social revolution that Khrushchev, for all his personal idiosyncrasies and limitations, was opening the way to. Even so, he expected the de-Stalinisation process to continue. It was another overestimation of the revolution's prospects.

— ✦ —

Pablo and his chief supporters remained suspended through 1964 and into 1965. In the March 1965 issue of *Quatrième Internationale*, Pierre Frank attacked Pablo and his supporters as 'rightists' and virtually uncritical allies of Khrushchev and Tito. In the next issue, the majority announced that Pablo had put himself outside the International by refusing to observe their discipline. His supporters, it was announced, could save themselves by disavowing their leader and submitting to the majority.[30] None did. It was only now, in the May 1965 edition of *SDS*, that Pablo went public with his criticism of the majority. The reaction was swift. In July, the International Executive Committee ruled that all supporters of the Pablo current had put themselves outside the International. It was expulsion without actually being expelled.

Pablo reacted with increasing anger at what he considered political blindness and organisational bullying. He penned and published a furious broadside to the majority after his exclusion. Under the heading *A necessary response*, he branded as a lie the public announcement that he had 'broken' with the International when in fact he had been administratively or organisationally excluded.[31] He then proceeded to lay out his disagreements with the policies and behaviour of the majority. He promised an extended critique of 'the systematically refractory attitude they share towards, in a word, every new revolutionary fact', and of 'the hardened defenders in their ranks ... of a dead and futureless past'. He singled out the Socialist Workers Party of the United States for particularly savage criticism for its 'legalistic' tactics in opposing 'the dirty war' in Vietnam (by which he meant the absence of any calls to

## 13 . PARALLEL DEFEATS (AND ROSA) 1964-65

industrial action in support of the Vietnamese or for fraternisation with the Vietnamese partisans) and for their attempt to bundle Malcolm X and the black power advocates into the white-led American workers movement, and thus diminish the black rights movement. He threw in a scornful reference to the American Trotskyists sending their condolences to the family of President Kennedy after his assassination.

Coexistence within a single organisation was clearly all over. When the Fourth International held its 8th World Congress at the end of 1965, some delegates from Pablo-supporting sections – such as the Australian Denis Freney – were barred from entry. A few others were admitted and protested the bans and suspensions, but to no avail. By then Pablo and his comrades were operating as a separate organisation outside the International. They held their first international conference in the month after the mother organisation's 8th World Congress.

Still, every cloud has a silver lining. Pablo would later claim that his ousting from the International restored his theoretical and practical freedom.[32] He had always been something of a heretic, he claimed, but his organisational responsibilities and need to be sensitive to the sensibilities of more conservative colleagues had curbed his own thinking and writing. Beyond the immediate issues in dispute, Pablo was developing ideas on self-managed socialism, the transitional economy and the concept of the revolutionary party that were in advance of – or if you prefer, different from – those of the International's majority. These ideas certainly put him at odds with Mandel, then the chief theoretician of the majority.

Despite this new freedom, he never took his eyes off what was happening inside the International, which splintered again in the 1970s. Right down to the 50th anniversary, in 1988, of the founding of the Fourth International, he wrote lengthy accounts of the issues involved in his exclusion and the subsequent development of the International.[33] The name adopted by his political current after their exclusion – *Tendance marxiste révolutionnaire de la Quatrième Internationale* – retained that link to the old body for the next seven years before belatedly dropping it. Nevertheless, he had clearly been realising, even before the break, that the Fourth International would not be the framework for the coalescing of the world's revolutionaries, whatever the pretensions of the trio-SWP leadership.[34] The majority's official divorce from the International's historic leader and his supporters had been preceded by a 'spiritual separation' on his part. And now he was a free man.

While Pablo seriously doubted revolution was imminent in Europe and the US, he still kept a watchful eye the engine room of global capitalism. As a man schooled in classical Marxism, with its emphasis on the central importance of the European socialist revolution, he could do no other, whatever the immediate prospects might be. In the summer 1964 issue of *Sous le drapeau du socialisme*, he published a long and favourable review of André Gorz's *Workers Strategy and Neo-capitalism*. The review certainly upset Ernest Mandel who described it as 'dithyrambic' and dismissed Gorz's ideas as unoriginal and no better than neo-reformism.[35] This was less than generous and far from accurate.

Gorz acknowledged that the continued development and prosperity of European capitalism demanded a new strategy from socialists and communists. He proposed that the labour movement focus on the quality of work and life in the new capitalism, and aim for the expansion of democracy and collective solutions rather than individualised and consumerist ones. He advocated the development of 'workers power' in the workplace and the economy. Through democratic organisation, workers could intervene in the organisation of work, decisions over what to produce and the kind of society they wanted to live in. In that way, via structural changes, the alternative to neo-capitalism would take shape. Gorz's approach was to gain a sympathetic hearing in radical and revolutionary circles in the years to come. Pablo's aim in the review was to endorse and popularise the value of it, while mentioning, but not overemphasising, his differences with the approach. Gorz did appear to be arguing for the progressive emergence of the new society within the body of the old. Pablo, on the other hand, thought it could only emerge in conditions of an active mass movement demanding a government of labour/socialist/communist parties.

The last word on the value of Gorz's work remains to be said. In the years that followed, Gorz became an early advocate of ecological issues and the value of utopian thinking. What catches the eye of a reader of the review today is Gorz's prediction of the alternative future if the labour movement didn't adopt his approach and continued to put the emphasis on wage demands. Concentrating only on the price of labour, Gorz writes,

> ... will allow industry (in a process we can call Americanisation) to manufacture a new mass of lobotomised proletarians among whom eight hours of daily brutalisation and work against the clock leads to a desire for an escape, which the marketeers and manipulators of leisure and culture will sell to them, on credit if necessary, persuading them in the process that they live in the best of all possible worlds.

The other noteworthy aspect of the review is Pablo's plea for more theoretical analysis of modern capitalism. He was still moving away from the congenital expectation of stagnation in the developed capitalist countries. In doing so, he laid particular emphasis on the expansion of the world market as the key to the continuing capitalist boom. The figures for this speak for themselves. As the *Financial Times*, for instance, reported in 1993: 'Over the whole period between 1950 and 1991, the volume of total world exports grew twelve times, the world output grew six times. More startling still, the world volume of manufactures [exports] rose twenty-three times ... while [manufacturing] output grew eight times'.[36]

Pablo didn't ignore the role of state intervention, arms spending, and the scientific revolution and its impact on production, but in emphasising the expansion of the market and the new regions of private capital accumulation, he acknowledged Rosa Luxemburg's pioneering work. 'I am constantly astonished,' he wrote in 1962, 'by the reserved reception which the fundamental work of Rosa Luxemburg on "the accumulation of capital" has found in Marxist circles.' He went on to dismiss the criticism of this work by Otto Bauer and Nikolaï Bukharin. 'In my opinion any serious study of the contemporary evolution of capitalism must take comprehensive account of the analysis of Rosa Luxemburg ...'[37]

This championing of Rosa Luxemburg was longstanding. He had cited her conception of the Marxist method as shaping his own in his first serious writing for the International. In 1970 he was to return to the subject of Rosa with an essay on her and Trotsky.[38] In that essay he argued she was the equal of Lenin and of Trotsky with whom she shared many things, including a fierce commitment to artistic freedom, the scope of the Marxist method and a talent for great writing. In one vital respect she was superior to both: 'Of all the great Marxists it fell to this exceptional woman – whom Franz Mehring in 1907 deemed the "most brilliant mind" among the heirs of Marx and Engels – to defend most consistently not only the correct democratic conception of the party in its dialectical relationship with the class, but also that of proletarian and socialist democracy in general.' For Pablo this was no small distinction. Her warnings about 'substitutionism' and bureaucratic dictatorship were sadly prescient in the Russian case.

As for Gorz, he certainly appreciated the review. He wrote to Pablo, 'Thank you for the outline you published of *Workers strategy* ... the best which has appeared, in my opinion, because you have generously given the right interpretation (meaning *revolutionary*) of the numerous passages and aspects of the book.'[39] The connection with Gorz confirmed

Pablo's belief that his elimination from the leadership of the International restored his intellectual freedom. The review also indicated he was still wrestling with the revolutionary strategy appropriate to the flourishing new capitalism. Expelled to Europe after the Boumediene coup, he could not escape thinking about these problems now he was back in the capitalist heartland.

CHAPTER 14

# 'The Gypsy Years' 1965-1968

PABLO RECALLED THE decade after the fall of Ben Bella as his gypsy years. Denied permission to permanently settle anywhere, he and Elly moved frequently. Later Pablo was to rejoice in this transient lifestyle:

> … in all of Europe I remained a wandering foreigner, moving every few months, a fact that did not at all annoy me, on the contrary, I consider that this exercise contributed to my retaining psychological and physical good health.[1]

He was much on the move and not just in Europe. He made visits to the Middle East and Latin America as well. It meant he witnessed many of the great moments in the revolutionary history of the era. He was on the spot in Paris for May 1968, in Jordan for the rise of the Palestinian resistance, in Chile at the time of Allende, in Portugal for the 'carnation revolution' and finally back in Greece after the sudden fall of the junta of the colonels. And he saw too, the emergence of the mass women's liberation movement that he had anticipated in the late 1950s. The Algerian door had closed, but others opened.

In the decade famous as 'the Sixties', the wave of radicalisation that swept across developed capitalist countries, buoyed up the young, racial minorities and women in particular, and, in some European countries, the working class. The tumultuous times made Pablo even more convinced of the centrality of *autogestion* – of self-management as the central and common aspiration of the working class, blue- and white-collar, of the 'wretched of the earth', of women and the young, of citizens of the East and the West. (In these years he was to translate *autogestion*' exclusively as 'self-management' but in later years he was to alternate between 'direct democracy' and 'self-management'. By either term he meant decisions being taken by the people involved in any activity or institution. His model, as we've seen, was the Athens of 4th and 5th century BCE.)

The first stop for Pablo and Elly in this peripatetic decade was Switzerland. The Swiss authorities did not exactly welcome them, however. They were warned their stay was conditional on no political activity. When they sought, for economy reasons, to move from their hotel to an apartment, the police denied them permission. They were told that they needed a residence visa to move and they were not going to be issued with one. Pablo persisted and the police agreed to look the other way, but warned him that if the immigration service discovered they had taken an apartment, they would be expelled. The immigration officials duly arrived after 12 months and served them notice to quit Switzerland. 'But such are the advantages of a democratic country like Switzerland that I engaged a lawyer and appealed against the expulsion and won a six-months extension,' Pablo recalled. 'However, the appeal was then rejected.'

Switzerland wasn't an ideal home anyhow. The bulk of his supporters lived in France. In the next two decades they numbered, at most, roughly 300. They strived to play a role in the life of the Left with the aim of assembling, by various combinations, a larger force committed to self-managed socialism. With their collaboration, Pablo continued to publish *Sous le drapeau du socialisme* (and its successor) for the next 25 years.

In the mid-1960s the problem for Pablo was how to regularly meet these supporters in Paris, given he had no rights of entry into France because of his Algerian activities. Once again an old friend came to the rescue, allowing him to travel to and from France without drawing the attention of the police. As he told Gilly:

> I have an old friend, an anar [anarchist] whom I love dearly, who is truly a perfect anar, who was completely on side. I knew him from the time of the Algerian war. He's a Swiss, and he knows all the ways to get people in and out, and he worked, including during the war, to smuggle people to safety, including Jews. A perfect type, and of extraordinary loyalty; that is to say, he was a man I could call at any time of the day or night, at two or three in the morning, say to him, "André, here I am, I need help" and he would come. So thanks to this man, I entered and left France as I wanted, despite being persona non grata …

This was almost certainly André Bösiger, a legendary Swiss anarcho-syndicalist.

However, with continued residence in Switzerland ruled out, the need for a convenient place of residence arose once more. That problem, too, was solved by an old friend, David Rousset, the Trotskyist comrade from the 1940s and survivor of Buchenwald, who in Pablo's view wrote 'the best account of life in the camps in world literature'. Rousset was now a Gaullist MP, and he and Pablo remained friends if not comrades. Rousset approached Christian Fouchet, one of de Gaulle's ministers – and possibly de Gaulle himself – and secured agreement that Pablo could stay in France on the understanding that he would never be given rights of residence and could thus be expelled without any legal impediments.[2]

Before that arrangement came to pass, Pablo did manage to attend the first international conference of the *pabliste* Tendency, in November 1965 in Paris. This conference adopted *Marxism and Our Time*[3], the platform he drafted whose aim was to set the political bearings for the small cohort of *pablistes* in a handful of countries. It embodied many of the themes that Pablo had already enunciated over the past decade. It acknowledged the long and accelerating boom in the advanced capitalist countries and set out the reasons. There would be occasional recessions and political crises in these countries but there would be no repeat of the Great Depression. The interwar assumption that capitalism was a decaying system was no longer the case. He argued that the technological and scientific revolution had so super-charged the productive forces in the world that a society of egalitarian comfort and freedom was now possible – if the social and political structure of the world could be changed and democratised, if there was international planning and if (a big if at the time) nuclear war could be avoided. Just as there were 'fetters' on egalitarian economic growth in the West, so there were in the East. Both needed a revolution based on *autogestion*, sweeping away the current ruling class and power structure.

The working class remained the essential revolutionary class in both the first and second worlds, and he repeated the 'Gorz thesis' that the long boom was creating new needs and aspirations among workers and citizens that neo-capitalism could not satisfy. In the Third World it was the poor and landless peasantry who were the revolutionary force. Pablo did not resile from his belief that the strongest revolutionary prospects remained in the Third World, particularly in Latin America. The social conditions there were as grim and explosive as they had been in 19th-century capitalist countries. (During 1966 a note of pessimism about revolutionary progress in the Third World would be struck in the light of the Indonesian massacres in particular.) Developments in each of these three sectors, or 'worlds', had an impact on the others. For instance, the process of de-Stalinisation, which he considered 'irreversible' even if 'not rectilinear and automatic', by redeeming the image of socialism, would reduce the understandable distaste among much of the working class and intellectuals in the West for 'communism'.

*Marxism and Our Time* also carried a section on the transitional, post-revolutionary economy, which remained a preoccupation for Pablo. In the case of economically backward countries aiming to transition to socialism, he never tired of advocating a version of New Economic Policy that Lenin had inaugurated in the Soviet Union in the 1920s. He warned that the nationalisation of everything in the economy was a political and economic error and only laid the basis for a new bureaucratic ruling class. It was enough to nationalise the key sectors, provided they were managed by their workers, the whole economy was democratically planned and political power was in the hands of the producers. That would check any tendencies towards capitalist restoration, as well as ensuring maximum growth. An essential part of this transitional economy was 'material incentives', which of course pitted him against such 'pure' Marxists as Mandel and Guevara. In other words, it was unrealistic to expect workers to work only for the glory. Probably the best justification of his position was written at this time:

> It is pure bureaucratic idealism to believe that you can make the masses work productively for a whole historic period by making an appeal exclusively or principally to 'ideological motivations' and not to 'material stimulants'. As it is a pure illusion, intrinsic to a bureaucratic interest and mentality, to believe that you can 'plan' by administratively 'suppressing' the 'laws of economics', the survival of the commodity market and money during the period of transition. All those who have experimented with such methods: Russians, Yugoslavs, Cubans etc have had to recognise their failure directly or indirectly. The Chinese will inevitably be obliged to do as much in the not too distant future. The 'materialist' corruption doesn't flow from 'material stimulants' recompensing the real work furnished by the workers organised in their self-managed units, but from the exorbitant nature of the bureaucracy's privileges, enjoyed without any relation to productive work.[4]

*Marxism and Our Time* accepted the 'irreversible integration' of the European economy via the Common Market or EU. In so far as it lifted productivity, it was laying the basis for a socialist Europe. Of course its political control by corporate interests had to be contested and the labour movement organise itself on a pan-European level. This would lay the basis for political contagion. Struggles and campaigns that began in one place, or region or country, could cross borders and fire up advances at the European level.

One Bolshevik article of faith that could not be discarded was the need for a world party of revolutionaries, although its mission would be to aid and ensure the transfer of power to citizens everywhere and not to appropriate power for its own ends. In other words, to expand democracy, not suppress it. Pablo still thought that the Fourth International could play the role of catalyst for this world party if it could slough off its conservatism, sectarianism and dogmatism.

— + —

In view of the events of 1965, the wandering revolutionary had to face up to the trifecta of setbacks, occurring almost simultaneously – Khrushchev's fall in the Soviet Union,[5] the coup in Algeria, and 'exclusion' from the Fourth International. At the beginning of that year, he had declared the 'international situation … the most revolutionary in the history of humanity'.[6] How was he now to explain what was turning out to be annus horribilis? Pablo sought to understand the less than encouraging evolution with a mixture of stubbornness, optimism (and its close cousin, delusion), and new thinking.

As he put it, 'battles were lost but by no means the inevitable final victory'. He continued to think that the cultural and economic development of the Soviet Union, and the end of its isolation, would lead to a lesser Stalinism that ruled as much by concessions as repression. This new period would be marked by division and conflict within the high bureaucracy, and this would lead to 'irreversible' liberalisation in the Soviet Union, thereby opening up the way for intellectuals, youth and the working class to intervene and create a democratic socialist future. It would likely lead to more militant and consistent support for revolution abroad. With the fall of Khrushchev, however, he realised he had underestimated the strength of the 'heterogeneous' alliance between those associated with heavy industry, the military, the armaments industry as well as the police and party apparatuses. These were precisely the bureaucrats threatened by 'the ceaseless reforms' of Khrushchev. As he would later admit, his analysis seriously underestimated the weight of the Stalinist past on the Soviet state and society and overestimated the capacity of the Soviet working class.

What he expected in the Soviet Union, in fact, unfolded in Czechoslovakia, however briefly – the Prague Spring was to be cut short by the Soviet-led invasion in August 1968, organised by that same 'heterogeneous' alliance that had organised the fall of Khrushchev.

In the case of the fate of the Algerian Revolution, Pablo had realised early that the central conflict was between the bureaucratic and democratic wings of the movement. He had not been over-confident of the self-managed current emerging victorious. He had written as much in that letter to Ben Bella in August 1963[7], trying to convince him that self-management was already being distorted and undermined by ministerial and party bureaucrats. The future had always been contingent. He did not have any regrets about supporting the Ben Bella-Boumediene combination in 1962 as it had assured Algeria's genuine independence and blocked the neo-colonialist path taken by its neighbours. He did regret, however, that Ben Bella's imprisonment from 1956 till 1962 had prevented the future president building his own independent organisation or current within the FLN, assuming any such current could have avoided the same traps of bureaucratisation.

Characteristically, no sooner had the coup occurred and he was safely away, Pablo produced an analysis of the fall of Ben Bella, but not before he had drafted the manifesto for the new Algerian underground Left. The downfall of Ben Bella was for him, in his congenital optimism, another setback rather than a more permanent defeat. He would not allow himself to entertain the conclusion that the coup was in fact the Thermidor (or conservative phase) of the Algerian revolution which had run its course for at least a generation. This usurping coalition, led by the army chief Boumediene, had been visible for some time. Ben Bella's intention to deprive some of its leading members of their ministries (which was on the agenda of the meeting of the FLN Political Bureau scheduled for the day of the coup) and Ben Bella's chairmanship of the second world conference of the Non-Aligned Movement a week later, which would have further consolidated his power, prompted the timing of the coup.[8]

There were other underlying causes. Ben Bella had played a Bonapartist role, balancing and strengthening his own position in 'palace manoeuvres' in a game of competing clans and interests. His personal regime had itself accepted and nourished a bureaucracy. The only antidote was to democratise the regime as quickly as possible by a radical land reform, by freeing self-managed enterprises from bureaucratic constraints, by encouraging cooperatives, by installing democracy in the FLN and the unions, by creating (at last) democratic communal councils, by forming a militia based on these communal councils and by elaborating a Plan for economic development. All these things Pablo had been advocating since the beginning and, for many of them he had in fact drafted legislation – in response to requests from Ben Bella himself.[9]

The fact that these democratisation measures had not been pursued by Ben Bella required explanation – and Pablo located it in the limitations of the petit-bourgeois revolutionary nationalist leaderships. Courageous and sympathetic as they could be, it was rare that such leaders could rise above their political conditioning. Castro had done it, but even in that case there were serious limits. As for Ben Bella, he 'learnt constantly from the exercise of power which became his veritable political school. From this point of view he surpassed all the other political men of the Algerian Revolution. But he didn't learn sufficiently quickly or completely, victim of his antecedents and the backward context of the Algerian society.'[10]

So Ben Bella switched or hesitated between those Bonapartist manoeuvrings and the occasional democratic initiative. The Algerian Left had been well aware of Ben Bella's limitations. Pablo himself was well aware of them. The main attacks and criticisms of Ben Bella at the meeting of the central committee of the FLN a week before the coup had come from the left and had concentrated on his immobilism in advancing socialist democracy. For most of his presidency, Ben Bella had chosen to support old comrades of 'the first hour' who in the end betrayed him. It was Tahar Zbiri, for instance, whom Ben Bella had appointed head of the armed forces, who awoke and arrested the president at gunpoint at 2 am on 19 June 1965.

The point was, revolutionaries had no other choice but to support Ben Bella in the circumstances of Algeria at that time. There was no other force capable of propelling the revolution forward and Ben Bella had demonstrated an instinctive sympathy for the Algerian poor. For those purists who scorned working with the material at hand, Pablo would respond:

> But the art of revolutionary politics in a situation such as Algeria consists of patiently forging all the necessary links in the chain permitting an advance – or simply avoiding in a given moment serious reverses. It isn't revolutionary Marxism to stand apart from the struggle or to jump over stages, losing links with the realities and proving incapable of throwing bridges from the given situation to a possibly more advanced one. All demarcation from sectarians and primitive "ultra-leftism" consists in that.[11]

He also defended his earlier positive estimation of the army whose officers had quickly evolved into a privileged elite, by claiming that in the army ranks there was still sympathy for Ben Bella and the socialist measures of his presidency. He knew, however, that any reliance on an army, no matter how sympathetic, could only be short-term and no substitute for basic democracy, with power in the hands of the people. Part of that would entail creating a people's militia as counterweight to the professional army.[12]

To the Algerian Left now fell the task of leading the opposition to the new military dictatorship. Pablo counselled it not to turn its back on Ben Bella and the popularity Pablo believed the deposed leader retained among the mass of the population. Daniel Guérin, who had followed developments in Algeria closely, made the same point.[13] However, he knew one of the main components of this Left was the pro-Moscow Algerian Communist Party (PCA) and, within two years he realised this party was flirting with supporting the so-called progressive wing of the regime and thereby weakening the resistance. In each issue of *SDS* for the next few years there was a 'Letter from Algeria', written by him, assessing with measured optimism the prospects of overturning the regime. It's still in power today.

In the immediate aftermath, Pablo was more intent on organising the defence of Ben Bella and the other political prisoners. The effort started the day after the coup with a telegram from Gilbert Marquis to Boumediene demanding the release of Ben Bella and the other political prisoners. A simultaneous media release canvassed the same demand. On 5 September, two of Pablo's lifelong supporters, Pierre Avot-Meyers and Simonne Minguet, were arrested in Algiers. In the same month Mohammed Harbi and Hocine Zahouane were captured. So was the communist party leader and writer Bachir Hadj Ali. Pablo believed these arrests were the tip of an iceberg. Once again, the great and the good of French society and beyond – Sartre, de Beauvoir, Simone Signoret, Yves Montand, Françoise Sagan, Daniel Guérin, Aimé Césaire, Alain Resnais et al – were mobilised in their defence, petitioning for respect of the prisoners' human rights. Sal Santen made it onto the lists as well, along with the likes of Isaac Deutscher. Although badly beaten and roughed up, Meyers and Minguet were released after a month of captivity. Harbi and Zahouane had to wait seven years before Pablo could successfully arrange their escape.

It was months before the whereabouts of Ben Bella emerged – imprisoned in the south of Algeria on the edge of the Sahara. For both political and personal reasons, Pablo was not content that Ben Bella remained prisoner – his friend could be killed at any moment and Algeria and Africa could not afford to lose another leader of such sympathy and standing. One Patrice Lumumba was enough.[14] Defence campaigns were good, but escape would be better.

## 14 . THE GYPSY YEARS 1965-68

In his political autobiography – and he would expand on this episode in his interview with Adolfo Gilly 30 years later – Pablo recounts being approached by an Algerian businessman in Paris who told him he was in touch with army officers – former *maquisards* or guerrillas of the interior – willing to help in the release of Ben Bella. He hinted that the French secret service, of all people, would connive at such an escape. Pablo insisted that Ben Bella be consulted before the plan went any further. He contacted Ben Bella's lawyer, Madeleine Lafue-Véron, who brought out word that Ben Bella agreed to the attempt. Such things weren't impossible. Ben Bella, after all, had escaped from a French colonial prison in Algeria in 1952. However, it required means that Pablo and the businessman did not have. Pablo takes up the story in the Gilly interview:

> **Pablo:** Ben Bella was held very tightly. There were three military circles around his prison. It was a very difficult business … So we needed material help. Ben Bella said, "Go to Tito first and ask Tito to help me. Then you'll go to Nasser, and then to Castro." So we went to Tito.
> **Gilly:** You went? You?
> **Pablo:** No, not myself.
> **Gilly:** People in contact with you?
> **Pablo:** Yes, of course. And Tito said "yes, I will do it for Ben Bella, but I don't do anything in Arab affairs without consulting Nasser. If Nasser is okay, I agree." We found that quite normal, and we went to see Nasser. So Nasser, when he listened to this plan, without counting anything at all, without making calculations, without thinking that his friend Boumediene could be very angry, he said yes.
> **Gilly:** Did he say yes? Nasser said yes?
> **Pablo:** Immediately. He said "Ben Bella is my brother", he even started to cry —"Whatever you want, you'll get it really quickly." And he did. He sent all the material help we asked for. After that, it wasn't even necessary to go to Castro. But we went. So Castro …
> **Gilly:** Hey … I know! I do not know, but I suspect.
> **Pablo:** He said "no, no, no, yes – I'll see." I think he warned [Boumediene] right away … To each his own.
> **Gilly:** Did he warn him right away?!
> **Pablo:** I am sure.[15]

And so the plan was scuttled. There are other versions of this episode that don't indict Castro. In those, it is the accidental sighting of Algerian dissidents at the Cairo airport by the Algerian ambassador that alerts the regime that something is afoot.[16]

Ben Bella remained in detention until after Boumediene died. He was not released until 1980, when he went into exile in France and Switzerland. Pablo's implication of Castro might have been an embellishment, but the fact that Ben Bella never made a trip to Cuba after his release, despite the strong fraternal relations of the revolutionary era in Algeria, may be indirect corroboration of the Pablo version. For that matter, Pablo himself was to grow more critical of Havana despite a few years of hoping the Cubans would create the basis a new revolutionary international.[17] The August 1967 conference of OLAS (Organisation of Latin American Solidarity) assembled representatives of revolutionary movements in both south and north America and seemed to lay the basis for such a new revolutionary International. However, by 1968, Castro was toeing the Moscow line, approving the Warsaw Pact invasion of Czechoslovakia to suppress the experiment of 'socialism with a human face'. Pablo happened to be in Havana in August 1968 at the time of the invasion and recalls the sense of shock of Cubans when Castro lined up with the Kremlin.[18] In the face of the American sanctions on Cuba, Castro apparently considered himself too dependent on Soviet aid and protection to do much else.

The disappointment over Algeria did not end Pablo's commitment to the colonial revolution. In Geneva he renewed his friendship with Mehdi Ben Barka, the exiled socialist leader of the democratic opposition in Morocco. Ben Barka was then one of the chief organisers of the Tricontinental Conference of anti-imperialist movements, to be held in Havana in January 1966. Pablo saw Ben Barka just before he disappeared in October 1965. Ben Barka had told him he was leaving to meet representatives of the Moroccan king in Paris. He never returned from the meeting and his disappearance has never been fully solved. It appears to have been a joint operation of the French and Moroccan police forces.[19]

— ✢ —

By the mid-60s the extraordinary resistance of the Vietnamese to the American bltzgreig was front and centre of world politics. Like everyone else on the Left in these years, Pablo was full of admiration for the heroism of the Vietnamese, appalled by the scale of the loss of human life – 'the unprecedented calvary' was his phrase – and angry and frustrated at the limited support from the Soviet Union and China.[20] A united front in support of Vietnam, he believed, was their elementary duty. He also worried that the ascendant war party in the United States might be reckless enough to start a war with China. At the very least, Washington aimed to demonstrate in Vietnam that 'revolution doesn't pay' and to secure for themselves bases in South-East Asia from which to wage a future conflict with China. His declarative style of thinking, often tinged with extreme apocalyptic overtones, was much in evidence in these years. On the outcome in Vietnam, he wrote in an editorial in *SDS* in October 1966, hangs 'the future of the Revolution and Socialism. It is a question of the future of the world communist movement, which is now experiencing the greatest crisis since its birth. It is a question of the future of humanity.'[21]

He did not go as far as Sartre in advocating Soviet rocket attacks on US bases in Thailand from which US bombing attacks were launched – he was conscious of the need to avoid nuclear war – but he did wonder in editorials in *SDS* why the Soviet air force was not scrambled over North Vietnam to meet the American fighter bombers that were wreaking such destruction on a fraternal socialist country, or why there was no 'second front' to relieve the pressure on the Vietnamese. Like Che, faced with the assault on Vietnam, he extolled the creation of 'one, two, three, many Vietnams'.

Vietnam was a crucial battlefield for the world revolution – 'let it not be forgotten, it is the defeat of imperialism in Vietnam that will be the real turn in the world revolutionary situation, launching the new inevitable upsurge.' A victory in Vietnam would make up for all the 'depressing' setbacks elsewhere, particularly to the colonial revolution – Indonesia, Brazil, Peru and elsewhere in Latin America, in Algeria and throughout Africa.[22]

Predictably, he wanted to be involved in the Vietnam struggle in practical ways. He advocated the widest possible unity in support of Vietnam, and for that aid to take as many forms as possible – up to and including industrial action and sending volunteers. In September 1966, he went to Brussels to attend the European conference of anti-war and solidarity organisations. He represented the Greek Committee for Aid to the Vietnamese People – the other delegate was Helene Kazantzakis, widow of Greece's most famous novelist. In addressing the conference in favour of volunteers for Vietnam, he argued:

> The significance of such a measure, independent of its immediate practical effect on the actual ground in Vietnam, will be very great. It will show that the resistance to imperialism in Vietnam isn't the exclusive affair of the people of Vietnam, but of the peoples of the world, and that their active solidarity with the Vietnamese is real and doesn't hesitate to pursue, if appropriate, any form of action.

His old comrade, Jacques Grinblat (party name Privas), spoke in similar terms, that rhetoric and demonstrations were not enough, and raised the example of international volunteers going to the aid of the Spanish revolution in the 1930s.[23] Organising volunteers for Vietnam, Grinblat argued, would help emphasise the significance of the struggle there and help fuel other forms of intervention. 'Remember the stir caused by the brigades in Spain. Some thousands said "we are prepared to die for the Spanish Revolution", and millions believed in the importance of Spain and did all they could for it.'

By the spring of 1967, this campaign to raise a corps of volunteers had been endorsed by leading French intellectuals and artists – Simone de Beauvoir, Simone Signoret, Sartre, Laurent Schwartz et al – and adopted by France's anti-Vietnam War movement. By March, Grinblat and others were claiming more than 200 young French and Western Europeans had volunteered to serve in one form or another in Vietnam. The Vietnamese decided to refuse international volunteers – their hard, authoritarian nationalist regime was not a good fit with the presence of a cosmopolitan corps of varied leftists. Nor did they want to import squabbling Russian and Chinese volunteers. They never did complain about the limited aid from other 'workers' states', or the disruption by China of Soviet aid passing through that country.

The Vietnamese fought on alone with limited aid but, in Pablo's estimation, they did reveal the real limits to American military and economic power and provoked the national crisis that the United States endured in this decade. By 1969 he was referring to Vietnam as American imperialism's 'lost war' and the anti-war movement as 'irresistible'.[24] Nevertheless the war, as we know, was to drag on interminably and cost the lives of millions before a devastated and grim Vietnam triumphed. The long-delayed victory did not ignite a 'new inevitable upsurge' of revolution in the colonial and dependent countries as Pablo had once expected, but when the victorious Vietnamese tanks entered the US embassy compound in Saigon on 30 April 1975, Pablo was in Portugal in the midst of that country's revolution.

But whatever happened in Moscow and Beijing, Pablo in these years advocated creating a united international revolutionary front, possibly based in Havana, that would support the colonial revolution, particularly in the Middle East and Latin America, and thereby relieve the pressure on Vietnam. As for the Middle East itself, in the wake of the devastating defeat of the Arab nationalist regimes (and their Soviet sponsor) in the Six-Day War of 1967, he came to bank on the Palestinians, the Democratic Popular Front for the Liberation of Palestine in particular, to inspire the next stage of the Arab revolution. For the next four or five years he had multiple contacts with the PDFLP until its leadership opted for close links with Moscow.[25]

— ✧ —

In these gypsy years he heard again the call of his homeland. After the doomed civil war from 1946 to 1949, Greece had become something of a political cemetery. However, with the 1963 election victory of the centre-left Centre Union, Greek society had come alive again in a period of political and social ferment captured in the Costa-Gavras' film Z. At that time, involved as he was with the Algerian struggle, Pablo had also closely followed the democratic reawakening of Greece. He visited the country for only the second time in nearly 30 years, in October 1964, en route to Cyprus and reported that his conversations with comrades on the Left went long into the early hours. The conservatism, or more precisely the 'parliamentary cretinism', of the leading centre-left political leaders annoyed him. He felt it granted the rightist forces, centred on the Palace and in the American-funded and trained army, plenty of scope to plot the suppression of the new-found liberty of the people and a return to the dark years of post-1944 reaction.

When the mild, centre-left government was duly stripped of office in a Palace-engineered manoeuvre in 1965, he saw the consequent mass protests and strikes as the arrival of a pre-revolutionary situation. The radicalism of the people – demanding, for instance, a plebiscite for the return of the republic – far outstripped the timidity of the centre-left leaders. The advent of a situation ripe for radical change, and under conditions of relative economic prosperity, also proved a larger point: it was possible for internally or externally generated political crises to spark revolutionary situations in prosperous capitalist countries. However, such crises occurred only rarely in a lifetime. Making the most of the opportunity depended on the presence of a political force up to the challenge. The *raison d'être* of the revolutionary party and its leadership is 'to exist only for such moments in order to attain the desired end. All their patient preparation, even if it takes decades, must be focused on this perspective.' A tall historical order.

The replacement of the centre-left government with a palace-friendly administration failed to calm the unrest in Greece. In April 1967, a corps of hard-right colonels seized power and set up a junta which would rule the country for the next seven years. Three days after this coup, Pablo issued a communiqué on behalf of the 'Revolutionary Marxist Tendency of Greece' calling for a united front of the radical left. This united front would work to form a new Resistance based on democratic local committees and a platform of the abolition of the monarchy, a transitional government based on the Resistance and the calling of a constituent assembly to be elected to draw up a new constitution. This Front would be open to all those who subscribed to this platform. 'This Front, without excluding other forms of struggle, would make the armed struggle, adequately organised in the mountains and the towns, the principal form of the combat for the overthrow of the dictatorship.'

This call was very much influenced by Pablo's nostalgia for the extraordinary wartime resistance of the Greeks against the German occupation. Outside of Yugoslavia and Poland, there had not been a resistance to the Nazis as widely supported and as heroic as theirs. Down the years since the war, Pablo had continually insisted there had been a Tito-ist potential or current in that resistance which had been suppressed and ultimately betrayed by the notoriously Stalinist leadership of the Greek Communist Party. Now, in the resistance to the Junta, Pablo harboured the wish that the non-Stalinist Left would be more deeply involved and a revolutionary social democracy would emerge. Nothing of the sort happened, as we know. Later he was to acknowledge that such moments as 1941-44 in Greece occur only once in an historical period. The wartime resistance, its betrayal and denouement in the doomed civil war of 1947-49, had apparently exhausted the Greek people's capacity for heroics.

In the summer of 1967, some 6,000 leftists and democrats were arrested and imprisoned or banished to the islands. The repression was heavy-handed, torture became routine, censorship was strict, the universities and schools were purged and the courts handed down heavy sentences to active oppositionists, although there were no death sentences. In response, resistance groups soon emerged and the Greek diaspora in Western Europe swelled with critics and resistants. Pablo was in his element. He aimed to create a broad movement of all those who were willing to take action against the regime, as he later explained to a Greek audience:

> When a bourgeois democratic parliamentary system functions, struggles for higher forms of political and social democracy must, in my opinion, be carried out through peaceful and democratic means. When, however, an open dictatorship arises, then our memory of the oath taken by Athenians in the beginning of the fifth century BCE must be reawakened. We need to recall that they considered it the duty of a citizen to include bringing about

## 14 . THE GYPSY YEARS 1965-68

the tyrant's death. My view was, and remains, that citizens must engage in all means of resistance and struggle against dictatorship or tyranny.[26]

Many of those determined to build an underground resistance to the Junta turned to Pablo. Even a major centre-right politician such as Constantine Mitsotakis – future foreign minister and the father of the current Prime Minister of Greece – advised the writer Elias Kulukundis that if he wanted to rescue his father-in-law and leading centre-left politician, George Mylonas, from his prison island, he should contact Pablo. Pablo was also a source of good forged passports – his closest collaborators had retained the skills used to help the Algerian activists during the Algerian war for independence.

Chief among them was Pierre Avot-Meyers. "Piero" had a heroic recent past. During the period of the Algerian revolution, he was the main person who organised the necessary papers, work permits, IDs, passports and so on for thousands of Algerian fighters, protecting them from prosecution by the French police, and allowing them to move about, Pablo recalled. In the years of the Junta in Greece, 'he made repeated trips to Greece to deliver and arrange false passports on behalf of Maria Becket, Amalia Fleming, Stathis Panagoulis and Andreas Papandreou's PAK and others.'[27] Pablo also had contacts with friendly socialist leaders such as Vassos Lyssarides in nearby Cyprus. Decades later, Elias Kulukundis published his rather sour account of collaborating with Pablo in the successful rescue of Mylonas.[28] Pablo did supply him with a false passport, but it was a Danish one and Kulukundis was dark and bearded; in other words, a very Greek-looking Dane.

Pablo's most fruitful collaborators appear to have been two remarkable Greek women – Maria Becket and Amalia Fleming. Maria and Jim Becket were his and Elly's neighbours in Geneva, and their apartment was one of the main centres for organising the resistance. Maria Hary Becket (1931-2012) was from an upper-class Greek family and had previously been married to a Greek shipowner. The coup and the repression that followed rapidly radicalised her. Jim was a rich Connecticut Yankee with enough legal training – he had a Harvard degree – to be described as a human rights lawyer. With another American lawyer he travelled to Greece on behalf of Amnesty International to investigate and collect evidence on the use of torture by junta police. However, if Amnesty or some other body was to bring a case against the junta before the European Commission of Human Rights, there would need to be victims and witnesses willing and able to testify. The colonels were not likely to let such people leave the country. The Beckets relied on Pablo to produce the false passports that were carried into Greece by sympathetic 'tourists' to be given to the witnesses. This successful smuggling operation, and the subsequent testimonies of the victims in hearings in Strasbourg, led the Scandinavian governments to move a resolution that the Council of Europe expel Greece for its use of torture. Seeing the writing on the wall, the junta resigned before being pushed.

This successful diplomatic isolation of the regime has justly been credited to the Beckets. As one Swedish diplomat put it:

> An important and often crucial role in mobilising European opinion against the Greek junta and exposing its human rights abuses was played, both openly and behind the scenes, by Maria Becket, a Greek citizen, and James Becket, an American. Seldom has the engagement of two private individuals had such an influence on a major issue of European democracy and human rights. The contribution of this couple, who lived at the time in Geneva, to the efforts of the Nordic countries to convince the Council of Europe about the human rights violations of the junta, tipped the scale from failure to success.[29]

Without taking anything from the remarkable Maria Becket[30], it's true to say that behind the Beckets were Pablo and his comrades. The collaboration also involved smuggling arms and *plastique* [explosives] into Greece.[31] Theirs was a friendship that persisted after Greece returned to normalcy in 1974, with Elly and Michel visiting and staying with the Beckets when they spent their summers in Horefto near Zagora on the east coast of Greece. 'It was hard not to be fond of Michel,' Jim Becket would recall.[32]

There wasn't as much success on other fronts. Pablo published *Antistasi* (Resistance) and sought to unite – with little or no success – the various resistance groups whose main activity appeared to be planting bombs to blow up US and junta targets in Athens – propaganda of the deed, as the anarchists called it.

In 1968 Pablo joined forces with the Independent Left led by Giannis Galanopoulos (1917-1993). In July 1968 he travelled with Galanopoulos and filmmaker Nikos Papatakis to Cuba as guests of the Cuban government in search of aid for the underground armed struggle. Pablo's two companions had personal histories almost as rich and extraordinary as his own. Galanopoulos was 'a daring, free-spirited *kapetanios* in the ELAS resistance during the war. He was imprisoned by the Right from 1945 till 1960 but shunned by the KKE [the Greek Communist Party]'.[33] He had escaped to Italy in the wake of the coup. Papatakis was born in

Addis Ababa in 1918, the son of a Greek father and an Ethiopian mother, and had fought in the Ethiopian army against the Italian invaders in 1935. He made his way to Paris in 1945 and became a budding left-wing film director. He was very handsome – his nickname was 'Beau' – and he had a series of French actresses as partners, including Juliette Greco. Despite the impressive CVs of this trio, the trip doesn't appear to have yielded any real benefits. A year later Pablo was arranging travel for young recruits, not to Cuba but to Palestinian military training camps in Lebanon.[34] This activity was also done in close partnership with the redoubtable Maria Becket and Amalia Fleming.

The resistance – left, right, royalist and centrist – remained hopelessly fragmented and disunited. There was the occasional spectacular failure such as the bomb set off by Alexandros Panagoulis in August 1968 which missed blowing up the car carrying the leader of the junta by seconds. Daring as this was, Pablo editorialised against assassinations in the pages of *Antistasi* in classical Marxist terms; the priority must be to mobilise the greatest number and aid the masses in their own liberation.[35] In that same month the Greek Communist Party split over the Soviet invasion of Czechoslovakia, which further weakened their already feeble, underground activity. In any case, both parties advocated a popular-front-type resistance, cosying up to the centre-right and the king and playing down any radicalism – even stopping short of demanding a republic.[36] The repression of the junta was very effective against all-comers and the economy continued to grow at a healthy rate, further dampening any enthusiasm for sacrifice on the part of most Greeks.[37]

The most high-profile figure on the Greek Left during these years was Andreas Papandreou. He and Pablo were comrades after a fashion. As a young man, Papandreou had briefly been a supporter of Pantelis Pouliopoulos, the legendary revolutionary Marxist who had also inspired Pablo. This affiliation had taken place after Pablo had gone into exile and so they had not met then. More significantly, Andreas was the son of the former historic leader of the Centre Union, George Papandreou, who had been prime minister from 1963 till 1965. In the wake of the coup, Andreas was arrested but, after an international campaign calling for his release, he was sent into exile in Sweden. He formed PAK (the Panhellenic Liberation Movement) and later PASOK, the Greek Socialist party, which was to become the major political party in Greece for a generation. As a resistance organisation, PAK was to be another brake on the emergence of a radical resistance inside Greece, as it preferred to concentrate on political and diplomatic activities outside Greece.[38] Pablo later recounted rather wryly that Papandreou had accept his suggestion that PASOK adopt the ideal of self-managed socialism as its goal, but spurned his other recommendation that PASOK should be a broad, socialist tent. After the junta fell in 1974 and parliamentary democracy was restored, Papandreou soon purged Pablo's supporters from PASOK.[39]

While the movement in Greece fell short of his hopes, events in France would soon turbocharge those revolutionary expectations. And Pablo, naturally, would be on the spot in Paris for what would turn out to be the most inspiring month in the second half of the 20th century.

— ∻ —

Before moving on to that heady time, it's worth mentioning the untimely loss, in that same year, of two men Pablo regarded as comrades. In 1967, Isaac Deutscher died in Rome on August 19, only 60 years old and 'in full intellectual activity'. He had been working on a biography of Lenin planned for the centenary of the Bolshevik leader's birth in 1970. Pablo paid handsome tribute to his 'eloquent' biography of Trotsky while noting it didn't exhaust the subject, and some conclusions were contestable. He acknowledged Deutscher's recognition of the socio-economic roots of bureaucracy and its rule in transitioning societies, but he dissented from Deutscher's conclusion that this rule was inevitable. Deutscher's view had led him to hesitate in condemning the bloody and violent collectivisation of agriculture in the Soviet Union, as he was not convinced that the alternative of consent from the peasantry was 'realistic'. Pablo felt this was symptomatic of Deutscher's tilt towards a 'Jacobin' view of history, 'which puts the emphasis on the role of the "elites" and "strong" personalities'.

Two months later he marked the early death of Che Guevara (he was not yet 40), murdered by his American and Bolivian captors in Bolivia.[40] Che and Pablo had differed over the economic strategy to pursue in the transition to socialism, and in Pablo's view there were reckless aspects to the Bolivian intervention (he had tried to point out the deficiencies in the Castro-Guevara concept of guerrilla warfare in 1966).[41] But those differences paled in the context of Che's courage, his love for the damned of the earth regardless of their nationality or race, his self-abnegating commitment to their emancipation and his urgent advocacy of an International of active revolutionaries.

It was hard to avoid the conclusion that he was now closer to people such as Deutscher and Guevara (and in some respects, to theorists such as André Gorz and Daniel Guérin in France, and Paul Baran and Paul

Sweezy in the United States) than he was to his former comrades in the Fourth International. Certainly by December 1968 he was proposing to his comrades that they drop any reference to the Fourth International in their title: 'Its behaviour not only on the Chinese question, the question of the Angolan revolution, self-management etc ... but also during the May [1968] events, has illustrated the ideological sterility of this tendency and its organisational sectarianism'.[42]

Praising and engaging with these non-Trotskyist sources was the intellectual equivalent of his political conclusion that revolutionary political forces had emerged in the world beyond the Fourth International. The revolutionary forces were now more diverse and plural than ever before. May 1968 in Paris and the Prague Spring were to confirm this.

CHAPTER 15

# Great expectations: Paris, Prague and Palestine 1968-1969

*Never, until now, have our ideas found such an echo and been taken up on such a scale. Notions, of 'Trotskyist' derivation, on Stalinism, on bureaucracy, on socialist democracy as we conceive it, of self-management, arouse and mobilise very large vanguard forces and even, in the case of some of them, millions of people. In this sense it is a complete triumph of our long ideological combat.*

**Sous le drapeau du socialisme**
September 1968

THE MAY EVENTS in France in 1968 were in Pablo's view 'more revolutionary than the Paris Commune'.[1] It was a conclusion he pronounced at the time and continued to claim right up until his death nearly 30 years later. It's true that in terms of numbers, extent, 'dreams' and spectacle, it did overshadow the Paris Commune of 1871. Millions of French men and women, young and old, threw themselves into mass protests all over France. Graffiti and inspiring posters of startling originality began appearing on the walls of Paris and other towns and cities:

*Imagination to power;*
*Under the streets, the beach;*
*Take your desires for reality.*

It was a time of heightened aspirations and, as Pablo noted in the immediate wake of the uprising: 'Never before have so many talked of 'self-management' in an advanced capitalist country ... In the space of several weeks, the idea of self-management has taken hold in diverse milieux right up to the peak of power in the person of de Gaulle, who now poses as the advocate of "participation".'

The Paris Commune of 1871 had inspired Marx to declare that it was the prototype for the socialist society of the future. For Pablo, it was the May events of 1968. It is worth quickly recalling the main events of that extraordinary month – and the responses of Pablo and his supporters at the time.[2]

During the first 10 days of May, students had skirmished with the police around the Sorbonne in central Paris. At the time university authorities were holding disciplinary hearings over student defiance of restrictions on their sexual and political activities. Hundreds, sometimes thousands, of students crowded the Sorbonne in solidarity with the activists who had been singled out. The fierce clashes with police culminated in the 'night of the barricades' on the Friday night of 10-11 May. Thousands of students built scores of imposing barricades composed of cars, trees, street furniture and building materials in the streets of the Latin Quarter and in a fog of tear gas fought the police block by block until the early hours of the morning. The brutality of the police that night aroused many local citizens to support the young people and so shocked France that the government promptly ordered the release of the hundreds who had been arrested and dropped all charges. It was not enough. The union federations called a protest general strike on Monday and students across France occupied their campuses and their schools.

At this stage the *pablistes* were calling the situation 'pre-revolutionary', but with the potential to quickly become 'revolutionary' if the workers were to join the youth uprising. They urged the students to make contact with workers, wherever and whenever, with the aim of explaining to them the essentially democratic aims of the movement of students and teachers – and inspiring the workers to take the same path. The students themselves needed to convene an 'États Généraux' (shades of 1789) to draw up a charter of transitional demands for the reform of education. And on the organisational level, a single 'revolutionary and democratic youth organisation' needed to be formed. The *pabliste* leaflet of 15 May concluded:

> Forward to the juncture with the working class in a single movement pivoted around the self-management of workplaces, schools, universities and public services by workers and citizens.

By the end of the week after 'the night of the barricades', the wished-for happened. The fire took off. Here and there, and then everywhere throughout France, workers decided to continue the protest strike and occupy their workplaces, often locking their bosses in their offices. By the following week, some seven to 10 million French workers were on strike. Hundreds of workplaces were occupied. It was not only a matter of the usual suspects. Librarians, actors, scientists, pilots, shop workers, journalists and civil servants joined the well-organised union workers at the big car factories, the rail workers, miners and steelworkers – the whole gamut of the modern working class came out. Their demands tended to be vague and qualitative – they wanted a change in the way they worked and the way society operated. As Pablo noted, there was no economic crisis or even recession to trigger the rebellion, even if there was an understandable desire for improvements in wages and working conditions. Pablo and his supporters, in adopting their platform *Marxism and Our Time* in 1966, had insisted that the days of revolution were not over in advanced neo-capitalist societies just because of the new prosperity enjoyed by the working class.[3] The point was, this new level of wellbeing fell short of what was possible and workers could fight for a more egalitarian society. The rising educational and cultural level would sharpen discontents with 'alienation' and the lack of genuine democracy and freedom at work and in the wider society. The general strike of May confirmed these prognostications.

The powerful Communist Party, after condemning the students, in the early days of May, as agents provocateurs and the spoilt brats of the bourgeoisie, rapidly mobilised its powerful and well-staffed apparatus to catch up with the workers' rising, take control, limit its aspirations to wage rises and prevent any 'contamination' by contact with the students.

The *pablistes* – in common with most of the revolutionary Left – did their best to counter this intervention by the communist party leaders. They urged the workers to 'follow the example of the students and of the Czech workers' by forming workers' councils ready to manage their workplaces, and to form coordination committees with the students and teachers at the local and regional level. In their leaflet of 18 May, they also raised the demand for the election of a revolutionary constituent assembly which, in coordination with the democratic councils, would draw up the constitution for 'the new revolutionary socialist and democratic France demanded by the situation'. Five days later they also called for the urgent establishment of 'a revolutionary council of Paris', made up of all the radical groups and parties, to give leadership to the uprising.

By the last week of May it was clear the Gaullist government was paralysed, and for a few days then, at the height of the crisis, it seemed that President de Gaulle would abandon office.

Once everything had stopped and the usual ways of doing things thrown up into the air, the question was: What next? On 27 May the *pabliste* leaflet declared that in response to this 'unprecedented revolutionary crisis' it was now time to proceed to the actual beginnings of the new society:

> *Comrade students and workers of France,*
> Aim high, aim for power
> Take the immediate organisation of social life into your own hands
> Manage the fields in which you exercise your profession
> Run the factories, universities and social services yourselves
> Everywhere take the place of the failing capitalist state
> Do not allow the strike and the struggle to rot in paralysis.

Pablo was present in Paris throughout May-June, writing leaflets and communiqués, attending the huge marches and speaking at mass meetings. He noted and regretted at the time that there existed no large political and social movement prepared for such a 'moment' as this – what other Trotskyists regretted as the absence of a revolutionary party. He called for an ad hoc alliance of leftist groups to fill the vacuum. He proposed that this alliance encourage the beginning of real self-management in the occupied schools, universities and workplaces and in towns and villages. In other words, begin to create the new society based on actual, working, direct democracy. The revolutionary alliance would also demand that the Socialist and Communist parties immediately form a coalition government to take charge of the country and convene elections for a constituent assembly to draw up a new radical constitution.[4]

It was as good a left-wing program as it was possible to imagine at that time, but getting it off the ground, getting enough people to take practical steps towards self-management, was another matter. Trotskyists, anarchists and Maoists might have a mass following among students, but they were all marginal when it came to the wider society – even if they had agreed with Pablo's ideas about actually pursuing self-management. The movement wallowed in indecision and vague slogans. There were exceptions – at Nantes, for instance, a central strike committee took charge of the city, assuring food supplies and the operation of vital public services.

Meanwhile, de Gaulle rediscovered his nerve, met with the army chiefs, rallied the Right (including pardoning the worst fascist putschists and terrorists of 1961-62), and fostered a deal with the Communist-led unions for wage rises and a resumption of work. He scheduled parliamentary elections which the communists and other left parties immediately agreed to. On 30 May there was a huge pro-de Gaulle demonstration in Paris. The next day Pablo and his supporters called for an immediate riposte, a mass counter-demonstration. It was not to be. The Communists and various left-wing parties preferred wage deals, retreat, compromise and the electoral game. Once the main bodies of workers were convinced to return to work, de Gaulle sent the police against recalcitrant holdouts among the workers and students. The Sorbonne was re-occupied by the police. In the elections at the end of June, the Left parties were heavily defeated.

Pablo would go on advocating this 1968 formula in other promising historical circumstances where there was more spontaneous take-up – Chile in the early 1970s and Portugal in the mid-1970s – but always there was the handicap of the absence of a large, conscious organisation ready to put into action the ideal of a new self-managed society.

When it came to reviewing the raft of books on the May events which publishers rushed into the bookshops, Pablo chose to single out *Mort d'une révolution* ('Death of a Revolution') by the *France Soir* journalist and radio commentator Jean Ferniot.[5] The book carried a double bonus: a detailed account by a mainstream journalist who had no vested interest in embellishing the events and yet who agreed in broad outlines with Pablo's conclusions about the failure of leadership and the basic, near-universal aspiration for 'self-management'. As Ferniot put it:

> From the student movement emerged one key demand: self-management, a word that flourished on all the barricades, in the amphitheatres where they fashioned the world of tomorrow, on the walls where the graffiti expressed not only the awesome rebirth of a new Dadaism or the old battle cries of [the legendary anarchist] Ravachol but the hitherto unknown desires of a generation. This questioning of social structures extended far and wide, from the students to the workers, signalling that they too believed they were entitled to demand self-management.

Ferniot nailed the efforts of the Left politicians, including the PCF and the CGT leaders, to suppress these aspirations as unrealistic:

> What these political and union organisations couldn't accept was ... that the movement starting in the faculties and reaching into the factories, before expanding out into the whole of society with lightning speed and force, expressed a revolt against authority, against the adult, against the father,

against the boss, against the gerontocracy which dominates the State, the civil service, the corporations, the churches, and the university, a revolt which also strikes out at the paternalistic and bureaucratic structures of the [Left] parties and unions themselves, the Communist Party [PCF] and the CGT in particular.

Little wonder, Ferniot concluded, that the PCF and CGT bureaucrats did their best to stop fraternisation between the workers and students.

In this review, Pablo mentions a 'remarkable' book by philosophers Edgar Morin, Claude Lefort and Jean-Marc Coudray (*Mai 1968: la brèche*, Éditions Fayard, Paris) which, according to Pablo, argued that the working class were not at all disposed to go as far as the students and drew 'pessimistic conclusions about its revolutionary potential'. This argument 'merits serious discussion', Pablo says, but, annoyingly, we never get it. "Jean-Marc Coudray" was one of the pseudonyms used by Cornelius Castioradis, a former Greek Trotskyist, one of the founders of *Socialisme ou barbarie*, a sociologist and who by 1968 was moving 'beyond' Marxism. Pablo prefers to dwell on Ferniot's conclusion that it was a failure of leadership that stymied the revolutionary potential of May.

In the wake of the Communist Party leadership's 'great betrayal', Pablo persisted in his advocacy of 'entrism sui generis'. He expected that a discontented, disillusioned left-wing – basically 'left centrist' in Marxist terms – would develop in the Communist Party and that it could make common cause with the far Left. Eventually, and it was a long-term aim, a revolutionary party with significant working-class following would emerge from this juncture. This continued attachment to entrism-plus-independent-sector marked him off from most of the rest of the revolutionary Left (and some of his own supporters) which now wrote off the Communist Party in its entirety as a brake on any revolutionary developments.

In the wake of the May events Pablo was keen to clarify the role of students. For the old Stalinists of the Communist Party, they were bourgeois or petit-bourgeois elements. For many leftists, they were essentially a political force, created by the times, inspired by external events – the Berkeley students, the Provos of Amsterdam, Black Power, the Cubans, Che and the Vietnamese. But in Pablo's view, while recognising the inspirational factors from abroad, they were a social force, a new and necessary element in the technologically charged neo-capitalism of the post-war decades, a new highly educated and trained strata of the working class. Moreover, while Marxists had always insisted history was made by the interaction between the material base and the superstructure of society, the May events confirmed the importance of superstructural factors, or what was present in people's heads. The cultural tenor of the times, if you like. And in the 60s, that tenor swung toward radical change. May resulted from 'the interaction of an ensemble of internal and external factors belonging essentially to the domain of political, ideological, and cultural 'superstructures' characteristic of French society at present.'[6]

— ❖ —

The other half of the revolutionary double act of 1968 was of course the Prague Spring, the hope-filled label given to the accelerated de-Stalinisation in Czechoslovakia. Pablo saw events there as the twin to the May events in France. Both shared the aspiration for a self-managed socialism. In 1968 in Czechoslovakia censorship was reduced, steps were taken to create 'workers councils' with some powers in workplaces, and the ruling Communist Party relaxed the police regime and authoritarianism in favour of advocacy and a freer political life. When Pablo passed through Prague on his way to Cuba in July, he noticed the freer atmosphere and the sudden possibilities of widely supported socialist democracy breaking through. It confirmed his analysis of de-Stalinisation – that it was fuelled by economic and cultural development and was a result of pressure from below on the factions within the bureaucracy. It was no accident that the Prague Spring was taking place in the most economically developed of the workers states and one which historically had a genuine mass communist party. In fact, its communist party had received significantly more votes in the relatively free post-war elections than either the Italian or French communist parties which then boasted significant popular support.[7]

All the developments in Prague alarmed the neo-Stalinist faction of the bureaucracy in charge in Moscow, who tried by threats and bluster to 'persuade' the Czechoslovak 'liberal' faction to retreat from their current course. This wasn't just a conflict between national bureaucracies, but between different transnational factions of the bureaucracy. There was, in Pablo's, view a 'Czechoslovak' faction in the Soviet party also, which would only be emboldened by any success in the smaller bureaucratic state, and the dominant neo-Stalinist faction in Moscow was well aware of this. This possibility was partially confirmed by Gorbachev in the 1980s – one of his closest friends at the time of the Prague Spring was one of the leading Czech reformers.

## 15 . GREAT EXPECTATIONS: PARIS, PRAGUE AND PALESTINE 1968-69

In his layover in Prague on his way to Cuba, Pablo sought out the Greek 'Tito-ist' Andreas Tzimas, the political advisor to the most formidable of the wartime resistance chiefs, Aris Velouchiotis. While he wanted a historical discussion with Tzimas, the old revolutionary strayed on to current events and warned him that only a Soviet invasion could stop the momentum towards a socialist democracy.[8] This is of course what happened on 21 August while Pablo was in Havana. But Pablo clung to the belief that the victory of neo-Stalinists was only temporary and more 'de-Stalinisation' struggles would soon erupt.

He felt this continued unrest in the workers states would in turn stir up debates in the Western and Third World communist parties. These parties could either further degenerate into stricter dependencies of Moscow or begin to detach themselves and differentiate between a social democratic wing and a left centrist wing. Again, 'the pursuit of the entrism sui-generis tactic' was vital.[9]

Overall his reading of events in 1968 was more optimistic than ever. 'Only' the problem of a global revolutionary leadership remained to be solved. Such a leadership would be able to decisively aid the interaction of revolutionary developments across the three sectors of the world revolution. Initially, in his view, it would be a process of collaboration and mutual aid rather than fusion and merging, more like the First International of Marx – the International Workingmen's Association – than the Third International of Lenin and Trotsky. In passing he had hoped that the Cubans, Vietnamese and North Koreans would form an independent, revolutionary anti-imperialist wing in the official world communist movement and constitute an element in this new 'International'.[10] This illusion was dashed by their support for the crushing of the Prague Spring.

— ✦ —

If Pablo was buoyed by the events in Paris and other pockets of advanced capitalism in the late 60s, he still saw the colonial revolution as the main motor of the world revolution.[11] The key theatres were Latin America and the Middle East. While most hopes were invested in the former, the aftershocks of the Arab defeat in the Six-Day War of 1967 were expected to strengthen revolutionary challenges to existing Arab regimes, whether they be nationalist republican as in states like Egypt or obscurantist monarchical as in Saudi Arabia.

As far as the Palestinians were concerned, he saw their struggle as the frontline and catalyst for the wider Arab Revolution without which the defeat of imperialism and Zionism would not be possible. To lock the Palestinians in the ghetto of their own struggle in the Occupied Territories was to doom them to defeat. The Palestinians and the Arabs more generally had to prepare for a long revolutionary process in which the elimination of regimes such as the Egyptian, Saudi and those in the Persian Gulf would be necessary. Realistically only a long struggle such as that taking place in Indochina could lead to the emancipatory solution of a federated, socialist united states of the Middle East and North Africa. Such a setup would, of course, protect the rights of minorities such as Israelis and Kurds.[12] However, by the early 1970s that 'classic' perspective of Arab revolutionaries, which Pablo shared, was being deeply interred.

In August 1969, Pablo went to Jordan as the guest of the Democratic Popular Front for the Liberation of Palestine (PDFLP). He went to participate in their cadre school and learn about their operations, drawn to this organisation in the Palestinian resistance because its ambitions were pan-Arab.[13] It was not only involved in guerrilla operations against the Israeli occupation, but also committed to overturning existing Arab regimes whose failure to develop modern and capable societies was so grievously on show in the Six-Day War. The DPFLP stood for the revolution of the Arab peasantry and workers to create a secular, democratic, socialist federation encompassing the whole of the Arab world. It had no truck with the borders drawn up by the colonial powers in the wake of the First World War. Only such a historic movement would attract a significant section of Israelis to abandon Zionism in favour of forming a secular Palestine and becoming part of this 'united socialist states of the Middle East'. In such a new regional union, minorities such as the Jews, Kurds and Berbers would be guaranteed equal rights. In other words, the PDFLP had seemingly taken up the analysis and ideals of Pablo's pamphlet of a decade before.

But at the same time, he was aware of the dangers to the Palestinian organisations in Jordan. Palestinians made up a majority of the Jordanian population and the armed resistance groups were the de facto government in their villages and towns. This meant there was a situation of dual power in the country and Pablo was aware that such situations inevitably come to a head. The king and the Jordanian army, supported by the Americans and Israelis, had already made tentative moves to rein in the power of the Palestinians groups. The chief Palestinian organisation in the country was Fatah, and its political line was strictly no criticism, opposition or interference to existing Arab regimes. The following year, Pablo's fears were realised, what Pablo had anticipated happened, in

## 15 . GREAT EXPECTATIONS: PARIS, PRAGUE AND PALESTINE 1968-69

a bloody crackdown that came to be called 'Black September'. In that month, the Jordanian armed forces launched frontal attacks on the largely unprepared Palestinian groups, killing hundreds of fighters and civilians, although those who could fought back and blunted the initial attacks. A truce followed, but in 1971, with the existing Arab regimes looking on, the king, with American and Israeli support, renewed the attacks until the Palestinian resistance was defeated and forced to relocate to Lebanon. In Jordan, there had been more than two million Palestinians, in Lebanon 300,000. It was a signal defeat and one that Pablo was reluctant to acknowledge.[14] By then, however, Chile was on the radar.

CHAPTER 16
# Close escapes and Chile 1970-1973

*He was not a conspirator, or an adventurer, but a kind of explorer of revolutions, such as they presented themselves. As soon as an opportunity arose, he went to meet processes – invariably "sui generis", as he might have said – to examine them closely. He then acted, as far as possible, consistently with his ideals.*

David Maurin[1]

*What died in Chile was the attempt to bring a revolutionary process to a victorious conclusion by avoiding a revolution.*

Michel Raptis
*Revolution & Counter-Revolution in Chile* (1973)

IN THE FEW years that followed the May events in Paris and the Prague Spring of 1968, Pablo continued to be immersed in organising his corner of the Greek resistance, encouraging solidarity with the Czechoslovaks and Soviet dissidents, working on the platform of the International Revolutionary Marxist Tendency (*TMRI* or *Tendance Marxiste Révolutionnaire Internationale* in French) which held its 3rd and 4th international conferences in November 1970 and May 1972, keeping up the campaign for Ben Bella's release, organising escapes for key Algerian comrades and maintaining contacts with the more radical Palestinians. All this while keep an eye on events unfolding in Chile. But, with so much to do, his entry into Chile was delayed.

By 1973, Pablo's old Algerian comrades Mohammed Harbi and Hocine Zahouane had been released from close imprisonment but were still confined to house arrest in their respective hometowns. Their long-term safety was in doubt, given their history, and Pablo set about organising their escape with the crucial help of two young *pablistes*, Lucie Maiques Grynbaum and François Leclerc. They volunteered to go to Algeria and carry out a daring plan. Both were dissident offspring from Communist Party families, radicalised by the Algerian and Vietnam Wars. Grynbaum's father had been a pilot in the Republican air force during the Spanish Civil War. When the fascists won, he fled, flying his fighter across the border and landing in Toulouse. He and Lucie's mother had been active in the Resistance. Leclerc's parents had similar if less dramatic lives rooted in the Communist movement. Leclerc was 25, Grynbaum 31, and both had been recruited into the pabliste ranks by Michel Fiant when students at the Sorbonne in the 1960s. They had the insouciant bravery of youth and a loyal faith in Pablo's planning.

The pair were to work simultaneously from different directions. Leclerc was to enter Algeria from the west via Morocco and contact Zahouane, while Lucie Grynbaum travelled from the east via Tunisia to pick up Harbi. The escapes needed to take place at the same time lest the escape of one lead to tighter surveillance of the other. In Grynbaum's account, she arrived in Tunis only to find the approaches to Algeria had been flooded and all roads closed. When she contacted Pablo, he ordered her to return to Paris. Three days later, however, when the flood waters receded, she was on her way back to Tunis. These comings and goings aroused the suspicion of the Tunisian police but she convinced them she was a genuine tourist and was allowed to rent a car. At the border, she was asked to give one of the Algerian police a lift back to Constantine, which was close to Skikda where Harbi was under surveillance. The cool-headed Grynbaum did as asked, dropping him off before proceeding with the strategy. Harbi, alerted to the escape plan, slipped away from his home in the early hours of the morning and was picked up in Constantine at 4am by Grynbaum. They drove south to make the Sahara crossing from Algeria into Tunisia. Grynbaum had brought a forged Turkish passport for Harbi and it worked. Leclerc's rescue of Zahouane followed the same procedures and escape route. They safely exited Tunis for Geneva, even though the police in Tunis again questioned Grynbaum about her short-stay tourism. The immaculate planning threatened to unravel in Geneva where the two Algerians found themselves stranded without support, until the redoubtable Annette Roger (nee Anne de Beaumanoir) intervened with money and transport to take them into France.[2]

The men were free and safe, but that show of loyalty put a price on Pablo's head, or a higher one, at least. He later observed that the operation was 'another unacceptable provocation on my part for Boumediene ... Consequently he had good reason to want to pay me back if by chance I fell into his hands. So I took certain precautions, such as never taking a plane that would fly over Algeria, as Boumediene was capable of forcing it to land and to settle accounts with me.'[3] This was reasonable paranoia. Two of the regime's high-profile opponents, Mohammed Khider and Krim Belkacem, had already been assassinated; Khider in Madrid in January 1967 and Belkacem as recently as October 1970 in Frankfurt. In 1965, the Moroccan secret police had kidnapped and murdered Ben Barka, the leader of the Moroccan Left. Mossad was not the only secret service murdering opponents.

David Maurin [not his real name] recalled Pablo's constant vigilance in regard to Boumediene, even in far-off Cuba during a visit in 1968:

> I remember this large dining room of the "Habana Libre", the old Hilton, where the Cubans used to treat their guests. It was in August 1968 and I had an appointment there with Michel who had just arrived in Cuba.
>
> The room was full of revolutionary militants from all over the world and officials from "friendly" countries of the time. Dozens and dozens. I recognised Michel at the back of the room by his felt hat, which alone emerged from the pages of a newspaper wide open in front of him, probably *Granma*. He was loyal to the hat, he always wore one when I knew him.
>
> When I joined him, he made me sit in front of him, and without lowering his newspaper he said to me: "Shh, at the table behind you, there are Algerian soldiers. Don't look back. They are the kind who were looking for me the day after the coup against Ben Bella, let's go elsewhere ..."[4]

Incidentally, Maurin had more to say about the hat (and the relationship between Michel and Elly):

> This same hat, I also remember it in Chile. It was before the 1973 coup d'état and the atmosphere was very tense in the small, discreet apartment, a hideout, where the Chilean SP [Socialist Party] had lodged him, and where we were waiting for him with some leaders from the left of the SP. Coming in, he threw his hat on the bed to come and sit at the table with us and start the meeting. It was without reckoning with Hélê, his wife, known to be a stickler for certain principles, who asked him to take the hat off the bed before we proceeded, which he did.

It may have been a mark of Elly's aristocratic upbringing, or perhaps it was prompted by some unconscious fear for her husband's safety. It's an old superstition that putting a hat on a bed courts bad luck, even death.

— ✢ —

Incidentally, one of the more bizarre Algerian escapes Pablo was caught up in, in 1971-72, concerned Eldridge Cleaver, the fugitive Black Panther leader and writer. In the late 1960s, Black Panthers and other imprisoned or hunted Afro-American rebels managed to escape the United States and make their way to refuge in Algeria. In a handful of celebrated cases, this involved hijacking passenger planes in the United States and even ransoming the passengers before flying on to Algiers. This modus operandi, and the unsolved crimes committed in Algeria itself, eventually made the fugitives, especially Eldridge Cleaver, who was their unofficial leader, unwelcome guests.

Elaine Mokhtefi, a remarkable American working in Algiers at the time and a friend of Cleaver's, tells the whole history of this souring of the Black Panther-Algerian relationship in her autobiography, *Algiers, Third World Capital* (Verso, 2018). Her portrait of Cleaver is devastating and essential reading for anyone who wants to understand the evolution of Black politics in the 1960s and '70s.

As Mokhtefi relates, conflicts between Eldridge Cleaver and other Black radicals and the regime itself became so dangerous that he needed to flee Algeria. Cleaver appealed to Mokhtefi to arrange it. On a visit to Paris [in the autumn of 1972] she turned first to de Beauvoir and Sartre, who refused to get involved. Then she mentioned her problem to Ben Bella's lawyer, Madeleine Lafue-Véron. The lawyer knew just the person to help.

> She asked whether I would be willing to meet Michalis Raptis, better known as Michel Pablo. "Of course I would!" … Pablo's activism with the FLN is legendary: he was a hero. … Pablo was waiting for me at the Café Cluny, on the corner of boulevard Saint-Michel and boulevard Saint-Germain. I recognised him under his fedora and headed for his table towards the back of the café's outdoor terrace.
>
> He was curious to know how the Panthers had arrived in Algiers. "What kind of people are they? Their backgrounds? Who is Cleaver and what is the Split [in the Black Panther party] about?" We talked about the hijacking. Then came the sixty-four-thousand-dollar question: what was their future?
>
> I explained that Ben Bella [through his wife, Zohra Sellami] had suggested that I contact his lawyer because after the hijacking money was returned to

the airlines, the situation of the Black Panthers had become increasingly precarious. They required air to breathe – and financing.

I had no idea where this contact would lead. When Mokhtar [Elaine's partner] joined me in Paris, he too met Pablo … In the early days of independence he had taken part in meetings with a group of progressives held in a quiet downtown Algiers café for discussions of government policy, in-depth criticism and planning. Pablo had led those sessions. He remembered Mokhtar and was delighted to see him again …

In December 1972, I went back to Paris to make arrangements. Michel Pablo, our Trotskyist contact, helped me lay plans. We decided that Eldridge would be less exposed travelling from Tunisia. Paul Roussopoulos volunteered to drive him from Algiers to the oasis in Tozeur, where he and his wife Carole owned a house. Border controls would be lax there; they would spend the night there in that otherworldly setting of date palms and desert and then drive to Tunis.

To fly into Switzerland from Tunis would be less risky. Pablo gave me the phone number of a 'passeur' who would rendezvous with Eldridge at the airport in Geneva. He would drive him into France, skirting the official border posts …

Pablo had one more favour to offer:

> When everything was wrapped up, Pablo handed me a classy British passport with a photo of a Black man who could have been a younger Eldridge. It was brand new, "clean", and safer than the stolen, doctored American one.[5]

When she went to farewell Cleaver: 'I couldn't believe what I saw. Eldridge was transformed, his big frame clothed in a heavy, long dark-grey chesterfield. His face was clean-shaven and he was wearing a homburg …'

Despite the incongruity, everything went to plan. Cleaver arrived safely in France and soon began his sad and rapid descent to the Right.

— ⁎ —

By 1970 Pablo, along with much of the international Left, had turned his attention to Chile. In September of that year, Salvadore Allende, the perennial socialist candidate, was narrowly elected president. (In fact, a Chilean comrade had raised the prospect of Allende's election leading to revolutionary developments in an article in *Sous le drapeau* in 1964, an article which had drawn Mandel's ire for its revisionism.) Chile was noteworthy in Latin America for being more like a European than a Third World country. It had a large working class, an extensive labour movement, well-established Socialist and Communist parties, and an active Christian Left. There were also Trotskyists or ex-Trotskyists active in the Socialist party who remained broadly sympathetic to Pablo and his politics. *Sous le drapeau* carried reports and analyses written by some of these sympathisers – incidentally, the quality of the writing was out of the ordinary – and Pablo himself saw great prospects for revolutionary socialism in the 'triangle' of Chile, Peru, where a reforming military regime was carrying through land reform and national development projects, and the ever-turbulent Bolivia. Again, what was 'indispensable' if revolutions were to be successful was the continued development of bodies of active democracy in workplaces and localities – the embryo of a new socialist democracy. Likewise, it was essential to develop worker and peasant militias to defeat the 'absolutely inevitable' attempt by elements in the armed forces, encouraged by Washington, to put an end to any experiments of a radical socialism.

It wasn't until August 1972 that Pablo headed for Chile, invited by an old friend, Pedro Vuscovic, who was then the executive vice-president of CORFO, the coordinating body for the nationalised sector of the economy. (Once again, the historian is struck by the sheer breadth of Pablo's contacts.) Elly had preceded him by visiting Peru and he headed there first. Elly was again his essential partner as she spoke Spanish fluently, while he understood it but spoke it only falteringly. In Peru he was keen to gauge the impact of the Nasser-esque regime of leftish army officers led by General Velasquez. The visit confirmed his view that without the democratic participation of the workers and peasants, then there could only be very limited and transient progress towards socialism. He was confident that a very different situation awaited him in Chile. Reports of the spontaneous formation of self-management bodies in workplaces and localities 'gave me wings', he later recounted.[6]

He flew into Santiago in the last week of August 1972 and 'immediately loved' the city as much for its 'distinctive beauty … as for the happy atmosphere which prevailed among a people with a long democratic tradition … and known as the most sophisticated of Latin America'.[7] He had arrived in time for the parade marking the second anniversary of Allende's victory. He was invited to the official reviewing platform and witnessed the estimated 700,000 march past – 'I saw the crowds in one of their rare charismatic moments when they see the future with unalloyed optimism and feel that they are participating in direct people's power'.

He was introduced to Allende. In a note in his autobiography which will provide fodder for those who see him as more oriented towards leaders ('counsellor to the Prince' is the critical phrase used) than the nameless workers and citizens he championed, he recalls that, on an official photograph of himself that the new president gave to him, 'Allende dedicated two most friendly phrases with the date of our first meeting and his signature'. He kept the photograph all his life: 'a reminder of an historic moment and of him'.

The official reason for Pablo's visit was to study and report on the model of workers participation in management that had been introduced by the new government. It was essentially 'co-management' (authority shared between managers and workers representatives) but there was a clear tendency for it to be pushed further by the workers themselves. There were also similar participatory bodies being established in localities and all kinds of institutions. Pablo, of course, was interested in promoting a wider and more full-blooded transition to self-management.

He was by no means in the same influential position that he had occupied in Algeria, but his aim was the same:

> If one had restricted oneself to making forecasts based exclusively on the state and official leadership in Chile, one might have easily come to the conclusion that the game was fixed in advance, which would have left little room for hope. But as long as one looked at the situation from the point of view of the unceasing interaction between 'base' and 'summit', as long as one sought to strengthen the process at the base as much as possible, then one stood on revolutionary Marxist terrain.[8]

An acceleration of this 'process at the base' was not long in coming, provoked by 'the strike of the bourgeoisie' as it was called. In the second week of October, employers, led by those in the trucking and bus companies, declared a strike against the government's nationalisation measures and its economic policies, which they blamed for spiralling inflation and other economic problems. They were soon joined by other businesses, shopkeepers, doctors, dentists and bank employees. There were violent anti-government demonstrations by the 'golden youth' of the better-off suburbs in Santiago. The leaders of the conservative National Party and the Christian Democrats, who commanded a majority in the parliament, formed a 'Democratic convergence' to give political leadership to the strike.

The working class and poor rose to the challenge, organising their own transport, commandeering vehicles, walking to work if necessary, ensuring supplies, organising famers' markets and protecting shops that remained open, and cooperating with sympathetic medical students who offered their services. They took over more than 100 factories whose owners had decided to close them. All this was accomplished by newly created and elected bodies as workplace and local self-management took a huge step forward. This resistance was encouraged mostly by the left wing of the Socialist Party and the Castroist MIR, the main organisation of the far left. The Communists and Allende himself were keener to come to an arrangement with the Christian Democrats who, as the strike of the bourgeoisie faltered towards the end of the month, were anxious to secure some benefits from the bosses' offensive. In the first week of November, as the strike began to collapse, a peace deal was struck by incorporating three generals into Allende's cabinet. It was a troubling concession by Allende and took some of the gloss off the victory of the government and its mass base.

During his three-month stay, Pablo travelled far and wide, meeting and talking with workers in a range of industrial settings:

> During the time of 'the strike of the bourgeoisie' I had for once in my life the unique opportunity to visit many factories and speak with the workers. With Elly I visited the most important factories in the cities and nearby towns, and we travelled north to the mines near the border with Bolivia. Here were impressive sea views and complete desert, where under burning sun or bitter cold wind, workers far from any town and village toiled through unending hours in clouds of dust for the most miserly of daily wages ... Everywhere the workers received us initially with some hesitation, but in time we won their confidence and then they freely expressed their opinions about the government's policies and the future. Generally, their demand was for greater democratic participation in the management of the businesses they worked for and in the life of their country. They displayed a deep awareness of the significance of the experiment which they had started with the Popular Union, but also of the dangers that threatened it.

He also attended more formal meetings: addressing the annual conference of Latin American sociologists on the subject of self-management and socialism and participating in meetings of the Socialist Party and of MIR. He attempted to bring these parties, along with MAPU,[9] together on a platform of developing direct democracy and an economic policy that would tackle the disruption and earn the cooperation 'not of the sum total of the middle class, something that was really unattainable, but with that part closest to the material and ideological level of the working masses'.[10] Such a political and social united front could offer an alternative to Allende's personal alliances and illusions. He concentrated his efforts on the Socialist Party as the most radical and influential part of the governing coalition, but to no avail, as he later acknowledged:

... As in Algeria, I confirmed yet again how difficult it is to organise a consistent leftist tendency within the framework of a party in government – one that is willing to wage battle against its own leadership and to escape from the routine of daily preoccupation with the everyday policies and governance problems, with the trees that hide the forest.[11]

He handed in his report on self-management to Vuscovic in December, noting that the workers he met were anxious for more participation, for more elected workers on the administrative committees in enterprises and for more information and education to help them shoulder their responsibilities.[12] He noted the resistance to this wider participation on the part of managers and technicians who were jealous of their prerogatives and scornful about the ordinary workers' abilities. They also feared for their material privileges. His solution was twofold: an effort to persuade managers and technicians that rank-and-file workers were now their allies and to drop their old paternalistic and authoritarian attitudes; and to introduce opportunities for workers to pursue further general and technical education. He noted as well that trade union officials too often considered their presence on management bodies equalled workers' presence. Generally, he advocated the three-tier system established in Algeria – general assembly, elected workers council and executive committee.

Self-management, he reiterated, meant more than workers' management of the enterprise. Power needed to be devolved to democratic local governments. Here also, he noted the spontaneous creation of 'commandos', or local and regional assemblies of delegates from committees formed for food distribution, health services and education. These assemblies, which had suddenly flourished in response to the bosses' strike, had begun to play the role of actual local and regional self-government.

A huge part of the solution was political. He acknowledged that the ad hoc system of co-management was messy. It would be a huge step forward if the legislation setting up a nationally uniform system of workers' participation were to be passed by the Chilean Congress. The opposition parties commanded a majority and had to date refused to pass the legislation.

Pablo left Chile in December to return to France, determined to write a book on developments in Chile. Before setting to work on that, he wrote a report on the situation in Peru and Chile for *Le Monde Diplomatique*.[13] He was impressed by the Velasco dictatorship in Peru which had carried through a radical land reform, nationalised key companies and set up a range of cooperatives. It was also promoting peasant and workers' participation in the management of what it called socialised enterprises, in a conscious effort to create an alternative to capitalism and existing bureaucratic socialism. All this while leaving basic civil liberties intact. Pablo's main concern was the general apathy of the workers and citizens, because the pattern in such regimes was for the initial radical strongman to be followed by a more conservative figure keen to dismantle his predecessor's radical schemes, as had happened in Egypt after Nasser died. Only an active democratic breakthrough could prevent such an outcome in Peru.

By contrast, his hopes for Chile were reasonably high. If one of the spurs for the strike of the bourgeoisie had been workers' takeovers of companies and the limiting of traditional prerogatives of employers, then that strike had further accelerated and spread the phenomenon. There was a wide and active sympathy for such a 'self-managed' future and strong support for it in the left-wing of the Socialist party and in MAPU. What worried him in the *Le Monde Diplo* article was the introduction of the army generals into the cabinet and the continued attempts to appease the Christian Democrats. The turn to the army had been justified as a check on the violent activities of the fascist Patria y Libertad, but it also curbed more radical initiatives among workers and peasants, with the army raiding working-class suburbs to confiscate arms and arrest militants. The officer corps, drawn overwhelmingly from the better-off classes, was committed to upholding the constitutional order which included existing property and social relations.

The presence of the generals only put more pressure to the brake already applied to the revolution by Allende, the right-wing of the Socialist Party and the Communist Party. The powerful Communist Party was adamant that efforts in Chile should be limited to creating an 'anti-imperialist, anti-monopoly, anti-oligarchy democracy' in partnership with the Christian Democrats. Of course, as Pablo noted, there was little evidence the Christian Democrats or the 'bourgeois oligarchy' or Washington were interested.

Pablo wrote his Chile book quickly – he seems to have completed the book in March – and it was published in France in the summer of 1973 under the title *Quel socialisme au Chili?* Beyond detailing the spreading democratisation and the political constraints, he noted the deterioration in the economy, which also threatened support for the revolutionary process. As he pointed out, the transition to a more socialised economy dislocated the normal functioning of the capitalist economy. There was a flight of capital and an investment strike leading to shortages, inflation and a black market. Washington naturally turned the screws, cutting any aid or relief to Chile, and the CIA and other agencies continued to conspire with the right-wing elements in the country. The Soviet Union gave only limited economic support to the Allende government. The Allende government urgently needed to pursue economic policies that would satisfy at least the less well-off part of the middle class without sacrificing its core supporters.

For all the problems, support for the Allende government continued to grow. Allende had been elected in 1970 in a three-way contest with 36 per cent of the vote. In the parliamentary elections in March 1973, the Allende alliance secured 44 per cent. Even before the election, the Communist Party suggestion – that the hundred or so companies that had been nationalised from below during the strike of the bourgeoisie be handed back to their owners – was defeated. This swing to the left, combined with the defeat of the strike of the bourgeoisie, signalled to Washington and the Right that there was no way the government could be overthrown by 'civic' means. On the odd occasions when Allende and the Communist Party leaders of the union federation agreed to mass demonstrations of support in the centre of Santiago, huge crowds and detachments of workers and citizens participated. These forces could have been called into action to sweep the fascists off the streets in the capital Santiago, but Allende and the government refused to mobilise them. Later Pablo speculated that such actions could have been useful as a dress rehearsal for countering any attempted coup.

Returning briefly to Chile in July 1973, Pablo witnessed one of these huge demonstrations. He was struck by the numbers of workers and peasants brandishing sticks and calling for firmness and the formation of a peoples' militia. Allende preferred to trust in his seemingly good relations with generals of the armed forces, appointing Pinochet – the architect of the coming coup d'état – as head of the army. Many in the Popular Union, the alliance of parties supporting Allende, continued to sow illusions about the generals' respect for the constitution and legality. The communist-led union federation appointed Pinochet as its military counsellor. On the very morning of the coup of 11 September, the Italian Communist Party's daily newspaper published a commentary by a Chilean Communist senator, Volodia Teiteboim, extolling the army's loyalty and love of democracy.[14] Not surprisingly, then, the president and government, and the mass of their supporters, were unprepared for the devastating coup of 11 September.

Pablo returned to Paris some weeks before the fatal blow. But Elly and friends were still in Santiago when the coup broke. Elly was left holed up in their apartment, which had served as a discreet meeting place for leaders of the Socialist Party but was only a few blocks from the presidential palace that was suddenly being bombed by air force jets and attacked by tanks. Allende had died there earlier that day, resisting the coup. Pablo – stranded in Paris – grew increasingly alarmed as reports flooded in of raids, round-ups, arrests, murders and torture of left-wing activists. For three days Elly stayed indoors, ready to suicide, as Allende apparently had, if the soldiers were to come for her (she had a collection of pills). Fortunately, an unknown and unnamed French 'acquaintance', with no political links to them, 'thought of looking for her ... He sheltered her and helped her cross the border into Argentina, taking advantage of the terrible confusion that still prevailed in Santiago'. Pablo described it as 'heaven-sent luck'. Indeed. And it was not the only example. Taking advantage of the confusion, a young doctor and supporter of Pablo made his way to Chile and helped in the escape of leftists such as Mac Ginty, who also crossed safely into Argentina.

Pablo himself underestimated the savagery of the army's coup, although he had anticipated there would be one. When 'the expected coup' did come, it was 'a bloody and unprecedented repression, the extent and horror of which no one had foreseen ...'[15] The force of the coup matched the revolutionary threat to the existing order in Chile and beyond. However, the popular forces were not prepared to react immediately and collectively. Even out in the industrial working-class suburbs where the workers were organised into networks of workplace and local elected bodies, 'the great majority ... waited passively for the barbarians to come and attack them in their factories'.

Pablo's Chile book was being translated into English when the coup occurred, and he quickly wrote a final chapter, summarising the main events after March and emphasising the lessons learned, in terms of the role of revolutionaries when a real opportunity arose. One of the lessons was clearly the need for creating and arming a people's militia. All the revolutions, from the American one of 1776 onwards, had demonstrated that need.[16] However, in the wake of the defeat, he was more focussed on the orientation the Left should pursue in an unfolding revolutionary situation. The Chile experience had shown that the radicalising workers and peasants would look to 'their' traditional parties, while at the same time organising themselves into new bodies marked by participatory democracy. The situation would progress through the interplay of parties and the mass of their supporters, and the role of the revolutionaries was to recognise this and become involved in this process. It would require as much cooperation as possible around the aim of strengthening the nascent economic and social democracy. In this unfolding scenario, elements in the traditional parties would join the alliance of revolutionaries in the pursuit of certain objectives, as had happened during the bosses strike in Chile. He was, in the end, most concerned to combat any ultra-leftist and messianic illusions that would-be revolutionaries might have of short-circuiting such a process, mistaking their dreams for reality.[17]

— + —

The time in Chile was part research and part advocacy. In Santiago he delivered a paper, 'Self-management in the struggle for Socialism' to the 10th Latin American Congress of Sociology in Santiago.[18] In it he outlined what became what we might call his "working hypothesis for revolution in Europe". He was to expound, refine and attempt to apply this hypothesis over the next decade. The version he delivered in Santiago is the fullest we have and was inspired by developments such as May 1968, the hot autumn of 1969 in Italy, the miners' strike in Britain in 1972 and the unfolding events in Chile itself. It was formulated before the downturn in the world economy that followed the oil shock of 1973. The ending of the *Trente Glorieuses* (as the French call the post-war three decades of rising prosperity) only confirmed him in his expectation that there would be socio-economic crises that could develop into pre-revolutionary situations of the sort he outlined in the 1972 paper. Such opportunities arose only rarely and if they were missed, or bungled, then revolutionaries would probably have to wait decades before another presented itself.

The 1972 paper covered the two basic challenges for revolutionaries – the first was the successful revolution which would transform property and social relations, and the second was to construct a transitional society to socialism that was worthy of the socialist label. The key feature for the successful completion of both tasks was the institutionalisation of mass participation, or the creation of a wider participatory democracy. He repeated his argument that the failure of May 1968 was due to the fact that the seizures and occupations of that month remained passive and, except in isolated instances, did not proceed to actual self-management. As for the society that would follow any successful revolt, it was not enough to nationalise the commanding heights, to transfer the source of workers' wages from the boss to the state. That did not represent a social revolution. In fact, the old model of a state-run nationalised economy and the rule of a single party was a recipe for the creation of a new ruling bureaucratic class. Certainly, in existing societies there were objective conditions – significant cultural and educational disparities – that led to the emergence of ruling bureaucracies, of directors and directed, of governors and governed. But there was also a subjective factor, and that was the commitment to the Stalinist model of the so-called existing socialisms. That model led straight to bureaucratic dictatorship.

The new model would depend on commencing self-management immediately in the socialised, publicly-owned sector of the economy; developing cooperatives, especially in agriculture; strong local and regional communal governments; a flexible and democratically elaborated and articulated socio-economic plan and an educational revolution. Of course, Pablo spelled out that mouthful in greater detail and emphasised that such a democratic model would always be a work in progress. There was, he said, no perfect ready-made system of self-management.

He put a great deal of emphasis on two key features. The first was that the method of payment for workers – collectively and individually – should be based on the wealth they produced. Although he admitted this might be difficult to estimate when it came to teams and to individuals, he believed that democratic discussion and determination by the workers, or producers, in each undertaking could achieve this. This method of payment, along with actual decision-making, would constitute the abolition of the proletarian condition. Equally, if not more important, was permanent or continuous education. This education would be general and technical, and be part of the paid working week, which would be made up of direct productive labour and educational labour. This continuous education would be necessary both for overcoming the gap between intellectual and manual labour, which was at the root of hierarchy and bureaucracy, and for rising productivity that would flow from a better educated workforce.

This paper was a companion piece to some ideological housekeeping on the nature of the so-called 'workers states'.[19] Pablo concluded in the early 1970s that the state ownership and control of the economy, in combination with the one-party state controlling all of social life, led to a bureaucracy emerging as a new ruling class. In the wake of the Russian Revolution, this is what had occurred in the Soviet Union in the space of three decades. Trotsky had labelled the rise of Stalin and the bureaucratic dictatorship as the Soviet 'Thermidor', after the conservative regime that stopped, reversed and consolidated the French Revolution after the overthrow of Robespierre. For Pablo, time had made this analogy invalid. More than a political counter-revolution was involved in the decades that followed Lenin's death. By monopolising political power, the bureaucracy had created a new ruling social class and form of economy and society.

The traditional Marxist idea that capitalism would be followed by socialism was a case of schematic over-simplification. The 20th century had witnessed anti-capitalist and anti-imperialist revolutions which had given rise to regimes that did not lead on to socialism, by which Marxists meant an expansion of democracy, the withering away of the state and the age-old division of labour. No matter what they claimed, the ruling bureaucracies had erected fundamental blockages to that evolution. (By labelling their regimes 'socialist', they also gave 'socialism' a bad name among workers and citizens in advanced capitalist countries.) The earlier conclusion, so stoutly defended by Pablo himself, that state ownership and planning equalled a 'workers' or proto-socialist state was erroneous. The nationalised, centrally planned economy could deliver the basic infrastructure of a modern economy, even high rates of growth initially, but at a certain stage it became a brake which only democratic liberalisation could overcome. The evidence for this was clearly visible in the stagnation of the Soviet Union from at least the early 1970s onwards.

In coming to these belated conclusions, Pablo and his friends did recognise that the bureaucratic autocracies flourished more in economically backward countries without democratic traditions. They thought the bureaucratic dictatorships in the Soviet Union and China were more solid and enduring than in the Eastern European countries where lingering knowledge of democratic institutions and resentment of national repression in the Stalin era made the chances of a political-social revolution more likely.

— ∻ —

At the end of 1973, twenty years after convincing the majority in the International to adopt 'entrism sui generis', he returned to the issue. He was responding to the 'slow and insufficient growth' of the revolutionary Marxist tendency in what he termed 'favourable' circumstances. He submitted a paper to a meeting of the international leadership of the Tendency (TMRI, its initials in French) in December 1973, a meeting called to consider the organisation's growth problems.[20] Reading it 50 years later, one cannot fail to be struck by the purely intellectual cast of the argument. There were, of course, other reasons why people joined organisations – the promise of activism, of emotional bonds, the reputation and ambience of an organisation, among others. The three Trotskyist organisations in France, for instance, which were all significantly larger than the *pabliste* organisations, did offer such a home away from home, a world or tribe to belong to, a comforting niche. Pablo did not consider those factors in his paper. In setting them aside, he was in effect saying he didn't want people to join on those bases. It made his pitch all the more challenging.

In essence, he was consolidating all his previous thinking, thinking that had been challenged or confirmed over the decades as world events unfolded. He accepted that a viable revolutionary Marxist party of hundreds, or thousands, of activists could only be created by alliances and fusions. Its strategy in the long haul would be to link with radicalising currents in the traditional mass parties of the working class.

For the entrism into this mass movement to be effective, however, it required hundreds and ideally thousands of revolutionary Marxists:

> It is obvious that 'entrism' makes no practical sense if we are, for example, too few or if the prevailing or conjunctural conditions in the mass organisation or movement are unfavourable. But in such cases it is not entrism which is in question, but simply its efficacy or the timely opportunity for its application.

His version of entrism now envisaged assembling the core of such entrist forces prior to or simultaneous with the actual entrist activity:

> … it is necessary that the organisation acquires first of all a mass base, becomes a genuine force composed initially of some hundreds of militants, then thousands …

Clearly, they were not yet available in the thousands that he envisaged, even in France which was always the major base for his supporters. The point he danced around was how to create them, although he did try some practical advice. In France he advocated a fusion with the Parti Socialiste Unifié (PSU) in the hope that a force of some thousands committed to self-management, to entrism, and the perspective of electing a PCF-PS government based on united front committees in workplaces and communities, could be assembled. The French supporters and their organisation, Alliance Marxiste Révolutionnaire, soon after initiated successful negotiations with the PSU to merge with them.[21]

In Greece, he thought that it would be possible to create a left socialist party with a mass following and membership, including a significant presence of revolutionary Marxists. After the 'Commune' of the Athens Polytechnic in November 1973, he was convinced the days of the junta were numbered. It was likely that the Americans and elements in the army would attempt a safe transfer of power to a conservative government led by Constantine Karamanlis. He wrote as much to Andreas Papandreou and proposed transforming PAK, the resistance organisation Papandreou led, into a left socialist party with self-managed socialism in its platform and with a democratic structure. In Pablo's view, the Greek members of the Tendency should be in the forefront of advocating and launching such a party.[22]

Like the French comrades, he and his Greek comrades were very soon to get the opportunity to put this advice into practice. But events at the other end of the Mediterranean world were to intervene. Portugal's 'Carnation Revolution' began.

CHAPTER 17

# The turn to Europe 1970s

*For the first time in a very long time, a conjuncture with very great
revolutionary possibilities has appeared in capitalist Europe ...
It is a matter of a battle of genuine historical importance.
For on its issue depends whether humanity can avoid the choice
between decadent capitalism and bureaucratic 'socialism', and
have instead the alternative of a socialism of self-management*

'Pour la révolution européenne'
Editorial, *Sous le drapeau du socialisme* 67
December, 1975

AFTER THE TRAGEDY in Chile, Pablo's primary focus switched to capitalist Europe. He shared the high hopes of the rest of the European Left following May '68 in France and the 'hot autumn' of 1969 in Italy. The old continent was now the 'epicentre of the world revolution'. To be precise, it was a time of possible 'revolutionary openings' in western Europe – particularly in Portugal, Spain, Italy and France.[1] These countries were 'ripe' for a self-managed socialism. As he wrote in analysing the significance of LIP, the watch manufacturer in France that the workers took over in 1974 and managed after the owners announced they were closing it:

> Generally speaking, in the advanced capitalist countries, various fundamental factors converge to make the case for a self-managed socialism. In these countries it is 'natural' for ever larger layers of the workforce to question a life based on dreary work, work not of their own choosing, in order to consume a range of products and services ultimately imposed by capital. Equally it is resented ever more keenly that this production relies on the

democratic collaboration and collective effort of these intellectual and manual workers ...

Added to these sources of discontent was a new factor:

And now, in addition, increasing numbers of workers and citizens are becoming aware of the disastrous ecological effects of the unrestrained growth [*croissance sauvage*] of this system.[2]

He sketched out the path forward. Sudden national crises could lead to governments of the traditional parties of the working class taking office. In such crises, networks of committees of workers and citizens could be organised in workplaces, localities and institutions and these committees – open to all – would press 'their' government to resolve the crisis by implementing measures that led in the direction of a self-managed socialism. This scenario had unfolded in Chile and, as early as 1972, Pablo was convinced that there was now a strong possibility of this pattern repeating itself in parts of capitalist Europe.[3]

This possibility was all the more likely with the gloss coming off capitalism with the end of the long boom – the *Trente Glorieuses,* as the French termed it – and the arrival of persistent inflation and significant unemployment. The shock oil price rise of 1973 decreed by the oil-producing countries had provoked a major recession in Europe. A potent mix of traditional working-class militancy, aspirations for workers control, women's liberation, student demands for self-management of universities and schools, and the claims of national minorities for self-determination, would, in his view, propel traditional working-class parties into office. This was on the agenda for countries such as France, Spain and Italy. Unforeseen detonators could also provoke revolutionary or pre-revolutionary situations elsewhere – Portugal and Greece would provide such examples in 1973-4.[4]

Pablo was explicit that such revolutionary openings would follow this pattern and these openings would mature over time. As the resulting governments wrestled with the problems and challenges facing them, as they attempted to implement their program and satisfy their base, institutions of dual power would develop as workers and citizens organised themselves to support the government and ensure the realisation of their demands. In such a process, a revolutionary formation could emerge with a significant mass following. While he didn't cite it, he was aware of the history of the Bolsheviks in 1917; at the outbreak of the revolution in

February they had 25,000 members, by October that membership had increased tenfold.

In this scenario, however, there would be no repeat of the rapid evolution of the Russian Revolution of February-October 1917, even if there would be decisive, even insurrectionary moments in the process of transition to a self-managing socialism. The process would, by definition, be democratic. This democratic evolution would be on two tracks – via electoral victories, which were necessary to win middle-class support (or neutrality) and via the development of self-managing institutions in every sphere and at every level.

The possibilities Pablo sketched out would require a great deal of patience and maturity on the part of would-be revolutionaries. As soon as possible, they needed to regroup, combine and coalesce so that they could be more than just marginal players. And they would have to respect the choices and the activity of the citizenry – including the radical currents in the traditional parties. Their role was not to substitute themselves for the working class, but to aid its efforts aimed at the wider democratisation of work, culture and social life.

The Pablo hypothesis assumed unprecedented mass politicisation and public activity (millions of Pablos, if you like). This was the least heroic of the assumptions underlying this working hypothesis – after all, such sudden awakenings of a whole society were not unknown in the 20th (or even this) century. France in May 1968 and Italy's 'hot autumn' of 1969 were examples or premonitions. What was more unlikely was the possibility of the traditional mass socialist and communist parties responding positively to mass demands for radical change and a more genuine and participatory democracy. True, in Chile there had been some goodwill and sympathy to this possibility, at least on the part of the Socialist Party and the Christian left-wing party MAPU. However, the same combination of such relatively open and independent parties scarcely existed in Western Europe, where the two superpowers, the United States and the Soviet Union, obviously wielded great influence – one on the social democrats and the other on the communists. Neither would stand idly by or facilitate the evolution-revolution Pablo envisaged. As Pablo himself pointed out on numerous occasions, Washington would defend capitalism against the spread of the red menace and the Kremlin would hardly welcome a model of socialism that was an indictment of the Soviet system. Nor could the intervention of the police and army on the side of the status quo be ruled out.[5]

The more pressing problem, of course, was how to stimulate the emergence of a united revolutionary formation – as a party or alliance –

with even a small mass following and a realistic strategy for revolutionary change. By 1977 there would be a certain pessimism (or realism) about the prospects of such a development, especially when those earlier opportunities had come and gone. Still, the working hypothesis continued to be expounded.[6] The problems on the revolutionary Left were – in Pablo's view – at least threefold: a mature attitude towards the mass parties and their government as the first stage of the revolutionary process; the challenge of elaborating a relevant contemporary program; and the bridging of the gap between the 'political Left' and the 'social Left' which had developed because of the suspicion of much of the Left towards movements such as the women's liberation movement. The failure to develop a mass revolutionary socialist party (or alliance) in the present decade would mean missing the current opportunity. If this was the unfortunate upshot, then revolutionaries could always wait and prepare for the next opening. But if this was to be the case, 'we risk waiting a long time'. [7]

Portugal turned out to be a dress rehearsal for the worth of the Pablo hypothesis. In April 1974, the world's longest surviving fascist regime (initiated in 1926 by Antonio de Oliveira Salazar who exercised power himself until 1968 before he handed power to a hand-picked successor) was overthrown in a military coup. The coup was organised by young army officers disillusioned and radicalised by their participation in Portugal's colonial wars in southern Africa. 'The military which overthrew the Portuguese dictatorship,' Pablo pointed out, 'had matured in the distinct experience of a long colonial war in Africa, so the founding of a democracy in their country was an added service which the colonial revolution rendered the mother country …'[8]

Organised in the Movimento das Forças Armadas (MFA), these radical junior officers promised a transformed and democratic Portugal. They immediately released political prisoners, restored civil liberties and legalised political parties and free trade unions. They also began negotiations with the independence movements in Portuguese colonies. This revolutionary opening was followed by an outburst of mass participation in politics and the democratisation of economic and social life. Little wonder that when he first read news of this coup and the progressive role of the military, Pablo thought 'O lucky country', so glaring was the contrast with Greece.

That summer of 1974, Pablo made his way to Lisbon.[9] From his period in Algeria at the time of Ben Bella, he knew many of the leaders of the colonial independence movements and the internal left opposition to the old regime. They had found refuge and support in Algiers and there, they had set up pirate radio stations to beam dissident news and views into Portugal and its colonies. In Lisbon, there were many reunions with these former neighbours from Algiers, and it was through them that Pablo started to meet the army officers who had led the coup. The negotiations for the independence of Mozambique actually began in the rooms next door to where Pablo was staying in a small Lisbon hotel.

From his memoirs it appears that his first and best audience for his ideas was among naval officers with whom he spent 'a memorable day' discussing revolution and socialist self-management at the naval academy overlooking Lisbon harbour. As the officers and sailors described the elected committees that were now running the navy, his mind conjured up images of the battleship *Potemkin* and the great naval uprisings of Russia in 1905 and 1917. In the audience that day was Otelo de Carvahlo, the chief organiser of the coup and the most left-wing of the army officers. Either that day, or soon after, he also made the acquaintance of other leaders of the MFA – Ernesto Melo Antunes, in particular. If Otelo was the most left-wing of the officers, Antunes was in Pablo's view the shrewdest. Despite what was to become an enduring friendship with Carvahlo, that officer was then surrounded by other 'advisors', most of whom appeared to be 'Maoists', and whom Pablo complained had more influence.

In line with the working hypothesis, Pablo advocated a Socialist-Communist-MFA government based on open committees in localities and workplaces (and the armed forces). Elections held for a constituent assembly in early 1975 indicated a clear electoral majority for such a government, but none of Pablo's wished-for components were willing partners. The socialists and communists were under the influence of foreign actors and their local leaders who had no interest in the government Pablo advocated. In the absence of such a willing coalition, Pablo advocated grassroots campaigns to bring together members and supporters of all the left parties, to press for this united front government pursuing socialist policies and based on a network of committees open to all. The disparate revolutionary left groups showed little interest in the idea, preferring to chase the illusion that the masses would soon turn to them for leadership.

Confusion – and a traditionalist backlash in the north of Portugal – reigned until November 25, 1975. At that point, the more conservative army officers in alliance with the socialists, easily the biggest party in the country, took control of the government, re-established order and organised new parliamentary and presidential elections. In the wake of these elections the Socialists formed a coalition, not with the Communists but the main conservative party. The 'moderate' head of the MFA, Antonio Eanes, was elected president with 62 per cent of the votes, far outstripping Otelo de Carvalho's 16 per cent. Carvalho had run as an independent, revolutionary socialist and as a champion of direct democracy. Pablo and his supporters made it clear that this was the second-best option – a single candidate of the labour movement and its parties being infinitely preferable.[10] Nevertheless, Carvalho was now becoming something of a *pabliste*, telling an election crowd: 'We should harness the spontaneity and creativity of the masses, which gives them the ability to solve their own problems. I saw, during the Portuguese Revolution, the power of this creativity in the streets and the towns and the fields.' His reasonable vote – the Communist Party candidate had received 11 per cent – underwrote a certain optimism in *Sous le drapeau du socialisme* about Portugal well into 1976, if only the revolutionaries could discard their ultra-left illusions.

By now Pablo and Carvalho were firm friends. After Carvalho was sentenced in 1985 to fifteen years jail on murky charges that he was the secret leader of an urban terrorist group[11], Pablo visited him regularly, organised international solidarity campaigns, lobbied President Eanes and Prime Minister Mario Soares for his release and, being Pablo, got involved in escape plans which Carvalho himself eventually vetoed. Writing of these plans in the 1995 epilogue to his memoir, Pablo enthuses: 'the opportunity was given me again to meet people who had played a decisive role in the international movement and, in spite of the new difficult times of disorganisation and discouragement, were ready to imperil their own freedom and lives to liberate the symbol of one of the last revolutionary outbreaks in Europe ...'.

Otelo de Carvalho was for him, like Ben Bella, an historically exemplary revolutionary leader who deserved support and honour even in defeat. Carvalho was pardoned and released in 1990 and within months he was in Athens visiting Pablo. (Another imprisoned dissident leader, the Moroccan, Abraham Serfaty, was also the subject of similar efforts by Pablo during these years. Serfaty was at this time the longest-serving political prisoner, after Nelson Mandela, in Africa. Jailed in 1974, he was released and expelled from Morocco in 1991.)

– ÷ –

Even before the disappointing denouement in Portugal, Greece beckoned. One hot summer night at the end of July 1974 in Lisbon, Pablo was at a friend's house when 'I learned from the television of the dramatic events in

Cyprus and the liberation of my country that followed. As if electrified, I rushed off to Paris and there waited impatiently to go down to Greece.' As we have noted, the resistance to the Greek junta never rose to threatening heights but there was one exception – and it was a heroic one.

The Polytechnic uprising took place in Athens in November 1973. Thousands of students occupied their campus in downtown Athens and via their own radio station called for the overthrow of the junta, the creation of a radical democracy and a break with the Americans and NATO. Thousands of people flocked to join the Athens 'Commune', as Pablo dubbed it, and similar occupations took place in other Greek cities. After three days, the junta sent in the tanks and hundreds died. Similar crackdowns took place elsewhere. Short-lived as it was, the Polytechnic Commune was an encouraging indication of the future politics of Greece. It also exacerbated the internal tensions within the junta between the hardliners and the moderates, with the hardliners emerging in control. This faction, in the hope of garnering mass (and American) support, attempted to occupy and integrate 'non-aligned' Cyprus into Greece in the summer of 1974. It was this failed adventure – it provoked Turkey's seizure of the north of the island where most of Cyprus's Turkish residents lived – that led to the collapse of the junta and the army generals' decision to recall Constantine Karamanlis as head of a transitional government which would hold elections and re-establish parliamentary government.

Pablo had anticipated just such an outcome. Papandreou's resistance organisation, PAK, had adopted a very radical orientation during the junta years, with Andreas writing that only the creation of a 'politico-military national liberation movement crafted after those of the third world' waging a multiform campaign, including armed struggle, could overthrow the colonels.[12] After the Polytechnic uprising, Pablo wrote to Andreas Papandreou to warn him that that classic Third-World national liberation struggle would not happen. Not only that, but it was highly likely that the bourgeoisie would dispense with the junta and turn to Karamanlis to bring Greece in line with the rest of Western Europe.[13]

This letter proved prescient and the drift of Pablo's thinking about Greece in the next decade was that the immediate future was one of modernisation and democratisation. Karamanlis started the process and Papandreou and PASOK (Panhellenic Socialist Movement) accelerated it when they came to office in 1981. This was not something that the radical Left should undervalue or threaten, in Pablo's view. However, for the next 28 years, Greece was to be the home of Europe's longest active terrorist group. The shadowy 17 November organisation used a leftist rhetoric to justify its string of assassinations – starting with the CIA station chief in Athens in 1975 – and in sensational circumstances Pablo was to be accused of being its secret leader.

His return to Greece from Lisbon, in 1974, wasn't exactly a hero's welcome, with scarcely anyone there to greet him at the airport in Athens. The country and its people had changed enormously in the four decades he had been absent, and he was initially disoriented. There were difficulties finding suitable accommodation until Amalia Fleming, the widow of Sir Alexander Fleming (discoverer of penicillin), came to the rescue. Once settled in comfortable, bourgeois Kolonaki, Pablo immediately wrote a long analysis of the socio-economic evolution of Greek capitalism since the war, noting the urbanisation, the growth in the services and construction sectors, weak industrial growth and the dependence on shipping and tourism to cover part but not all of the stubbornly large trade deficit. The most noteworthy social change was the reduction in the size of the poor peasantry, which had been the backbone of the revolutionary resistance of the 1940s.[14]

The old revolutionary generation was also passing. Those Greek comrades of his youth who had survived dictatorship, war, the prospect of murder at the hands of Nazis or Stalinists, and domestic reaction, were now departing. Pablo was not yet the 'last of the Mohicans' but the process had begun. In 1973, he paid tribute to Mitsos Chilios, a blue-collar worker and *pabliste*, who had remained an active revolutionary right through the junta era, providing support for members and supporters of the resistance and circulating underground literature. Another death noted at this time was that of Lazarus Tournopoulos, apparently a more orthodox Trotskyist but a comrade from the 1930s who had maintained the underground organisation and press of the Trotskyists during the periods of post-war illegality.[15]

Pablo was, as ever, hopeful. There was scope for a revolutionary Marxist party with thousands of members, he claimed, as well as a larger left socialist party which could accommodate a range of socialists and social democrats. 'Such a party could be created by the current represented by Andreas Papandreou, and it would draw in a great number of the activists who had struggled in Greece against the dictatorship. It would be thanks to the interaction between these two forces, an independent revolutionary Marxist organisation and a left socialist party, that it would be possible to act efficaciously so that the process triggered in Greece with the fall of the military dictatorship takes a revolutionary path, capable of successfully undertaking the project of self-managed socialism.'

As for the first option, there was the usual problem of a cluster of competing Trotskyist groups, all keen on exclusively pursuing their own line. But on the second possibility, things looked more hopeful. Andreas Papandreou was already turning PAK into PASOK (the Greek Socialist Movement) and in Pablo's view, this could be the mass left socialist party.

Initially, PASOK did situate itself as a left socialist party. The ideal of self-managed socialism was adopted by Papandreou, and some of Pablo's closest collaborators held influential positions in the new party. Dimitris Livieratos, for instance, was employed in the party's executive bureau and in the policy unit, the grandly titled Centre for Research and Enlightenment.[16] Along with a handful of other Pablo supporters, he was deeply involved in the spread of PASOK clubs and branches throughout Greece – something he remained ever proud of.[17] Later Pablo recalled that he had proposed to Papandreou that he form a mass left socialist party committed to self-managed socialism and to internal democracy, and that Andreas accepted the first idea but not the second. Indeed, the fatal flaw in Pablo's expectations was that they all depended on the gift of one man. As the historian of PASOK notes '… PASOK was the creation of A. Papandreou and he was ultimately its sole source of power'.[18]

The first free national elections held in November 1974 were disappointing for PASOK – and for Pablo. The result was a landslide win for prime minister Constantine Karamanlis and the conservatives. PASOK came in third on 14 per cent of the votes, trailing the old shell of the Centre party on 20 per cent. The two communist parties garnered some ten per cent. PASOK did much better in the local government elections in April 1975, winning the mayoralty in almost all the cities and big towns. However, by then Papandreou had decided to tighten his control over PASOK and move it to the right. He adopted a more strident nationalist and anti-Turk position in the continuing clashes with the neighbour over divided Cyprus and territorial rights in the Aegean Sea.

While warning of the dangers of this nationalist turn and internal anti-democratic practices, Pablo remained hopeful through 1975 that the formation of a government of the Left led by PASOK was still a real possibility. Papandreou's purges of liberal and radical elements were even presented as being partly brought on by 'sectarians pursuing their own confused, to say the least, goals'. The wars between the Papandreou machine and these sectarians hindered the growth of PASOK among the working class and poor peasantry. In any case, political developments in Greece depended as much on what happened elsewhere in Europe.[19] However, the purges continued throughout 1976 and included Pablo's supporters. By September 1976, he had shed most of his illusions about PASOK. 'Its chances of evolving into a left centrist formation, a sort of left socialist party,' he wrote, 'are now considerably diminished.' He added that only his own organisation, which published a journal *For Socialism*, 'struggles against the chauvinist currents which have swept up the Maoists and certain Trotskyist groups'.[20]

Now more than ever he divided his time between his national roots and international interests. He lived in Athens but spent much of his time in Paris. He became a regular columnist for *To Vima* and *Ta Nea*, the two centre-left dailies in Greece which supported PASOK. This engagement as a regular in the centre-left press seems to have occurred very quickly after his return. For instance, 'Greek newspapers' sent him to Spain to cover developments after the death of the fascist dictator Franco in 1975.[21] Over the next twenty years he wrote thousands of columns and articles for these two mass-circulation papers. There was no slackening of his analyses and writing for *Sous le drapeau du socialisme*, but even there his Greek roots started to show.

He continued to travel widely in Europe – and beyond. He was a guest of honour at the Sinn Fein conference in Dublin in October 1978.[22] Sinn Fein was the political arm of the Provisional IRA, then fighting for the independence and unity of Britain's oldest colony, and had recently adopted a federalist, democratic socialist platform. Judging by one journalist's report, this visit must have been a morale-boosting occasion for Pablo:

> The fraternal delegates at the Ard Fheis [Sinn Fein's annual conference] represented an eclectic mix, a bit like the political *pot-pourri* within the Provisionals themselves: there were purely nationalist Bretons and Welsh language campaigners, socialists from the Basque country and from the Portuguese United Workers' Organisation (OUT), as well as the legendary Trotskyist revolutionary, Pablo. Few of the delegates can have had an idea of the historical resonance of his name. Risteard Behal, head of the Foreign Affairs Bureau, proudly presented a summary of Pablo's 50-year career in revolutionary politics – indeed he did it twice – his record of imprisonment and deportation, and of assistance to independence movements, and the crowd loved it.[23]

The reception is not surprising. Greece had been the Ireland of the Turkish empire and Algeria the Ireland of the French empire. The Greco-French Pablo was Irish twice over.

The following year he was in Mexico City with Elly for the commemorative conference marking the centenary of Trotsky's birth.

## 17 . THE TURN TO EUROPE 1970s

The other guests included Tamara Deutscher, Marguerite Bonnet, George Novack, Raymond Molinier, Pierre Broué and Adolfo Gilly. He spoke at some of the seminars and at the concluding public meeting. One of his earlier interventions had to do with basic civil liberties which the Left could be too silent about:

> It appears necessary to me to draw the following from the terrible experience of the Moscow Trials [*which condemned to death Lenin's closest comrades on the basis of confessions extracted by torture – HG*]: to remain ever critical and vigilant in relation to analogous experiences elsewhere. I am personally struck and concerned by the apathy of the international intelligentsia, as at the time of the Moscow Trials, on the subjects not only of what is happening in Cambodia, Laos and Vietnam, but also in China itself.

He went on to cite the persecution and trial of Maoists in China. Whatever one's views on their politics, we 'must make known our opposition to all persecution for political reasons, and demand from the authorities clear and transparent accounts of what people are arrested for, their treatment and their trials.' At the final meeting he introduced the concept, borrowed from the East German dissident, Rudolph Bahro, of women and men with an 'excess of consciousness' (*l'excédent de conscience*) and their role in facilitating the ultra-democratic revolution necessary to avoid the possibilities of ecological and nuclear disasters in wait for humanity. Trotsky was cited as an inspirational model of such human beings – 'not as gods, or heroes, or mythical leaders, but as examples of real men and women, of true combatants for the genuine liberation of humanity'.[24] This idea of people with an 'excess of consciousness', by which he meant those able to stand critically outside the prevailing culture, was to become a leitmotif of his writing for the time he had left.

— ✢ —

In a major essay on self-management published in 1977, Pablo elaborated his argument that the concept of socialism based on generalised self-management, or direct democracy, was an essentially new development in socialist politics. There had been earlier manifestations of such an aspiration, but now the aspiration had a real material basis. Capitalism had super-charged the productive forces with the application of advanced technology which required a workforce with a higher cultural and educational level. This in turn enabled mass participation in the management of the economy and society, although that participation, of course, was not encouraged under capitalism. That potential coincided with the emergence of movements such as the women's movement and the student movement whose basic aspiration was for self-determination, via forms of direct or participatory democracy. These phenomena were common to a host of advanced industrial countries, so the ideal was not confined to one city or one country. The times were now right for self-managed socialism like never before. In a review of the memoirs of de Gaulle, he had made it a virtue of the great man that he recognised the need to introduce some democracy into the workplace.[25]

In acknowledging that the self-management ideal had a prehistory, Pablo harked back to the Paris Commune of 1871, and Russia between September 1917 and the spring of 1918 when workers, soldiers, sailors, and peasants created a whole universe of elected committees to run their affairs and the whole country. But, as we have observed, he was also keen to trace the ancestry right back to fourth- and fifth-century Athens where direct democracy had taken its classical forms. He also drew attention to the philosophical justification for direct democracy that underwrote the Athenian model. The key philosopher in that respect was Protagoras. No fragments of his writings survive, although Plato allows Protagoras in the eponymous dialogue to expound on his theory that direct democracy flows from the nature of man as endowed by the gods. Apparently Protagoras' view was that humans are born with the capacity to participate in governing society and this trait can flourish if cultivated by education and application. For Pablo, this philosophical belief in humanity's capacity was confirmed by the operation of Athenian democracy over nearly two centuries. He also endorsed Aristotle's point that it also required a certain homogeneity in the cultural level, or genuine equality in society.

His admiration for Protagoras went so far that on his return to Greece, Pablo formed a 'Protagoras circle' in Athens, as a meeting place for advocates of self-management. It was this organisation that organised the campaigns and meetings in support of Polish solidarity in the 1980s, for example. One of their meetings, Pablo boasted in 1983, drew 5,000 people.[26]

Pablo's turn to Europe had more twists in store. The working hypothesis for the anticipated social and political advances of the 1970s remained unfulfilled. The possibilities that had flared in Portugal and Greece died away and resulted in social democratic governments that promised much but delivered less. Spain looked to be following a similar pattern after the fall of the fascist regime in 1975. In Italy, the radicalisation of the working

## 17 . THE TURN TO EUROPE 1970s

class and youth had receded and any existing chances were frittered away by a Communist Party anxious for an alliance with the governing Christian Democrats. A united socialist-communist government was elected in France in 1981, but workers and citizens were relatively quiescent and there was no united or significant formation of revolutionaries. At the first economic crisis, this government turned right and embraced austerity and neoliberal solutions.

Meanwhile, would-be revolutionary groups remained small and divided. In 1974, Pablo's French co-thinkers had amalgamated with the PSU and hoped that a similar junction could be worked out with the Ligue Communiste Révolutionnaire (LCR), the Mandel-influenced French section of the Fourth International. The LCR was not interested, however, and, when the PSU majority decided to uncritically support the election program of the Socialist-Communist alliance in 1977, the Pablo supporters in the PSU left to join with dissidents from the LCR to form the Committés communistes pour l'autogestion (CCA).

In turn, the CCA divided in 1981 over the importance of work in and around the PCF, (the French Communist Party) which Pablo himself considered a priority. After his intervention in the 1979 conference of the CCA, the two sides had agreed to work together and they settled on a common conference resolution. However, an issue that might have helped keep both sides together went missing from the attempted consensus. Pablo warned the conference about the short-ranged, nuclear-armed American Cruise missiles and Soviet SS-20s being deployed in Europe in the bizarre belief that using these weapons in limited nuclear exchanges was feasible. He advocated that his supporters approach 'various revolutionary groups' with the aim of launching a campaign against the deployment of such weapons. Yet there is no mention of it in the final conference resolution. It was, of course, a key issue that fired up huge public campaigns in the next decade in Europe, and led to the formation of the Greens in Germany and elsewhere.[27]

In the 1970s Pablo encountered two major difficulties with his supporters, particularly in France. The first was their reluctance to abandon the characterisation of the Soviet bloc as 'workers states'. His own conclusion, also late in the piece, that a new ruling bureaucratic class or bloc had taken power in these countries was only slowly accepted. The 5th international conference of the Tendency held in 1975 agreed only to continue discussing the 'the re-evaluation of the character of the "workers" states and the bureaucracy'.[28]

Still, he had more success in convincing the hold-outs on that issue than he had in the second dispute, over where the *pablistes* should concentrate their energies. He had recognised and supported the new social movements of the 1970s and argued they were an essential element in any revolutionary movement. However, he insisted that the main game was still the mass labour movement. He explained that the pivot to 'entrism sui generis' in 1950 was essentially recognition that the bulk of the working class retained its loyalty to its traditional parties and unions and that revolutionaries must turn their attention to them for the 'longue durée' (long haul). Entrism, moreover, would only make sense if it was undertaken by hundreds or thousands of revolutionary socialists and it was always the priority to assemble such a force. Due to the Algerian work and then the new social movements of the 1960s and '70s, this appreciation and commitment to the working class and its politics had been diluted or put to one side. The problem was that some of his supporters wanted to continue this 'neglect' in favour of the new movements and the new strata of the working class.[29] This was to be a recurring dispute and problem for the rest of his life.

— ❖ —

Among the 1968 generation, the disappointments and dashed hopes of the 1970s led to the emergence of left-wing terrorist groups, principally in Germany, Italy, Spain and Greece. The targets of groups such as the Red Army Faction in West Germany, the Red Brigades in Italy, the Basque ETA in Spain and *17 November* in Greece, were typically capitalist institutions and members of the ruling class and its servants. They bombed American-related companies and bases, robbed banks, kidnapped industrialists, assassinated CIA, army and police officers and torturers, and on occasion murdered hostages. Many a daring prison break was organised. Some tried to avoid killing, others took that option and indefensible acts were committed. Similar phenomena arose, too, in the United States and in Latin America, particularly in Uruguay, Argentina and Peru, where they were more like urban guerrillas as they enjoyed a wider support than in Europe. In some leftist circles there was a romantic aura surrounding these avenging, if outgunned and doomed Robin Hoods, and many on the Left admired their more extraordinary exploits.

It was impossible for serious left-wing militants not to take a position. Pablo tackled it in *Sous le drapeau* in 1977 in the wake of the 'suiciding' of the Baader-Meinhof group in a West German prison. Three of its members had been found dead in their cells in Stuttgart on 18 October that year, and Ulrike Meinhof was said to have earlier hanged herself while in custody. Any judgment about terrorism, by which Pablo meant armed action by small groups or individuals, depended mainly on context. Such action in the Third World, in places like Palestine, South Africa and South America, or in Eastern Europe or the Soviet Union, where there was relatively little or limited political freedom, would be viewed differently from that in Western Europe. Here, the turn to terrorism was the result of the frustration and desperation of young people confronted by the 'blockage' to political and social change in their societies. The responsibility had to be sheeted home to traditional socialist or communist parties. For instance, in West Germany the social-democratic SPD was an immovable supporter of the status quo, despite the hold-outs from the Nazi era who infested its police, army, judiciary and corporations. Its support for imperialism in its wars was equally staunch.

Naturally, Pablo reasserted the classic Marxist position of giving primacy to mass political work and the belief that socialist revolution would be the work of a conscious majority of the working class rather than a Jacobin minority. Nevertheless, he concluded that in the current circumstances, the attitude to these marginalised 'terrorists' should be one of understanding but not complaisance, of 'practical solidarity' when they were being hunted and persecuted, and dialogue with them in the hope of winning them over to the struggle for self-managed socialism.

Through all of this, Pablo continued to follow events in the Third World. One victory in the Indochina wars was, however, to lead to one of the worst regimes of all, in a century replete with them. In 1977, details of the genocide carried out by the Khmer Rouge were revealed to the world in *Cambodge année zéro* by the missionary François Ponchaud, who had lived in Cambodia from 1965 to 1975 and spoke Khmer. Here is not the place to regurgitate the evasions, hesitations and denials on the Left concerning Pol Pot and the Khmer Rouge.[30] It is however to Pablo's honour – and testimony to his intellectual integrity and astuteness – that he was not one of them. He faced the horror of the 'killing fields' full-on, in a prompt review of *Cambodge année zéro* and its first-hand accounts of what was happening in Cambodia.[31] The extent of the slaughter was difficult to believe, he admitted, but the evidence was impossible to ignore. The fact that it what had been happening in Cambodia had been covered up by the Chinese was not surprising. What was really discomforting for the international Left was that the Vietnamese had also stayed silent. The Khmer Rouge regime clearly had more in common with the despotisms associated with the Asiatic mode of production (for example, pharaonic Egypt) than socialism. It was certainly an anti-capitalist regime, but it had shown itself to be a world away from genuine socialism.

— ♦ —

Into this grim landscape in 1981 burst the workers' revolt in Poland. It reignited Pablo's hopes. A regular incantation in his *Sous le drapeau du socialisme* contributions in the 1970s had concerned the 'explosive contradictions' building up within the bureaucratic straitjacket of the Soviet bloc and China.[32] This regime was responsible for the slowing economic growth and blocking the way for them to reach the economic development of advanced capitalist countries. Poland, in his view, was already a basket case economically.[33]

One of the hoped-for effects of the advance of self-managed socialism in Western Europe would be that it would help undermine authoritarian regimes in both the East and West. The French *pablistes* had been very active in organising support for the Czech oppositionists and persecuted Soviet dissidents. Pablo himself had written elementary defences of Solzhenitsyn and others who were being persecuted in the Soviet Union. The Russian writer's retrograde political and philosophical views were used to attack him by official communists and others in the West, but his views were the very point according to Pablo. Socialism must stand for all the democratic rights conquered under capitalism and expand them. This meant that everyone had the right to expound and publish their views no matter what they were. Nor should it surprise people in the West that intellectuals like Solzhenitsyn and others espoused anti-socialist views after their experience of the terrors and miseries of the bureaucratic absolutism that called itself 'socialism' or 'communism'.[34]

The anti-system dissidence of the intellectuals was a common phenomenon in the Soviet Union and its satellite countries in the 1970s. It spread to other social strata and almost universalised in the eastern marches of Europe in the 1980s. These countries were now to occupy centre stage in Pablo's thinking and hopes.

CHAPTER 18

# End of an era 1980s

*From the years around 1789 to those around 1989, revolutionary politics maintained an actuality and dynamic potentiality, but since the 1980s it has been defamed, antiquated, unlearned and turned unreal.*

**Andreas Malm**[1]

THE 1980S WAS the decade in which Pablo prepared himself for death. In 1981 he reached 70, the Biblical finishing line for a life of three score years and ten. Elly was five years older. In 1983 they were the subject of a documentary on their lives that was shown on national television in Greece. The following year, prompted by his newspaper editors, he wrote his political memoirs (in Greek). He had decided to go quietly into the night when the time came. As he concluded his memoir, 'Animals end their lives naturally without prayers, but also without cowardice, cries, laments or tears. After so much travail, they lie on the ground and calmly surrender to the mystery of the Great Silence.' In the documentary, which took the form of a first-person narration, he had declared that he had no regrets:

> I think now that both of us are approaching the point of farewell, the farewell to beautiful 'Alexandria' – and truly Alexandria was a beautiful city and with terrible sadness we will farewell her, but without tears, without hesitation, without complaint. We feel that this 'Alexandria' has given us whatever it could give a person. And from this point of view, our farewell to 'her' entails naturally a certain sadness, but at the same time also the feeling that our life was, in the final analysis, considerably full and satisfying, and [besides] 'she' does not brook complaint and false consolation.[2]

In the meantime, he would continue to live life to the full, which was his motto after all. That meant, as always, analysing the world as it was emerging and acting accordingly. There was the added duty in his mind of repelling the counter-attack on Marxism that marked that decade, particularly in France. There was in fact no slackening of his political and intellectual activity. Happily, there was also the consolation of a new close friend in his life, Marika Karageorgiou.

He began the decade by arguing that developments in cybernetics reinforced the possibility for self-managed socialism. In an essay, *Autogestion et télématique*,[3] he sketched out this confidence that advances in science and technology made redundant all the old arguments among Marxists – which had begun between Bolsheviks and Mensheviks over the nature of revolution in Russia – about whether you could have socialist revolutions in underdeveloped countries. Now it was possible to have a global economy that opened the way to material abundance, a constantly rising educational and cultural level and an expansion of free time for everyone. These had been considered the *sine qua non* for socialism by Marx and now they were possible. Cybernetics (or telematics – the more limited sense of its application to machinery and storing information) was the latest factor making this possible. Pablo pointed out that Marx, principally in the *Grundrisse*, had predicted a capitalism in which production was largely automated and allowed for an expansion of labour-free time which was essential for the full development of the individual. Capitalism's social and political structures severely deformed the emancipatory potentiality as could be seen in the arms industry, space exploration, and developments in biological and genetic research. 'A new technocratic elite, linked to capitalist power centres, is able to manipulate information ... and increase the secret, elitist and authoritarian character of the system.' (As is now abundantly clear.) The same situation prevailed even more in the bureaucratic states, although the development of cybernetics lagged considerably.

How was this gross and dangerous distortion of potentiality to be overcome and the emancipatory potential realised? In answering that question he now employed (or borrowed) concepts that he was to return to again and again in the years he had left. They added up to a call for an almost religious renaissance rivalling the advent of the great religions. He clearly had in mind something like St Paul and his followers who freed Christianity from its Jewish exclusivity, or the 'parfaits' of the Cathar phenomenon that swept southern France in the 13th century, or even the Narodniks of 19th century Russia. Once again there are echoes of his

Tolstoyan youth in his prescriptions. This is how he saw the freeing of the genuine utopian potential occurring:

> The hope consists in the amplification and liberation among men and women of what Rudolf Bahro calls an 'excess of consciousness' and Henri Laborit the capacity – human, *par excellence* – of the 'imagining cortex'. They refer to the social and biological capacity of human beings, placed in social conditions favourable from the material and cultural point of view, to imagining a new social project.

These new revolutionaries, endowed with an 'excess of consciousness' and liberated imaginations, exist and will exist in increasing numbers in 'the most diverse social categories'. Often reformist initially, they will become more revolutionary with experience. This new vanguard 'cannot act as a new intellectual elite cut off from the mass of workers living in "subalternity" (or in a subordinate or excluded or oppressed social condition):

> On the contrary, integral to their 'surplus of consciousness' is the deep understanding that liberation cannot be achieved by this 'avant-garde' acting alone in an ocean of 'subalternity' perpetuated by the age-old division of labour and growing state control of social life.

Pablo concludes by proclaiming that 'their real mission' is to politicise, arouse, and aid workers and citizens to shake off the mindset of their subaltern status and to persuade them of the possibility of creating democratic self-management and self-managed socialism.

Such messianic visions did not mean that the 'Wretched of the Earth' left his field of vision. His solidarity with the Palestinians, for instance, continued into the 1980s. When the Israelis launched their 1982 invasion of Lebanon and facilitated the infamous massacre of Palestinian civilians at the refugee camps of Sabra and Shatila, Pablo organised a call for international volunteers to go to Lebanon to support the Palestinians. Associated with this call were Maria Becket, Mohammed Harbi, Nico Papatakis, the dissident French general Jacques de Bollardière, the Argentinian Marxist Hugo Moreno, Sinn Fein leader and founder of the Provisional IRA Ruairí Ó Brádaigh, and French left-wing intellectuals such as Michel Leiris and Gérard Molina.[4] Such volunteers were for both military and non-military service on the model of the International Brigades in Spain during the Spanish Civil War of the 1930s. The war in Lebanon concluded with the evacuation of the bulk of the Palestinian forces and leadership from besieged Beirut to Tunis, and the call for international volunteers did not proceed. Any direct link between this call and the later corps of international volunteers, of which the courageous Rachel Corrie was the exemplary figure, is unlikely, but the idea was now in the ether.

Concern for the fate of the Palestinians continued and three years later he was writing in *Sous le drapeau* an indictment of the Shiite attacks on Palestinians in Lebanon.[5] Much as it was needed, the Arab world was a long way now from the hopes of just twenty years before of a pan-Arab democratic socialist revolution. Accepting the ebbing of hope, Pablo argued that it was up to the Palestinians to determine their stand on any peace agreement, including acceptance of a mini-state – as long as this acceptance was arrived at democratically.[6]

Thanks to the ideological housekeeping in the 1970s, Pablo was well-placed to respond to key political developments in the 1980s, particularly those in Afghanistan, Poland and the Soviet Union itself.[7] Having cast off illusions about the bureaucratic states – the Soviet Union and its satellites, as well as China, Cuba, Vietnam and North Korea as 'workers states' or 'socialist' – the *pablistes* could be clear-eyed about the Soviet invasion and occupation of Afghanistan: it had nothing to do with socialism or even the defence of the Soviet Union. It was therefore a straightforward decision to oppose the invasion and back the Afghan resistance.[8] To those who hesitated because of the nature of the Afghan resistance, the *pablistes* could always point to how the invasion and occupation was further entrenching the traditionalists and fundamentalists. Pablo's position may strike many readers today as natural enough, but it was far from universal on the Left, and orthodox Trotskyists tied themselves in all kinds of knots in either justifying the invasion or hesitating to criticise it. The *pablistes* not only called for the immediate withdrawal of Soviet troops, but broadly supported the Afghan resistance.[9]

The invasion of Afghanistan was another example of the great power aggressiveness of the Soviet Union.[10] Its ruling bureaucracy now commanded military power almost the equal of the United States and was not afraid to use it. Examples of this were Angola and Ethiopia where Soviet military capacity ensured the victory of "the revolutions" there, although the price of that aid was ensuring that the post-revolutionary regimes were patterned on the Soviet model and were in that way obstacles to the socialist transition in those post-revolutionary societies.

In Pablo's view, this Soviet military power and its projection masked extreme economic enfeeblement as the Soviet regime could neither adequately feed its population, let alone integrate the scientific and technological revolution into its productive apparatus as capitalism was doing. The military strength was a result of the focus that central economic planning could achieve and the investment of huge resources (estimated as high as 17 per cent of GDP each year). Nevertheless, at the beginning of the decade he believed the prospect of a capitalist restoration in the Soviet Union was non-existent and that we were faced with the likelihood that the bureaucratic society would spread and endure. In fact, he considered the military expansion could bring economic advantages to the Soviet Union in terms of access to raw materials and energy.[11]

His focus, however, was principally on Europe in this decade.

His view of capitalism and its immediate future was finely balanced between his estimation of its current strength and its difficulties.[12] He was not yet sure of capitalism's complete victory and extended life – that would come in the 1990s. In the 1980s he recognised that capitalism was undergoing a fundamental pivot towards a dominant financial sector, an extension of the market into hitherto insulated sectors of the economy, an advance in automation and an even more globalised and abstract structure. This had effects on the social structure. The decline of traditional industries and/or their automation reduced and broke up the traditional working class that had been the bedrock of left politics from the 1920s to the 1950s. Now the Left had a trio of challenges. It had to assemble a bloc out of the heterogeneous, more differentiated working population, to respond (initially defensively) to the new culture that flowed from the neoliberal turn in capitalism and to seek to integrate the aspirations of the new social movements, particularly the women's, peace and ecological, into the post-Fordist, post-Stalinist labour movement. He remained convinced that the aspirations of such a multifaceted movement, or 'revolutionary subject', would find a common, unifying goal in the 'self-managed republic', which he saw as a national, regional and global project.

The weaknesses and dangers for capitalism were that it was creating a dual society on both the national and international levels. In the advanced capitalist societies, the duality took the form of a good half or more of the society enjoying stable and secure prosperity. On the other side of the coin, a 'new poor' made up of minimum-wage workers, those in precarious jobs, the unemployed, social welfare recipients, immigrant workers and national minorities, constituted the lesser half. This dual pattern of privileged and underprivileged was repeated in Third World countries, with the difference that the prosperous section was a distinct minority. On a global scale, the duality expressed itself in the prosperous advanced capitalist countries in the midst of vast Third World penury and immiseration, where anti-imperialist and anti-capitalist revolutions were still possible in his view.

This whole shaky, unjust edifice was threatened by a looming major economic downturn. It was in his mind a crisis of overproduction. As he put it in 'Rediscovering Marx'[13], composed in 1983 for the Marx centenary:

> We are today faced with a new crisis of the capitalist system, an economic crisis on a world scale which has so far failed to produce any perspective of recovery in the short term … It is in the last analysis a crisis of overproduction. The difficulties arise from a fall in the rate of profit, linked on the one hand to an increase in the organic composition of capital, and on the other hand, to a narrowing of the world market's capacity for absorption.

In this respect it is worth recalling the mass unemployment of the 1980s in core capitalist countries and the stock market crash of 1987. This fragility of capitalism was to prove temporary (or periodic).[14]

In Western Europe these were watershed years. A huge anti-nuclear movement arose in response to the deployment by the United States and the Soviet Union of strategic, short-range nuclear weapons in Europe. The old continent was now being conceived as a theatre for limited nuclear war. Many in the movement, including Pablo and his supporters, reached out to dissidents in the Soviet bloc to join the push for a demilitarised Europe from the Urals to the Atlantic. Out of this resurgent peace movement emerged the Greens and a wider preoccupation with ecological issues. On the other side of the ledger, neoliberalism continued to gain ground and the socialist governments in France and Greece quickly succumbed to this new orthodoxy. The revolutionary Left in Western Europe remained divided and of declining significance compared to the two preceding decades.

Pablo's reception to the Greens was critical and tinged with disappointment. Initially the Greens were confined to Germany, but they ran a list in the 1984 elections for the European parliament in Strasburg. Their election manifesto drew some sharp criticism from Pablo in *SDS*.[15] Their claim that the manifesto was the first such comprehensive and radical manifesto for Europe in over a century stuck in his craw – what of the revolutionary left in those years? While their defence of the biosphere was welcomed, their argument that it was the result of 'consumerism' and 'productivism' did not go far enough. Similarly, it was excellent that they raised the issue of the poverty and immiseration of much of the Third World, but their solutions – principally debt cancellation – were nowhere

## 18 . END OF AN ERA 1980s

near comprehensive enough. Their vision for a future Europe also fell short of the revolutionary Left's goal of a united federation of states and peoples. He couldn't accept the Greens' absolute pacifism either.

All of this critique was valid enough, but it was difficult not to read into it the disappointment that it wasn't the revolutionary, 'self-management' Left that was reaping the electoral support going to the Greens. The conclusion of his article listed the positive parts of the Greens platform and called for support for the Greens where no better alternative existed. Finally, it expressed the hope that, in the near future, an alliance of the Greens, the new social movements and what he called the 'social workers movement' could run on an agreed platform in future elections. The pages following his critique did reprint the Greens' electoral platform.

— ✦ —

The one inspiring revolutionary development in Europe was in Poland with the emergence of *Solidarnosc* (or Solidarity), the free trade union. Here was the opportunity to crack open the world of the bureaucratic autocracy and begin the advance to the self-managed socialist future.

What is striking about Poland in the early 1980s is how classical, or even antique, its industry and economy were. It appears to have been characterised by huge workplaces in shipbuilding, steelmaking, coal mining and car manufacturing. It was a world straight out of Marx's *Das Kapital*. In other words, there was still a classic proletariat, and it was these workers who rose against the bureaucracy that ruled Poland in the shadow of the Red Army.

Major strikes broke out in Poland in the summer of 1980 in protest against the stagnation in real wages and rising food prices. The phenomenon was so widespread that the bureaucracy made many, if sometimes transient, concessions to contain the strikes. In August the strikes became quasi-political, as well as economic, when the shipyard workers in Gdansk struck. They not only demanded wage rises and increased family allowances, but the right to form what they called 'independent and self-managed' unions, the right to strike, the reinstatement of sacked militants and the release of political prisoners. The strikes were launched and continued by practising the utmost democracy. It seemed like 4th century Athens had come to Poland. General assemblies initiated the strikes and continued to make decisions about the demands and conduct of their strikes. The elected strike committees established city-wide and region-wide links. The union-cum-social-movement, 'Solidarity', also began to take shape as a national organisation.[16] When the government agreed to negotiations with the workers' delegates, the negotiations were broadcast on radio so that the assembled workers knew what was going on.

Pablo and the International Revolutionary Marxist Tendency immediately announced their 'total support' for what they saw as the 'beginning of the Polish Revolution'.[17] This turned out to be an accurate enough reading of what was to unfold in Poland in the next decade, but they were wrong about the kind of revolution it would ultimately be. 'In reality we are living through a revolutionary process in Poland which aims to install self-managed socialism on the ruins of the bureaucratic state,' Pablo wrote in October 1980. When Solidarity adopted as its aim 'the self-managed republic' a year later, this hope for a democratic socialist breakthrough was complete.[18]

Pablo wasn't wrong about the implicit challenge to the existing order. The strikers this time did not, as in the past, take to the streets to sack party offices and torch police stations. The discipline and coordination were exemplary. It meant that the people didn't tackle the regime head-on. In fact, in winning their demands for free unions, the Solidarity negotiators conceded "the leading role of the party" and explicitly accepted the country's existing alliances. But for all that, the challenge to the regime was fundamental. Direct democracy and bureaucratic dictatorship were in open contradiction. While a Dubcek, or Nagy, or 'liberal communist' faction could come forward, it was more likely the dominant faction of the regime would attempt to reassert itself by violence using the police and army. 'In any event,' Pablo wrote, 'it is illusory to think that the Polish Revolution will triumph without a decisive combat, not only against the Kremlin but also their allies on the ground in Poland itself.' And he concluded: 'It is necessary to prepare for this eventuality.'[19]

Right from the start Pablo and his comrades acknowledged the influence of the Catholic Church in the situation. It was the only institution to maintain some independence from the regime and the visit of the Polish pope, former cardinal Wojtila, in the previous year had certainly raised the spirits of the Polish people. The *pablistes* were under no illusion that the Church hierarchy was friendly to a self-managed socialism – precisely the opposite:

> … its ideological influence will allow the Church to play a decisive political role, if an autonomous and revolutionary political vanguard does not emerge from the workers movement, for in the end the project of the Church hierarchy and the self-managed socialist project are incompatible … [20]

As for this 'autonomous and revolutionary political vanguard', it didn't exist although the search for it went on throughout the decade.

In the autumn of 1981, first the Polish communist party and then Solidarity held their national congresses. In the case of the first, the reformers failed to carry the day and the hardliners, in which General Wojciech Jaruzelski was prominent, retained a strong position. In the case of the second, the union delegates adopted a program of self-management and an economy which would still be highly regulated, despite the opposition of Lech Walesa and the executive. It appeared that the secular Left had prevailed over a leadership that was strongly influenced by the Church hierarchy and ideas of a liberal, market economy. As a leader of the Solidarity Left was to recall, after the Left had won the vote on self-managed socialism, one of the Walesa team sneered to him, 'So what?'[21]

As 1981 progressed, Solidarity was beginning to implement its program in practice – free unions, free media, political pluralism, and workers control. A classic dual power situation was emerging.[22] The bureaucracy's grip on power was being eroded and Moscow was sounding the alarm. In November the Party's hardline faction led by General Jaruzelski launched a coup d'état, imposed martial law and arrested or drove underground the bulk of the leading Solidarity activists. The Polish Spring, which for Pablo was the culmination of a historic movement towards self-managed socialism which began with May 1968 and the Prague Spring, and evolved via Chile and the 'carnation revolution' in Portugal, was now cut short.[23]

But the East continued to be a source of revolutionary hope. While Polish developments were delayed by the Jaruzelski coup, developments in the Soviet Union itself demanded attention. Mikhail Sergeyevich Gorbachev became leader in 1985 and soon emerged, in Pablo's view, as a new and more radical and consequential Khrushchev. Gorbachev embarked on a reform program under the twin names of 'Glasnost' and 'Perestroika'.[24] The first was a commitment to end the secrecy and censorship that prevailed in the Soviet Union and the second was essentially a loosening up of the bureaucratic straitjacket, which had trapped the Soviet Union in its economic backwardness, in favour of political democracy, autonomy for enterprises and farms and the introduction of markets. What was most surprising was not that Gorbachev and the more enlightened elements in the Soviet ruling class had decided on *perestroika*, Pablo wrote, but that it had taken so long for them to do so.[25] He noted the not insignificant conservative opposition to Gorbachev in the bureaucracy and was not hesitant in declaring his support for the new party general secretary and Soviet President in the face of that opposition.

The fatal flaw in the new leader's program, in Pablo's view, was that he hoped to accomplish it by mobilising the ruling communist party which was in fact a bastion of the status quo. You could not break the iron grip of the bureaucracy with the party of that bureaucracy. Nevertheless, Gorbachev was right to believe that a new version of Lenin's NEP (New Economic Policy) of the 1920s was necessary to rejuvenate the Soviet economy. In other words, more market and less central administration. The danger in this, Pablo frankly admitted, was the development of capitalist forces in the economy and society. As he wrote in November 1988:

> An unbridled NEP, applied empirically, can lead to the emergence of neo-capitalist forces ... it is easy to transform bureaucrats managing a nationalised and state-owned economy into neo-capitalists ... in reality no one knows any longer what will be the ultimate results, either in the Soviet Union or the other so-called 'socialist' countries, of the course now embarked upon.

The only way to check the slide to capitalism was democratic planning to ensure the socialised and cooperative elements of the economy were fully supported. This in turn required free trade unions and a multiparty system. There was now a race in the Soviet Union and Eastern Europe between the emergence of capitalist restoration and a truly democratic and socialised economy and society, what he called the 'Self-managed Republic'. He continued to insist on the possibility that a reawakened Soviet working class could intervene to install a genuine socialism and he drew hope from the fact that *glasnost* was resurrecting the ideas of the Bolsheviks on the transition to socialism and socialist democracy that had been so long suppressed.[26]

But he eventually expected the collapse to the right. As the editorial in *SDS* 110-111 of May-June 1989 concluded:

> The foreign policy triumphs of Mikhail Gorbachev play well internally and internationally and help maintain him in power. But by themselves they will not be sufficient. In the absence of palpable results on the economic front and an elaboration of the precise content of his economic, political and social reforms, a clarification of the type of society he's aiming for now that the Stalinist model is buried, then all the efforts of Gorbachev risk destabilising the existing 'communist' regimes, freeing up uncontrollable neo-capitalist forces in the USSR and the other countries of the East. Some Westerners are betting on this dynamic. It is high time that that Marxist-Gorbachev wing, in the USSR and internationally, fully understood the historic contest underway and clarified its own projects, thereby restoring confidence in its ranks.

His analysis was already pessimistic and prescient when it came to the Soviet buffer states. The high probability was that these states would seize the opportunity to break away and install pro-capitalist and pro-Western regimes.[27] 'Objectively', Poland was still seen as 'the best placed' to transition to a 'Self-managed Republic', but the absence of a 'conscious political leadership' favouring this outcome was acknowledged, as was the fact that 'pro-Western' and 'pro-capitalist' forces were (to say the least) equally strong. Those states which had imitated the Soviet big brother – Cuba, Vietnam, Angola, Yemen etc – would also now have to reassess their model of development and 'the danger existed that imperialism would profit from their crisis'. Certainly he never expected the collapse of Stalinism to the 'right' to occur so suddenly and so completely. But when it did, he accepted that he was spending his last years in a completely new era.[28]

—+—

Western communism was also being shaken and shattered by the Gorbachev innovations. Pablo argued for a focus on encouraging the renovators and reformers in the European communist parties, which still had significant mass support, with a view to regrouping with them. This was a realistic possibility, particularly in France where there were scores of *pabliste* activists and where an opportunity presented itself when Pierre Juquin, a prominent Communist Party leader and now party dissident, declared himself a candidate in the presidential elections of 1988. Already in France, in response to a *pabliste* initiative, a number of small organisations had come together in the FGA – the Federation of the Alternative Left – in 1986. When Juquin announced his intention to run for president, the FGA, the PSU and the LCR (the Fourth International affiliate in France) agreed to support his bid and united in a network of campaign committees open to all supporters. *Pablistes* such as Maurice Najman, Michel Fiant, Gilbert Marquis, and Frederic Brun became key organisers. Local campaign committees proliferated all over France. Thirty years later Brun disclosed that Pablo arranged with Ben Bella to help fund the campaign.[29]

Despite an enthusiastic campaign, the results were disappointing. Juquin received just 2.1 per cent of the vote compared to 6 per cent for the official Communist Party candidate, nearly 2 per cent for the orthodox Trotskyist candidate (from Lutte Ouvrière) and 3.8 per cent for the Greens candidate. Nevertheless, after the election, such was the positive feeling flowing from the united effort, that a convention of supporters decided to keep the campaign committees together as the basis for a new political formation called the Nouvelle Gauche (New Left). This was very much an initiative inspired by the *pablistes* and Juquin himself. The PSU were also favourable to this convergence, although the LCR pulled out, preferring to preserve their own organisation.

These developments seemed to offer some support for Pablo's advocacy of a politico-social movement which would unite the old and new working class and the social movements, and be spearheaded by a coming together of political currents from the Left, the labour and social movements. Trouble was there was an alternative radical option: the Greens. Emerging out of anti-nuclear movement in the early 1980s, the German Greens had almost immediate electoral success, topping the five per cent barrier at the 1983 federal elections in West Germany and entering the Bundestag. Very soon after, Die Grünen was winning seats in German state elections and joining coalition governments with the Social Democrats. In the 1987 federal elections, their vote topped 8 per cent. By the mid-1980s, Green parties started to appear in other Western European countries.

The question of how to relate to these parties was to be at the centre of a sharp conflict between Pablo and his younger supporters. This conflict – along with his failing health – helped confirm him in his determination to consolidate and update his Marxist view of the world.

— ✢ —

Naturally, he convened and spoke at the international conference in Athens commemorating the centenary of Marx's death in 1983. This was as much a riposte to the stepped-up anti-Marxist ideological offensive that marked the 1980s as it was a tribute to his Master. The venue was apposite, he claimed, because Marx considered Greece his second homeland. His paper to the conference emphasised the open-ended process of understanding Marx's approach and how new advances in the sciences modified and supplemented it. He took up the discussion about what Marx meant by 'class' and 'mode of production', arguing that for Marx, definition of class flowed from the social division of labour more than the question of ownership of the means of production. The dominant or ruling class was composed of those who governed or directed or managed as against those who were governed, ruled and directed. He insisted, too, that Marx shared the same goal as the anarchists – the abolition of wage-labour and the State. The difference being that Marx conceived these as processes or transitions, rather than overnight acts. Given the rise of the environmental movement in Europe and the US, he mentioned Marx's awareness of the destructive impacts of capitalist industrialisation. He finished by reminding people of Marx's insistence that communists did not set themselves apart as an elite, but saw their role as acting in the mass organisations of the labour movement.[30]

In the middle of the decade, a British connection was established with about 30 young Marxists, mostly in their twenties and thirties, many of them recent graduates of universities in London and Oxford. Prominent among the group was a young Keir Starmer, the future right-wing British Labour Party leader (and now Sir Keir Starmer). They produced a journal, *Socialist Alternatives*, which went through half a dozen issues in 1986-87. Starmer was the major contributor, alongside 'Harry Curtis'. It was Pablo's advocacy of 'self-management', his ideological boldness, his early commitment to social movements (such as the women's liberation movement) and the life he'd led, which seems to have attracted the British adherents.

In 1986 they invited him to England to give talks on Marxism and self-management. These seminars were invitation-only affairs and were held in London and Oxford. The advertised basis of the seminars was a discussion of his paper 'Imagination, Utopia, and Socialism'[31] which appeared earlier that year in *Sous le drapeau*. This essay aimed to save utopian visions and imagination from the 'condescension of posterity', to paraphrase E.P Thompson – and from crudely materialist Marxists. He pointed out that utopian visions of the future were the product of the play between an ethical or moral rejection of the status quo, critical thought, social practice and the exercise of imagination. Although any such projections would be shaped – and limited – by the conditions the utopian thinkers found themselves in, the work of the imagination would be transformative:

> Thanks to imagination, to the creative transformation of the data drawn from our senses and thinking, we go beyond the present and we find solutions which in the beginning outline themselves as visions, as a utopia, and acquire little by little flesh and blood, ripening and becoming the direct line to the reality of tomorrow.

In socially quiescent periods, utopias are the property of the most radical thinkers, but when revolutions occur, the most radical social strata push forward the most daring utopias. This tendency was evident in the English Revolution of the 17th century, and in the French and Russian Revolutions of the 18th and 20th centuries. Marx had essentially attempted to systemise and ground any utopian goals in a dialectical materialist or sociological understanding of the status quo and its revealed possibilities. But Pablo argued that for all Marx's care not to provide hard and fast blueprints for the socialist and communist futures, Marx's concept of socialism and communism contained a large dash of utopianism, of imagining. Moreover, for Marx there was nothing automatic about this future; it had to be made by men and women seizing the opportunities presented in and by history.

Pablo's essay sought to champion what he called "the utopian disposition". 'All those who strive to kill the utopian disposition in men and women in the name of a cold objective science, are objectively the eternal promoters of social conservatism, the Epimetheuses of the social status quo, now particularly common in the advanced capitalist countries.' In Pablo's view, the utopian disposition, Marxist analysis and contemporary social and ecological struggles lead to the utopia of the self-managed republic on a global stage. It is not a matter, he concluded, of immediately creating an ideal society. There is no blueprint, only past experiences and future possibilities ' – with the aid of the imagination'.

The importance Pablo attached to this essay is testified to by the fact that he chose it as his contribution to the new magazine his supporters launched in France in 1993.[32] The new magazine took as its title, and this underlined the direction of the thinking of his comrades as well at this time, *Utopie Critique*.

As it was, that was not to be the subject of the main lecture he gave. The London-Oxford lecture was entitled *What does it mean to be a revolutionary Marxist today? (Qu'est-ce qu'être marxiste révolutionnaire aujoud'hui?)*.[33] Written in his straightforward and confident style, it noted the ideological offensive against Marxism that marked the intellectual life in the West in the 1980s, an offensive that piggy-backed on the clear and present failure of the Soviet bloc countries to deliver either material comforts or political and cultural freedom. To identify Marxism with the bureaucratic states was for Pablo the equivalent of blaming early Christianity for the Inquisition, or Nietzsche for Nazism.

The real meat of the essay was his attempt to reconcile Marxism with advances in the physical sciences and other schools of social science such as structuralism. Marxism did not provide all the answers, and the idea of Marx as 'god-thinker' ('penseur-héro') was alien to Marx himself. Revolutionary Marxists, and he based this portrait on his own life, started with an ethical rejection of the world as it was and with an aspiration to the 'absolute' – or, more precisely, the elimination of exploitation of labour by capital, its substitution by free associated labour, the withering away of the State and the expansion of free time. From that ethical rejection flowed an adoption of the Marxist method to understand society, underpinned and tested by practice. Marxism was for Pablo, as he would repeat endlessly, an experimental science, a continuous, and imaginative, attempt to grasp the main features of a constantly developing and infinitely complex social whole. As such, it must welcome any scientific or philosophic advances. If Freud and Levi-Strauss, for instance, could help in understanding the social whole ('le fait social de masse'), so much the better. This did not undermine the central efficacy of dialectical and historical materialism as a method for understanding reality. Moreover, Marxism was not vulgar economic determinism. He pointed to Marx's *Eighteenth Brumaire of Louis Napoleon* and Trotsky's *History of the Russian Revolution* to illustrate his point.

He concluded, as he would invariably, by reminding the listener/reader of the injustice, inequalities and dangers of the present world and referring to the extraordinary advances in science and technology, and the promise this held for a materially sufficient world of the free and equal.

In closing, he championed the worth of the revolutionary life. His writing in this decade is full of advertisements extolling its virtues, in the hope of encouraging his heirs. The revolutionary – 'the most complete type of human', he says in his autobiography – is impelled by an age-old set of values:

> Mankind's 'Christian' inclination is much older than that of the Buddhists: we come across it the more we understand world cultures millennia earlier ... I was charmed when a female friend, recently returned from New York where she had revisited the amazing Metropolitan Museum, had stood ecstatically before an ancient Egyptian column bearing the following inscription: 'I gave bread to the hungry and clothes to the naked. I ferried in my boat those who had no means to cross the river.' These were 'Words of an Evangelist' in the Ninth Dynasty, 2160-2130 BCE, well before the god of the Christians!

The revolutionary is in this tradition. Moreover those values can now be the basis for the future:

> ...for the first time in history, the objective potential exists for a real self-managed democratic society on a world scale. A society free of the long hours of waged labour and a state free of an oppressive centralised political power which essentially continues to primarily serve the interests of privileged social minorities.

But another future also lies in wait:

> Real 'power' is now more than ever concentrated within small, privileged minorities on a global scale ... these minorities, which are divided within themselves into even smaller, closed and antagonistic 'centres', have been overtaken by the forces they possess and which they mistakenly believe they control. Our world in its totality is being swept along towards an unknown future, which no one can define or predict. The culmination of this paranoid course and development manifests in multiple ways: the rupture which is widening between the developed world and the growing Third World; the accelerating destruction of the ecological environment; and the perennial arms race of atomic and conventional weapons in general.

If humanity survives this 'explosive mix' it will be 'a miracle'. The solution lies in a general democratic awakening to which his heirs must commit themselves.

— ✦ —

In the 1980s, Pablo returned briefly to the topic of women's liberation. On this subject, the 'iconoclastic' work of Elisabeth Badinter prompted him. In *SDS* 104 (May-June 1987) he devoted a sympathetic review of her book *L'Un est l'autre*. Daniel Guerin added a note to the review. Badinter argued that the material basis for the sexual division of labour was disappearing and that genuine equality, and interchangeability, between the sexes was now a fact of life in Western societies. The death of the patriarchy had begun with the French Revolution and had accelerated enormously over the past two decades, according to Badinter. It set the stage for an emerging androgynous or bisexual human being, where the binaries were left behind and people were distinguished by their personal and individual characteristics rather than sex- or gender-based ones.

As the evidence, Badinter pointed to the common education of boys and girls, the legal and economic equality between the sexes, the influx of women into all parts of the workforce, the control over their bodies and sex lives that women had attained in the past 20 years, the decline in the importance of marriage, the discovery of parenthood by many men, the enlistment of women in the military and the fact that most jobs now didn't require distinctively different sex or gender skills – computers, for instance, didn't care whether you were male or female. All this, wrote Badinter, 'brings the sexes together in the greatest possible resemblance. In doing so, it allows the expression of all personal differences. Humanity is no longer split into two heterogeneous groups, but is made up of a multiplicity of individuals who both resemble each other and are distinguished by all sorts of nuances.' Yes, this emergent egalitarian reality was still largely confined to the West but it represented an irreversible historical trend, in Badinter's view.

Pablo and Guerin were broadly in agreement with Badinter's thesis. Guerin was disappointed that she didn't recognise homosexuality as the precursor to this universal androgyny or bisexuality. Pablo parted company with Badinter over her uncritical acceptance and celebration of individualism, of the 'me' narcissism typical of neoliberal capitalist societies, a trait she saw accompanying the rise of the society of free individuals. She seemed unaware of the dangers, in his view:

> … if it turns out to be true that our Western society is deprived of God, of the father, of marriage, of the family, of maternal love and even of the love of the couple, and that the individual is increasingly locked up in the solitude of its hypertrophied "me", cutting it off from any impulse towards sacrifice, generosity, and broader social solidarity, then civilization would be heading towards an impasse. Such a humanity would be capable of turning towards generalized psychosis, or towards other more brutal and murderous "evasions".

Pablo insisted on the importance of love for the 'other' – the moral health of the West, for instance, depended on developing this feeling towards the Third World.

What Elly made of Pablo's estimation of the women's movement and its impact is not known precisely. In the 1983 documentary on their life, she touched on their occasional differences of opinion. 'For my part I believe we shouldn't be one hundred per cent in agreement because things would become boring. Besides,' she added, 'I have some of my own activities. For example, the women's movement of which I'm a supporter, a hundred per cent, a thousand per cent, a million per cent. I'm not sure if Michalis [Pablo] is a million per cent.'[34]

Elly herself in this decade translated into Greek Trotsky's *La révolution défigurée*, which was his little-known account of the intra-party struggle against Stalin and in which he lays out his policy ideas for an economy like the early Soviet one, isolated and undeveloped. Pablo provided a preface in which he critically discussed Trotsky's proposals which were promising, but far from finished, prescriptions. However, these alternatives to the Stalinist model, as outlined by dissidents in the 1920s, had yet to be tried anywhere in the wake of an anti-capitalist revolution. The economic basket case of the then Soviet Union was the result of the economic course taken by Stalin. Gorbachev was now dismantling the centralised and state-owned economy inherited from Stalin in favour of market mechanisms, without a clear realisation that capitalist restoration was the likely outcome – unless, of course, the Gorbachev team went back to the ideas of Trotsky and the other anti-Stalinist Marxists of the 1920s.[35]

— ✦ —

If his almost valedictory essays showed Pablo's more appealing side, there were other aspects that were less straightforward. His friendly relations with the Libyan regime of colonel Gaddafi in the 1980s was a source of unease among supporters. In the past, he had been excoriating about the pusillanimity (particularly in response to Israeli aggression against Palestinians) and lack of any democracy of Arab regimes, including Gaddafi's.[36] However in the 1980s this regime became something of a *bête noire* to Washington and a source of financial support to various left-wing movements (while still selling its oil to capitalist Europe and Western oil corporations). After the American attacks on Libya in the wake of the terrorist outrages at the Rome and Vienna airports in December 1985 – actions described by Pablo and his comrades as 'thoughtless and hideous' and damaging to the Palestinian cause – the *pabliste* TMRI issued a solidarity statement:

> The Libyan regime continues to be hunted and threatened by imperialism. Despite the fact that no evidence could be provided to substantiate the accusation that Libya is the hotbed of "international terrorism", or a key base for it, Washington continues its campaign of disinformation, as it does its preparations intended to bring about the fall of the Libyan regime and even the assassination of its leader. The Americans could thus move more freely along the path of "settlement" in their favour of the Palestinian question and the Middle East.
>
> It is therefore the duty of the world revolutionary forces to resolutely defend the Libyan regime threatened by imperialism, without succumbing to the pressure of the reactionary international campaign, which, by exploiting the real weaknesses of this regime, deliberately obscures its overall nature in order to bring it down.[37]

In Pablo's view, the 'overall', and positive, nature of the regime lay in Libya's status as something of a mini welfare state and 'the last bastion of Arab radicalism', as far as opposition to imperialism and reactionary Arab governments was concerned. In the same optic, he noted its more progressive attitude to rights for women than elsewhere in North Africa or the Middle East. With acute historical foresight he predicted a dire future for Libya if Gaddafi was overthrown:

> The eventual fall of the Gaddafi regime, far from opening up Libya to Western-style "democracy", would once again deliver it to the despotism of neo-colonialist clans, eager to squander the country's wealth, under the protection of imperialism. Arab reactionary regimes, and even some African regimes, would breathe more freely, freed from the daily subversive propaganda that Libya directs at them through its media and its actions.[38]

That, in fact, has come to pass.

In 1989 Pablo organised dozens of supporters to go to Libya in a show of solidarity to mark the regime's 20th anniversary. It appears to have been an uncomfortable experience for them. Serge Marquis related how they were expected to wear T-shirts lauding Gaddafi to a rally, something the French comrades refused to do. The presence of American neo-nazis was also something the French delegates objected to and secured their ejection.[39] The Argentinian Guillermo Almeyra, then living and working in Italy, explained that he went out of loyalty to Michel but afterwards considered it a bridge too far.[40] Nevertheless, Pablo published his speech to the Greek delegates justifying an attitude of understanding for the Libyan regime.[41] Both Gilbert and Serge Marquis continued some liaison with the Libyan regime for a while longer, but Serge is adamant there was no financial support forthcoming.[42]

There were suspicions at the time that the Libyans had channelled funds to the *pablistes*, but no evidence has surfaced that that happened.[43] There were no offices opened or staff hired, and *SDS* went on being published as before. There was one exception: issue 103 of *Sous le drapeau*, published as a slick 180-page book at the end of 1986. Titled, *Vers une république autogérée* (Towards a Self-managed Republic), it contained all the conference documents from the 8th international conference of the TMRI, held in June 1985, plus several articles by well-known figures from the radical left in France, Europe and Latin America. However, it contained no encomiums to Libya and it could have been financed from the resources of Pablo and his comrades. On the other hand, Pablo never shrank from unpopular or difficult alliances and, in his final interview with Adolfo Gilly, he freely mentioned Libya as a possible source of funding for a centre of revolutionary Marxist research and activity.

All in all, the 1980s turned out to be a busy decade for Pablo. Clearly, even a ready and conspicuous acceptance of death looming did nothing to reduce his appetite for the revolutionary life. He did find, however, by the end of the decade, that times had changed and convincing his younger supporters of his vision of the revolutionary life was not as easy as it had once been. The rise of the Greens played a key part in that. But before turning to an account of Pablo's final political battle – with many of his more recent and youthful supporters – an account of his relations with friends and comrades in these final years is in order.

CHAPTER 19

# The fate of friends and comrades
## 1980s

*I'd like once again to salute them all, to tell them that they remain unforgettable in my memory, symbols of our common, steadfast ideals and struggles.*

**Michalis Raptis (Pablo)**
*My Political Autobiography*[1]

PABLO WAS A man who took friendship seriously. His political memoir ends with that salute to comrades past and present, and it was more than a passing elegiac gesture. Pablo rarely forgot a friend and, as such, was a good friend to have. Right to the end of his life he had friends dating back decades. In the case of comrades like Mitsos Soulas, the connection went back to the 1930s, when Soulas was a bakery worker and union organiser in working-class Athens. In each of the decades since, new and enduring friendships had been forged. With a few exceptions, even when there had been differences, even betrayals, some connection remained. Those longstanding comrades encompassed the famous and the obscure, and they came from many cultures.

In the 1980s, he renewed friendships and embraced new friends and comrades, but it was also a time for farewells. Memories and nostalgia were very much on his waking and dreaming mind. In 1987 he tried his hand once more at fiction with a rather bleak short story entitled *Nocturne*. It was about death and friendship. Jaime, the central character, is in Paris and alternates between dream and wakefulness, thoughts of death and joys of continuing life. The 'petite' is back in Greece and her phone calls recall him to optimism and remind him of the joys of young love, of walking through the Swiss Alps during the war. Out in the street he meets 'Mado' who has recently attempted suicide because of her husband's refusal to forgive her for adultery. Then he encounters 'the Albanian' who tells him he has bought a plot in a Paris cemetery so that his family trapped in Albania will know where to find him after his death. He visits the ailing writer 'James' who has devoted the family fortune to the pursuit of social and sexual liberation (Daniel Guérin comes to mind), but who now asks why one should go on living when desire and pleasure have passed. Old memories surface – of 'Alvarez', an old Spanish friend who used to take him to the Spanish republican club where the exiled fighters meet every year to remember those who have died. And so the story continues.

Pablo read it to his close friends and they pressed him to publish it, but he never did. (However, his old comrade Spiros Bafaloukos published it in Greek in a handsome edition in 2005, along with a *Ta Nea* column from 1990, *Exit by the sea*, about a dying ship captain on the island of Andros who decides he will die where he has lived and loads his pockets with stones and swims out to sea to drown.)

Ben Bella, his old friend and comrade, had eventually been freed in October 1980, after 15 years of prison and house arrest. Pablo had been foremost among the dwindling numbers who kept Ben Bella's fate in the public arena, and Ben Bella sought him out when he came to France, and exile, early the following year. They were to remain close friends and allies until they fell out over the war in Bosnia.

Ben Bella had evolved politically. He admitted that in his years in power he should have been more supportive of 'self-management' and independent democratic organisations. He now embraced the concept of a multi-party democracy. On the other hand, he had become more religious, although Pablo thought this might not be a negative factor. Noting the rise of Islamist fundamentalists in Algeria, as elsewhere, Pablo hoped that a democratic Islamist like Ben Bella would realise that Islam alone could not provide the answers to the problems of Algeria and might form an alliance with secularists like Mohammed Harbi and Hocine Zahouane. Initially that seemed unlikely, as bad blood persisted from the post-independence years. Pablo acknowledged in his first article on Ben Bella's release that the Algerian leader had not wanted to meet Harbi. With some relief he reported they had eventually met. The ball, in Pablo's view, was now very much in Ben Bella's court: 'It is to be hoped that Ahmed Ben Bella can make the choices that are required.'[2]

## 19 . THE FATE OF FRIENDS AND COMRADES 1980s

Ben Bella's stay in France was cut short when the socialist government ordered his expulsion in January 1983, claiming that his organising work among Algerian workers in France was 'Islamist' in character. Pablo believed that Paris was responding to pressure from the government in Algiers worried by Ben Bella's recruiting in France. Protests were to no avail and Ben Bella was forced to settle in Switzerland. Nevertheless, Ben Bella persisted in the work of making alliances with other democrats and historic leaders of the FLN, such as Ait Ahmed, the leader of the *Front des Forces Socialistes* (FFS), with its support base among the Berber minority in Algeria.

Showing opposition to the Algerian regime continued to be dangerous. In 1987 Ali Mecili, the editor of an opposition journal published in France, was assassinated in a Paris street. The well-founded suspicion was that the hit was carried out by servants of the Algerian regime. The regime was subsequently severely shaken by demonstrations and strikes in Algeria in 1988 and forced to concede free elections. However, it was not the democrats or the Left that the elections favoured but the Islamic fundamentalists. The regime responded by reimposing its military dictatorship and a savage civil war ensued.

Meanwhile, Pablo's other friend among past revolutionary leaders, Otelo Saraiva de Carvahlo in Portugal, had his turn in prison. Carvahlo and scores of his comrades – at least 45 others were arrested and imprisoned – had been swept up in an 'anti-terrorist' operation in June 1984. By no reasonable stretch of the imagination could Carvalho be deemed a terrorist. The police classed his political organisation as terrorist because it was committed to revolution, or more precisely to the fulfilment of the promise of the Carnation Revolution of 1974 which Carvalho had led. As the *New York Times* recognised: 'Mr Saraiva de Carvalho stood trial in 1985, accused of being the "intellectual author" of terrorist attacks.' The document the prosecution relied on was drafted in 1977 as a strategy paper on how to respond to a fascist coup.[3] Carvalho and his comrades did not go on trial on terrorism charges until 16 months after their arrest. The trial itself dragged on for some 17 months before a guilty verdict was handed down in 1987 and Carvalho was sentenced to 15 years imprisonment. As the *New Yorker* noted, the verdict was a rare example of a point of agreement between the Portuguese Communists and the old Portuguese Right.[4]

Pablo was deeply involved in the campaign to free Otelo (as Carvahlo was widely known) and his comrades. While this solidarity campaign found some support in Scandinavia, France and Germany, this support was mostly confined to radical intellectual and political circles. In Greece, on the other hand, it became something of a mass movement, with big public meetings, mass petitions, street marches and protest delegations to the Portuguese embassy. The central committees of PASOK and the Communist Party (Interior), as well as the trade unions and local councils, protested the arrest and trial.[5] The extent of the campaign in Greece is captured in an anecdote in an interview the former political prisoner, Isabel Do Carmo, gave to the major Portuguese weekly magazine *Expresso*:

> I was in a museum in Athens with my family and we started taking photos, which was against the rules, and a security guard came to tell us to stop. But in the middle of speaking to us he asked, 'Do you support Otelo or not?' After I said 'Yes', he told us it was okay to continue to take photos. That's how things were in Greece.[6]

Pablo was the inspirer of this campaign, visiting Otelo many times in jail. He was naturally a conspicuous part of the large Greek delegation that arrived in Lisbon for the opening of the trial in 1985. He was a member of the international defence committee which was headquartered in Paris. He was again in Lisbon in November 1988 for the forum on an amnesty for Otelo and fellow political prisoners. Other foreign delegates, including a handful of MPs, came from all over Europe. The amnesty campaign received the official support of the German Greens and, to the consternation of some, of Colonel Gaddafi. Ben Bella weighed in, too. After the forum, Pablo had a three-hour visit with Otelo, whom he found in good spirits, preparing an appeal to the constitutional court as well as being optimistic about the amnesty campaign that now had substantial support in Portugal itself after a slow start.[7]

Otelo's appeal, along with that of 16 of his comrades, did succeed the next year – the police and prosecution had violated provisions for a speedy and fair trial. Despite a continued campaign for amnesty, the comrades who remained in prison had to wait until 1996 for the amnesty. The first country a free Otelo visited was naturally Greece, where Pablo organised the usual array of press conferences, public meetings and private audiences. Never one to lose an opportunity, he also got Otelo involved in the campaign to free Christos Roussos.

Roussos had been condemned to life in prison without parole in 1976 for the murder of his friend and lover. He was just 19. As a serving soldier in the navy at the time, he was judged and convicted by a court-martial which refused to admit any extenuating circumstances. Roussos claimed the lover had prostituted and humiliated him and he reacted by stabbing him to death. In 1986 Roussos went on what was to be a 73-day hunger strike appealing for a reduction of his sentence to 20 years. The Minister for Justice supported his cause but in the new year, President Christos Sartzetakis rejected the plea on the grounds that there was no new evidence and in the absence of a previous 'honourable life' (presumably because Roussos was homosexual).

After the president had refused the pardon, a hunger strike of well-known writers and intellectuals in support of Roussos began at the gates of the University of Athens. Pablo was among them.[8] As one participant, the well-known Greek filmmaker Vasilis Raphailidis, recalled, 'It was astonishing for Pablo to lie down beside you, with his age and authority, and in his incongruous elegant and expensive clothes …'[9] In the wake of the protests, Roussos's sentence was suspended for 30 days to allow him to recover from his hunger strike, but he had to wait another three years before the election of a new president – Karamanlis again – led to a pardon.

It wasn't just a matter of sit-downs and signing appeals; Pablo was in direct contact with Roussos and he took his friend Otelo along on one of his visits.[10] When the pedantic and flinty Sartzetakis' term drew to a close and a new president was about to be elected, Roussos wrote and cabled Pablo (and Otelo) to step up the campaigning. Pablo said he would ask Stavros Psycharis, the influential editor-in-chief at *Ta Nea* and *To Vima*, to intervene with Karamanlis. Whether that had any impact on Karamanlis' decision is unknown, but Roussos certainly believed it did. The friendship between these two unlikely comrades continued after Roussos' release, with the latter making periodic visits to Elly and Pablo.[11]

It is to Roussos' credit that he did not forget the prisoners he left behind and he recruited Pablo to their cause. There is a letter from a long-term prisoner called Thanos in the Pablo archive saying he's writing on Roussos' advice and appealing for Pablo's help in his upcoming appeal. Another letter from Thanos thanks Pablo for paying for his new dentures – noting, 'at least now I can chew the prison food'. Pablo didn't have much luck with Charis Temperekidis, an anarchist whom he helped to have released. He was shot dead soon after by the police, during a bank robbery.

In these years Pablo also renewed another older friendship. After 20 years of frosty relations, things thawed with Ernest Mandel – on a personal level at least. The occasion was the tragic death of Mandel's partner, Gisela, in early 1982. Pablo travelled from Athens to Brussels for the cremation and Mandel sent him a handwritten note of appreciation for his attendance along with 'comrade Marquis'.[12] It was a sign of how distant their relations had become that the note was sent care of the Paris address of *Sous le drapeau*. Their correspondence before then had been very formal.[13] The following year, Mandel accepted Pablo's invitation to be one of the key speakers at a centenary conference of the death of Marx that Pablo organised in Athens. Mandel's paper was subsequently published in *Sous le drapeau*.[14] When news reached Mandel in 1987 that the health of Pablo and Elly was in decline – Pablo had been warned of a weak heart and Elly's legs and brain were giving out – he sent a note of concern.[15] Similar friendly inquiries would follow in the years to come.

Their relationship never returned to its former closeness. Pablo could not forget what he considered Mandel's stab in the back after he was arrested in 1960.[16] In his view, Mandel had compounded it on occasion. After Pierre Frank died in 1984, the Fourth International published a book of reminiscences and appreciations of Frank, including one from Mandel, which certainly annoyed Pablo. Mandel wrote that over their long friendship he differed from Frank in only one important respect: the exclusion of the French majority in 1952. Frank continued to defend it while Mandel described it as a grievous error. Mandel, Pablo noted, had raised no objection at the time, when the decision was finally made. Moreover, the exclusion had been preceded by three years of internal, free discussion. The International had taken the view that the Trotskyists in France should concentrate their efforts on working in the CGT, the main and communist-led union movement, and not the minority, anti-communist and American-sponsored Force Ouvrière. Furthermore, in Pablo's view, Mandel's late repentance for such heavy centralism was also very selective. It had not stopped him excluding Pablo and his supporters in 1965 and he was yet to express any regret over that.[17]

The fate of other old comrades was never far from Pablo's consciousness. He hadn't yet started to talk of himself as 'the last of the Mohicans', but he was conscious of the shrinking circle of historic Trotskyists and fellow revolutionaries. Besides Pierre Frank, there were other departures – Juan Posadas, CLR James, Leslie Goonewardene, George Breitman, Agis Stinas, Roger Foirier[18] and Daniel Guérin among the most noteworthy.

The remarkable Guérin, though never a Trotskyist, had long been a comrade in the larger sense. Guérin shared with Pablo an interest in anti-colonial politics, self-management and sexual politics. Both of them were anarcho-communists. Pablo welcomed Guérin's contributions to *Quatrième Internationale* in the 1950s and then to *Sous le Drapeau* – even when those articles were criticising his positions. One of the last pieces of Guérin's that he published was an historical essay pointing out that

## 19 . THE FATE OF FRIENDS AND COMRADES 1980s

Marx and Engels had deliberately scuttled the First International when it looked like they were about to lose control.[19] When Pablo learned that Guérin was gravely ill, he hurried to Paris and visited him daily during the last weeks of his life. His obituary for his old companion *En marche* is redolent with love and admiration.[20]

He also acknowledged Franz Modlik (1902-86), the veteran Austrian communist, who as 'Lerze', had been such a strong defender when the trio were busy ejecting Pablo from the International. This obituary was rather shamefaced, as it was belated. Pablo had lost touch with Modlik, and he hoped – in vain, as it turned out – that someone else would supplement his rather scant knowledge of Modlik's life. Modlik had been one of the organisers of the first Trotskyist Left Opposition in any Communist Party outside the Soviet Union – for this sin he was expelled from the Austrian Communist Party in 1926. He had remained a revolutionary Marxist to the end – right through the Nazi years. After the war he continued to translate and distribute the International's and then the Tendency's documents and publish *Arbeiterkampf*, a regular bulletin on local politics and campaigns. His fellow Trotskyists and *pablistes* in Austria were never very many, but apparently he never let his lonely vigil dishearten him.[21]

The contact with Sadik Premtaj (1915-1991) was never broken. He had been one of the founders of the Albanian Communist Party and the wartime resistance against the Axis occupation, but had fallen out with party boss Enver Hoxha, who at war's end accused him of treason and Trotskyism. Neither charge was of course true – Premtaj had no idea what Trotskyism was – but the charges were a death sentence. Warned in time, Premtaj and two comrades had managed to escape through the mountains into Italy. Arriving in Paris in 1947, he learned at last what Trotskyism was and, soon after, joined the Fourth International. He had left behind his mother, a brother, wife and daughter and was to see none of them again. He had become the official hate figure of the regime, Hoxha's 'Snowball' from Orwell's *Animal Farm*. His brother spent 25 years in jail for his refusal to denounce him. As Hoxha's Albania began to unravel in the late '80s, Pablo wrote a wonderful portrait of Premtaj for *To Vima*, relating how the Albanian was now calling him at all hours to relay optimistic news of what was happening in Albania. He recalled, too, his comrade's insistence over the years that he and Elly join him on summer holidays on Corfu so that he could look across the water at his native land. Sadly, Sadik was to die before being able to set foot again in his homeland.[22]

In was in these years that Pablo began referring to himself as 'the last of the Mohicans',[23] appropriating the title of James Fenimore Cooper's novel set against the background of the defeat, dispersal and destruction of the Indian tribes of north-eastern United States in the 17th and 18th centuries. His Mohicans were basically the comrades who had assembled in Paris in 1938 to found the Fourth International, or those who had joined in the hard years of the war. He knew that a handful of others were still alive, but he was the only one still active.

A ghost from his first years as a revolutionary died in this decade – Agis Stinas (b. 1905) in Paris in November 1987. Stinas had come to France after the war, a survivor of the Metaxas dictatorship, of life in prison during the German and Italian occupation, and of the Stalinist death squads and rightist repression of the 1940s. Pablo described him as a 'red monk', who lived on coffee, austerely and alone with his rejection of a world which did not move quickly enough in the direction he desired and hoped for. Pablo had collaborated with him in the early 1930s after he had left the Archeio-Marxists. Stinas, expelled from the Communist Party for his sympathies with Trotsky, had briefly been something of a political elder brother. However, he harboured a personal dislike of the more charismatic Pantelis Pouliopoulos, so when Pablo and his small group decided in 1935 to merge with Pouliopoulos' group, Stinas cut off any relations with Pablo. It was a personal separation that Pablo clearly regretted. He paid him tribute by writing a warm preface to the French translation of Stinas' memoirs: '… independently of any judgement on him and his politics, I would now rather see in him one of the many faces of the revolutionary human being, one who is distinguished above all by his faith, his monastic frugality, and his courage in the face of the Praetorians of the bourgeois order and the fanatical devotees of Stalinism.'[24]

— ✢ —

While his principal collaborators in Greece in these years were his old comrades Dimitris Livieratos, the cardiologist Spyros Bafaloukos and the school principal Christos Gogornas, they were joined by Marika Karageorgiou, a psychiatrist, who quickly became part of his inner circle. When old friends such as Otelo, Ben Bella and his wife Zora, or Adolfo Gilly came to Greece, Marika would join Michel and Elly in entertaining and hosting them. She was included in the delegation that travelled to Paris in 1992 for the talks with the leadership of the Fourth International. His will made her his principal legatee and executor. (According to Savas Matsas, when his father asked Pablo the secret of his continuing good health, he replied: 'one main meal a day, walking and falling in love'.)

Karageorgiou's family background embodied so much of Greece's extraordinary and heroic history. Pablo had met her through her father Konstantinos (1909-1984), a doctor in Zagora in north-east Greece, near the seaside village of Horefto where Pablo and Elly usually went for their summer holidays – as did the Beckets. Konstantinos, it appears, was the doctor who defied the Resistance in bringing medical help to the local Italian garrison during their wartime occupation. A contemporary of Pablo's, Konstantinos had studied medicine at the University of Athens between 1927 and 1934 and had been a supporter of the Archeio-Marxists. A clue to his politics, which he expressed in the life he lived rather than by membership of any political organisation, can be glimpsed from the core of his library as recalled by his son:[25]

> Apart from the medical books in his library (Freud's works included) there were nine translated books that he was never separated from and kept revisiting: Spinoza's *Ethics; The Gambler* by Feodor Dostoyevsky; *The Right to Heresy: Castellio against Calvin* by Stefan Zweig; the *Art of being right* by Arthur Schopenhauer; Nietzsche's *Will to Power*; Charles Baudelaire's *Les Fleurs du mal*; Maxim Gorky's *The Mother*; Tolstoy's *Resurrection;* and a well-hidden translation of [Leon Trotsky's] *The Revolution Betrayed* translated by Pantelis Pouliopoulos.

It is little wonder that Pablo and Konstantinos hit it off.

Konstantinos had not only survived his participation in the war, the Resistance, and the civil war but also the rightist ascendancy in the post-war period. He had been elected mayor of Zagora in 1950-54 and 1954-56 and again in 1964-67 when Greece swung to the left. After the colonels' coup in 1967, he was dismissed as the local mayor. When the junta fell, he teamed with Andreas Papandreou and helped organise PASOK in the north of Greece. Such was the history of the doctor from Zagora. As his son put it:

> I think that in the personality of my father, Pablo saw an authentic and modest "local hero", a fierce opponent of injustice but not an easy fellow. Being of the same age as him, a man whose non-cosmopolitan but turbulent biography, less "important" of course than his, contained riches of a work ethic, a fighting spirit full of humanistic values and a strong will to fight for the common good and not for his self-interest. In other words, a fellow Greek of his generation that he would like to have had as a lifetime comrade. Both of them were always aware that:
> *Tis the day of the chattel,*
> *Web to weave, and corn to grind,*
> *Things are in the saddle,*
> *And ride mankind* (Ralph Waldo Emerson)

It was the kind of friendship that honoured both men. It found its continuation in the friendship of Pablo and Marika.

On the eve of the war, Konstantinos had married into the Cassavetes, one of the best-known liberal bourgeois families in northern Greece. The Cassavetes' celebrated history went back to before the 1821 revolution in which they played an active role, and they continued to be an important player in Greek politics right up till the 1930s. On his return to Zagora, Konstantinos had become the family doctor and fallen in love with the beautiful daughter. The match between the town doctor and the daughter of its leading citizen went against the wishes of the family patriarch and the couple had had to elope. After having three children (the daughter was Marika), Konstantinos and Angeliki divorced in 1949. Marika went to live with her mother in Athens, but she was her father's daughter in politics and personality, with a strong streak of historical romanticism, something she shared with Pablo. Her beauty and intelligence would have played a part in their friendship, too. Given all these revolutionary antecedents, it is not surprising that Pablo would help Marika buy back the Cassavetes family mansion in Zagora with the intention of establishing a museum and a historical archive.

Around that time, there were the occasional bitter disappointments, too. Jacques Grinblat (1917-1997), whose party name was Privas, found himself beyond the pale when he decided that there were inadequacies and dangers in the thought of Karl Marx. Pablo regretted this crucial rejection of revolutionary Marxism as he and Jacques had been close comrades for 40 years. As we have seen, Jacques played a key role in initiating the defence campaign when Michel had been arrested in 1960, and it was Jacques that he could call upon for delicate missions such as driving an ailing Sherry Mangan from the cold of northern France to the warmth of Spain in 1958. (Grinblat, incidentally, prolonged the life of Joe Hansen. In the heat of the political battle with the *pablistes* in 1964, Hansen, very much the chief *anti-pabliste*, collapsed with a heart attack. It was Grinblat who understood the danger and rushed Hansen to hospital. When he recovered, Hansen recognised he owed Grinblat his life. The grateful letter acknowledging this, written by Reba, Hansen's wife, but dictated by Hansen, has found its way into the Raptis archive in Athens.)

But there was nothing sentimental about Pablo's response to Grinblat's expectation that he could continue as a member of TMRI and argue his case within the organisation. He had, in Pablo's view, crossed a bridge too far and put himself outside the organisation by his repudiation of Marx, even if he still claimed to be a revolutionary. These were the years of the 'new philosophers', led by Bernard-Henri Lévy and the Black Book on Communism, when Marxism was held to be a totalitarian ideology that led adherents straight to the gulag (not as prisoners but as guards!). With Marxism and revolution under sustained ideological assault and in need of defence, it was in Pablo's view sheer foolishness to expect a revolutionary Marxist organisation to indulge a renegade member, no matter how esteemed.[26]

Moreover, Grinblat's critique was misconceived and invalid, Pablo argued. The year before, at a centenary conference marking Marx's death, Pablo had testified to his still growing admiration for the genius of Marx. In his response to Grinblat, he summarily stated his position that Marx's thought had to be appreciated in its evolution through its philosophic, historical, social and political phases and dimensions. The starting point had been Marx's determination that man's exploitation by man had to be abolished. In his study of industrialising, capitalist countries, he had identified the working class as the force to carry out this task. It would, in Pablo's view, still play a central role. Grinblat's alternative, the social movements and minorities, were not enough. They had neither the social weight nor fundamental interest in overthrowing the existing system. As for less developed societies, it followed logically – and history had confirmed it – that the poor peasantry would play the role of revolutionary force. This scenario would not unfold to its completion without the participation of a conscious force armed with the ideas, ideals and tools of analysis that Marx and his heirs had elaborated. The aim of such an organisation would be to aid the working class and the mass of poor peasants and their allies to take over the democratic management of their societies. Grinblat had given up on that vision and, to the consternation of some of Pablo's supporters, Pablo cut him dead.[27]

— ✢ —

By the last decade of his life, Pablo was an established public figure in Greece.[28] Right up until his death, and over 20 years, he wrote two columns a week for *Ta Nea* and another for *To Vima*, the two main centre-left newspapers in Greece, owned by the Lambrakis family. It can safely be said that he was the only avowedly revolutionary Marxist in any country of the world to have a regular column in a major newspaper – and not just in one, but two.

He was hired to write on international events and doesn't appear to have strayed too far from that brief, although he was free to comment on

Greek affairs in interviews and forums published in the Lambrakis and other newspapers. Mind you, it didn't take much imagination to transfer his comments on developments elsewhere, say the attempt at a socialist-communist united front in France, to Greek politics. He was certainly the ideal candidate for the role of international commentator: a well-connected, cosmopolitan internationalist with decades of involvement in world politics. Recall that this was before the internet; Pablo was a kind of human, walking, talking Wikipedia. He wrote for an audience that had been starved of world news but for which there was a growing appetite. Greece was now opening up to Europe and also living on the doorstep of the region most wracked by civil strife, wars and superpower rivalry.

Pablo's columns combined reportage, analysis and philosophical reflection. It helped that he was a polished writer in Greek. His prose was spare, limpid with a colourful turn of phrase. Saddam Hussein, for instance, was the Imam of Baghdad. He did name-drop on occasion, but it was just as likely to be relatively unknown, but colourful characters, such as Sadiq Premtaj, the exiled Albanian guerrilla fighter and archenemy of Enver Hoxha, as Ben Bella, who admittedly made frequent appearances. Marx, Lenin, Trotsky and Rosa Luxemburg were also introduced to readers. Concision, with a dose of elliptical or oracular declaration, was required because of the constraints of the word-count. The twice-weekly *Ta Nea* columns were usually about 300 words. The weekly *To Vima* columns, on the other hand, could run to 2000 words. They were peppered with quotes from the classical and modern Greek poets. He rarely missed a chance to advocate for deeper and wider democracy, or deliver over-optimistic predictions of revolutionary developments. He indulged his fondest dreams, too, such as his longstanding vision of a united, federated Arab republic stretching from the Atlantic to the Tigris. After noting the rise in the oil price, the demographic explosion and the continued threats from Israel, he continued in a 1990 column:

> The Arabs still have immense problems to resolve. To unite as a nation and as a market. To tame an extremist Islamism which develops a little everywhere, supported financially and politically by Saudi Arabia and the Americans. To democratise their societies and their regimes. To recognise the inviolable rights of women, who are at the centre of a growing social movement. To invent, at least in certain regions, the human resources for a rapid and balanced ecological and economic development. [All this] Before emerging in all their new grandeur, united, independent and free, contributing their own values to the new civilisation of a universal and democratic society. Inshallah.[29]

## 19 . THE FATE OF FRIENDS AND COMRADES 1980s

Inshallah, God willing, indeed.

Much of what he wrote in these newspaper columns remains topical and valid: the ceaseless waves of desperate refugees heading towards Europe; the rise of neo-fascism in Europe and toxic nationalism in the old Soviet bloc; the overweening military power of the United States; the colonising and aggressive orientation of Israel; German domination of the EU; the centrifugal forces and deep discontents in a China in urgent need of democracy; the deepening ecological crisis endemic to capitalism; and the urgency for the Left to re-analyse capitalism and how to replace it with an egalitarian and sustainable system.[30] Rereading these columns today is a matter of *plus ça change, plus c'est la même chose.*

The same preoccupations had prompted him to form the Protagoras circle with close friends in 1978. Over the next decade it organised forums on key international developments. Protagoras brought representatives from Polish Solidarity, the Iranian opposition, the guerrilla movements of El Salvador and Guatemala, the Sandinista movement in Nicaragua and Soviet dissidents to address what were major events in Athens. The forum on Solidarity, for instance, drew an audience of thousands. Pablo made a point to involve as many of the parties and groupuscules of the Left as possible. In this way, the Protagoras forums were to be the model for the united front of the Left and workers' parties that he continued to advocate for Greece and France; open, participatory, inclusive.[31]

There were other attempts to regroup the Left, one of which came to grief because of Elly's wild intervention. *For socialism*, the bi-monthly magazine Pablo and his supporters published between 1975 and 1980, had been wound up in favour of devoting energy to Protagoras. In 1984 a collection of Marxists of various persuasions came together to found *Spartakos,* resurrecting the name of the group and journal founded by Pantelis Pouliopoulos in the 1930s. Pablo's participation, however, lasted only one issue. As Tassos Anastassiadis recalls it,[32] Elly, who had little direct involvement in the group to this point (although she was the legal publisher), demanded that Tassos Goudelis be excluded from the group because she was in a legal dispute with his father, Yorgos, a lawyer who had managed her real estate when she and Pablo were in exile. The group refused and Pablo resigned. Tassos tried to get him to stay on, but Pablo was immovable. His and Elly's relationship was like that. (It is, of course entirely possible that Elly was correct about irregularities and/or laxity in the management of her estate in her long absence.)

Pablo might no longer have been a Trotskyist in the generally accepted definition, but he retained an immense affection and admiration for Trotsky. In 1990 he was invited to speak at a conference on 'The heritage of Trotsky', held in Budapest. In Eastern Europe, these were times for tasting the forbidden fruit of the Stalinist decades. The subject was too big for one speech, Pablo told his audience, and he would focus on the principal contributions of Trotsky and what in his legacy remained worthwhile.[33]

He praised Trotsky's support for the New Economic Policy in the Soviet Union in the 1920s (so brutally and disastrously cut short by Stalin) as the model – provided it was accompanied by democratic planning and socialist democracy – for undeveloped countries aiming to transition to socialism. The mess the Soviet Union found itself in was proof of the superiority of Trotsky's model, even if the great revolutionary put too much emphasis on the role of a reformed Bolshevik Party. He acknowledged, too, Trotsky's analysis of the roots of the ruling bureaucracy in the Soviet Union.

Switching to the global stage, he highlighted Trotsky's understanding of fascism and particularly his advocacy in the early 1930s of an active united front among the German working-class parties to stop Hitler — as opposed to Stalin's policy of attacking the Social Democrats as "social fascists". Hitler's victory had not been inevitable. At the time Trotsky had warned that the Nazi victory would hasten the outbreak of the Second World War. Historians, Pablo argued, had been slow to acknowledge Trotsky's historic perspicacity.

It was the end of Pablo's speech that brought listeners back to the contemporary scene. Living through the Great Depression, Trotsky had concluded that capitalism had exhausted its capacity to develop the world's economy. It was seen as a brake on progress. Developments during and after the Second World War proved this demonstrably false – capitalism had fostered an amazing spurt in economic development in the decades that followed the war. On the other hand, it wasn't beyond being wounded. In the 1970s, the boom ground to a halt and stagflation set in, and in the 1980s capitalism had had to re-group its forces and restructure.

Now the question facing critical Marxists was: would the long expansion of capitalism that Trotsky had not foreseen continue? The challenge to a 'new generation of Marxists' was to write an updated version of Marx's *Capital*. Pablo's own hunch was that capitalism could not prevent 'the enlargement of zones of "poverty", including in the so-called developed countries, nor provide a way out of the extreme distress in the Third World'. The 'world self-managed republic' he dreamed of was 'not only more than ever necessary but, for the first time in history, possible'.

## 19 . THE FATE OF FRIENDS AND COMRADES 1980s

Possible, and necessary, but a long way from being achieved:

> We are witnessing an accelerated development of the world's problems, something which necessitates global solutions. Yet we cannot seriously speak of these being implemented by a worldwide self-managed republic We are still very far from this objective, which however constitutes the only efficacious 'solution' capable of warding off the primordial threats of nuclear war, ecological catastrophe and the monstrous manipulation of the biogenetic sciences.[34]

For that matter, Pablo and some of his more recent comrades had very different ideas on how to arrive at this 'solution'.

CHAPTER 20

# The last battle: how Green is my party? 1988-1989

IN THE LAST years of the decade, Pablo faced a fundamental challenge to his strategy within his own organisation, the TMRI or Association marxiste révolutionnaire internationale (AMRI) as it had become. It was his final political or ideological battle. It was to pit him against the younger cohort of *pablistes* over organisational questions and the importance of the Greens. In the long debate that unfolded over years, there would be no winners. Even if Pablo had the better of the argument, it is an argument which still has reverberations today.

Essential to Pablo's whole political *raison d'être*, as we have seen, was the necessity to organise a distinct, global association of revolutionary Marxists, acting collectively and inspired by the goal of generalised self-management on a world scale. However, his latter-day fraternal opponents in the AMRI – and they were mostly young – argued for a loose network of individuals working principally in the Green parties and alternative movements in Europe. This was too narrow a focus in Pablo's eyes. As early as April 1987, Pablo had tried to head off these notions at the pass by circulating a broadside entitled 'Préalable: maintenir et renforcer la TMRI'[1] (The prerequisite: to maintain and reinforce the TMRI).

It probably wasn't a good idea – as he did in the second paragraph – to link the dissent of his own youthful supporters to Alain Finkielkraut's *Défaite de la Pensée*, a then best-selling critique of, as Finkielkraut would have it, the general decline in education and culture among the young. It made Pablo look like an old-fashioned fuddy-duddy. He wasn't against change per se – open, for example to a modernisation of political language or changing the name of *Sous le drapeau du socialisme* to something more contemporary. But he did oppose capitulating, as he saw it, to the surge of social movements – phenomena, he argued, which were confined to Western Europe and the United States – at the expense of abandoning the traditional Marxist commitment to the working class and the wider Third World. 'On the world scale it is still the poor and working masses who constitute the crushing majority of the forces able to acquire a revolutionary disposition ... to aspire to a radical changing of society.'

As for the social movements, he went on to spotlight the loss of revolutionary elan in the women's movement: it was, in his view, resting on the laurels of the enormous, 'epochal' advances it had made in the past 15 years in terms of women's legal equality and control of their sexuality and reproduction. The ecological movement, for its part, was a perfectly legitimate reaction to the careless and destructive industrialisation of the capitalist and bureaucratic states, but it ignored the positive potential of the new productive and technological forces that accompanied this industrialisation. As for the youth movement, it did the young no favour not to introduce them to Marxism and the history of the workers movements. How healthy were the new social movements, he asked, if it was necessary to hide or abandon your revolutionary Marxist beliefs. 'We don't want to preach to anyone, to "manipulate" or "'infiltrate" and we are willing to discuss issues "pedagogically" so as not to "shock" the "innocents" ... But surely they can accord us the elementary democratic right to have a distinct cultural and political identity and to display it without any embarrassment.'

Revolutionary Marxists needed their own organisation, he insisted, to discuss their priorities and further their own project. This could not be done if they were to dissolve themselves into some rainbow or green organisation or movement. The *pabliste* current was distinctive, he reminded them, and had much to be proud of. It had been decided at the 8th international conference in 1985 to concentrate on building the TMRI as an organisation but now 'we are in the process of dissolving whole sections for the illusory benefit (illusory for us) of a "larger" work' in the Greens and other alternative movements. In his view, the TMRI also needed to move away from the current 'eurocentrism' and to develop centres for its work in the Third World and the Soviet bloc.

The pre-emptive attack didn't work. Younger members and supporters could not withstand the lure of the Greens – for very natural reasons. The members of these Green parties were generally fellow radicals of 1968 and its aftermath. Among the reasons the younger supporters had been drawn to Pablo was his insistence on integrating the social movements into an alliance with the labour movement and its parties, and of course his advocacy of self-management. The Greens championed these same social movements and were committed to participatory democracy. On the face of it, they were a natural fit for Pablo's supporters. Maurice Najman, who emerged as the spokesman for the younger dissidents, advocated becoming the revolutionary Marxist wing of the new Green parties.

At the 9th international conference of the TMRI held in Paris in June 1988, this 'Greens' current was much in evidence, spearheaded by the younger *pablistes*. They dissented from both the general political resolution and the adoption of a new Declaration setting out the political position of the AMRI. The dissent was substantial, garnering almost 40 per cent of the votes. Both the resolution and the Declaration had been drafted by Pablo. Such was the dissent that the final adoption of the Declaration was postponed to another meeting in February 1989.

There had been fireworks at the conference that had not shown Pablo at his best in the view of some.[2] He could be impatient with dissent on what he considered to be crucial questions, and the gentleman revolutionary could give way to the rough-house factional fighter.[3] Pablo had offered to integrate the amendments to the general political resolution moved by Yves Sintomer – on condition they didn't alter the general thrust – but this dubious peace offering was rejected.

In the political resolution he had nuanced some of the polemical positions he took in his first broadside, but without abandoning them. On the women's movement he added that in some countries, the laurel-resting meant the achievements were at risk of being reversed. Furthermore, in the workforce, women's employment was likely to be precarious and concentrated in the lower-paid occupations. In daily life and in general political matters, their power was still inferior to that of men, and they needed to keep challenging that situation. 'Revolutionaries will not progress if they do not make those struggles their own.' On the ecological movement, he conceded that a pause or moratorium on fundamental issues such as genetic engineering was logical while the impacts of this and other 'advances' were considered. He still insisted that technology had the potential to be used in a sustainable way that would benefit humanity as a whole. Any political party or movement that confined itself to only ecological issues would flounder. It was necessary to tackle the social issues thrown up by capitalism, and he acknowledged the German Greens had recognised this.

These "concessions" did not alter his overall conclusion that 'in the advanced capitalist countries the true alternative political and social movement can only be a movement rooted in the totality of the social forces that are potentially anti-capitalist and oriented to self-management.' Those social forces included the traditional working-class unions and parties. In countries like France, that meant 'attaching particular importance to the crisis in the Communist Party ranks and to their convergence with the alternative movement'.

Those parts of the resolution dealing with the European Union, Eastern Europe and the Soviet Union and the Third World aroused little or no opposition. A unifying theme there was the support for wider federations and common markets around the world. The problems facing humanity demanded a breakout from confined national boundaries. '… There is a globalisation of problems and solutions that it is necessary to recognise everywhere; society is rapidly becoming planetary and ruled by planetary forces. The free and constructive development of those forces demands a global self-managed republic.'

The conflict simmered after the conference, and stayed on the front burner even after the acceptance of the Declaration at the February meeting. The February issue of the *Lettre internationale pour l'autogestion*, the TMRI's internal newsletter, carried a report from Najman about the British group's interest in joining the Greens and excerpts from papers by George Shaw, Derek Wall and Keir Starmer which appeared to favour abandoning work in the Labour Party in favour of the Greens. The May issue carried further pieces along the same lines from German and Italian members. Clearly, the central question of the priority to give the Greens had not been settled. After the good showing of the Greens – particularly in Britain, France and Italy as well as Germany – in the European parliamentary elections in June 1989, the conflict broke out again, fiercer than ever. It pitted Pablo against Maurice Najman in a bitter war of words.

Maurice Najman was an extraordinary character.[4] In some ways he was the Pablo of his generation. In answer to the question of what was the meaning of life, Pablo would respond, 'the only answer is that the meaning of life is life itself. You should live as much as you can.' Najman certainly lived by that credo. His family were of Polish Jewish origins, his mother, a survivor of the Nazi extermination camps, still spoke Yiddish to her children; and the Najmans were reputedly related to Rosa Luxemburg on his mother's side. An uncle, Maurice Najman, had died in Spain fighting for the republic in 1937. The Najmans were well-off but also

Communist Party supporters. Maurice met François Leclerc in the young communist movement in 1965 and it was François who introduced him to Gilbert Marquis and Michel Fiant. In 1966 he formed a group at his high school in support of the NLF in Vietnam and in 1967 in his final year at school, he became one of the founders of the Comités d'Action Lycéen (CAL), the national movement of high school students, which organised support for the Vietnamese resistance and the right of political activity and dissent in schools. CAL was a major force in the May days of 1968 and Maurice was by then fully committed to the self-managed socialism and internationalism of Pablo.

An eloquent speaker, indefatigable organiser, filmmaker and impressive writer, he soon became the best-known and respected of the younger generation of Pablo supporters. His taste for drugs and rock'n'roll added a patina of counterculture to his image. Christophe Nick dubbed him the leader of the 'red dandies', Pablo's young French followers so named (by Nick) because he claimed they shared a 'look': long hair, leather coats, jeans and cowboy boots. A style which was, of course, very common at that time.

In many ways, Maurice Najman showed the same flair for revolutionary initiative as Pablo. This was particularly the case with the democracy movement in Czechoslovakia in the 1970s. Najman made contact with Charter 77, the organisation of Czech democratic reformers, and established friendships with some of its best-known members, such as Vaclav Havel and Petr Uhl. Uhl became an occasional contributor to *SDS* and Havel invited Najman back to Prague to organise a convention of citizens after the 'Velvet revolution', which saw the peaceful overthrow of 'communism' in Czechoslovakia in 1989. Najman had something of the Marxist impresario about him (it is claimed, for instance, that he wanted to form a Rock Liberation Front). He organised the release in France in 1977 of recordings by the persecuted Czech underground rock group, The Plastic People of the Universe. The disc came with a 50-page booklet which included the history and demands of Charter 77. The profits, along with false papers provided by Pierre Avot-Meyers, helped in the escape of Pavel Zoricek, one of the band members who had been imprisoned and tortured in a psychiatric hospital.

A younger comrade, Patrick Serand, encountered Najman in the mid-1980s in the organisation IDEO. IDEO sought to publicise the activities and fate of dissidents in the Soviet bloc and establish bridges between the pacifists and leftists in Western Europe and those dissidents. 'What is there still to be said about Maurice?' he writes in his 2018 memoir. 'A dazzling operator, often difficult to follow (literally as well as figuratively) with a sharp sense of the innovative and an often unquestionable flair for political action.'[5] Elsewhere he notes that Najman is 'across everything and in touch with everyone'. In his biography of Najman on Maitron (the online dictionary of biography of the French Left), Jean-Paul Salles concludes: 'Everyone who met him recognised his charm, his intelligence, his vivacity, his incredible energy and his sense of humour.'

Now he was to bring out the best and worst in Pablo. Sintomer was to recall the conflict as a generational one and involving the issue of what kind of organisation the TMRI (or AMRI) was: a congenial club or a disciplined party.[6] It was possible to view it as simply a club of like-minded, free-floating radicals where nothing concrete was achieved. Patrick Serand described a meeting of leading delegates in 1987:

> The TMRI was a circle of various characters and activists from skeletal organisations ... I met there Michel Raptis, "Pablo" ... who gave a long report on developments in the USSR which was ultra-Gorbachev. The attendees represented disparate groups: the French and German, Theo Blom (the last of the Dutch comrades of the TMRI), some Latin Americans, some British if I recall correctly, and Mohammed Harbi who seemed to be present as 'counsellor to the prince'.[7]

It corresponds to this writer's memories of such meetings from 1968-69, except that appearances can belie reality. Real practical decisions could be and were taken and followed through. In my case, for instance, one task was the printing and circulation of a Greek resistance newspaper in London. Another was translating and publishing Pablo's analysis of May 1968 and the Prague Spring.[8]

The conflict in 1989 took place within an organisational framework that formalised this informal but real International. The 9th conference of the TMRI had unanimously adopted new rules and a new name, henceforth it was the International Association of Revolutionary Marxists (or Alliance marxiste révolutionnaire internationale). The new organisational rules made it clear that the AMRI was a free association of revolutionaries on the basis of shared ethical and political beliefs, with few or any detailed by-laws spelling out rights and duties. This may have suggested "a club" but it was clear from the new rules that the aim was for a global organisation that did things together. It was not just a talk shop: 'Internationally and nationally we act together in a coordinated, efficacious, militant manner ...'

Pablo always dreamed of a properly international organisation. The TMRI or AMRI was internationalist but its membership was essentially western European, with friends and supporters in some Eastern European, North African and Latin American countries. But it was essential that the analysis of an international organisation be global and its political platform reflected that. His oft-repeated criticism of Mandel and the United Secretariat Fourth International, which did have a much wider global spread of members, was that it was just a federation rather than a cohesive world party.

This international dimension was paramount, as it always had been for him. In the conflict with the younger *pablistes*, it became a sticking point. Of course, it was always possible to argue that Pablo conveniently identified his view as the 'international' one when it was arguably the case that the opposition had more accurately captured the international situation and its demands. Certainly, Najman and the others argued this was the case – that we were entering the age when ecological concerns were the new global issue and that the Green parties had tapped into this new reality. For Pablo, always conscious of the Third World where the bulk of humanity still lived in poverty and oppression, this was arrant European provincialism.

Just how deep the divisions ran became obvious in the exchange between Pablo and Najman after the February 1989 conference. In a statement he issued,[9] Najman and his supporters argued that 'pabloism', having accomplished much historically in terms of updating revolutionary Marxism (support for the colonial revolution, clarification of the nature of the bureaucratic states, new thinking on the nature of the revolutionary party), had now 'stagnated'. The need was for a redefinition, a re-founding, a new leap forward (all these phrases were used). The Tendency's own openness to new developments had encouraged some *pablistes*, at least, to understand what was now needed: 'our ideological, political, organisational and cultural repositioning for the tasks of the future: to assemble the eco-socialist, Marxist wing of the alternative movement.' As Najman pointed out, the conservative old guard were resisting this turn.

The young French, English and German comrades argued that Greens were the future and that they already completely occupied the 'alternative' political space. In the wake of the conference, they outlined five propositions which needed to be considered: 1. 'strategically determinant as it remained', the capital-labour contradiction was no longer as central. 2. The collapse of the bureaucratic states and the communist parties would end in total failure and would not lead to a transformation of the labour movement. 3. The Greens, on the other hand, would shape the future on a worldwide scale. 4. Left to themselves, the Greens would become radical reformist parties helping to regulate and stabilise the capitalist world. Although that was still far from the case, the possibility existed that the Greens could 'participate in the reformulation of a revolutionary project for the 21st century'. 5. It was up to the Tendency or Association to try to 'maximise' that transformative possibility by joining the Greens and contributing to its political evolution.[10]

This 'turn' to the Greens was, the 12 signatories argued, a natural next step for the AMRI which had completely moved beyond the old Trotskyism and Third International thinking. They proposed that the *pablistes* now participate in establishing a global 'eco-socialist' forum. They declared themselves against forming a faction in the AMRI because they were not absolutely sure where their thinking would lead them and, besides, they had too much respect for the organisation and its achievements to engage in a 'degrading' factional battle that would risk disrupting the continuity of the current.

Nevertheless, many of the comrades advocating this turn to the Greens had already taken the step. In England, for instance, they had left the Labour Party to join the Greens. This was also part of a wider debate in the French far Left at this time. By mid-1989, Juquin himself had abandoned the idea of the Nouvelle Gauche and announced his intention of applying to join the Greens – it took another two years before he was admitted.

Pablo's initial reaction to this alternative position was finely balanced between civil and scornful. In June 1989 he intervened with a nicely written essay '*L'herbe et le grondement*' ('Green Shoots and Rumblings'). It was in response to a Najman contribution, the title of which carried a quote from Lenin: 'Put your ear to the ground and listen to the grass grow'. What Najman heard was the growing pains of a new multi-faceted, 'alternative' movement in which the Greens were a major component. He argued that the *pablistes* should become a network grouped around a weekly paper, active in all aspects of this new 'alternative' movement (including the disintegrating labour movement). They should also help convene an annual 'eco-socialist forum' to bring all parts of that movement together.[11]

With his own ear to the ground, Pablo insisted on the adequacy of Marxism as a tool to understand the ecological catastrophe brought on by capitalism; the urgent need for a deep analysis of the new stage of financialised and global capitalism; the inadequacy of the analysis and solutions of the Greens leaders; the disintegration of Stalinism; the misery of the Third World; and to cap it all, the serious economic difficulties of capitalism. In other words, he could hear more than the ecological crisis and the Greens' response, and argued that a Marxist framing was as relevant as ever. For good measure, he characterised Najman as a 'centrist' (someone unable to make the leap from radical reformism to revolution), an old charge from the Trotskyist movement thrown at anyone judged to be drifting to the right.

Najman seized on the "centrist" charge to pour disdain on Pablo's desperate tactic of resorting to shop-soiled polemical clichés. In a letter of 12 September, 1989, circulated to all members and supporters of the Association (Tendency), Najman declared that he wasn't prepared to involve himself in the 'degrading' dispute that was wracking the Association. Nonetheless, he proceeded to characterise Pablo's argument as 'reactionary' and accused him and Gilbert Marquis of hijacking the organisation and its publications, and repudiating the decisions of the 9th conference.

For Najman, the polemics were degrading, 'above all for Michel, from whom we expect better and more than an orthodox defence of Marxism, without a dialogue with the really existing forces whatever their baggage and limitations (which are anyhow equal to ours)'. It appeared to Najman that Pablo was turning his back on the 'alternative' movement that had emerged in Europe, in favour of an old-fashioned, conservative Marxism which could result, as Pablo had already indicated, in a return to the Fourth International. Najman expected that the division between the two sides would persist. However, he thought it 'necessary to maintain, as least for a period, a current that had emerged from the critique of Trotskyism', from the 'qualitative leap' animated by Pablo in the 1960s and since deepened (more pragmatically) by those younger comrades who emerged out of the movements of the 1970s and 1980s. One can only imagine how that characterisation of 'pablism' as a two-stage affair which had become the property of a wider number than its 'historic' initiator, would have gone down with that same comrade.

As the months wore on and Najman and his supporters persisted, Pablo became impatient, even exasperated. In October, in a document entitled 'Let's get it over with' (*En finir*)[12], he rounded on Najman. It was hard not to read the argument as personal, as far as Pablo was concerned, and he did not hold back. The sharp tone of the document is a reminder that he was not always the avuncular, patient, gentleman revolutionary. At its core, his argument was valid enough but contained a fair degree of polemical injustice.

He began by declaring that Najman's propositions about the need to join the Greens were 'comical if they were not so tragic'. The only (and it was minimal) credit he would give Najman was that he was now openly making the break with those he called 'ideologically sterile', 'conservatives' like himself and Gilbert Marquis. He attributed the appearance of the Najman alternative to the 'incredible organisational laxity' of the Tendency. He took a lot of the blame on himself. He had tried to promote a new organisation of revolutionaries based on freely associating comrades who came together to advance agreed objectives based on thorough analysis and discussion. However, too many members observed the rights and not the duties of such an association.

Revolutionaries, like people generally, were now being buffeted by a storm of changes, he acknowledged, brought on by the new stage in capitalist development and by the unravelling of the Stalinist world. This posed a formidable intellectual challenge, essentially to understand the emerging 21st century world, a new situation he would later say posed the need for a new *Capital*. Instead of analysing these changes in depth and cleaving to the revolutionary forces emerging from the recomposition of the workers movement and the wider global revolutionary movement – in the Third World and Eastern Europe as well as the developed capitalist countries – Najman and his supporters were caving in to ephemeral ideological and political fashions in a handful of western European countries. They had latched onto 'epiphenomena' such as the ecological consequences of capitalism. Such political and ideological 'levity' and 'impressionism' was to miss the wood for the trees. 'The challenge is to struggle against the totality of the system, not against the epiphenomena of the system, as important as they are.' The point was to explore the new forms a resurgent capitalism was taking:

> Far from fixing our attention ... on the new phase attained by the hyper-concentration of capital following, on the one hand, its penetration into the spheres of health, education, tourism, leisure and so on, and on the other, the globalisation of the new abstract form of capital (exempt from all control, whether it be taxation or inflation) ... and investigating its 'civilisation', the mentality and culture fashioned by this new phase of capital, we've fallen into focusing on ecological epiphenomena and its vogue among certain circles in a handful of countries.

Najman, he charged, wanted to abandon the Tendency's proud and historic commitment to a global movement in favour of a western Europe-centric focus. They wanted the *pablistes* to 'rush frantically after the

Greens', rather than attempt to assemble a global 'New Left'. He added, for good measure, that capitalism would 'recuperate' the ecological crisis, conceivably by making it a new market.

He finished his counter-blast on what he called a personal note. Perhaps the Tendency, or Association as it now was known, has served its purpose. He didn't have many years left and he was inclined to devote himself to study and writing. He even talked of winding up the Association for the same reasons Marx and Engels had wound up the First International – the presence of too many comrades with contrary 'anti-Marxist' ideas. Certainly, Najman and any co-thinkers should leave the Association forthwith. Those comrades who wanted a more comforting and stable organisational life would, he counselled, be better off joining the Fourth International rather than 'running after' the Greens. While he despaired of its 'organisational pretensions', the 'anachronism' of its functioning and the retention of too much 'traditional ideological baggage', the Fourth was at least a 'rampart' against capitalist triumphalism. But it seems he wasn't quite ready to retire from the field himself. He called for an extraordinary world conference of *pablistes* to 'reorganise and rearm'.

Patrick Serand, an admittedly unfriendly source who was present at the 9th conference, recalls Pablo 'freaking out' at the persistence of the turn-to-the-Greens argument and savaging Yves Sintomer. He puts it down to the 'aging' Pablo panicking that his 'frail skiff had lost any following wind' and was about to lose its dwindling crew.[13] This ignores the question of how right Pablo may have been about the Greens. Pablo continued to emphasise the ecological danger that capitalism represented but he never resiled from his doubts about the Greens' ability to respond to that danger. In the light of subsequent political history, it might even be said that characterisation of the Greens (certainly in contemporary Europe) as 'radical reformers' was an overestimation. Serand's own memoir – he went on to join and leave the Greens – might even be said to bear out this judgment.

Over the next decade, Pablo's supporters divided roughly three ways – forming the Alternative Rouge et Vert (formed out of a merging of the Nouvelle Gauche and the PSU), or going back to the Fourth International, or joining the Greens. It is fair to say that all of them continued to hold, as central, their commitment to self-management or revolutionary participatory democracy .

In the longer view, this conflict represented the earlier and ongoing tension in Pablo's corps of fellow-thinkers between its Trotskyist antecedents and its openness to new developments, between its labour

## 20 . THE LAST BATTLE: HOW GREEN IS MY PARTY? 1988-89

movement orientation and support for the new social movements, its Third World sensitivity and its European roots. Integrating these 'moments' had always been a challenge.

As for Maurice Najman, despite the spats, he remained associated with the AMRI. As a journalist and filmmaker, he reported from Eastern Europe on the fall of the Wall, notably writing a book and making a film about Markus Wolf, the East German spymaster. Back in Paris he helped form 'Right to Housing' and with organising squats. His last major interest was the phenomenon of the Zapatistas, the peasant 'commune' in Chiapas in Mexico, and subcomandante Marcos. (This was an interest he shared with Pablo.) Sadly, Najman died aged 50, in 1999 – his radical personal life catching up with him.

Pablo, for his part, had already begun to spell out his final vision of revolutionary Marxism in a series of lectures and essays. Despite his age, his heart problems, his expectation of imminent death and the 'frail skiff' of his organisation taking on water and losing crew members, he was to be as active as ever both on the Greek and the international stages in the last years of his life. But he knew he was in a very different world now.[14] What Eric Hobsbawm was to dub 'the Short Twentieth Century (1914-1989)' was now over.

CHAPTER 21

# A new era: the final years 1989-1996

*I would like to close my eyes far away from the daily scenes of the unbearable barbarism into which I see our world sinking at the moment (and who knows for how much longer). At the time of my life when I woke up to this world, I did not approve of it, and I have tried with so many other people to change it – at the beginning in a radical way, then, and based on the experience that we gained, only to a degree, but still in a substantial way, without ever compromising with it.*

**'Overtime'**
epilogue to My Political Autobiography
(Athens 1997)[1]

WHEN HE WROTE his memoir in 1984, Pablo and Elly expected they were nearing the end of their lives. Instead, as he wrote 10 years later when the memoir was republished, there was 'an unexpected extension ... another chapter and one of the most interesting of our lives in the country to which we belong'.[2] He was a prodigal son returned to the fold – to Attica if not Ithaca. As well as being a recognised public figure in Greece, he became something of a sage, writing on subjects as diverse as a 'good death', the value of Freud, the need for a new *Capital* in recognition of the fact that capitalism had entered a new stage – and even a new *New Testament,* comparing the need for an awakened ecological sensibility to the advent of new religions.

He became a fixture at academic conferences, some of which he initiated and helped organise; in 1990, for example, he addressed academic conferences on Marx and technology (in Crete), Literature and

Revolution (in Greece), and Trotsky's heritage (Budapest, and in Germany, October 1989). The following year there were conferences on Lenin in Germany and Greece. The papers he delivered, like many of his articles, elaborated his argument that Marx and Marxism retained their relevance despite the likes of Francis Fukuyama and François Furet, who claimed that the sudden (and welcomed) collapse of the 'communist' states in Europe represented the end of Marxism as well as of History. This status as something of a grand old intellectual of the Greek Left culminated in the conferring of an honorary doctorate by Ioannina University in 1995, just months before he died.

Naturally, none of this intellectual activity detracted from his continuing activism. Nor, it must be said, did the deteriorating health of Elly and of his brother Kletos, for whom he was the principal carer. In the end, they were both to outlive him but only by a year or two. His responsibility for them did curb his travel but appears to have had only a minor impact on his journalism and his organising. His energy and taste for political activity remained undiminished.

Of course, he wasn't universally loved. The decade had begun not with honours but with the sensational accusation that he was the secret leader of a terrorist gang. The charge that he was the real brains behind the 17 November (17N) terrorist group was made in a book published in September 1990: *17N: the Leader* by Dimou Markus Botsaris, a right-wing defector from PASOK. Fifteen years after the restoration of parliamentary democracy, 17 November was still operating, having defied the extensive and Clouseau-like efforts of Greek and American police to discover and arrest its members.[3]

While Botsaris was a self-aggrandising and unreliable figure – he had not a skerrick of evidence for the allegation – Pablo reacted with fury in an immediate double-page reply in *To Vima*.[4] He saw the book as inspired by the reactionary security services that had fed Botsaris all kinds of fake news. It was certainly true, as Pablo pointed out, that the police and security services in Greece had never been purged of the extreme right-wing personnel who had been recruited during the Nazi occupation and in the civil war, Cold War and junta periods. Moreover, they had close relations with the CIA and Mossad. Pablo's extensive links with revolutionaries and rebels in Europe, North Africa and the Middle East made him an obvious target of their surveillance and paranoia, some of which was revealed in the subsequent court case.

While he was a critic and opponent of the urban terrorism of 17N, Pablo did have some sympathy for the persecuted members of organisations like the Italian Red Brigades and the Red Army Faction (RAF), better known as the Baader-Meinhof group, in Germany. Gilbert Marquis, for instance, agreed to his request to hide a woman fugitive of RAF in Paris in the late 1980s.[5] There was a minimum of solidarity that was owed to such wayward comrades. 'Even though I could not at all accept some of their ideas and actions,' he wrote in his *Political Autobiography* of the Red Brigades in particular, 'I have ascertained that within their ranks are militants of exceptional human qualities from the point of view of disinterestedness, daring, heroism and self-denial.' Despite their 'political immaturity', despite their 'impatience', 'when persons from these circles knocked at my door for a discussion, they always found it open. I consider that the best way for one to help the correct political orientation and the maturing of a person with redoubtable revolutionary orientation and higher active human qualities, is to show understanding and solidarity towards them'.[6] Such empathy and generosity did not extend to 17 November, who, rightly or wrongly, he situated on the extreme right.[7]

17 November had a good deal of blood, much of it innocent, on its hands and Pablo had spoken out against it. After the shooting of two prosecutors on 10 January and 18 January, 1989, Pablo led a forum on urban terrorism that ran over three days in *Ta Nea*.[8] He noted that the leader of the most famous urban terrorist group of the last third of the century, the Tupamaros in Uruguay in the 1970s, had since admitted the error of the strategy as it helped destroy the country's parliamentary democracy and ushered in a right-wing dictatorship. The Greek terrorists were following the same disastrous path, he pointed out. It was possible to see them as expressing the blind rage of many Greeks at the seeming corruption their politics were mired in. Nevertheless, the main result of their activities was the strengthening of the police and their repressive powers. Moreover, Pablo suspected that 17N was manipulated by the security services.

He could not have made his disavowal of 17N clearer. Moreover, his whole political philosophy was in opposition to individual terrorism. He stood for the greatest possible involvement of the greatest number of people in political activity, now and in the future society. 'How was it possible for me to be a theorist of direct democracy and to lead a terrorist organisation at the same time?' he asked. 'It would amount to the self-destruction of my contribution to the global revolutionary movement. I would have to forsake my entire life.'[9] Not surprisingly, the terrorist group itself issued a media release rejecting Botsaris' claim, saying that with his views, Pablo 'could not be a supporter, let alone a leader'.[10]

Given all this, Pablo argued that the accusation that he was the secret leader of this gang not only painted him as a hypocrite, but could prompt someone to kill him as an act of vigilante justice and vengeance. 'He has set me up as prey to be avenged by any honest or pretended outraged citizen who might meet me on the street.' He announced he was commencing legal action, confident that he could secure 'a huge financial compensation … if the Greek and European judicial system do their duty as I think and hope they will …'[11] That was an overconfident assumption for a revolutionary to make, something he recognised later.

The complication was that in vehemently denying the charge (which Botsaris and his supporters continued to make), he called Botsaris 'a worm' (it can also be translated as 'a piece of nose snot'). Anger is never a good master, and in this case it wasn't only his own amour-propre that was outraged but Elly's too. Botsaris' one piece of actual 'evidence' was a claim that Elly's fingerprint had been found on the media release sent to the Paris daily *Libération* after the assassination of the CIA station chief by 17N in 1975.

In response to Pablo's defamation action, Botsaris counter-sued for 'insult'. By what appears as a bizarre process, to eyes used to British legal procedures, the two claims were heard simultaneously. The five-day court battle in May 1991 garnered huge publicity in Greece as both sides mobilised star witnesses. Botsaris' included a former interior minister and the current head of the prime minister's media office (he happened to be a former Stalinist). Pablo's included his editors at *Ta Nea* and *To Vima*, the mayors of Athens and Syros, Manolis Glezos, as well as an array of writers, academics and union officials.

Messages of solidarity flowed in from friends and comrades (including Ernest Mandel and Alain Krivine, as well as Zora and Ahmed Ben Bella, Laurent Schwarz, Félix Guattari, Gilles Perrault, Claude Bourdet). In the end, Botsaris was found guilty of 'malicious slander' and fined 1.5 million drachma and sentenced to 12 months imprisonment. However, Pablo was convicted of 'insulting' him, fined 400,000 drachma and sentenced to four months in prison. It was a dual judgment which Pablo ironically described as 'a truly Solomon-like decision', reflecting the pressure from conservative circles whose disproportionate weight in judicial circles he now acknowledged.

While Pablo's was the greater victory, he could not yet reap any financial benefits from it, because Botsaris appealed the verdict in his case. By this stage Pablo had wearied of the fight and agreed to a settlement 'whereby Botsaris withdrew his book and Raptis withdrew his insult'.[12]

It was 'a compromise that I accepted, not wishing to prolong the case,' he explained later, as it was 'an unpleasant experience which had lasted two whole years'.[13] He soon after thought it was an error to have accepted the deal. However, with time now in short supply, there were other more important battles to fight.

— ✦ —

For Pablo, the final disappearance of the Soviet Union in 1991, following hard on the heels of the collapse of the bureaucratic states in Eastern Europe and the first Gulf War, signalled a whole new historical period. The 'Short Twentieth Century' was now over. The age of revolutions might not be over but it was in abeyance. The United States was enforcing a *Pax Americana* on the world. In the first Gulf War of 1991, Iraqi soldiers were massacred en masse, the country's military power and the infrastructure of its economy destroyed, along with it any Arab challenge to American and Israeli domination of the Middle East. Meanwhile, a brutal capitalist regime was being imposed on Russia and Eastern Europe; vicious ethnic nationalism was emerging in the old Soviet world and in parts of the Third World; regional wars were becoming frequent; economic and social inequalities within and between nations were widening; and ecological destruction was unceasing. The advance of science and technology may have made utopia a realistic option in Europe, for instance, but the political preconditions were not present. The 'revolutionary subject', the politico-social force that makes a revolution, had not been formed, let alone taken to the field of battle.

Humanity faced an age of barbarism. In this reading of the future, 'the consolation of radical militants … must stem less from the perspective of the nearness of 'utopia' as from the ethical necessity to resist by an exemplary and coordinated struggle the barbarism that global capitalism and imperialism maintains and perpetuates'.[14] Utopians and revolutionaries must act in the mass movements with a consciousness of reality and 'the extreme relativity in which we find ourselves for a long period still'.[15] While the times certainly curbed his optimism, he never did drop reference to the utopian possibilities he believed existed in the world, however distant.[16]

In 1992 the International Association of Revolutionary Marxists, as it was now called, held its 10th and penultimate conference and issued '26 theses'. Drafted by Pablo, the theses attempted to describe the new situation in the world and its possible evolution.[17] Despite the victory of capitalism, there was no slackening of the critique, for obvious reasons. Capitalism brought with it gross inequalities, mass poverty in the Third World, wars, recrudescent fascism, and ecological devastation. More than ever Rosa Luxemburg's choice – socialism or barbarism – confronted humanity.

In retrospect, what strikes the reader immediately in the '26 theses' is the absence of any emphasis on the rise of China. Pablo still saw the capitalist world as being composed of three blocs – North American, Europe (namely the EU) and Japan. He believed their competition would shape the immediate future. He did venture the possibility that this rivalry could be superseded by a *Pax Americana* and the appearance of global technology and financial corporations, but he preferred the inter-imperialist rivalry thesis. Russia and its former satellites would be sunk in the miseries of capitalist restructuring for some time – as, indeed they were – and the Third World would remain mired in stagnation despite occasional and short-lived 'miracles'. In his view, China, in the wake of Tiananmen Square, faced an unstable and oppressive future.[18]

Despite the contemporary pessimism his utopian hope persisted. Europe was the logical starting place for the utopian transformation:

> For the first time in the history of humanity (and for almost thirty years) the objective possibilities exist, either in the USA or in Europe, to attempt by successive approximations to begin to build "utopia". Compared to the USA, Europe has the advantage, with a practically equal technological base, a higher cultural, humanistic level – thanks to the heritage of ancient Greek civilisation, the Italian Renaissance, the French Enlightenment, 19th century German philosophers (including Marx and Freud) – and a labour and social movement rich in experience and history. Admittedly Europe's ethnic diversity is a handicap – a handicap that only its true democratisation could progressively neutralise.[19]

The unknown factor was the revolutionary 'subject' that would bring about this 'realistic' utopia. In the three decades after the Russian revolution, it had been the traditional proletariat, according to the '26 theses'. Since the Second World War, however, capitalism had changed due to a quickening scientific revolution and its practical application to the economy. Society had become more complex and it was no longer the proletariat alone which created value. It was now the case of the 'collective worker' with input from scientists, technologists and highly skilled operatives, in an increasingly automated economy in which 'fixed capital' was more central than ever. So, the new 'subject' must reflect this complex social reality.

The '26 theses' warned against any 'economism' or new 'workerism' – a predominant emphasis on wages and conditions, in other words – arguing that ideas and social values would play a central role in the creation of that subject. Here again were the ideas of a 'surplus of consciousness' and the emphasis on the moral and ethical dimension of Marxism.

As for the scattered and dispirited elements of the revolutionary left, they needed to circle the wagons, to come together, initially in forums, campaigns and journals, to pursue prospects for radical change and push back against the neoliberal onslaught against Marxism, the possibility of a different world, and even the Welfare State. This was what Pablo had been practising in Greece for some time via Protagoras. The theses also floated the idea of a coordinating 'centre', although there was no flesh on the bones of that idea. By now Pablo and his comrades were on the threshold of admitting defeat in their own organisational efforts, even applying to rejoin the Fourth International from which they had been unceremoniously excluded in 1965.

Despite their best efforts, Pablo and his supporters never managed to build a strong organisation. Their numbers were always modest – they had perhaps 250-300 members of their French section in the 1970s at the height of their influence, and in the handful of other countries where there were supporters, they rarely went beyond double figures. By the 1990s, only France and Greece could be said to have something resembling an organisation of *pablistes*. Supporters and sympathisers in the Netherlands, Denmark, Austria, West Germany, Spain and Britain had all created organisations, or established journals, but they had either dispersed after brief existences, or persisted around only a handful of individuals. Right-wing coups in Chile, Argentina and Peru in the 1970s put an end to any organisation in those more promising arenas.

In other words, much as they were needed, the *pabliste* heralds of 'the human socialist city of tomorrow' were still in very short supply. This was in contrast to the other currents that could trace their origins back to Trotskyism. Their memberships were much more numerous and they boasted continuing organisations. True, most of them had a significant churn of members and their ideology and practices were not something the *pablistes* envied – far from it. It is fair to say each of these currents made a priority, or even a fetish, of organisation. The trouble with *pablistes*, maintained Jean-Pierre Hardy, a critical communist for self-management, was that they tended to make a fetish of non-organisation.[20] This is harsh, but it is true that in the wake of May 1968, they were the last of the revolutionary currents involved in that momentous month to create a formal public organisation – the Alliance marxiste révolutionnaire in July 1969. Even then, they kept one eye on events inside the French Communist Party (PCF) because they had not given up on 'entrism sui generis' which saw the emergence of a mass revolutionary party as linked to developments inside the PCF.

There were other reasons for this laxity about organisation. The Bolshevik emphasis on the Party and its primacy had been a contributing factor in the creation of the one-party state dictatorship that had facilitated the rise of Stalin. Pablo and his supporters accepted that the Bolshevik party had been essential for the victory of the Russian Revolution and that any successful revolution would require revolutionary leadership. However, the substitution of the party for the class was always a danger. In order to avoid it, a new conception of revolutionary leadership was needed – the revolutionary party had to aid the people to take charge of society. In other words, the emphasis was on the people as revolutionary subject, to whom the party was subordinate. The party should also separate itself from day-to-day management of the state as soon as possible.

That perspective meant there was an underlying suspicion of party organisation and an overestimation of the revolutionary consciousness of the masses. Hardy has many labels for this way of conceiving the party and its role – 'neo-spontaneism', 'organisational dilettantism' and so on. They all add up to an underestimation, in his view, of the need for a stable, continuing organisation of revolutionaries. In his final interview with Adolfo Gilly, Pablo echoes something like Hardy's critique, allowing that the critique of the Jacobin/Bolshevik concept of the party too easily slid into a distaste for hard organising.

None of the *pablistes* considered that any of the self-styled revolutionary parties of the 1970s and 1980s would morph into the new Bolsheviks of a new 1917, despite the common self-delusions of those parties that that they could. It was why the *pablistes* had advocated an alliance and convergence of the would-be revolutionary currents as the only realistic solution to the need for an authoritative revolutionary leadership. As we know, they were ready at any moment to merge their organisation into a larger organisation which accepted the model of a self-managed socialism and a government of the traditional worker parties, supported by a network of committees open to all workers. Waiting for that opportunity, however, was another source of organisational laxness. Any organisation was transitory, ad hoc and a step towards a larger outfit. (This ambivalence towards organisation took a symbolic form. When the AMR adopted a logo in the early 1970s, they chose a stylised hammer and sickle. The sickle was stood straight up and bore an unfortunate resemblance to a question mark.)[21]

Despite these phobias about too much organisational chauvinism, Pablo himself was committed to forming a continuous and strong organisation. It was at the 9th conference in 1988, that the *pablistes* eventually transformed themselves into the AMRI, Association Marxiste Révolutionnaire Internationale (or International Revolutionary Marxist Association), a title Pablo had suggested 20 years before. And it was at that conference that they adopted a set of rules or statutes that corresponded with Pablo's long-held conception of a revolutionary party as an active, disciplined organisation, composed of critical-minded, but responsible comrades who each had the right to dissent from the organisation's political positions.

He had spelled out this position in 1976 in his obituary for Georges Vereeken, the prickly, veteran Belgian Trotskyist.[22] Georges was the very epitome of a militant with his own opinions and a reluctance to remain silent in the face of perceived errors. Nor was he a respecter of persons. In the 1930s he had crossed swords with Trotsky himself, telling the Old Man that if there was GPU infiltration of the movement it was probably in the circle around his son in Paris. (He was, tragically, right.) He also had a higher estimation of the value of POUM's role in the Spanish Revolution than Trotsky and said as much. He had been excluded from the nascent Fourth International for such outspokenness. Late in life he had developed an obsessive concern about the continuing infiltration of the Trotskyist movement by Moscow's agents and the movement's laxity in security matters – including in the years that Pablo himself had been the secretary. Yet he had been an accepted pillar of the TMRI.

Pablo's obituary for Georges was fond. He recounted the story of his last visit to the old comrade in a Brussels hospital. Georges told him the bed opposite was occupied by a paratrooper, who had participated in the counter-revolutionary putsch against independent Congo in the early 1960s that resulted in the murder of the country's elected prime minister, Patrice Lumumba. The previous night this dying putschist had collapsed on the floor on his way to the bathroom and had been unable to get up. Rather than let him wallow in his shit and piss, Georges had got up and helped him to the bathroom and back to bed. In the end, his compassion and humanism had taken pity on the ailing enemy. But the main point Pablo made in his obituary was that any decent revolutionary movement must have room for difficult customers such as Georges, for comrades who reserved their right to think and speak out if they deemed it necessary.

Such an organisation as conceived by Pablo and his allies turned out to be attractive and congenial for individuals who had a taste for adventure and radical ideas, but it was not conducive to solid, or stolid, organisation building. Decades later, Didier Leschi penned this (self)-portrait of the *pablistes* of the 1970s and 80s:

> … the supporters of Michel Raptis known as "Pablo", were called "*pablistes*" but preferred to define themselves as "revolutionary Marxists" or as "communists for self-management". I saw them from afar, with their intimidating top-of-the-class, rhetorical style, without thinking that one day I would end up being a *leader* of this strange movement. Constantly in search of innovation, the *pablistes* were animated by an optimism that sometimes blinded them. They saw the revolution everywhere and every sign was over-interpreted on the positive side even when it was ambiguous …
>
> Polyglot in the great tradition of internationalists, Pablo's curiosity about the United States had made him recognise the importance of what were not yet called new social movements and lifestyle issues, feminism among others. His supporters, excited by these issues which, they hoped, would regenerate a Marxism ossified during the Stalinist night, loved to join these new movements, at the risk of being diluted within them. Immersed in these movements they were less a group than a collection of brilliant, extremely cultured individuals, often shod in Mexican boots, with at their fingertips a book by one of the thinkers of the Frankfurt School. Maurice Najman was the typical model of the *pabliste*, ready for all experiences, even the most extreme, which ended up carrying him away.[23]

This seconds Hardy's severe judgment, essentially that they were a club of brilliant individuals more than a party.[24] In the absence of its own substantial organisation, Pablo and his supporters were often reduced to auxiliaries or advisers in revolutionary situations. Pablo himself was described, admittedly by his enemies, as a 'counsellor to princes'. We know that is far from the whole picture, but there is some truth in it – and that truth flowed from the weakness of his organisations. He periodically talked of overcoming this weakness but no real progress was ever made. In his defence, however, it's fair to say it was a general weakness on the Left – no one had built a significant revolutionary party.

Tellingly, the '26 theses' contained positive words about the Fourth International and its political evolution – namely, that it now presented itself as a component of a necessary wider convergence and there was an underlying identity in its political positions and those of the AMRI. These were reasons to re-join the Fourth International. As Pablo admitted, it was a much larger organisation.[25] Before the 10th conference of the Association, Pablo had written privately to Mandel, although he did add a note that he could show the letter to Daniel Bensaïd (the leading thinker of the younger cohort in the Fourth).[26] Mandel had sent him the draft of a new 'manifesto' to be adopted by the Fourth and Pablo's letter was basically a commentary on the new platform. Pablo made the elementary point that it lacked a dramatic peroration:

> The 'Manifesto' must straightaway be dedicated, like the overture of Beethoven's Fifth Symphony, to the 'New Historic Period' which we are now entering, facing either unprecedented liberation or the descent into the worst barbarism, alternatives which coexist in uncertain combat. We cannot limit ourselves just to mentioning that, to diluting it, to minimising it in the text by emphasising only the negativities of the current historic process and its real dangers.

He thought the new Manifesto tended to idealise the current working class, underestimating its stratification and the attachment to capitalist culture of the new-technology workers. He reiterated that the assembling of a socio-political movement, encompassing the majority of society, with the necessary 'surplus of consciousness', would be a long process.

He took up, as was inevitable, the question of the Soviet Union and the responsibility of Lenin and Trotsky for this disaster. He acquitted them on the grounds that neither of them believed that a backward and isolated country like Russia was ready for socialism. In making the revolution in Russia, they had banked on its extension to economically developed Germany. As this was delayed, they took what measures were necessary to win some time. If Lenin had survived, Pablo was convinced he would have, like Trotsky, espoused a united front of the German labour movement against Hitler and the Nazis in the early 1930s. In the resulting civil conflict they would have 'almost certainly' risked everything on the armed intervention of the Red Army to prevent the triumph of the Nazis. Trotsky had advocated this at the time. It would have changed the course of world history.

In the admittedly remotely analogous situation of Nicaragua, Pablo had already acknowledged the Sandinistas had saved the honour of the revolutionaries by permitting democracy, elections and then the transfer of power after they lost the 1990 elections. Those elections had been held in the most disadvantageous conditions: not just isolation and economic underdevelopment, but armed subversion and embargo carried out by the United States. The majority had voted to end hunger and war. In this case, the international Left had not been strong enough to deliver to the Sandinistas the aid they needed and deserved.[27] As he put it: '... in order to resist, a revolution needs international support, and the consciousness of the best part of the population is not enough to sustain it. In this sense, the Sandinistas have been the victim of Stalinism, before and after perestroika, and of the weakness of the international Left which has fallen short in its task of solidarity with a small heroic country like Nicaragua.' All talk of "the errors" of the Sandinistas obscured this fact of isolation and ignored the extraordinary maintenance by the regime of a liberal democracy. These Sandinistas had 'preferred to cede power than install a dictatorship'.[28]

The talks about Pablo and his supporters rejoining the Fourth continued for another six months. He had signalled to Mandel in his July 1992 letter that the regrouping was not proceeding smoothly either in Greece or France, due to 'bureaucratic or sectarian pettiness'. In May 1993, he travelled to Amsterdam with Elly and Marika to seal the re-entry. He, Gilbert Marquis and Guillermo Almeyra represented the AMRI at the meeting of the Fourth's International Executive Committee (CEI). While the French difficulties were resolved, problems persisted with the Greek Trotskyists due, in Pablo's view, to their 'incoherent isolation' from relations with PASOK. But this did not prevent a successful conclusion to the negotiations. The AMRI was offered two seats on the CEI. Gilbert Marquis and Guillermo Almeyra were proposed but the latter was ruled unacceptable because the Fourth had no section in Argentina, and to accept Almeyra would be to endow him with a representative status he did not have. Pablo was pressed to take his place, although he was reluctant for reasons of his and Elly's health. According to the report of the meeting from the AMRI delegation, Mandel 'rendered an homage to Michel' at the conclusion of the negotiations.

As it turned out, Pablo's membership was half in, half out. The Greek Trotskyists objected very strongly to his admission, on the grounds of his 'nationalism' and support for the Serbs in the wars that accompanied the break-up of Yugoslavia.

Pablo had long been a critical supporter of the Yugoslav communists. A supporter because of their defiance of Stalin and their initiatives in workers' self-management in workplaces. But critical because the party bureaucracy retained overall control of the economy and society, meaning Yugoslav self-management remained ghettoised in the factories and offices. Tito's foreign policy twists and turns to appease imperialism also drew his criticism. However, Pablo opposed the breakup of Yugoslavia because it had in his view been engineered by imperialism. The United

States, Germany and Turkey, between them, were carving out spheres of interest in the Balkans, and only Serbia opposed the carve-up.

This sympathy and support for the Serbs, including in Bosnia, was something he shared with the bulk of Greek society. He acknowledged that there had been terrible atrocities committed by the Serbs, but this was also true of their adversaries. Moreover, there was a history of the Serbs being on the receiving end of atrocities during the Second World War. This support for them led to a breach with his old comrade Ben Bella, who saw the conflict in religious terms and sided with the Muslims in Bosnia against their Orthodox Christian enemies. For Pablo this was a complete misreading of the Balkans conflict, which arose essentially from the Serb resistance to the attempt by Berlin and Washington to divide the old Yugoslavia into their respective spheres of influence.

Pablo had no time for Milosevic whom he considered quite capable of selling out the Serbs, but he does not appear to have the same critical attitude towards Radovan Karadzic and General Mladic, respectively the political and military leaders of the Serbs in Bosnia.[29] Pablo regretted that things had come to ethnic cleansing – he located the reasons for it in the different responses of the various national groups to the Nazi occupation and the unequal economic development since – but he accepted the circumstances had made it an inevitable outcome. History had regrettably ordained a future where each community had its own distinct geographic region within Bosnia. Asked about the dream of a multinational Bosnia, he responded: 'Unachievable for now. So much blood has been spilled, so much hatred created. These things do not get solved easily.'[30] (These views were formed before the details of the massacre at Srebrenica became fully known.)

The other outlaw peoples to receive his strong support in these years were the Iraqis, Cubans and Libyans. For him the Gulf War of 1991 represented a new stage in imperialist warfare – and barbarism. 'I followed it day by day ... the bombardment which day and night, for a month, attempted to return a small Third World country to the pre-industrial age. It was the trial run for a new type of computerised warfare ... against which a long-term war of resistance was not able to exist'.[31]

The destruction and the terrible massacres of Iraqis were followed by a comprehensive economic embargo. Pablo could not remain passive. He created and became president of the Greek-Iraqi Alliance of Friendship and Mutual Aid. It was in this role that he organised international conferences in 1993 and 1995 in Athens against the sanctions and blockade imposed on Iraq, Libya and Cuba. Margaret Papandreou, the former wife of Andreas and the mother of the future Prime Minister, George, was the other high-profile Greek sponsor of these conferences. International sponsors included Ramsey Clark, the former Attorney General of the United States; Tony Benn, the leader of the Left in the British Labour Party; writer and polemicist Christopher Hitchens; and Ben Bella. Among the dozens of lesser-known sponsors was Marcel Bleibtreu, a surgeon and Pablo's chief critic and opponent in the crisis in the French Trotskyists in 1951-52. This was another example of the fraternity that was reasserting itself among some of the old, historic comrades.

The first conference focused on all embargos but the second was purely on Iraq and the devastating impact the US-instigated embargo was having on the most vulnerable Iraqis. 'Thousands of Iraqis – especially women, children, the elderly and the chronically ill – are dying every month,' announced the program for the second conference, 'due to the shortages of food and lifesaving medicines.' While some medical aid was organised and sent to Iraq as result of these efforts, this was symbolic rather than substantial. The explicit aim of the conferences, and follow-up sessions in other European cities, was to shift public opinion and undermine support for the embargo. The conferences also organised delegations to visit Iraq to gather first-hand evidence of the embargo's impact. The state of Elly's health prevented Pablo from making these visits as he explained in letters to Tariq Aziz, the Iraqi foreign minister.[32]

Pablo was on stronger ground in this cause. As he explained to Gilly:

> We are not supporting Saddam Hussein. The aim was to lift the embargo which strikes the Iraqi people. On that basis we have taken the position to be against all economic embargoes, against no matter what people, because the result of an embargo is, on the one hand, to increase the suffering of the poorest people of the country, and on the other hand, to encourage the proliferation of mafia-like neo-capitalist groups who specialise in contraband, smuggling and black markets.

Pablo emphasised proudly to Gilly that the conferences had been financed by donations raised in Greece. It seems he was sensitive to any rumours about compromising subsidies from Gaddafi, which plagued parts of the far Left in these times.[33] Among the Greek sponsors of the second conference in February 1995 were Olympic Airways, Panteion University of Athens, the Athenaeum Intercontinental hotel, as well as an array of academics, doctors, journalists, lawyers, retired army officers, ship captains, mayors and PASOK MPs. (What he didn't mention publicly was that he sold one of Elly's apartments to make up a shortfall in finances.[34])

The inhumanity that was now evident in the world, as demonstrated by the Gulf War and the wars in Yugoslavia, sent him back to Freud ('who demythologised the dark world of our "soul"') and the Austrian's view of humanity's basic murderous nature. Freud, he recalled in a lecture at Athens University in 1993, had been swept up in the chauvinistic war fever at the commencement of World War I but had quickly recoiled before the mass killing that followed. It had forced Freud to think further about our basic biological urges:

> For example, delivering a talk at the Vienna University in 1915, Freud invited his audience to consider the bestiality and misery that had overwhelmed the world in the War and to accept that the instinctual disposition toward evil was a foundational component of human nature. It was, of course, not the only factor. Thucydides had already attributed wars to a similar vice of human nature towards evil.

'Freud argued,' Pablo explained, 'that primitive man killed his fellow man with pleasure, that we originate from a long line of executioners of our fellow human beings, that the drive to death and self-destruction lurks deep within our biology, that only thanks to our cultural Superego, our so-called civilisation and culture, do we manage somehow to master these innate urges.' The strength of those urges was evident in the 20th century and Pablo pointed to the development of the atomic bomb and the more recent 'advances' in genetics. 'Were the famous physicists,' he asked, 'who during World War II ultimately decided and succeeded in discovering and using atomic energy in the form of a bomb, not capable of resisting or being enticed by the demonic game of death and self-destruction?'

Pablo used this evidence of a still 'superficial' Superego, to argue the urgency and importance of rational thought and a humanistic education, once again referencing Ancient Greece:

> ... humanity has not managed yet to develop a cultural Superego capable of achieving an inner balance without feeling miserable or in a constant state of anxiety and insecurity. We know that the great Epicurus proclaimed that such a state could be achieved with a suitable philosophical education. In other words, with the training of rational thinking so that it can gently and pedagogically impose itself on our urges, convincing us that we can live fleeting life in relative happiness, and with great calm, free of prejudice and fears of Cyclops and Laestrygonians [a race of cannibalistic giants referred to in the *Odyssey*] that lurk within us, who, when knowledge shines its light on them, disappear like ghosts.

Freud was of course less optimistic than Epicurus, but his thinking went in the same direction. Freud's conceptions were for Pablo more relevant than ever,

> ... at the dawn of a new historical age, as is emerging after the collapse of the Eastern Bloc and the globalisation of the monetary economy, an age whose continuation may plunge us into greater barbarity and ignorance, it is necessary to look back to those Promethean characters in human history, who valiantly armed with rational thought and a deep humanistic education and understanding, stood as pioneers opening new roads, capable of leading to a higher form of human society that reconciles the individual and the totality [of humanity] towards a common fate.

And Freud, he concluded, should be regarded as one of these Promethean figures.

— + —

It was usual now for his conference papers and newspaper columns to allude to the literature and history of ancient Greece. On occasion, there would be reference to Rome too, but usually to figures inspired by Greece, such as Seneca. He had never been more Greek in the cultural and philosophical sense, something he recognised and revelled in, although he did regret that he had written thousands of articles in Greek that would never receive a wider audience.[35]

If he did not become what Australians call a 'national treasure' in his final years, he certainly evinced the respect and admiration in intellectual and political circles in his own country. Even Greece's main conservative newspaper called him 'our most courteous revolutionary', admittedly in announcing his death. A sign of this standing was the decision of the University of Ioannina in the autumn of 1995 to confer an honorary doctorate. He could not attend the ceremony in December 1995, for health reasons. The citation for the doctorate dwelt on his command of Hegelian logic and his utopian ideals as well as his political life.

The acceptance speech[36] he sent in his absence opened with a statement of his reluctance to accept the honour, which had been first proposed to him by Panagiotis Noutsos, a professor of philosophy at the university, as early as 1987, over coffee in a Paris café: 'I have always considered and still consider myself to be outside all systemic institutions, against which I have and still try to maintain a critical stance.' But he quickly added that he didn't want to tire the university audience 'with my reservations and dogmatisms'. He did add, however, another reason for his hesitation, by citing Cavafy's Manuel Komninos and that poetic character's desire to appear before his god without earthly honours and pretensions. 'I discern in Mr Manuel the feeling of futility that overcomes us in regard to our earthly ambitions, and the need, when on the brink of the great departure, to appear extremely modest, free of conceit and arrogance, the fate of mortals who consider themselves to be timeless and immortal.'

He confessed that it was only 'at an advanced age' that he had become aware of how important a part the political, philosophic and aesthetic values of Ancient Greece had played in his cultural formation. 'I gave a special place to the purely Greek notion of the Citizen who actively participates in public life, striving for substantive power and constantly being educated with the help of the Republic.' He singled out for mention Pericles and Protagoras and the concept of 'Agape', altruistic love or 'the expression of universal solidarity', championed by the Ancients and adopted by the apostle Paul as a constituent of Christianity. He went on to nominate 'the deep rationalism of Spinoza', the Enlightenment thinkers, the logic of Hegel (which 'I tried to decipher over one whole summer'), Marx and Engels ('in whom I found the basic elements of demythologisation and understanding of our social being and becoming') and, again 'at an advanced age', Freud, who like Marx also offered an approach to 'a deeper understanding of ourselves' even if one did not agree with his conclusions.

All this added up to a constant, unending quest to understand. 'I don't think that the search for an inaccessible holistic truth ever abates within us.' He finished with a lyrical reflection on the coming of death and life's lessons and an allusion to the nearby temple of Dodoni, located in Epirus, like the University of Ioannina:

> You undoubtedly acquire a more stoic approach to life and Destiny's fate that hangs inexplicably above it by deepening your humanistic culture. ... A tranquillity spreads through you, that highest of goods that the great Epicurus searched for; and when your end approaches you don't need to call on the oracle of Dodoni's false and timorous consolations. It would be enough just to visit the place, to bring to life with your imagination its imposing aesthetic beauty composed of the sacred oak's rustling leaves, the chimes of the copper bells when the wind claps them together, and the fluttering and cooing of the doves in the pale evening light.

Elsewhere, his critics argued that his return to his Hellenic roots had degenerated into a kind of Greek nationalism. 'I am not a nationalist,' he told *To Vima* in his last interview with the paper. 'I am an internationalist and I love my country.' Asked about the difference between nationalism and love of country, he explained it was matter of not supporting your country right or wrong, of being concerned with others and still having a justified pride in what your country might offer all humanity – and this was certainly true of Greece and its ancient civilisation.[37]

In his last years, he certainly believed that Greece was in danger of losing offshore islands and border areas to Turkey in a conflict over gas and oil reserves in the Aegean Sea. The danger arose from the politico-military complex in Turkey, which preferred to use military solutions to solve problems, demonstrated by its continuing war on the Kurds and its occupation of northern Cyprus. Pablo counted on a democratic mobilisation of Greek society to resist any Turkish attacks, attacks which he believed would be supported, or acquiesced in, by Washington.[38] His support for Kurdish self-determination was longstanding and he certainly had links with the Iran-based Kurdish movement led by PDKI (Democratic Party of Iranian Kurdistan). In the early 1980s he had hoped that the Kurds would form part of the coalition to oust the Khomeini regime as a result on the ongoing revolutionary process he anticipated there.[39]

— ✦ —

In these later reflective years, he revisited the islands of his youth and would spend as much of summer as he could with Elly in Horefto on the eastern shore of the Aegean. Marika seems to have been a constant visitor and Maria Bennet and her daughters summered here as well. It was here, too, during his last summer, that Adolfo Gilly caught up with him and conducted the long 'definitive' interview. These summers were times to relax, to read and to ponder the meaning of his life. As he wrote in *To Vima* in September 1990:

> We play no role in coming into this life, but in leaving it we are able to play a part. When the small light of our life begins to slowly fade, then you naturally wonder what it's all been about, what sense it has … and then you are seized with an irresistible urge to revisit all the best that humans have created in thought, art and beauty. I am particularly interested in the conclusions, the final opinions and acts which certain eminent thinkers have come to. It is this that I ponder, a branch of mandragora in the hand to numb me, during the last summer days that I will pass on this earth … [40]

On the second morning of the long interview/discussion with Gilly in 1995[41], Michel received a phone call with the news from Paris that Ernest Mandel had died, aged 72. His sadness was mixed with guilt. The previous day he had spoken of his lingering bitterness that Mandel had betrayed him over the forged money affair and had joined with Gilly in regretting Mandel's less than enthusiastic embrace of the colonial revolution. The Gilly interview had raked over the coals and revived some of the bitterness. Still, Pablo acknowledged Mandel's latter-day embrace of self-management and his gifts as an economist. He appreciated, too, that Mandel had welcomed him back into the Fourth International. He recalled his fondness for the younger Mandel, their long years of cooperation in the 1940s and 1950s and his belief – which may have been wishful thinking – that Ernest regretted the breach of the 1960s. Along with Gilly he expressed a mixture of surprise and disapproval at Mandel's loss of influence in the Fourth International in the past decade. The younger Trotskyists had joked about Mandel's over-optimism, something Pablo admitted was true but added, 'it was better than cynicism'. With these bitter-sweet memories he travelled to Paris the following week to attend Mandel's funeral at Père Lachaise cemetery where he spoke. He believed that the premature death of Mandel, who he was convinced had literally worn himself out in the service of his ideals, was 'truly the end of an era'.

Even before Mandel's death, Pablo had decided that the return to the Fourth International was a mistake. Despite his co-option onto the international executive committee, there was no intention to involved him in the leadership of the Fourth International. He complained to Gilly that he did not receive draft policy documents. In his view the Fourth International was being run by small-time bureaucrats. As for the official Greek Trotskyists, who barred his full entry into the Fourth, they were politically insignificant and had no public standing. Livio Maitan argued that Pablo's return to the Fourth failed because he could no longer work with people, but on Pablo's account it was because he was not afforded the opportunity. Given the sidelining of Mandel, it is probable that the same attitude would apply to Pablo. They were yesterday's men, 'dinosaurs' to borrow the label another veteran, Yvan Craipeau, applied to himself.[42] Whatever the explanation, he was not without friends, comrades and influence at the end of his life, but he was without an organisation. It didn't extinguish his hope, however.

Pablo had often observed that, from antiquity onwards, the idea of a world facing 'order' and 'disorder' was central to many philosophers' view of the world. Plato had sought to solve the disorder of declining Athenian democracy by introducing a dictatorship of the wise. At the end of the 20th century, the world was still wracked by disorder and the search for order, for equality, for freedom, elusive as those things might be, continued.

During his life, Pablo had often used Rosa's neat summary of the alternatives facing humanity as a touchstone: 'socialism or barbarism'. The choice was simple, even if the road to the self-managed utopia was rocky and filled with reverses and disappointments along the way. For Michel Pablo, there had never been any doubt that the journey was worth attempting. He had devoted his life to it.

Now, as the 21st century unfolds, as disorder continues and the planet plunges into deeper crisis, the goal seems more distant than ever, but just as necessary.

**(Research for this chapter was undertaken by Takis Katsambanis.)**

EPILOGUE
# A prophet out of time

*To articulate the past historically, says Walter Benjamin, means
'to seize hold of a memory as it flashes up at a moment of danger'.
The 20th century was not the century of enlightenment, nor of progress.
It was the century of that lightning-flash,
the memory and experience of which we will need to recover
in order to illuminate the present moment of danger.*

Adolfo Gilly[1]

*Don't stop thinking about tomorrow.*

Christine McVie
Fleetwood Mac

ON A BRIGHT and sunny morning in a café on Kolonaki Square in Athens in mid-February, 1996, Pablo suffered a massive heart as he talked with friends and comrades. It was apt that he died surrounded by those who loved and admired him. They accompanied him to hospital and kept vigil through the long night until he finally died at dawn the next day. His last thoughts were personal, appealing to his comrades to care for Elly. He uttered no injunction to political action or slogan about the future. He had lived his life to the full. He did not appear to have any regrets. Pablo was fond of quoting one of Lenin's favourite dictums for revolutionaries to the effect that if you don't succeed at first, rethink and reload, and try again, a thousand times if necessary.[2] His whole life could be said to have been summed up in that attitude. He never seems to have faltered, despite the failures and disappointments. It was a persistence that ultimately flowed from a profound moral and ethical rejection of the status quo – of capitalism and imperialism, of the whole division of the world into the rulers and the ruled, of oppressors and oppressed. It was state of affairs he would not and could not accept. The legendary Greek composer Mikis Theodorakis, recalling Pablo late in his own life, said Michel had always struck him as "a Biblical personage"[3], and there was something to that. Pablo never deviated from his conviction that revolutionary Marxism starts from a deeply moral place.

Moreover, Pablo believed there were viable social and political alternatives that humanity was forever reaching for – and on occasion attaining. In his own lifetime he had witnessed not just glimpses of a new society but permanent advances, such as the colonial revolutions. He had lived in a century which had begun with billions of people of colour ruled by white men. He had been more than a sympathetic spectator: he had played his part in ending that global reality. Likewise, there was women's rolling back of the patriarchy in Western societies, something he had anticipated and embraced.

Theodorakis's recollection of Pablo as 'Biblical' also suggests Pablo's descent from a long line of similar 'prophetic' figures who delivered authoritative judgements. Pablo certainly saw himself as part of the genealogy of classical revolutionary Marxism – not as one of the giants or prophets, but as a working partner in the project. He was also very New Testament in his forgiving nature, as David Maurin recalled: 'He was also a man tolerant of the opinions of others, whereas so many others in this milieu preferred to pursue differences and to pronounce excommunications'.[4] (There were exceptions to that generosity, of course, as we have noted.)

Pablo did live his life according to prophesies or, more prosaically, prognoses. For him Marxism was the best tool kit for arriving at those understandings of the world. He accepted those results would be approximations rather than exact predictions. But even on that criterion, it did let him down. (Still, it would be very hard to argue that the biblical or classical Marxist prophets, or even many capitalist economists were any more successful.) At the end of his life he had no choice but to recognise the durability of capitalism and imperialism, particularly American imperialism, despite the dangers it posed to the very conditions of life on the planet.

His earlier reluctance to recognise that, in the post-war decades, led him to overestimate the relative power of the anti-capitalist and colonial revolutions. That revolutionary challenge to capitalism existed – and he discerned it in the Third World, among the wretched of the Earth, earlier than most – but it was disfigured by the form it took in the Soviet Union and then elsewhere.

The alternative forms of post-revolutionary order he devoted his energies to, did not amount to more than suggestive if inspiring failures or, at best, those flashes of the future that Walter Benjamin described. Budapest in 1956, Algeria in the early 1960s, Paris and Prague in 1968, Chile in the early 1970s, Portugal in the mid-1970s, Poland in the early days of Solidarnosc. What was remarkable was his own participation in some of these events. As an artist friend once remarked, he was like a revolutionary Zelig. And what was worthwhile was his effort to ensure revolution remained the property of the greatest number, and was not confiscated and deformed by 'Jacobin' minorities. He knew his ventures were an uncertain wager. As he admitted, there was an element of bluff in his efforts to promote an alternative version of revolutionary socialism even in Algeria, which offered the best, hands-on opportunity to put his ideals into practice.

The failure in Algeria disappointed him but didn't crush his utopian spirit. He looked elsewhere for the emergent material and social forces that would make a truly democratic socialism possible, and there were some hopeful moments. May 1968 and the Prague Spring of the same year, the emergence of second wave feminism, and Solidarity in Poland, suggested the possibility of a revolutionary breakthrough to a mass participatory socialism or utopia in Europe. After 1968 he would persist in the belief that the material and cultural conditions for a truly utopian 'leap', leading to the beginnings of socialism, existed in Europe.

In his eagerness to find resistance to the triumphant world system of capitalism and imperialism, impossible to ignore, he sometimes established friendly contacts with the governments of 'outlaw' countries, even when those governments were at odds with his idea of democracy. It was an uncomfortable link that unsettled some of his friends and many of his admirers. He wasn't too comfortable either, as his final interview with Adolfo Gilly revealed. Why couldn't Gaddafi and Saddam have instituted a more social democratic regime, he wondered, as much in sorrow as in anger. Why did they leave the democracy card in the hypocritical hands of Washington and its allies?

The answer lies in the tragedy of the last century. The forces that were committed to a truly democratic society, in the Athenian sense, were too feeble to durably succeed anywhere. There is a great deal of truth in the observation a character in Sally Rooney's novel, *Beautiful World, Where*

*Are You*, makes of the past century: 'I think of the twentieth century as one long question and in the end we got the answer wrong.'

His belief in a new Jerusalem was 'biblical'. Equally biblical were his habitual references to the great prophets or apostles of the preceding revolutionary generation – Lenin, Trotsky and Rosa Luxemburg – and to his Athenian ancestors from the 4th and 5th centuries BCE. The conservative Athens daily newspaper, *Kathimerini*, wanted to situate Pablo in another, more contemporary, and Greek, line of disappointed prophets. Its front-page tribute at his death was headlined: 'A citizen of the world' and celebrated his internationalism and his Hellenism. No argument there, but it concluded:

> And if we would wish to find a distant equivalent to him, we wouldn't search for it in the life of Che Guevara, but probably in a meteor that traversed the political and literary sky in Greece in the last century. I am talking of the visionary from Patras, Andreas Rigopoulos. He, too, tried to discover fire in the ashes of a revolution which saw its glory darken and be defeated; he, too, was close to the radical spirits of the time in Europe and America, with Marx and with Manzini.[5]

The 'revolution' here was the Greek revolution, or war of independence, of the 1820s, one of the first anti-imperialist revolts of the modern era. The original impulse was to create a radical democracy but it ended with a (barely) constitutional monarchy imposed by the great powers of the time. Rigopoulos, however, maintained his faith in that original aim. Arguably, Pablo did try, like Rigopoulos and the Greek Revolution of the 1820s, to redeem the promise of the derailed Russian and German Revolutions of 1917-18 – 'the fire in the ashes of the revolution'. That 'fire' for him, and he was convinced it was for Lenin, Trotsky and Rosa too, was the international quest for the self-managed, socialist republic.

It is not that such judgements of Pablo are wrong so much as that they are incomplete and ignore the more contemporary elements in Pablo's thought and life. This is no more evident than in Adolfo Gilly's judgement. The famous historian of the Mexican Revolution travelled half-way round the world in 1995 to meet Pablo in his summer retreat at the far end of the Mediterranean, in order to record Pablo's valedictory thoughts on his life. While he and Pablo were talking, the phone rang with the unexpected news that Ernest Mandel, the other major figure in the history of the Fourth International, had suddenly died, aged 72. It was a few days later that they made their way across Europe to Père Lachaise cemetery in Paris for the funeral.

Afterwards Gilly decided to write an essay comparing the two old comrades. Gilly explained the division between Mandel and 'his Greek master' as between the proletarian revolutionary Belgian, Mandel, and the latter-day 'Narodnik' or Balkan conspirator, Pablo. The Narodniks were those Russian populist and democratic idealists of the 19th century who went into the countryside to organise the peasantry to overthrow Tsarism and establish a community-based economy and democracy.[6]

In an essay for *To Vima,* the Greek newspaper, Gilly attributed the division in part to their geographic origins:

> ... the Belgian believed the industrial proletariat was going to change the world. His thinking came from Marx in *The Communist Manifesto* and *Das Kapital*, and the workers in the industries and the mines of Belgium had further inspired his orientation. The other [Pablo], the Alexandrian and Cretan, having grown up in a European country on the borders, with a very long history of eternal battles for its national independence against the Turks, and closer to the so-called Third World and the Middle East than the West, saw that the large uprising that would shake the world was that which Trotsky had foreseen from Mexico in the final years of his life: that of the numberless humanity of colonial peoples ... of India, China, Indochina, Indonesia, Korea, the Middle East, Algeria, the Arab states, all of Africa, Latin America. His thought came from Marx in *Grundrisse* and the final letters to Vera Zasulich [1849-1919, a Russian social revolutionary and assassin who became a Marxist – HG].

Gilly saw them as two sides of the one coin:

> I don't want to say that the two thoughts were in competition or that one excluded the other. Simply, when the infallible proof of practice did appear which, unexpectedly as always happens, appeared between 1959 and 1960 with the war in Algeria, it would put them on deviating paths. The feature of the century was for one of them the proletariat and socialist revolution, for the other the national and colonial movements. From there came different priorities, visions, futures, forms of organisation and battle: one thought about, first of all, workers councils and general strikes, the other about conspiracies and national uprisings.[7]

Gilly used Pablo's own words to cement his case,

> Michel Pablo told me last summer: 'The deepest meaning of the 20th century was this huge movement of the liberation of the colonies, of oppressed peoples and of women, and not the revolution of the proletariat, which was our myth and our God.'

Without resiling from that irrefutable judgment, Pablo would have objected to it as a final word. Gilly's essay is a beautiful literary creation but an over-simplification. His characterisation of Pablo ignored the latter's lifelong championing of self-management as the core of socialism for our times. As we've seen, he regarded the social, cultural and economic development of capitalism, with its resultant educated producers and citizens and its advanced technological possibilities, as having prepared the ground for the growth of self-management, eventually on a federated, global scale – and starting in Europe.[8]

Gilly was partly right in that Pablo, in contrast to Mandel, had given up on the proletariat as the single ordained force that would make the revolution and set the world on the way to socialism. The world was 'over-ripe' for socialism, in Pablo's view, but the subject, the force, that would achieve this was nowhere in sight. The traditional proletariat would be part of that new revolutionary subject, there was no doubt in his mind, but not necessarily its privileged leading element.[9]

— ✦ —

Pablo admits in the final pages of his political autobiography to a renewed interest in the last days of his revolutionary 'heroes'. He recalls Marx's interest in the 1870s in the rural communes of Russia as a possible vehicle in the transition to socialism in that country without having to go through capitalism. He notes the last battle of the sick and dying Lenin 'to counter the bureaucratic distortion of power that he himself had established and Stalin who represented it'. He was interested, too, in Trotsky's late thoughts, 'when he returns to his youthful democratic views about the Party and poses the question of what future lies ahead for a revolution when "Jacobins" of the one and only "revolutionary party" have taken power'.

He went on to recall the leaders he had met and how they must be judged, in the end, by how they handled power – or what part they played in the 'comedy of power'. 'But in the long portrait gallery which I often see passing before my eyes when I recollect my life,' he wrote, 'always prominent are the faces of ordinary people, of fighters of every race, men and women with whom we were bound tightly in some moment of our life. I wish still once more to greet all of them, to tell them that they remain unforgettable in my memory, symbols of common, irrevocable ideas and of the common struggle.' It was with them that people like him, fortunate enough to have a 'surplus of consciousness' of the dangers and injustices as well as the possibilities, must work.

Perhaps the last word should be with 'David Maurin', an old comrade, whose description of Pablo inspired the title of this biography. He recalled the 'elegance' of the man in both dress and manners. He realised that 'elegant' was a surprising word to use 'but he was so, in his bearing as in his attitude towards others, a quality which was not so frequent in revolutionary circles.' Maurin went on to note Pablo's internationalism, his generous nature and tolerant spirit. Harking back to Pablo's political origins, he observed, 'He was a strange Trotskyist. In a movement divided into irreconcilable and most of the time sectarian and dogmatic factions, he was open to the most diverse winds, those of decolonization and of independence, of self-management in all its forms, of feminism …'

Maurin acknowledged there were 'legends' about Pablo, 'although he himself did nothing to cultivate them'. 'No doubt more was expected from him than he could do and which was encouraged by his strong, generous and open personality.' Politics was for Pablo a deeply joyful way of life. As Maurin recalled:

> I remember the succulent hot potatoes in the cafes of Kolonaki in Athens, which he introduced me to when the dictatorship fell and the songs of Theodorakis were playing loudly in every street; our night walks to the headquarters of the MFA (Movement of the Armed Forces) in Lisbon after 25 April 1974, before the independence of Angola and Mozambique was proclaimed; the "perros", the abandoned dogs of the gardens of Santiago of Chile, which he and his wife loved when we met there in the days before the fall of Salvador Allende; the way I was received in the Ceylonese National Assembly by the leaders of the LSSP, a mass party professing Trotskyism …
> 
> I remember our appointments in an incalculable number of cafes, his illegible handwriting with which he filled a huge number of little sheets, our larger meetings where the participants expressed themselves in a good dozen languages … And of all those who one day ended up in Paris, on the run, and for whom he organized the care and shelter, come what may. Where he campaigned for support, when they were in prison and in danger in their country, in order to give them a little protection.

Maurin concluded his memoir with the words, 'I no longer remember all those little secrets that Michel sometimes shared with me and remember only his broad and revolutionary vision of the world of which he was an elegant militant.'

That 'broad and revolutionary vision' was of a world that would ensure, as Pablo always emphasised, the best possible conditions for the flourishing of every individual human being. Such a world would be guaranteed by an enhanced and revolutionary democracy – and the mobilisation of the imagination and the creation of a space for utopianism. He will forever be associated with the term 'autogestion' – self-management. This 'socialisation' of management and government went hand-in-hand with socialisation of ownership of large-scale industry, essential services and what used to be called the commanding heights of the economy.

That dream is yet to be realised. Pablo, naturally, wanted us to continue in the attempt. His conclusion that the new advanced technological capitalism provided the social, material and cultural basis for the self-managed republic, for a new Athenian direct democracy, was much too broad-brush. Over the past four decades the reorganisation of work and the spread of a more individualist culture has complicated, if not fatally undermined, Pablo's optimistic expectation.[10]

As for Pablo's insistence that our political responses must now be internationalist, as the major problems facing humanity are global, that is more valid with every passing day. In his lifetime, Pablo's cosmopolitanism was unusual. Technologically infused capitalism has certainly made the world smaller and more accessible. In that respect it has made pabliste planetary politics more possible – and more necessary, as we realise the increasing dangers to the conditions for a good life for everyone on this planet. Or to paraphrase William Blake: The new Jerusalem and the planet's green and pleasant land are inextricably linked. The one necessitates the other.

## ACKNOWLEDGEMENTS

This biography has relied on the help and contributions of many people. Some of them are old friends and comrades, but others were completely unknown before I contacted them. The help of the former exceeded all my expectations. As for the latter, the kindness of strangers is not acknowledged enough and is one more testimony to the inherent possibilities for a more humane and cooperative society that exist in today's world.

From France I received information and materials from [in alphabetical order]: Gérard Grizbec, Lucie Maiques Grynbaum, Mohammed Harbi, Jean-Pierre Hardy, Patrick Le Tréhondat, Gilbert Marquis, Serge Marquis, 'David Maurin', Danielle Riva and Patrick Silberstein. Yves Sintomer read and commented on an early draft and offered critical encouragement, as did Marc Saint-Upéry.

From The Netherlands I am indebted to: Maurice Ferares, Ellen Santen and Alex de Jong. This book would not have been possible without the unfailingly courteous and helpful staff of the International Institute of Social History in Amsterdam. The Institute's archives were indispensable. At another archive, Penny Duggan from IIRE tracked down some hard to locate materials. Here I must also mention RaDAR Association for the scans of Fourth International publications from the 1940s, 1950s and 1960s which they have made available online. (RaDAR stands for Rassembler, diffuser les archives de révolutionnaires – Collect, publish the archives of revolutionaries.) Similarly the Autogestion Association has digitised valuable Algerian materials. The Warwick University Trotskyism archives also proved useful. From Germany, Klaus Dräger forwarded documents on the Algerian connection.

In Greece I would like to acknowledge Takis Katsambanis who introduced me to the Raptis collection in the Hellenic Literary and Historical

Archive (ELIA) in Athens. He uncovered a host of other materials and contacted past friends of Pablo's. His aid and encouragement have been vital. Giorgos Tsaknias and Mathildi Pyrli at ELIA were unfailingly helpful. The others who deserve my thanks in Greece – or for Greek information – are (again in alphabetical order): Tassos Anastassiadis, Hugh Barnes (the *Guardian* correspondent in Athens in the late 1980s, early 1990s), Daphne Becket, Jim Becket, Alexandros Karageorgiou, John Brady Kiesling, Dimitris Konstantakopoulos, Savvas Matsas, and Stavroula Panagiotakis.

Of course my translators from the Greek – Dorothy Economou, Petro Alexiou, and Denise Anagnostou – were absolutely indispensable. In this connection Marion Gevers deserves special thanks for transcribing the Gilly interview tapes and general encouragement. She also kindly proofread the penultimate draft.

Fred Leplat, of Resistance Books, urged me to use the Covid lockdown to write the biography which he knew I had long ago promised to do, but postponed to the Greek calends. If not for his intervention I would not have undertaken the task.

Sophie Bibrowska, Vangelis Calotychos, Lena Hoff, Lucy Neville Clarke, Sebastian Budgen, Peter Greenland, Winmarie Greenland may be surprised to see themselves listed, but they helped in small and vital ways. The late Alan Roberts was a long-time supporter of this project.

A sincere thanks to Adolfo Gilly whose long interview – occurring over 4-5 days – at the end of Pablo's life was an essential source. (On the other hand, in correspondence he initially set such intimidatingly high standards that it nearly succeeded in deterring me. Once I was well into the project, he urged me on.)

David Leser deserves thanks too for his practical advice and suggestions to make the book more accessible to a general reader. I hope some of that advice has made it to the final version.

Most writers benefit from encouragement and wise counsel. Michael Zerman provided both judiciously, as well as providing a close and helpful reading of all the drafts. I am certain the book benefited from that, although Michael, like everyone else who helped me, is not responsible for the shortcomings.

And finally and indispensably, I would like to acknowledge Fenella Souter, for her 'light' edit and as an unending source of joy, inspiration, frank advice and love. My own good fortune helped me understand the bond between Pablo and Elly.

# ENDNOTES

## GENERAL NOTES

This biography draws heavily on Pablo's autobiography: Michalis N. Raptis, Η πολιτική μου αυτοβιογραφία/My Political Autobiography (third edition Athens, 1997). The book, first published in 1984, was based on articles he wrote for the newspaper To Vima in that year. I commissioned an unpublished English translation which has formed a valuable basis for this biography. In his preface Pablo explains that he will not reveal anything about the internal workings of the various organisations he's belonged too. But he does promise to write about those matters later, although he never did in any comprehensive way. Nevertheless, there is enough material in archives and his own writings to fill many of those gaps. Incidentally, he warns in the preface that men writing their autobiographies are rarely capable of being objective about themselves and are prone to 'mythologising'. I have borne that in mind in composing this book. It's important to note that unattributed quotes are from the political autobiography; at the beginning of each chapter, I have indicated in the footnotes which chapter those quotes are drawn from.

The second general point about the footnotes that follow is that some of the sources are in the Raptis archive in the Hellenic Literary and Historical Archives (E.L.I.A,) in Athens. Unfortunately this archive has not yet been catalogued, which explains the very general reference to the Raptis archive.

Finally, both the tapes and the transcript of the long Gilly interview with Pablo conducted 20-24 July, 1995, are now held by the International Institute of Social History in Amsterdam. It is an invaluable gift to anyone studying the life and ideas of Michalis Raptis/Michel Pablo. See https://search.iisg.amsterdam/Record/COLL00595 Note that the final part of the interview is conducted by a person unknown.

## PROLOGUE

1. Personal communication 13 September 2020
2. Stavroula Panagiotaki, 'Love and Revolution', *Woman* (Gynaíka) magazine, August 1997
3. Obituary for Ferares (1922-2022) https://internationalviewpoint.org/spip.php?article7920
4. Interview with Maurice Ferares 2006
5. 'Manolis Glezos 1922-2020' by George Souvlis, https://jacobinmag.com/2020/04/manolis-glezos-obituary-greece-nazi-resistance
6. Dina Vayena, 'A comradely farewell to Pablo', *Eleftherotypia*, 22 February 1996
7. Ibid
8. *To Vima*, 30 April 1995, pp A4-A5
9. 'L'Europe introuvable', editorial in *Sous le drapeau du socialisme* (*SDS*), 122-123, November 1992
10. See, for instance, '1992', editorial in *Sous le drapeau du socialisme* 121, February 1992
11. Editorial, *SDS* 122-123, November 1992

## CHAPTER 1. IN THE BEGINNING WAS TOLSTOY 1911-1936

1. Biographical details are taken from Chapter 1 of his autobiography: Michalis N. Raptis, Η πολιτική μου αυτοβιογραφία/*My Political Autobiography* (third edition Athens, 1997). Quotes which are not specifically attributed are taken from this autobiography.
2. Manus Perakis, 'Muslim exodus and land redistribution in Autonomous Greece' (1898-1913), *Mediterranean Historical Review*, Dec 2011, 26:2, pp 135-150. See also Asli Emine Çomu, 'The Exchange of populations and its Aftermath in Ayvalik, Mersin and Trabzon', *International Journal of Turkish Studies*, Vol 18, Nos. 1&2, 2012.
3. See chapter 15 of Chris Moorey, *A History of Crete* (Haus Publishing, London 2019). 'On the whole, the Christians who settled in Crete were fairly easily assimilated into the general population.'
4. Summer issue 2014 Accessed at https://kedrisos6.webnode.gr/κεδρισοσ,-τευχοσ-γ΄-(καλοκαίρι-2014)/
5. This paragraph continues: 'For this religious phenomenon is the combined result of the biological anxiety of human beings faced with the mysteries of existence ('where do we come from', 'where are we going') and with their inevitable decrepitude and death, and the terrors and uncertainties generated during the course of their historical development from barbarism to the present day, when extreme alienation still persists.'
6. Mark Mazower, 'The Refugees, the Economic Crisis and the Collapse of Venizelist Hegemony, 1929-1932', *Bulletin of the Centre for Asia Minor Studies*, 9/1 (1992), pp. 119-34. The Morganthau quote is from his *I Was Sent to Athens*, (New York 1929), pp. 246-247.
7. Georgios Kritikos, 'From Labour to National Ideals: Ending the War in Asia Minor – Controlling Communism in Greece', *Societies*, 2013, 3, pp 348-382
8. Pierre Broué, 'Pablo est mort', *Cahiers de Léon Trotsky*, March 1996, p117ff
9. See Michel Pablo, Preface, A. Stinas *Memoirs*, translated by George Gordon (London 2004) Accessed January 2022 https://libcom.org/files/stinas_mem_en_v0_95.pdf
10. Ibid
11. See Pablo's funeral speech for Soulas (who died in 1992) in the Raptis archive in Athens.
12. An informative account of the operation of this legislation can be found in Bert Birtles, *Exiles in the Aegean: a personal narrative of Greek politics and travel* (Victor Gollancz, London 1938). Birtles, an Australian journalist, spent a year in Greece from the summer of 1935 and made an extended visit to the prison island of Anaphi to discover how exiles coped.
13. Letter in the Raptis Archive in the Hellenic Literary & Historical Archives in Athens. There is no indication who it's addressed to besides the sign-off: 'Donnez mes amitiés à Arlette' (almost certainly Arlette Laguiller, the perennial presidential candidate of the Trotskyist party, Lutte Ouvière).
14. Michel Raptis, 'L'introduction de l'année Karl Marx en Grèce', Raptis archive, Athens
15. See Michel Pablo, Preface, A. Stinas *Memoirs*, translated by George Gordon (London 2004) Accessed January 2022 https://libcom.org/files/stinas_mem_en_v0_95.pdf
16. Ibid
17. Sylvain Pattieu, 'Le "camarade" Pablo, la IVe Internationale, et la guerre d'Algérie', *Revue historique*, volume 619, issue 3, 2001, pp 695-729
18. Mohammed Harbi, *Une vie debout* (Paris, 2001), p 228
19. Peter Bien, *Kazantzakis: Politics of the Spirit* (Princeton, N.J. 2007) Chapter 5, pp 50-51

## CHAPTER 2. PRISON, ELLY AND EXILE 1937-38

1. This chapter draws on 'France on the eve of war', Chapter 2 in M. Raptis's *Political Autobiography*. Unattributed quotes are from this chapter.

# ENDNOTES

2   Chapter 2, P. Voglis, *Becoming a subject: political prisoners during the Greek Civil War* (Berghahn Books, New York, 2002) See also P. Voglis, 'Political prisoners in the Greek Civil War, 1945-50: Greece in comparative perspective', *Journal of Contemporary History*, volume 37 (4). 523-540. Voglis puts into perspective even the descent into savage repression of the post-war years in Greece by a comparison with Stalin's regime, Franco's and Nazi Germany. Between 1939 and 1953, for instance, it has been estimated that the Soviet gulag held between 400,000 and 500,000 'counter-revolutionaries'. Over 600,000 were executed at the height of the purges in 1937-8. The scale of the killing by the Nazis in their camps is even more horrific.

3   The Australian journalist Bert Birtles has left a detailed portrait of prisoners' life on the island of Anaphi in the year before Metaxas seized power. See *Exiles in the Aegean* (London 1938) chapters 12-20.

4   Stavroula Panagiotaki, (1997)

5   Isaac Deutscher, *The Prophet Outcast*, (OUP, London 1963), pp 417-18

6   See https://www.marxists.org/history/etol/revhist/supplem/wolf.htm Accessed 2 March 2020

7   See https://www.marxists.org/history/etol/revhist/backiss/vol4/no1-2/freund1.htm Accessed 2 March 2020

8   See Elizabeth Poretsky, *Our Own People: a memoir of 'Ignace Reiss' and his friends* (London 1969) Poretsky was the widow of Reiss.

9   The letter is reprinted in Elizabeth Poretsky, (1969), pp 1-3

10  See Isaac Deutscher, (1963), pp 388-390

11  See Poretsky, (1969), pp 236-241

12  Isaac Deutscher, (1963), p 401

13  See Pavel Sudoplatov's memoir *Special Tasks* (Little Brown, Boston 1994). Also Pierre Broué's account at https://www.marxists.org/history/etol/revhist/backiss/vol1/no1/klement.html

## CHAPTER 3 DANGEROUS LIAISONS 1938-42

1   Interview 'Le 3 Sept 1938 à Périgny', *SDS* 108-109, Nov-Dec 1988, pp 39-41

2   *The Prophet Outcast*, (1963), pp 423-4, 427-8, Chen's views get an airing in these pages too.

3   See Robert J. Alexander's 'Trotskyism in Greece' in *International Trotskyism 1929-1985: A Documented Analysis of the Movement* (Duke University Press, 1991) and the minutes reprinted in *Cahiers Leon Trotsky*, No.1, January 1979 pp 17-56

4   Isaac Deutscher, (1963), pp 257-260

5   Pablo's account of the founding and the first 10 years of the Fourth International can be found in the spring, summer & autumn 1958 and autumn 1959 issues of *The Fourth International*, the official organ of the Fourth international. The title of the series was 'the first 20 years of the Fourth international' but the series only reached 1948.

6   Cited in M. Pablo, 'The first ten years of the fourth international', *Fourth International*, https://www.marxists.org/history/etol/newspape/fi-is/index.htm Accessed 5 March 2020

7   Isaac Deutscher, (1963), pp 435-6

8   Alan Wald, *The New York Intellectuals: the Rise and Decline of anti-Stalinist Left from the 1930s to the 1980s* (University of North Carolina Press, 1987)

9   The following account of the flight from Paris and the return is based on Chapters 3 and 4, 'The Second World War' and 'The first years of the War', of *My Political Autobiography*.

10  The best discussion of Trotsky's evolving position on the war and the trials of the various Trotskyist groups in France during the Nazi occupation is in Jacqueline Pluet-Despatin's *Les trotskistes et la guerre 1940-1944* (Paris 1980). https://funambule.org/lectures/social-économie-politique/litterature-marxiste/Les%20trotskistes%20et%20la%20guerre%20 1940-1944%20-%20(Jacqueline%20Pluet-Despatin).pdf Accessed May 2022. Pablo's review of Pluet-Despatin's book can be found in *SDS* 86, Feb-Mar 1981.

11  Rodolphe Prager interview, 1977. Typescript in the Raptis Archive in Athens.

12  According to one of the survivors, Jean-René Chauvin, in Christophe Nick, *Les trotskistes* (Fayard, Paris 2002) p 317.

13 Simonne Minguet, *Mes années Caudron : Caudron-Renault, une usine autogérée à la Libération (1944-1948)* (Paris 2001) préface

### CHAPTER 4 . PABLO'S WAR 1943-46

Pablo's own account of the war years is to be found in *My Political Autobiography*, pp 78-111. Also 'La IIe guerre mondiale et la quatrième internationale : entretien avec Michel Pablo', *SDS* 100, June-July 1985, pp 20-25

1. Jacqueline Pluet-Despartin, (1980), pp 194, 233-234
2. See 'Les trotskystes et la Seconde Guerre mondiale : Un billet de Jean-Guillaume Lanuque et Jean-Paul Salles' (2016) at https://dissidences.hypotheses.org/7109 , p 4, citing Jean-Michel Brabant *Les partisans et la Quatriéme internationale en France sous l'Occupation*, Maîtrise Paris VIII, 1974
3. J-G Lanuque et J-P Salles, (2016), p 6
4. Pluet-Despartin pp 131-136 and pp 169-171, for instance
5. J-G Lanuque et J-P Salles, (2016), p 3ff
6. L. Trotsky, *Sur la Deuxiéme Guerre Mondiale* (edited by D. Guerin, Belgium 1970 & Paris 1974)
7. This was spelled out in his very last and unfinished article 'Bonapartism, fascism and war', 20 August 1940.
8. See P. Broué, 'How Trotsky and the Trotskyists confronted the Second World War', *Revolutionary History, volume 3, no. 4, Autumn 1991*
9. Michel Dreyfus, 'Les trotskystes français et la question nationale pendant la Seconde Guerre Mondiale', *La Revue d'Histoire de la Deuxième Guerre Mondiale* (Presses Universitaires de France), No. 103 July 1976, p 20
10. Pablo found confirmation of the potential of fraternisation in Liddel Hart's post-war conversations with German generals who claimed that such a policy would have ended the war in 1943. See *SDS* 86, Feb-March 1981 for Pablo's review of Pluet-Despatin, (1980). Also the interview with Pablo in *SDS* 100, June-July 1985
11. See the recent biography of Monath by Nathaniel Flakin: *Martin Monath: A Jewish Resistance Fighter Among Nazi Soldiers* (London 2019)
12. Prager interview 1977
13. Roger Faligot and Remi Kauffer, *Éminences grises*, (Fayard, Paris 1992), pp 287-326
14. Daniel Bensaid, *Les trotskysmes* (PUF, Paris 2006) pp 51-55
15. 'Le trotskyisme et l'Europe pendant la deuxième guerre mondiale', *Cahiers Leon Trotsky*, August 1989, pp 49-75.
16. See Association RaDAR (Rassembler, Diffuser, les Archives de Révolutionnaires) http://www.association-radar.org/?-Revues-129- for issues of *La Verité* for this period.
17. See the interview with Pablo in *SDS* 100, pp 20-25
18. Frédéric Charpier, *Histoire de l'extrême gauche trotskiste de 1929 à nos jours*, pp 144-157
19. Pluet-Despatin, (1980), pp 208-210
20. Yvan Craipeau, *Swimming Against the Tide; Trotskyists in German Occupied France* (London 2013) pp 271-2. Also by the same author, *Mémoires d'un dinosaure trotskyste*, pp 171-198.
21. See 'On comrade Morrow's reply', *Fourth International*, July 1946, pp 218-22
22. See 'La IIe guerre mondiale et la quatrième internationale : entretien avec Michel Pablo', *SDS* 100, June-July 1985, pp 20-25
23. See the preface to R. Prager, *Les Congrès de la IVe Internationale: L'Internationale dans la guerre, 1940-1946* (Paris 1981). Reprinted here: https://www.marxists.org/history/etol/revhist/backiss/vol1/no3/prager.html
24. 'Les Partisans à l'œuvre : La Libération massive du Puy-en-Velay', *La Vérité* 20 November 1943
25. A forensic and thorough account of this affair was published in 1997: Pierre Broué & Raymond Vacheron (en collaboration avec Alain Dugrand), *Meurtres au Maquis* (Paris 1997).

# ENDNOTES

26 See https://maitron.fr/spip.php?article17821 Accessed 31 March 2020
27 See entry in Le Maitron https://maitron.fr/spip.php?article18137
28 See Jean-Michel Krivine, *Inprecor*, March 2010, for the history of this term.
29 René Dazy, *Fusillez ces chiens enragés: Le génocide des trotskystes* (Olivier Orban, Paris 1981) p 274
30 Robert Alexander, (1991), 'Trotskyism in Greece'.
31 Adolfo Gilly, *'Deshoras' Souvenirs de l'oubli*, La Brèche numérique, 2009, originally published in 1997 as an obituary for Pablo and Mandel.
32 Gilly interview 1995
33 'La France devant la montée révolutionnaire et les tâches du P.C.I.', May 1944 cited in Pluet-Despartin, (1980), pp 218-220
34 *Quatrième Internationale*, January-February 1945 and October-November 1946
35 Communication with the author 2022
36 *Quatrième Internationale*, Jan-Feb 1945, pp 4-6
37 Winston Churchill, *The Second World War: Triumph and Tragedy* (Houghton Miffin company, Boston, 1953), volume 6, pp 198ff. Churchill's meeting with Stalin of October 9, 1944, in Moscow is famous for the so-called 'percentages agreement', where Churchill suggested that Britain and Russia agree 'spheres of influence' in the different countries of eastern Europe. He scribbled some figures down on a piece of paper (Romania 90-10, Greece 10-90, Yugoslavia and Hungary 50-50 etc.) and passed it to Stalin. 'He took his big blue pencil and made a large tick upon it, and passed it back to us. It was all settled in no more time than it takes to set down,' Churchill recalled. See https://en.wikipedia.org/wiki/Percentages_agreement An authoritative and detailed account of the betrayal of revolutionary possibilities in Greece is John O. Iatrides, 'Revolution or Self-Defense? Communist Goals, Strategy and Tactics in the Greek Civil War', *Journal of Cold War Studies*, Summer 2005, vol 7, No.3, pp 3-33 but particularly pages 13-18.

## CHAPTER 5. THE REVOLUTION WILL HAPPEN (BUT ELSEWHERE) 1945-50

1 See Pablo's reply to Felix Morrow in *Fourth International*, March 1946
2 Eric Hobsbawm has noted the 'mythological' French Resistance, especially in comparison to its Italian counterpart. See E. Hobsbawm, *Age of Extremes: the Short Twentieth Century 1914-1989* (London 1994) pp 164-165
3 These reflections taken from Pablo's *My Political Autobiography* (Athens 1997). All unattributed quotes in this chapter from Chapters 6 & 7.
4 This section is based on the resolution adopted at the January 1945 meeting of the European Executive Committee: 'The maturing of the revolutionary situation in Europe and the immediate tasks of the Fourth International'.
5 *Quatrième Internationale*, September 1943
6 Jeremy Black, *France – A Short History* (Thames and Hudson, London 2021) p 180 for details of the devastation in post-war France.
7 Mike Davis, *Old Gods New Enigmas: Marx's Lost Theory* (London 2018) pp 153-154
8 Eric Hobsbawm, *Age of Extremes: the Short Twentieth Century* 1914-1989 (London 1994) p 230.
9 Alexis Hen, 'Conflits et mémoires dans les Balkans : Les trotskystes grecs pendant la seconde guerre mondiale', *Cahiers balkaniques* 38-39, 2011
10 See, for instance, 'On comrade Morrow's reply', *Fourth International*, July 1946, vol 7, No.7, pp 218-222
11 Cited in David McNally, *Blood and Money* (Chicago, 2020) p 209
12 Pablo's economic analyses and predictions can be found in regular articles in *Fourth International* (published in New York) for the years 1948-51 and available on the internet.

13 Special Bulletin of the International Secretariat on the Second Congress of the Fourth International, December 1948 contains a summary of proceedings at the congress.
14 Livio Maitan, *Memoirs of a Critical Communist*, translated by Gregor Benton (Resistance books, IIRE, Merlin Press, London 2019) pp 26-44. Maitan's handsome tribute to Pablo's prescience on so many issues is all the more noteworthy because he became one of Pablo's fiercest opponents in the 1960s helping to drive him out of the Fourth International.
15 Eric Hobsbawm, *Age of Extremes: the Short Twentieth Century 1914-1989* (London 1994) pp 168-9, 232
16 'La Chine de Mao-Tse-Tung', *Quatrième Internationale*, Mars-Juin 1949, pp 12-15
17 Charles Wesley Ervin, *Tomorrow is ours: the Trotskyist movement in India and Ceylon 1935-1948*, (Social Scientists Association, Colombo 2006) pp 218-231
18 Gilly interview 1995
19 *SDS* 62, April 1974
20 'The Yugoslav Affair' (August 1948) in *Fourth International*, vol.9 No.8, December 1948, pp. 235–242.
21 Michel Pablo, 'The Yugoslav Affair', *Fourth International*, Dec 1948, pp 235-242. The article was dated August 1948
22 'The evolution of Yugoslav centrism' (October 1949) From *Fourth International* vol.10 No.10, November 1949, pp. 291–297
23 'Evolution of Yugoslav centrism', 15 October 1949 in *Fourth International* vol.10 No.10, November 1949, pp. 291-297
24 Michel Pablo, 'Korea and the "Cold War"', *Fourth International*, Sept-Oct 1950, pp 137-142
25 Jan Willem Stutje, *Ernest Mandel: A Rebel's Dream Deferred*, translated by Christopher Beck and Peter Drucker (Verso, London 2009) page 58

## CHAPTER 6 . MOHAMMED MUST GO TO THE MOUNTAIN 1950-55

1 *Quatrième Internationale*, March 1955
2 Gilly interview 1995
3 'Des précisions', *SDS* 78, May 1979
4 Those with a taste for closer examination can find commentary and documents in Rodolphe Prager (ed.), *Les Congrès de la IVe Internationale,* Paris : Editions de la Brèche, 1981-1989. (4 tomes)

   1. *Naissance de la IV internationale (1930-1940)*
   2. *L'Internationale dans la guerre, 1940-1946*
   3. *Bouleversements et crises de l'après-guerre, 1946-1950*
   4. *Menace de la troisième guerre mondiale et tournant politique, 1950-1952*

   https://archive.org/details/rodolphepragerlescongresdelaiveinternationale4tomes
5 The new entrist approach was first outlined to the 9th plenum of the International Executive Committee of the Fourth International in November 1950. (This committee was composed of delegates from each of the sections.) It was followed in early 1951 by a major essay of 8,000 words entitled 'Where are we going?', Pablo's analysis of the new post-war world and what it involved for the International. He elaborated further in *Trotskyism Re-arms*, circulated in the lead-up to the Third World Congress of the Fourth International in August. In early 1952 he combined these analyses into a pamphlet published in French as *La guerre qui vient* and in English as *The Coming World Showdown: Capitalism or Socialism?* He would forever explain that the original French title wasn't his. He had titled his prognosis on the outbreak of a global war and revolution, 'La guerre qu'ils préparent' or 'The war they are preparing', but Pierre Frank apparently thought 'The coming war' a more appropriate and appealing title and he substituted it. The new title did rather firm up Pablo's prediction about a global clash between imperialism and the revolution. As he told the International himself:

The war being prepared this time by a united imperialism under the leadership of the USA is the counter-revolutionary war which aims not at the punishment of the Soviet bureaucracy and the crimes of Stalin, but at the destruction of the workers' states, the reconquest of China, the crushing of all the colonial revolutions and of the world revolutionary movement … what is involved is the final struggle which brings an epoch to a close.

In Pierre Frank's defence, the new title did reflect the apocalyptic contents of Pablo's analysis, and his complaint appears as a mark of embarrassment at an erroneous prognosis. That said, there were some nuances. He was clearly writing of probabilities. He was well aware that his prognosis could be derailed by the conciliatory policies of the Soviet bureaucracy – or by the sheer destructiveness of any world war. 'To be sure,' he noted, 'the policy of the Soviet bureaucracy places in peril all the conquests up to now and can facilitate a new shift in the relationship of forces to the advantage of capitalism.' More seriously, he was aware that 'the danger exists that a general war may engender extensive destruction which will render still more difficult, more complicated and more protracted the socialist reconstruction of humanity. Under certain conditions, the theoretical possibility of a descent into barbarism is not excluded.'

6   See his disputes with Mandel and Jungclas below and *Sous le drapeau du socialisme* 37, Jan-Feb 1967 pp 19-21

7   Prager, tome 3, pp 284-307 for the preface and statutes adopted at the Second World Congress. Section 7 reads: 7) National Delegations immediately after the World Congress shall report to specially convened Plenary Assemblies of their National Executive Committees or to Congresses, with a view to ensuring democratic assimilation, wide publication and prompt and effective execution of the decisions of the World Congress. In the event of discrepancies, however serious they may be, between a Section and the World Congress, the Section shall, regardless of the position of its delegation, carry out the decisions of the World Congress, while having the right to appeal to the next regular or specially convened World Congress.

8   Michel Lequenne, *Le Trotskisme, une histoire sans fard* (Editions Syllepse, Paris 2005) pp 223-259

9   Declaration of the International Secretariat of the Fourth International, *La Vérité des travailleurs*, Aug 1952.

10   See, for instance, 'Sens et perspectives de la politique de la 4e Internationale', *Quatrième Internationale*, Dec 1954, pp 59-62

11   Trends in membership numbers for French Trotskyists can be found in Jean-Guillaume Lanuque, 'Le trotskystes dans le Maitron', *Cahiers Léon Trotsky*, December 2002, pp 47-54. Pierre Broué gives even lower figures, claiming that the majority PCI only retained a few dozen members and the minority a dozen, *Cahiers Léon Trotsky*, No.56, p 64

12   The whole 'entrist' experience in France from 1952 to 1965 is examined in detail in Gérard Grizbec's University of Paris VIII master's thesis (1976) '*Les trotskystes dans les organisations communistes françaises pendant les années cinquante*'. A copy forwarded by the author.

13   'Report on the international situation, presented to the 16th plenum of the International Executive Committee by comrade M. Pablo (extracts)', *Quatrième Internationale*, Dec 1955 pp 48-59

14   Pablo's emphasis on the preservation of the International as a democratic centralist world organisation runs through all this writing related to the conflict with the SWP majority. For instance: 'Letter to [SWP] National Committee majority', 24 Sept 1953; 'To the Leaderships of All Sections', 15 November 1953; 'They desert, we go forward', 20 November 1953; 'In the Defense of the Fourth international', December 1953 (with Pierre Frank and Ernest Mandel); 'The conception of the International and the struggle within it', 25 April 1954. Typescript copies from the Issy Wyner archive are in the possession of the author.

15   See François Moreau *Combats et débats de la Quatrième Internationale* (Paris, 1993) p 139

16   Maitan, (2016), p 52

17   See *Quatrième Internationale*, March-May 1954, pp 6-7 for the offer to the SWP of a role in preparing the Fourth World Congress and submitting proposals.

18   'Manifeste du 4e Congrès de la IV Internationale', *QI*, July-August 1954 p 4

19 'Report on the international situation', *Quatrième Internationale*, December 1955, pp 48-59. See http://association-radar.org/IMG/pdf/16-014-00071.pdf
20 See his essay 'The Dictatorship of the Proletariat' (1953) in M. Raptis, *Socialism, Democracy & Self-management* (London 1980) pp 17-34.

### CHAPTER 7 . VIVE LA RÉVOLUTION ALGÉRIENNE 1954-62

1 See chapter 8 'The Algerian Revolution' in *My Political Autobiography* (1997) pp149-173.
2 Sylvain Pattieu, *Les camarades des frères: Trotskistes et libertaires dans la guerre d'Algérie* (Paris 2002) see chapter 3 in particular.
3 Simonne Minguet, *Mes années Caudron* (Paris, 1997) pp 7-9 and 'Prologue' pp 11-16
4 All these quotes are from *My Political Autobiography* (1997).
5 See Martin Evans, *The Memory of Resistance* (Oxford 1997), for an account of the Jeanson, Curiel and *Voie communiste* networks which came into existence in 1956-57.
6 *Sozialistische Zeitung*, February 2005, p 20
7 Ali Manoun, *7th Wilaya* (Algiers 2005), 'Le nerf de la guerre', Chapter 18, pp 316-325, 489-491
8 'Les Trotskystes et la Guerre d'Algérie'. *Dissidences*, No.3, Printemps 2012
9 Ian Birchall, 'A note on the MNA', *Revolutionary History*, volume 10, No.4 (2012) p 161
10 Mohammed Harbi interviewed by Adam Shatz, *Historical Reflections/Reflexions historiques*, Summer 2002, vol. 28, No.2, pp 301-309
11 Martin Evans, *The Memory of Resistance* (Oxford 1997) pp 150-151
12 Gilly interview 1995
13 Sylvain Pattieu, (2002), pp 80-87
14 Sylvain Pattieu, *Les camarades des frères* (Paris 2002), footnote 13, chapter 8, p 275
15 The quotes from Pablo in this chapter are sourced from chapter 8 in *My Political Autobiography* (Athens 1997) pp 149-173
16 'Néo-réformisme, stalinisme et marxisme', *Quatrième Internationale*, October, 1955
17 *Bulletin interieur*, November 1958
18 See Christophe Nick (2002) pp 416-418
19 'L'importance internationale de la révolution hongroise', December 1956, *Quatrième Internationale*, vol 15 Nos.1-3 (77) March 1957
20 See *Quatrième Internationale*, October 1957
21 *Ibid*, 'Rapport sur l'activite de l'Internationale', in particular pp 115-116
22 *The Arab Revolution* (Fourth International Publications, Holland, 1959) p iii

### CHAPTER 8 . THE ARMS FACTORY IN MOROCCO 1955-60

All unattributed Pablo quotes in this chapter are from *My Political Autobiography*, (1997), chapter 8 'The Algerian Revolution', pp 149-173

1 S Pattieu, *(2002)*, pp 74-77
2 *Perspectives on Terrorism*, Vol.6, No.6, 2012
3 Mathilde Von Bülow. 'Myth or Reality? The Red Hand and French Covert Action in federal Germany during the Algerian War, 1956-61', *Intelligence and National Security*, vol. 22 no.6 2005, pp 787-820. See also her exhaustive *West Germany, Cold War Europe and the Algerian War* (CUP, Cambridge, 2016).
4 Ali Haroun, *La 7e Wilaya: La guerre du FLN en France 1954-1962* (Casbah editions, Algiers 2004) pp 127-128. Also Mathilde von Bulow, *West Germany, Cold War Europe and the Algerian War* (Cambridge, 2016) p 318
5 *L'usine invisible*, (Paris, 2012), p 131
6 Serge Marquis interview with Mohammed Harbi, September 2020

# ENDNOTES

7  Livio Maitan, *Memoirs of a critical communist* (first published in Rome 2006, English language version 2019) pp 102-106 in particular
8  Ali Haroun, *The 7th Wilaya* (2005, originally published in 1986) pp 329ff
9  Ali Haroun, (2005), p 330
10 Gilly interview with Pablo, track 3.2
11 Gilly interview
12 Ali Haroun, (2005), chapter 19 for the full account
13 *L'usine invisible*, (2012), p.87
14 Sal Santen, *Dapper zijn omdat het goed is*, p16. I am indebted to Alex de Jong for this information.
14 Personal interview by the author
16 Christophe Nick, *Les Trotskistes* (Paris, 2002) pp 408-409
17 This letter is in the Santen archive in the International Institute of Social History, Amsterdam.

## CHAPTER 9 . THE TRIAL OF PABLO AND SANTEN 1960-61

1  Certainly the Defence Committee suspected as much.
2  The indictment and copies of Pablo's various declarations are in the Pierre Avot-Meyers archive held in the International Institute of Social History, Amsterdam.
3  The final speech to the judges at the trial is in *Quatrième Internationale*, July 1961.
4  *The Militant*, July 24 & 31, 1962, page 6.
5  Cher camarade Sirio, 2 June 1962, the Santen correspondence held in the International institute of Social History
6  See the Jimmy Deane archive at the University of Warwick.
7  Gilly interview 21 July 1995
8  Maitan, (2019), note 163, page 375
9  'Pierre Frank has dared'. review of Pierre Frank, *History of the Fourth International, SDS* 48, May-June 1969, pp 30-31
10 Gilly interview

## CHAPTER 10 . PRISON WRITINGS – WOMEN, FREUD, CUBA, CLASSICAL ATHENS AND LATE MARX 1960-61

1  *The Liberation of Women & other essays* (Sydney 1965) p 21
2  *The Liberation of Women*, pp 11-12
3  They were published together with an essay on Plato and Vatican II as *The Liberation of Women & other essays* (Sydney, 1965). His essay on Freud was prompted by reading Ernest Jones' three-volume biography of Freud. The *Liberation of Women* essay, but not the Freud essay, is published in English online, see the Marxist Online Archive.
4  *The Liberation of Women & other essays* (Sydney 1965) p 7
5  See his review of *The Mandarins* in QI, December 1955
6  *The Liberation of Women & other essays* (1965) p 11
7  *The Liberation of Women & other essays* (1965) p 9
8  *The Liberation of Women & other essays* (Sydney 1965) p 10
9  Though not in this author's mother, who was a working-class militant and socialist. When I asked her if as a young woman she had read Pablo's essay would it have changed her life, she answered 'Yes'. To the further question of 'how?' she replied, 'I wouldn't have had you children'. (Hopefully, I took it to mean 'when I did'.)
10 *The Liberation of Women* (1965), p 14
11 Communication from Danielle Riva, 17 March 2021
12 See *SDS* 55, March 1971, pp 6-7

13 *Quatrième Internationale*, July 1962
14 The best exposition of this 'historicising' of Trotskyism is in *Lettre ouverte aux camarades de la Quatrième Internationale*, SDS 80, 1979
15 Only the letter to the Cubans was published. See *QI*, April 1962, pp 46-51
16 Dated 16 August 1961 and addressed to 'Chers camarades, chers frères du FLN'

## CHAPTER 11 . JOINING THE WRETCHED OF THE EARTH 1961-63

1  For Pablo's own account of these events, see the Australian journal, *International*, 15 November 1961, pp 1-4. The following paragraphs are based on this version.
2  See *Le Monde*, 20 March 1960 https://www.lemonde.fr/archives/article/1960/03/28/sympathisant-du-f-l-n-un-professeur-belge-est-tue-par-un-colis-explosif_2090893_1819218.html Accessed 14.11.2022
3  See *My Political Autobiography*, chapter 9 'Algeria under Ben Bella' pp 149-173
4  A. M Gittlitz, *I Want To Believe: Posadism, UFOs and Apocalypse Communism* (Pluto Press, London 2020), pp 76-77
5  Gilly interview, July 20, 1995, pp 10-11
6  Gilly Interview, July 20, 1995, pp 12-13
7  Livio Maitan, (2019), pp 87-92.
8  Letter in Santen archive in the International Institute of Social History
9  Santen to the IS, 15 March 1962
10 Santen to IS 13 March 1962, letters to Pablo 25 April 1962, 22 May 1962
11 Santen to Pablo, 22 May 1962
12 Pablo to Santen, 21 Jan 1962
13 Pablo to Santen, 17 Nov 1961, 27 Nov 1961, 20 Dec 1961
14 Pablo to Santen, 3 Feb 1962
15 Pablo's letter to Frank, Mandel and Livio, 2 June 1962 outlines all these practices. Also letter to this trio dated 5 July 1962. Similarly, Pablo's letter to a German comrade 30 June 1962
16 Letter from Pablo to leaderships and members of the International, 5 July 1962
17 Letter from Pablo to Pierre, Walter, Livio, 2 June, 1962
18 *Le Programme de Tripoli* (Parti Communiste International, Paris, September 1962) p29. The preface noted that this was the first publication of this program in France.
19 Clarissa Zimra, 'Afterword' to Assia Djebar, *Children of the New World* (New York 2005)
20 Jeffrey James Byrne, *Mecca of Revolution: Algeria, Decolonization & the Third World Order* (Oxford 2016),
21 The review is reprinted in '1962-2022/Algérie plus que jamais, rouvrir un avenir à la révolution', *Contretemps*, No 54, July 2022, pp 93-106.
22 Jeffrey James Byrne, (Oxford 2016), p 62, see also p 120 and p 126
23 Michel Pablo, 'Impressions et leçons de la révolution algérienne', *Quatrième Internationale*, No. 97, Dec 1962
24 'L'armée et la révolution', *SDS* 25, Jan 1966. p 10. In the same issue 'Ahmed Ben Bella et Houari Boumédiene' pp 6-8
25 *Quatrième Internationale*, No. 97 and *International*, September 1962
26 *La voie communiste*, 23 January 1963
27 Clarissa Zimra, 'Afterword' to Assia Djebar, Children of the New World (New York 2005) p 223
28 Letter to Sal Santen from Michel Raptis, 27 March 1983. A copy in the author's possession.
29 Elspeth Etty, Obituary, 'Gentle Trotskyist: Sal Santen (1915-1998)', *Europe Solidaire Sans Frontières*, https://www.europe-solidaire.org/spip.php?article37576 Accessed 14 November, 2022

# ENDNOTES

## CHAPTER 12 . PABLO'S WAGER: ATHENS IN ALGIERS 1962-65

There is a superb overview of the decline of agriculture, the burgeoning bureaucracy, problems of self-management, the population explosion and the drift to the cities and towns, in Mahfoud Bennoune, 'Algerian Peasants and National Politics' (Middle East Research and Information Project 1976, available at https://www.jstor.org/stable/3011103). There is a conservative but well-documented account of the fate of self-management in Algeria in these years in David and Marina Ottaway, *Algeria: the Politics of a Socialist Revolution* (University of California Press, 1970). Chapter 3, 'The March Decrees', pp 50-68. See Pablo's own account of these years in chapter 9, 'Algeria under Ben Bella', of his political autobiography (1997), pp 174-204.

1. Interview Mohammed Harbi by Serge Marquis, 2020
2. Interview Mohammed Harbi by Serge Marquis 2020
3. 'L'économie de l'Algérie de Tahar Benhouria', *SDS* 82-83, Jan-Feb 1980
4. Michel Pablo to Adolfo Gilly, 22 July 1995
5. M. Harbi, *L'Autogestion en Algérie : Une autre révolution?* (Syllepse, Paris, 2022) pp 18-20
6. See pages 36-42, Michel Raptis, 'Dossier de l'autogestion en Algérie', *Autogestion* No. 3, September 1967.
7. Michel Raptis, (1967), p 47
8. See Ottaways (1970) pp 66-67. Note too the decree of September 1963 which stipulated that 'In the pursuit of better production and increased returns, ONRA is empowered to decide the amalgamation or division of farms and the sharing, transfer and utilisation of livestock'. Other organisations reinforced this administrative tutelage, notably the Cooperative Centres for Agrarian Reform whose role in financial and accounting matters reduced the responsibilities and powers of self-managed enterprises ... Moreover, the Agricultural Machine Units controlled the use of all agricultural machinery. See *La voie algérienne* (Maspero, Paris 1974) 62ff.
9. Michel Raptis, (1967), pp 55-58
10. Michel Raptis, (1967), pp 60-64
11. International, No.33, 15 September 1963, pp 9-12
12. All quotes from the interview with Mohammed Harbi conducted by Serge Marquis, September 2020.
13. Marquis interview, (2020)
14. August 1963, p 8. Cited in Jeffrey James Byrne, *Mecca of Revolution: Algeria, Decolonization and the Third World Order* (OUP, New York 2016) p 171
15. David and Marina Ottaway, *Algeria: The Politics of a Socialist Revolution* (University of California Press, 1970)
16. Marquis interview, (2020)
17. Jeffrey James Byrne, (2016)
18. Gilly interview 1995
19. Pablo's *Political Autobiography*
20. *Sous le drapeau du socialisme* 2, Feb 1964
21. Gilly interview, July 20, 1995 pp 18-19
22. Michel Raptis, (1967), p 72
23. Serge Marquis interview with Harbi (2020)
24. *SDS*, Feb 1964, p 4
25. 'La chute de Ben Bella', *SDS* 19-20, Jul-Aug 1965, particularly pp 3-4
26. Gilly interview, July 20, p 23
27. Michel Raptis, (1967), p 73
28. *Sous le drapeau du socialisme*, Jan 1964, p 3
29. See the collection of observers' reports, annex vi, Michel Raptis, 'Dossier de l'autogestion en Algérie', Autogestion No.3, September 1967.

30  Michel Raptis, (1967), pp 67-69
31  *SDS* 11, Nov 1964, p 2
32  Michel Raptis, (1967), p 71
33  Grigori Lazarev, in his study 'Autogestion agricole en Algérie', published in *Le Cahier de la revue Tiers Monde* in 1965 confirms the picture being presented here.
34  Michel Raptis, (1967), pp 77-78
35  Michel Raptis, (1967), p 79
36  A copy of the draft is in the Raptis archive in Athens
37  Michel Raptis, (1967), p 84, pp 79-84 and pp 144-148 for the draft law
38  Michel Raptis, (1967), pp 85-88
39  M. Harbi, *L'autogestion en Algérie* (Syllepse, Paris, 2022) p 25
40  See Ottaways pp 7-8
41  'L'option du socialisme en danger', Supplément du *Sous le drapeau du socialisme*, 23 June 1965
42  H. Alleg, *The Algerian Memoirs*, translated by Gila Walker (Seagull, Calcutta 2012) pp 354-355
43  'Houari Boumédiene devra rectifier', *SDS* 23-24 Nov-Dec 1965, p 31
44  See chapter 9, *My Political Autobiography* (1997), 'Algeria Under Ahmed Ben Bella', p 203
45  'Le côté rouge de la frontière: Gilbert Marquis et Michel Pablo Raptis', *Autrement*, No.38, March 1982, pp 46-49
46  M. Harbi, *L'autogestion en Algérie : une autre révolution 1963-1965?* (Syllepse, Paris 2022) pp 13-31 in particular
47  'Letter from Algiers', *International*, November-December 1964, pp 14-15 in particular

## CHAPTER 13 . PARALLEL DEFEATS (AND ROSA) 1964-65

This chapter draws on chapter 10 'May '68' in Pablo's My Political Autobiography, (1997), pp 205-21

1  Michel Pablo, 'Notre ligne et la leur', March 1965 which spelled out this approach in some detail. Roneo-ed copy in Issy Wyner archives.
2  'Notre ligne et la leur', March 1965
3  Letter to Bob Gould, 26.8.1965, *Dossier Australie, IVe Internationale*, FD Res 494, BDIC (now La contemporaine), University of Paris Nanterre
4  Adolfo Gilly had also made this case for more active internationalism in the discussion leading to the 6th World Congress, 'Pour le développement de la IVe Internationale à la hauteur de ses possibilités' (16 Novembre, 1960). He quoted Trotsky on the responsibility of revolutionary Marxists in the colonial struggles: 'Bolshevism doesn't limit itself to advocating the granting of rights [to oppressed nationalities] or protesting about the trampling of those rights. Bolsheviks go into the heart of the oppressed nationalities, raising them against the oppressor, linking their struggle to that of the proletariat of the capitalist countries, conveying … the art of insurrection and assuming complete responsibility for this work vis-à-vis the civilised executioners.'
5  Jeffrey James Byrne, *Mecca of Revolution: Algeria, Decolonization and the Third World Order* (OUP, New York, 2016) This paragraph is drawn from that extraordinary study.
6  'It is high time to stop on the road of blind factionalism', September 15, 1962. I suspect this letter would have come to the attention of the SWP leaders in New York, then discussing rejoining the International, and have been very reassuring.
7  See 'On Four Major Problems of Our Time' that Pablo submitted to the pre-congress discussion for the 7th World Congress. It was particularly strong on its analysis of the Sino-Soviet conflict, the configuration and possible outcomes of the colonial revolution, and the pre-eminent importance of the movement for nuclear disarmament (which he argued could, inter alia, along with solidarity activity with the revolutionary movements in the Third World, radicalise the political environment in advanced capitalist countries).
8  Ernest Mandel, *On the Pablo Tendency* (IMG pamphlet 1977) Originally written and published in 1964.

# ENDNOTES

9   Letter to P. Frank 30.1.1964
10  See 'The most friendly relations – with whom?', statement of the majority of the United Secretariat on the political orientation of comrade Pablo, February 1964.
11  See for instance 'Pablo announce sa rupture avec la IVe Internationale', *QI*, June 1965 pp 48-53.
12  See Pablo's articles 'China, the USSR and the colonial revolution' in *SDS* 1, January 1964, and 'The Fall of Khrushchev' in *SDS* 11, November 1964.
13  'Notre ligne et la leur' March 1965. It was a response to Mandel's comprehensive critique of October 1964 which was circulated under the title 'Une tendance droitière' in English as well as French.
14  See Pablo's letter to comrades Pierre, Walter and Livio of June 2, 1962 which began: 'I have just learned that in your latest session of the "IS" of May 20, a session of which I had not been informed, the agenda of which I did not know and the minutes of which I have not yet received, you decided ...'
15  The United Secretariat's reply is dated 10 November 1963.
16  See his letter to the United Secretariat and the International Executive Committee dated 8 October 1963 protesting inter alia, the rejection of his article, the omission of the minority's document and resolutions from *QI* and the anti-Test Ban Treaty position. This and other supporting material available in the Issy Wyner archives.
17  See 'The Political Orientation of Comrade Pablo', Statement of the Majority of the United Secretariat, no date but apparently February 1964.
18  'La révolution angolaise au seuil de l'An II', *QI* April 1962, pp 38-41
19  Accounts of the politics of the Angola national liberation struggle can be found in John A. Marcum, *The Angolan Revolution*, vol II: Exile Politics and Guerrilla Warfare 1962-1976 (MIT Press, Cambridge, Mass., USA 1978) chapters 1-4 in particular; Arthur J. Klinghoffer, *The Angolan War: a study in Soviet policy in the Third World* (Routledge, New York 1981), especially chapters 5 and 8; Michael Wolfers and Jane Bergeroi, Angola in the Frontline (Zed Press, London 1983); and Kristin Reed, *Crude Existence: Environment and the Politics of Oil in Northern Angola* (University of California Press, Berkeley 2008).
20  See *QI*, July 1964 and March 1965. Detail of the majority's support for Holden Roberto spelled out in the letter to the sections from the African Commission, 10 Dec 1964.
21  Gilly Interview, July 20, 1995, pp 17-18
22  Ernest Mandel, (October 1, 1964. Reprinted 1977)
23  *SDS* 3 Mars 1964
24  'The meaning of the struggle' in *Documents on the IEC of May 1964* issued by Pablo's supporters gives the text of his 'declaration' to the plenum of the IEC. It runs to 9,000 words. The publication also carries the proposals from the minority for future cooperation.
25  See for instance his letter to 'the US comrades' dated 15 October 1964.
26  See Mandel's letter to Jimmy Dean, 21 May 1964, explaining the CEI/IEC decisions (the Warwick University archives).
27  Statutes, Section 7. 31(h)
28  Gilly interview 20 July 1995
29  Jean-Paul Martin, 'The Fall of Khrushchev', *SDS* 11, Nov 1964. It elicited another public condemnation from the majority which misrepresented the article's contents.
30  'Pablo annonce sa rupture avec la IVe Internationale', *QI* July 1965, pp 48-53
31  See *SDS* 19-20, July-August 1965, pp 18-19.
32  Gilly interview, track 6.1
33  See *SDS* issues in 1967 for the first series of these articles.
34  See, for instance, 'Realities, problems and perspectives of the new dynamic of the world revolution', December 1968: 'We must consider abandoning the name of Revolutionary Marxist Tendency of the Fourth International and simply calling ourselves, for instance, International Association or League of Revolutionary Marxists ...'

35  *On the Pablo Tendency*, (1964), p 14
36  *Financial Times*, 16 December 1993
37  'On four major political problems of our time', Internal Bulletin of the IS of the 4th International, Oct 1962
38  See *SDS* 57 January 1970
39  Quoted in '*Notre ligne et la leur*'

**CHAPTER 14 . THE GYPSY YEARS 1965-1968**

1  All otherwise unattributed quotes are either from Pablo's *My Political Autobiography*, (1997), chapter 10 'May '68' pp 205-215, or from the Gilly interview of 1995.
2  This and other information not specifically sourced is from Pablo's *My Political Autobiography* (Athens 1997) chapter 10.
3  Published in *Sous le drapeau du socialisme* 24 Dec 1965, also *International* No.48, January 1966
4  'Une réponse nécessaire', *SDS* 19-20, July-Aug 1965, pp 18-19
5  See 'la chute de Khrouchtchev' *SDS* 11, November 1964, and 'Après Khrouchtchev', *SDS* 12, Dec 1964
6  *SDS* 14, February 1965. See the editorial.
7  *SDS* 21 September 1965
8  See Pablo's full analysis in the editorial 'La Chute de Ben Bella', *SDS* 19-20, July-August 1965, pp 1-5.
9  Details of these draft laws were published in subsequent issues of *SDS*.
10  *SDS* 39, May-June 1967
11  *SDS* 39, p 17
12  See 'L'armée et la révolution', *SDS* 25, Jan 1966, p 10
13  See D. Guerin, *L'Algérie caporalisée ?* (Paris 1965)
14  The first elected prime minister of the newly independent Congo who was arrested and executed by pro-Western forces in 1961.
15  First track. Michel Pablo [Raptis] interview by Adolfo Gilly 1995 in French. Audio. International Institute of Social History, Amsterdam. Transcribed by Marion Gevers, copy in author's possession and copy forwarded to IISH. See: https://iisg.amsterdam/en/detail?id=https%3A%2F%2Fiisg.amsterdam%2Fid%2Fcollection%2FCOLL00595
16  Roger Faligot and Rémi Kauffer, *Éminences grises*, (Paris, 1992), pp 316-317. See also Gilles Perrault & Sylvie Braibant, *Un homme à part: Qui était Henri Curiel?* (Paris 1984)
17  'La conférence de l'OLAS – le regroupement des forces révolutionnaires mondiales est en marche', *SDS* 41, Sept-Oct 1967
18  Gilly interview 1995
19  See the Wikipedia entry https://fr.wikipedia.org/wiki/Mehdi_Ben_Barka.
20  See in particular the editorials in *SDS* 37, 38 and 39, Jan-Feb, Mch-April and May-June 1967.
21  Editorial, *SDS* 33-34, Sept-Oct 1966
22  See the editorial, 'Lignes de force de la situation internationale', *SDS* 30, June 1966.
23  *International* and *SDS* 40, July-August 1967
24  'La crise de l'impérialisme américain', *SDS* 49, Jul-Aug 1969, pp 1-3
25  Gilly interview, tape 7.2
26  *To Vima*, 23 September 1990
27  *To Vima*, 23 September 1990
28  E Kulukundis, *The Amorgos Conspiracy*, (2012), issued on Kindle 2020
29  Henrik Liljegren, *From Tallinn to Turkey, As a Swede and Diplomat*. (2006) p. 71.
30  See the website 'The Maria Becket Report' for more on this truly remarkable woman

## ENDNOTES

31 Interview with James Becket, 26/27 June 2021
32 Interview James Becket, June 26/27, 2021
33 John Brady Kiesling, *Greek Urban Warriors: Resistance to Terrorism 1967-2014*, (Athens, 2014) p 27
34 J Brady Kiesling, (2014), p 22
35 Lena Hoff (2003), 'Resistance in Exile – A Study of the Political Correspondence between Nicolas Calas and Michalis Raptis ([Michel Pablo]) 1967–72', *Scandinavian Journal of Modern Greek Studies*, 2, pp 17-41
36 See for instance *SDS* 42, November-Dec 1967 and *SDS* 44, March-April 1968.
37 Nicholas Gage & Elias Kulukundis, 'Report from Greece: Under the junta', *The American Scholar,* Summer 1970, pp 475-497
38 *SDS* 44, March-April 1968
39 Gilly interview
40 See 'À la memoire de Che Guevara', *SDS* 42 Nov-Dec 1967.
41 *SDS* 30, June 1966 in a downbeat survey of the international situation.
42 'Realities, problems and perspectives of the new dynamic of the World Revolution', *SDS*, December 1968

### CHAPTER 15 . GREAT EXPECTATIONS: PARIS, PRAGUE AND PALESTINE 1968-69

1 See *SDS* 45, Jun-July 1968 – his reflections were dated 21 June 1968. Also 'Apparition de nouvelles forces révolutionnaires sur l'arène mondiale', *SDS* 46 Sept-Nov 1968, pp 1-4. See also his 'May events – one year after', *SDS* 48 April-June 1969
2 See *Dossier: The revolutionary Marxists and the French Revolution*, published 1 July 1968 in London by the author and Margaret Eliot. It was a collection of translated leaflets issued by the Revolutionary Marxist Tendency of the Fourth International during the May events.
3 See 'Marxism and our Time', an *International* publication, Sydney 1967.
4 'L'autogestion comme mot d'ordre d'action', *SDS* 45 Jun-July 1968, pp 10-11
5 *SDS* 46, Sept-Nov 1968 pp 31-32
6 *SDS* 46, Sept-Nov 1968 pp 1-4
7 *SDS* 46, Sept-Nov 1968 pp 1-4
8 Pablo's account of his visit to Prague in chapter 11 of *My Political Autobiography* and the Gilly interview.
9 *SDS* 46, pages 3-4 in particular
10 'Sur les perspectives de la situation internationale et les taches des marxistes révolutionnaires', resolution adopted at the May 1967 conference of the TMRI.
11 See the platform of the tendency adopted at its 3rd international conference in November 1969, *SDS* 51, Dec 1969-Feb 1970.
12 'Révolution arabe: quelle stratégie?', *SDS* 60, April 1973, pp 11-13
13 'Un rapport sur la révolution palestinienne', *SDS* 50, Sept-Nov 1969, pp 9-15
14 *SDS* 54, Dec 1970

## CHAPTER 16 . CLOSE ESCAPES AND CHILE 1970-73

1. Pseudonym. Personal communication 2020.
2. Based on the accounts from Lucie Maiques Grynbaum and Mohammed Harbi in February 2023. The good doctor Roger (1923-2022) was a distinguished neurologist. As a medical student she rescued two Jewish children from the Nazi round-up in 1944 and transported them to safety at her parents' house in Brittany. Later she was a major supporter of the Algerians campaigning in France during the war of independence. Resident in Marseilles and then Paris she could always be counted on for shelter, transport or finance. Sentenced to 10 years imprisonment after her arrest in 1959 she managed to escape to Tunisia the following year. After independence she became one of the architects of Algeria's health system. Like Pablo, she was forced to flee when Ben Bella was overthrown. https://maitron.fr/spip.php?article150461
3. All unattributed quotations from Η πολιτική μου αυτοβιογραφία/*My Political Autobiography* (1997) particularly chapter 12, "Allende's Chile", pp 226-243.
4. 'Un révolutionnaire élegant', private communication 2020.
5. Elaine Mokhtefi, *Algiers, Third World Capital* (Verso, 2018) pp 160-161, 177-178
6. *My Political Autobiography* (1997)
7. *My Political Autobiography* (1997)
8. Michel Raptis, *Revolution & Counter-Revolution in Chile* (London 1974) pp 86-87
9. MAPU, Popular Unitary Action Movement
10. 'Chili : quelles perspectives', *SDS* 60, May-June 1973, pp 9-10
11. *My Political Autobiography*, p 242
12. A copy of the report is in the Raptis archive in Athens.
13. See *Le Monde Diplomatique*, February 1973
14. *My Political Autobiography* (Athens 1997) p 241
15. See chapter 7, 'The lessons of Chile', in *Revolution and Counter-Revolution in Chile*.
16. 'Armée et révolution en Amérique latine', *SDS* 60, May-June 1973, pp 9-10
17. 'La leçon chilienne', *SDS* 61, Nov-Dec 1973
18. Included in Michel Raptis, *Revolution and Counter-Revolution in Chile* (Allison & Busby, London 1974) pp 150-174. Also published in *SDS* 59, Dec 1972.
19. Michel Raptis, 'L'autogestion dans la lutte pour le socialisme', *SDS* 59, Dec 1972, pp 28-35. See also 'États ouvriers ou états bureaucratiques: il est temps de trancher', draft presented to 7th international conference of the TMRI, *SDS* 87, Jun-Aug 1981
20. 'Sur la construction de la tendance', *SDS* 62, April 1974, pp 37-39
21. See Jean-Pierre Hardy, *Les marxistes-révolutionnaires pour l'autogestion dits 'pablistes' : des 'pieds-rouges' d'Algérie aux altermondialistes* (Paris 2021) for a comprehensive and lively history of the *pablistes* in France from the late 1960s to the present.
22. 'Sur la chute de la dictature militaire grecque', *SDS* 63, July-August 1974, pp 38ff

## CHAPTER 17 . THE TURN TO EUROPE 1970s

1. 'Après la conférence d'Helsinki', *SDS* 66, October 1975
2. 'Autogestion et socialisme : levier du renouveau idéologique', *SDS* 61, Dec 1973
3. See 'La crise inédite du capitalisme', editorial *SDS* 62, April 1974. Also 'Réforme, révolution, socialisme', editorial *SDS* 63, Jul-Aug 1974.
4. See 'La crise inédite du capitalisme', *SDS* 62, April 1974
5. 'Une nouvelle conjoncture internationale', editorial *SDS* 75, Aug-Sept 1978
6. See the editorial dated March 1977 in *SDS* 72, 'Les perspectives révolutionnaires en Europe et la gauche révolutionnaire', July-August 1977. In the same issue 'Texte de préparation à la 6e conférence de la TMRI : Du "gouvernement des partis ouvriers de masse" à la victoire de la révolution'. See also *SDS* 68, March 1976, 'Réflexions sur la révolution socialiste européenne'.

7   See editorial, *SDS* 73, Jan-Mar 1978, p 2. Also 'Les perspectives révolutionnaires en Europe et la gauche révolutionnaire, *SDS* 72.
8   All quotes in this chapter, unless otherwise attributed, are from 'From the revolution of the red carnations to the return', chapter 13, in *My Political Autobiography* (Athens, 1997) pp 243-263.
9   'Rapport sur le Portugal', *SDS* 63, Jul-Aug 1974, pp 16-19
10  'Soutien à la candidature d'Otelo de Carvalho en développant la lutte pour l'unité ouvrière', *SDS* 70, June 1976
11  Peter Robinson, 'Obituary for Otelo de Carvalho', *The Guardian* 17 August 2021
12  Michalis Spourdalakis, *The Rise of the Greek Socialist Party* (London & New York, 1988), p 52. See also 'Grèce : instabilité explosive', *SDS* 62, April 1974 on the Karamanlis option. Provided it was a liberalising regime and not a return to the past, it was the only way to avoid more widespread uprisings than the Polytechnic commune of November 1973.
13  'A First Balance Sheet of the Greek Socialist Experiment: an interview with Michel Raptis', *Journal of Area Studies*, issue 8, Autumn 1983, pp 34-36
14  M. Raptis, 'La Grèce après la dictature militaire', *SDS* 64, Dec 1974
15  *SDS* 61, Jan-Mar 1974. Lazaros Tournopoulos was the leader of the trade union of shoemakers and a leader of the Trotskyist movement from the interwar period. He was also responsible for the printing of the illegal, post-war Trotskyist newspaper E*rgatiki Pali* (Workers Struggle), organ of the Communist Internationalist Party of Greece (section of the 4th International).
16  Michalis Spordoulakis, (1988), pp 64-69
17  Interview December 2021
18  Michalis Spourdalakis, (1988), p 124
19  *SDS* 68, March 1976
20  'Grèce : flambée chauvine', *SDS* Sept 1976
21  See *Éminences grises* (1992) p 322
22  'La radicalisation du nationalisme irlandais', *SDS* 78, May 1979
23  Brian Trench, 'Provisional Pot-pourri', Magill, 31 October 1978 https://magill.ie/archive/provisional-pot-pourri. Accessed November 2022
24  'La célébration du centenaire de Léon Trotsky au Mexique', *SDS* 82-83, Jan-Mar 1980.
25  See 'Theoretical Foundations of Direct Democracy' in Michel Raptis, *Socialism, Democracy and Self-management* (Allison & Busby, London 1980) pp 176-206. Also 'Memoires d'espoir et de Gaulle', *SDS* 55, March 1971, pp 25-26.
26  'A first balance sheet', (1983), *Journal of Area Studies*, issue 8, Autumn 1983, p 35
27  See *SDS* 82-83, Jan-March 1980
28  'Les travaux de la Ve conférence internationale de la T.M.R.I.', *SDS* 65, May 1975
29  'L'intervention de Michel Pablo au Congrès des C.C.A.', *SDS* 82-83, Jan-March 1980, pp 45-47
30  See for instance Michel Löwy, 'Heroism of reason', IIRE (Amsterdam), 20 Jan 2020 https://www.iire.org/node/900
31  *SDS* 72, July-Aug 1977, p 37
32  See for instance, *SDS* 59, December 1972, p 2. The same issue carried a strong solidarity response to the continuing repression in Czechoslovakia.
33  'La crise s'aggrave', editorial *SDS* 81 Oct-Nov 1979
34  'L'affaire Soljenitsyne', *SDS* 62, April 1974. The same issue carried an article by the dissident Soviet Marxist Roy Medvedev.

### CHAPTER 18 . END OF AN ERA 1980s

1   *How to blow up a pipeline* (London 2021) p 61
2   Vasilis Rafailidis, 'Michalis Raptis or Michel Pablo: The Upper Class Man who Served in the Labour Movement', *Ethnos*, 10 April 1983 pp 24-25

3 See *SDS*, 81, Oct-Nov 1979, pp 36-40. The essay is dated September 1979.
4 *SDS* 90-91, May-Jun 1982, p 2
5 'Tournant au Moyen-Orient', editorial *SDS* 101-102, Jan-Feb 1986
6 'Les nouveaux massacres de Sabra et Chatila', *SDS* 100, Jun-Jul 1985, p 6
7 See 'États ouvriers ou états bureaucratiques – Il est temps de trancher', draft presented to 7th international conference of TMRI, *SDS* 87, June-Aug 1981.
8 'Sur la politique de la bureaucratie soviétique et la question d'USSR à la lumière des événements d'Afghanistan', *SDS* 84, Jul-Aug 1980, p 30ff
9 See 'Oublier l'Afghanistan c'est préparer l'abandon de la Pologne', *SDS* 88-89, Nov-Dec 1981, p 4.
10 Déclaration du Secrétariat International TMRI, March 1980
11 'Une nouvelle guerre froide', *SDS* 82-83, Jan-Mar 1980. 'Sur la question de l'URSS et la politique de la bureaucratie à la lumière de l'invasion en Afghanistan', *SDS* 84, May-Jun 1980. 'Bilans 1980, perspectives 1981', *SDS* 86 Feb-Mar 1981
12 This composite view is based on the preface to *Vers une république autogérée* (*SDS* 103, Oct-Nov 1986), 'Perspectives et tâches de la TMRI' (8th International Conference of the TMRI, June 1985) and 'Résolution politique' (9th international conference of the TMRI, June 1988) and 'Déclaration constitutive de l'Association Marxiste Révolutionnaire Internationale (February, 1989)
13 *Socialist Alternatives*, July 1986, pp 26-30
14 'La crise s'aggrave', editorial *SDS* 81, Oct-Nov 1979
15 'Remarques sur le programme européen des Verts', *SDS* 97-98, June 1984
16 Matthias Werner, 'Pologne : une révolution en marche', *SDS* 85, November 1980 pp 10-15
17 'Soutien total à la révolution polonaise commencée', resolution of the international secretariat of the TRMI, 22 Oct 1980
18 See 'La révolution polonaise a commencé', *SDS* 85, Nov-Dec 1980 p 3, pp 31-36.
19 'La révolution polonaise a commencé', *SDS* 85, pp 3-4
20 'Soutien total à la révolution polonaise commencée', *SDS* 85, October 1980
21 Z. Kowalewski, 'L'autogestion au coeur de la révolution', *SDS* 88-89, Nov-Dec 1981, p 9ff
22 'Pologne : vers le double pouvoir' in *SDS* 88-89 – the analysis is dated 28 October 1981
23 Christian Mahieux, *Pologne : Combats pour l'autogestion, Solidarnosc* (1980-1981) (Syllepse, Paris, 2022) covers the rise and fall of Solidarity in general and Walesa in particular.
24 Pablo's main writing on the 'reform/revolution' of Gorbachev were 'Crise du régime bureaucratique et glasnost' (speech to the commemoration of the 50th anniversary of the Fourth International held in Paris 26-27 November 1988, see *Lettre internationale pour l'autogestion*, No 4, February 1989).
25 See 'La "Révolution politique" en URSS, ses effets et ses perspectives', 3, May 1988, in *Débat* : Préparation de la 9e conférence de la Tendance Marxiste-Révolutionnaire Internationale, pp 23-29.
26 See for instance, 'Sur la question de l'URSS et la politique de la bureaucratie à la lumière de l'invasion en Afghanistan', *SDS* 84, May-Jun 1980.
27 See documents of the 9th International conference of the TMRI, June 1988.
28 See for instance: 'L'écroulement du stalinisme', editorial *SDS* 112-113, Nov-Dec 1989. It begins: 'The end of this century will probably be marked above all by the spectacular collapse of Stalinism …'
29 See Jean-Pierre Hardy, (2019), pp 152-155.
30 'Le marxisme critique : une problématique actuelle', *SDS* 95-96, Dec 1983, pp 40-43
31 *Socialist Alternatives*, Oct-Nov 1986, pp 27-32; originally in *SDS* 101-102, Jan-Feb 1986, pp 32-34
32 See *Utopie Critique – revue international pour l'autogestion*, No.1 auttomne 1993, pp 25-36.

# ENDNOTES

33 Written in September 1986 and published in *Sous le drapeau*, 108-109, Nov-Dec 1988 pp 33-35.
34 *Ethnos*, 10 April 1983
35 The preface is reprinted as 'Actualité de *La révolution défigurée* de Léon Trotsky', *SDS* 112, Nov-Dec 1989 pp 37-39. Similar ideas about Gorbachev's economic course were outlined in 'Crise du régime bureaucratique et glasnost', *Lettre internationale pour l'autogestion* No.5, March 1989.
36 See I. Hashim, 'Les limites de Kadhafi', *SDS* 61.
37 Declaration of TMRI International Secretariat, September 11, 1986 Also editorial *SDS* 101-102, Jan-Feb 1986 p 2
38 'La Libye traquée par l'impérialisme', *SDS* 104 May-June 1987, pp 3-4
39 Cited in J-P Hardy, (2019) p 140. See also Serge Marquis, 'Libye : une lettre au PCF', *Mediapart* 20/23 August 2011; 'Gilbert Marquis, mon père', *Mediapart*, 9 Feb 2015.
40 Conversation with Yves Sintomer, 17 March 2022
41 'Les vingt ans de la révolution lybienne 1969-1989', *SDS* 112-113, Nov-Dec 1989, pp 27-28
42 Personal communication with the author (and others who questioned him on this matter).
43 Serge Marquis, (2015)

## CHAPTER 19 . THE FATE OF FRIENDS AND COMRADES 1980s

1 All unattributed quotes in this chapter are from Pablo's political autobiography published in Greek, from the third edition (1997).
2 'Ahmed Ben Bella à Paris : l'avenir de la révolution arabe', *SDS* 88-89, Nov-Dec 1981
3 'Freedom for Otelo', *Socialist Alternatives*, August/September 1987, p 7
4 *The New Yorker*, 30 November 1987
5 *SDS* 101-102, Jan-Feb 1986, p 40
6 'Otelo is against a pardon but in favour of an amnesty', *l'Expresso*, 12 November 1988
7 'Le credo d'Otelo', *Lettre internationale pour l'autogestion* 6, pp 3-4
8 See *Le Monde*, 1 February 1987 and *New York Times*, 8 February 1987. https://www.lemonde.fr/archives/article/1987/02/01/grece-remous-autour-d-un-condamne-le-president-sartzetakis-est-la-cible-d-un-large-mouvement-de-contestation_4020447_1819218.html https://www.nytimes.com/1987/02/08/world/killer-s-plea-imperils-a-greek-leader-s-prestige.html
9 'The patrician of revolution', *Eleftherotypia*, 11 February 1996
10 Interview with C. Roussos by Takis Katsabanis, 8 April 2022
11 All the correspondence is in the Raptis archive in Athens.
12 Mandel's note, 24 February 1982, Raptis Archive E.L.I.A. Athens.
13 See for instance Mandel's response to Pablo's invitation to the Fourth International to send observers to the 1981 conference of the Tendency, 14 March 1981, Raptis Archive Athens.
14 'La théorie marxiste des crises et l'actuelle dépression économique', *SDS* 97-98, June 1984, pp 40-42
15 Mandel to Michel [Pablo], 21 February 1987, Raptis Archive Athens
16 There are a number of critical references to this in the Gilly interview of 1995.
17 'À propos Pour un portrait de Pierre Frank', *SDS* 101-102, Jan-Feb 1986, pp 48-49
18 *SDS* 110-111 May-June 1989
19 *SDS* 108-109 Nov-Dec 1988
20 'Éloge de Daniel Guérin', *SDS* 108-109, Nov-Dec 1988, p 51
21 *Quatrième Internationale*, Jan-Mars 1973 has an article on Austrian Trotskyism by Raimund Löw. See also Fritz Keller, 'Trotskysme en Autriche 1934-45', *Cahiers Leon Trotsky*, No.5, 1980.
22 'Spring arrives in Albania too', *To Vima*, 5 December 1989. And the obituary for Sadik Premtaj, 'Victor' in *SDS* 118/119, 8 April 1991 p 39.

23 See his use of the phrase in the long interview he gave Roger Faligot and Rémi Kauffer, *Éminences grises* (Fayard, Paris 1992) pp 287-326.
24 libcom.org/files/stinas_mem_en_v0_95.pdf Accessed February 2022
25 Email to the author
26 J-P Hardy, (2021), pp 105-106, p 138. Pablo's criticisms of Privas/Grinblat, 'Pauvre Marx ! Réponse à Privas', were in the internal political letter circulated before the 8th international conference of the TMRI in June 1985.
27 J-P Hardy, (2019), p 140
28 'The bourgeois who served in the labour movement', *Ethnos*, 10 April 1983 pp 24-25
29 'Problems of the Arabs', *Ta Nea*, 28 July 1990
30 These were all themes taken at random from columns in *Ta Nea* and *To Vima* in 1990. French translations were provided by Gilbert Marquis. Copies of all the published columns are in the Raptis archive in E.L.I.A. (the Hellenic Literary and Historical Archives) in Athens.
31 The prospectus for the Protagoras circle and reports on its activities are in the Raptis archive in Athens.
32 Personal communication with author 2021
33 *SDS* 116-117, Jun-Aug 1990
34 General political resolution, 9th conference of TMRI, June 1988

### CHAPTER 20 . THE FINAL BATTLE: HOW GREEN IS MY PARTY? 1988-89

1 Discussion préparatoire à la conférence extraordinaire, *Bulletin Intérieur* No. 2
2 Patrick Serand's account, *Parcours en hétérodoxie : Fragments d'un itinéraire militant* (2018, available at the International Institute of Social History)
3 Compte rendu, IXème conférence de la TMRI, *Lettre internationale pour l'autogestion*, No 1, October 1988, pp 21-22 The new statutes are on pages 23-24
4 See Association Autogestion https://autogestion.asso.fr/maurice-najman-1948-1999/ and his biography on Maitron https://maitron.fr/spip.php?article23804
5 Patrick Serand, (2018), see pages 20-21
6 Conversation with Yves Sintomer, 19 March 2022
7 Patrick Serand, (2018), see page 25
8 See Michel Pablo, *World in Revolution* (London 1968) available at https://britishpabloism.files.wordpress.com/2016/09/world-in-revolution-michel-pablo.pdf
9 Declaration of 9th conference of TMRI, *SDS* 107, April-May 1988, pp 37-39
10 *Lettre internationale pour l'autogestion*, No.5, February 1989 pp 5-6. The 'Déclaration de 12 camarades' is in *Bulletin Interieur* issued by the Comité de coordination international of the Association marxiste révolutionnaire internationale, dated 28/29 October 1989
11 See the two articles in *Lettre internationale pour l'autogestion*, No. 9 Jun-Jul 1989 pp 16-20
12 AMRI Discussion Bulletin, October 1989 pp 7-9.
13 Patrick Serand, (2018), see page 29
14 'Effondrement accéléré', *SDS* 114-115, May-June 1990, pp 1-3

### CHAPTER 21 . A NEW ERA: THE FINAL YEARS 1989-96

1 *My Political Autobiography*, (1997), p 279
2 *Ibid*
3 The best account of 17N and other terrorist groups of this era is John Brady Kiesling's *Greek Urban Warriors* (Lycabettus Press, Athens, 2014) to which I am indebted for the bulk of the sources for this section though the judgments are entirely mine.
4 'Why they made me out to be leader of November 17', *To Vima*, 16 September 1990, pp 12-13
5 Personal communication to the author

# ENDNOTES

6 *My Political Autobiography*, chapter 13
7 *Éminences grises*, p 324
8 *Ta Nea*, January 30, 31 and February 1, 1990-91
9 *To Vima*, 30 April 1995
10 Many newspapers carried the declaration. Cited in *Greek Urban Warriors*, p 208.
11 *To Vima*, 16 September 1990.
12 John Brady Kiesling, (2014), p 208
13 *My political autobiography*, (1997), pp 274-275
14 Letter to Mandel, July 1992
15 L'Europe introuvable', editorial *SDS* 122-123, November 1992
16 'Se regrouper', editorial *SDS* 120, December 1991
17 *SDS* 122/123, November 1992
18 'Effondrement accéléré', *SDS* 114-115, May-Jun 1990
19 'Europe introuvable', *SDS* 122-123, November 1992 pp 1-2
20 Jean Pierre Hardy, *Les marxistes-révolutionnaires pour l'autogestion dits « pablistes » : des « pieds-rouges » d'Algérie aux altermondialistes* (4th édition, October 2021). See pages 58, 62, 66 and 67 for instance.
21 J-P Hardy, (2021), p 62
22 'Georges Vereeken est mort', *SDS* 75, Aug-Sept 1976
23 Didier Leschi, *Rien que notre défaite* (Les éditions du Cerf, Paris, 2018)
24 Hardy, (2021), pp 66-67
25 'Résolution interne de la 10e conférence internationale de l'AMRI'
26 Letter to Mandel, July 1992 Copy in Raptis archive.
27 'Nicaragua, Salvador, résister à l'imperialisme', *SDS* 114-115, May-June 1990, pp 5-6
28 *SDS* 114-115, May-June 1990 pp 5-6. See also 'The Defeat of the Sandinistas', *To Vima*, 28 February 1990.
29 A summary of the crimes Karadzic was found guilty of by the UN International Criminal Tribunal for the former Yugoslavia in The Hague can be found at: https://www.icty.org/x/cases/karadzic/tjug/en/160324_judgement_summary.pdf
30 'Pablo speaks about terrorism', *To Vima*, 30 April 1995. See also the Gilly interview, July 22, afternoon
31 See the epilogue to *My Political Autobiography*.
32 See the Raptis archive.
33 See Serge Marquis' account of a visit to Libya in 1989 and the repercussions of any hint of support from Gaddafi, J-P Hardy, (2021), pp 109-110.
34 Personal communication from Dimitrios Konstantakopoulos 17 Feb 2023
35 Gilly interview, 1995
36 'Surveying the articulations of my culture', from the Program for Award of Honorary Doctorate of Philosophy, December 6, 1995, translated by Petro Alexiou.
37 'Pablo speaks about terrorism', *To Vima*, 30 April 1995, p 1, A4-A5
38 *To Vima*, 30 April 1995, A4-A5
39 *SDS* 87, June-August 1981, p 4
40 'Exit by the sea', *To Vima*, 8 Sept 1990
41 Gilly Interview, the morning of July 21, 1995
42 *Mémoires d'un dinosaure trotskyste* (Paris 1999)

## EPILOGUE

1. 'What exists cannot be true', *New Left Review* 64, July-August 2010
2. For instance, *SDS* 100, 1985, page 31, a review of Rodolphe Prager, *Les congrès de la IVe internationale*
3. As reported by his nephew in an email 6 January 2021
4. Communication by email 13 September, 2020
5. 'A citizen of the world', *Kathimerini*, 20 February 1996
6. Adolfo Gilly, 'Ernest Mandel: Recuerdos del olvido (Memories from oblivion)', *Nexos*, December 1995. Published in Mexico. Savvas Michael told me how annoyed Pablo was with this narrow characterisation.
7. 'Trotsky's Orphans', *To Vima*, 19 November 1995
8. 'Le chaos', *SDS* 121, February 1992, pp 8-10
9. *To Vima*, 30 April 1995 pp A4-A5
10. Possibly his last letter to Ernest Mandel, July 1992

# NAMES INDEX

Please note: after the page number, 'ch' refers to the chapter number, and 'n' refers to the number of the endnote.

Abbas, Ferhat 100
Alexander, Robert 83, 349 *ch.3 n.3*, 350 *ch.4 n.30*
Alleg, Henri 177-178, 357 *ch.12 n.42*
Allende, Salvador 113, 240, 241-247, 342, 361 *ch.16 n.3*
Almeyra, Guillermo 141, 287, 327
Avot-Meyers, Pierre 3, 87, 103, 112, 185, 214, 221, 308, 354
Baader-Meinhof 266, 318
Badinter, Elisabeth 284-285
Bafaloukos, Spiros 3, 290
Bahro, Rudolf 263, 271
Baird, John 119, 139
Becket, James 221-223, 345, 360 *ch.13 n.31 & 32*
Becket, Maria 221-223, 271, 297, 345, 360 *ch.13 n.30*
Belkacem, Krim 238
Ben Bella, Ahmed 4, 88, 148-180, 184, 191, 207, 212-216, 236, 238, 239, 256. 258, 279, 290-292, 296, 300, 319, 328-329, 356 *ch.11 n.24*, 356 *ch.12 introduction*, 357 *ch.12 n.25*, 360 *ch.14 n.8*, 361 *ch.16 n.2*, 364 *ch.19, n.2*
Benn, Tony 4, 329
Benoits, Henri 85, 112
Benoits, Clara 85, 112
Bensaid, Daniel 326
Bleibtreu, Marcel 329
Bösiger, André 208
Botsaris, Dimou Markus 317-319
Boudaoud, Mansour 99, 101

Boudaoud, Omar 99, 101
Boumediene, Houari 150-152, 168-169, 176-179, 206, 212, 214, 215, 238
Bourdet, Claude 90, 113, 119, 319
Bourdet, Yvon 8-9
Bouteflika, Abdelaziz 176
Braslawski, Lucien 32, 85
Brausch, Gabrielle 44
Broué, Pierre 37, 263, 348 *ch.2 n.13*, 349 *ch.4 n.8*, 350 *ch.4 n.25*, 353 *ch.6 n.11*
Brun, Frederic 279
Bucholz, Mathieu 44-45
Cabral, Amilcar 191
Cammelbeeck, George 116, 139
Cannon, James 24, 56, 77-79, 144
Carvalho, Otelo S de 187, 188, 257, 258, 191-193, 296, 362 *ch.17 n.10 & 11*, 364 *ch.19 n. 3, 6 & 7*
Castoriadis, Cornelius 59, 62
Castro, Fidel 134, 136, 141, 152, 156, 166-167, 177, 213, 215-216, 224,
Chapelle, Albert 44
Chen, Duxiu (Tu-Hsiu) 25, 348 *ch.3 n.2*
Clarke, George 77
Cleaver, Eldridge 239-240
Cliff, Tony 62
Cochran, Bert 77
Cohen, René 32
Craipeau, Yvan 39, 40, 43, 85, 113, 334, 350 *ch.4 n.20*
'Curtis, Harry' 281

Dalmas, Louis 40
De Beauvoir, Simone 68, 90, 112, 113, 116, 127, 214, 218, 239
Demazière, Albert 44
Deutscher, Isaac 21, 25, 26, 27, 118, 119, 200, 214, 224, 348 *ch.2 n.5*, 349 *ch.3 n.4 & 7*
Diovouniotis, Helene (Elly) v, 1, 2, 17, 19, 20, 21, 23, 24, 29-30, 32, 38-39, 45, 51, 55, 68, 87, 92, 100, 103, 105, 106-109, 111, 117, 139-140, 154, 178, 179, 182, 185, 186, 192, 207, 208, 221-222, 238-239, 241, 243, 247, 262, 269, 285, 293, 294, 295, 297, 301, 316, 317, 327, 329, 333, 336
Djebar, Assia 155, 177
Douady, Daniel 32-33
Dubcek, Alexander 194, 276

Fanon, Franz 148-150, 191
Ferares, Maurice 2, 112, 157, 193, 344, 347 *Prologue n.3*
Ferniot, Jean 230-231
Fiant, Michel 87, 89, 92, 201, 237, 279, 308
Fleming, Amalia 221, 223, 260
Foirier, Roger 87, 112, 179, 294
Fontaine, Louis 87, 104, 185
Frank, Pierre 89, 106-108, 110, 121, 122, 133, 141, 142, 192-193, 202, 294, 352 *ch.6 n.5*, 353 *ch.6 n.14*, 355 *ch.9 n.9*, 356 *ch.11 n.15*, 358 *ch.13 n.9*, 365 *ch.19 n.17*
Freney, Dennis 185, 201, 203
Freud, Sigmund 4, 9, 12, 117, 125, 126, 129, 283, 297, 316, 321, 330-332, 355
Freund, Hans David 21, 348 *ch.2 n.7*
Frias, Ismael 185

Gaddafi, Muammar 286-287, 292, 329, 338, 367 *ch.21 n.33*
Galanopoulos, Giannis 222
Gaulle, Charles de 3, 31, 37, 99, 108, 114, 118, 119, 209, 227, 229, 230, 264
Gilly, Adolfo 1, 108, 114-115, 122-123, 140-142, 159, 166, 169-170, 188, 201, 208, 215, 263, 287, 296, 323, 329, 333-334, 338, 339-341, 345, 347 *endnotes introduction*
Giotopoulos, Dimitris 11-12, 39
Glezos, Manolis 3, 319, 347 *Prologue n.5*
Gogornas, Christos 3, 296
Gomulka, Wladyslaw 93
Gorbachev, Mikhail Sergeyevich 232, 277-279, 286, 309, 364 *ch.18 n.24*
Gorz, André 204-205, 209, 224

Goudelis, Sotiros 3, 301
Grinblat, Jacques (Privas) 40, 87, 112, 217-218, 298-299, 365 *ch.19 n.26*
Grynbaum, Lucie Maiques 337, 361 *ch.16 n.2*
Guérin, Daniel 36, 214, 224, 284, 285, 290, 295, 365 *ch.19 n.20*
Guevara, Che 141, 167, 191, 210, 224, 339, 360 *ch.14 n.40*

Hansen, Joe 30, 120, 298
Harbi, Mohammed 15, 17, 85, 88, 89, 90, 107, 110, 148, 155-156, 158, 160, 162, 165-166, 168-169, 176, 178-180, 214, 236-237, 271, 290, 309, 344
Hardy, Jean-Pierre 322, 323, 325, 344
Haroun, Ali 109-110
Havel, Vaclav 308
Hegel, Georg Wilhelm Friedrich 13, 33, 68, 125, 331, 332
Heijenoort, Jean van 44, 56
Hic, Marcel 35, 37, 40,
Hitchens, Christopher 4, 62, 329
Ho Chi Minh, 156, 177
Hompe, Hubertus 11, 118-119
Hoxha, Enver 295, 300
Huberman, Leo 137
Hussein, Saddam 4, 300, 329
Jaruzelski, Wojciech 277
Joffé, Jules 32
Juquin, Pierre 279-280, 311

Karageorgiou, Marika 4, 170, 188, 270, 296, 298, 327, 333
Karageorgiou, Konstantinos 297
Karadzic, Radovan 328, 367 *ch.21 n.29*
Karamanlis, Constantine 252, 259, 261, 293
Kazantzakis, Helene 217
Kerr, Anne 139
Khider, Mohammed 238
Khrushchev, Nikita 77, 93, 133, 194-195, 199, 202, 211-212, 277
Klement, Rudolf 23, 76, 348 *ch.2 n.13*
Krivine, Alain 92, 319, 350
Kulukundis, Elias 221

Laperches, Georges 102
Leclerc, François 237, 308
Le Gre've, Pierre 102
Leiris, Michel 113, 119, 271

# NAMES INDEX

Lenin, Vladimir 14, 22, 25, 26, 30-31, 36, 59, 60, 61, 125,132, 134, 144, 153, 196, 205, 210, 224, 233, 250, 263, 278, 300, 311, 317, 326, 336, 339, 341

Leon, Abraham (real name Wajnsztok) 40, 45

Lequenne, Michel 74, 352 *ch.6 n.8*

Leschi, Didier 325

Livieratis, Dimitris 48, 102-11, 261, 296

Lumumba, Patrice 214, 324

Luxemburg, Rosa 25, 26, 46, 66, 134, 144, 168, 191, 205, 300, 307, 321, 339

Lyotard, Jean-François 62, 155

MacArthur, Douglas 65-66, 80

Maitan, Livio 78, 106-110, 121-123, 133, 142, 190, 192, 197, 201, 334, 351 *ch.5 n.16*

Mandela, Nelson 191, 258

Mangan, Sherry 54-55, 87, 298

Maniadakis, Konstantinos 19-20

Mandel, Ernest 40, 45, 48, 58, 60, 66, 68, 76, 77, 90, 106-109, 110, 114, 121, 122-123, 133, 140, 142-144, 192-193, 196, 199, 203, 204, 210, 240, 265, 293-294, 310, 319, 325-327, 334, 339-341

Mao, Zedong 60, 65, 74, 140, 156, 202, 229, 257, 262-263, 351 *ch.5 n.13*

Marquis, Gilbert 2, 64, 87, 107, 112, 196, 200, 201, 214, 279, 293, 308, 312, 313, 318, 327, 344

Marquis, Serge 287, 344, 354 *ch.8 n.6*, 356 *ch.12 n.1 & 2*, 357 *ch.12 n. 12 & 23*, 364 *ch.18 n.39 & 43*, 367 *ch.21 n.33*

Marx, Karl 33, 54, 69, 75, 125, 158, 159, 227, 233, 270, 274, 276, 280, 281, 282, 283, 294, 296, 298, 299, 300, 314, 316, 317, 321, 332, 339, 340, 341,

Matsas (Michael-), Savvas 2, 3, 345, 267

'Maurin, David' 1, 2, 14, 236, 238, 337, 342, 344

Melnik, Constantin 101

Mercader, Ramon 30

Mercier, Marcel 102

Merleau-Ponty, Maurice 90

Messali, Hadj 84-86, 88, 89

Mills, C. Wright 137

Milosevic, Slobodan 328

Minguet, Simonne 3, 32, 79, 85, 87, 89, 112, 185, 201, 214, 349, *ch.3 n.13*

Mitsotakis, Constantine 221

Mladic, Ratko 328

Modlik, Franz (aka Lerze) 142, 295

Mokhtefi, Elaine 239-240

Monath, Martin (aka Paul Widelin) 38-40, 349 *ch.4 n.11*

Moneta, Jakob 87, 331

Moreno, Hugo 3, 141, 271

Morrow, Felix 56

Najman, Maurice 279, 306-315, 325

Najman, Charly 187

Nasser, Gamal 97, 152, 160, 166, 177, 215, 241, 245

Neto, Agostinho 190

Noutsos, Panagiotis 3, 331

Ó Brádaigh, Ruairi 271

Oeldrich, Albert 103-104, 110-11, 114, 118-120

Origlass, Nick 144

Pablo, Michel *see chapter outlines* pp 373-376

Papandreou, Andreas 3, 221, 223, 224, 252, 259-261, 297

Papandreou, Georges 3

Papandreou, Margaret 4, 328

Papatakis, Nikos 222, 271

Pinochet, Augusto 246

Ponchaud, François 267

Posadas, Juan (Homero Cristalli) 82, 113, 122-123, 138, 140-141, 142, 143, 144, 196, 294

Pouliopoulos, Pantelis 13-15, 20, 45, 223, 296, 297, 301

Prager, Rodolphe 40, 43, 45, 349 *ch.3 n.11 & 23*, 352 *ch.6 n.4*, 367 *ch. 6 n.2*

Premtaj, Sadik 295, 300, 365 *ch.19 n. 22*

Protagoras 264, 332

Raphailidis, Vasilis 293

Raptis, Michalis *see chapter outlines* pp 373-376

Ravelli, Michel 87

Rein, Heinrich 51

Reiss, Ignace 21-22

Riva, Danielle 344, 355 *ch.10 n. 11*

Roberto, Holden 190, 198-201, 359 *ch.13 n.20*

Rousset, David 172-173, 186, 209

Roussos, Christos 292-293, 365 *ch.19 n.10*

Santen, Sal 82, 103, 107-109, 111-112, 116, 118, 120, 122, 139, 141, 143-144, 156-157, 184, 191, 192, 193, 196, 214, 354 *ch.8 n.14 & 17*, 354 *ch.9 n.5*, 355 *ch.11 n. 8-14 n.28 n.29*

Sartre, Jean-Paul 68, 90, 112, 113, 116, 214, 217, 218, 239
Schlüter, Otto 101
Schneeweiss, Helmut 11, 118
Sedov, Leon 22-23
Sedova, Natalia 62, 92, 94, 119
Seidenfeld, Barbara 44
Serand, Patrick 308, 309, 314
Shachtman, Max 59
Sintomer, Yves 306, 309, 314, 344
Sneevliet, Henk 21, 141, 191
Solzhenitsyn, Aleksandr 194, 268
Soulas, Mitsos 12, 289, 348 *ch.1 n.1*
Souzin, Henri 32
Spinoza 118, 297, 332
Spoulber, Nicolas 39, 40, 45
Stalin, Josef 11, 21, 22, 23, 26, 29, 30, 31, 36, 47, 48-49, 60, 61, 62, 63, 76-78, 92, 132, 194, 197, 250, 286, 302, 323, 327, 341
Starmer, Keir 281, 307
Stinas, Agis 11, 13, 14, 294, 296, 365 *ch.19 n.24*
Schwartz, Laurent 90, 113, 119, 218
Sweezy, Paul 137, 225

Tresso, Pietro 44
Trotsky, Leon 11, 14, 20, 21, 22, 23, 24, 25, 26, 27, 29, 30-31, 36, 37, 44, 47, 50. 51, 52, 56, 61-62, 69, 92, 119, 122, 128, 132-134, 144, 153, 168, 205, 224, 233, 249, 263, 283, 286, 296, 300, 302, 317, 324, 326, 339, 340, 341
Truman, Harry 79
Tzimas, Andreas 49, 233

Uhl, Peter 308

Velouchiotis, Aris 49, 233
Vereeken, Georges 324, 366 *ch.21 n.22*
Vitsoris, Georges 11, 32, 40
Vuscovic, Pedro 241, 244

Wald, Alan 27
Walesa, Lech 277
Wolf, Erwin 21

Zahouane, Hocine 179, 214, 236, 237, 290
Zborowski, Mark (aka Etienne) 22
Zeller, Fred 39
Zilliacus, Konni 119
Zwart, Joop 11, 119

## CHAPTER OUTLINES

### PROLOGUE **A DEATH IN ATHENS** 1996

A well-dressed Greek suffers a heart attack on stylish Kolonaki Square in Athens. He is Michalis Raptis, aka Michel Pablo, or as one conservative outlet describes him, 'our most courteous revolutionary'. Obituaries appear on the front pages of local newspapers and feature in radio and TV news. *Le Monde* and the *Guardian* carry obituaries. At his funeral tributes are delivered by Greek and European comrades, the Greek prime minister sends his regrets, anarchist bank robbers and police ministers rub shoulders, and ambassadors from 'revolutionary' or 'outlaw' regimes crowd the chapel. The remarkable odyssey of this cosmopolitan Greek started 85 years earlier on another fabled Mediterranean shore. *Pp 1-5*

### CHAPTER 1 **IN THE BEGINNING WAS TOLSTOY** 1911-1936

Early life and dream-like childhood of Michalis Raptis in Alexandria, Cairo and Crete. The literary activities and 'religious' Tolstoyan interests of his youth. University in Athens and entry into leftist and labour politics – from the 'Archeio-Marxists' with their semi-mystical guru to 'Spartacus' and its polymath leader, Pantelis Pouliopoulos. Forges friendships that will last decades. *Pp 6-16*

### CHAPTER 2 **PRISON, ELLY AND EXILE** 1937-1938

The advent of the Metaxas military dictatorship in Greece. He is arrested and sentenced to a prison island, where he is re-united with a wealthy and radical Hélène (Elly) Diovouniotis. After his transfer to a prison-fortress, contracts TB. Release and exile to Switzerland and Paris where he helps organise the Trotskyist Fourth International. *Pp 17-23*

### CHAPTER 3 **DANGEROUS LIAISONS** 1938-1942

In Paris and elsewhere Stalin's secret police are murdering leading Trotskyists. He attends the founding conference of the Fourth International, inspired and led initially by Leon Trotsky. At the conference he raises two issues – the role of the peasantry and the centrality of democracy in any transition to socialism. At the outbreak of war he flees (temporarily) Paris. He is gravely ill with TB and Elly manages his escape from occupied Paris to a sanitorium on the Swiss border. *Pp 24-33*

### CHAPTER 4 **PABLO'S WAR** 1943-1945

Recovered from TB, he returns to Paris. He now takes on the nom de guerre 'Michel Pablo'. He joins the Trotskyist underground resistance – publishing an illegal newspaper and helping organise fraternisation and dissent among the German troops. Reorganises and unites French and western European Trotskyists, and prepares for the expected end-of-the-war revolutionary wave. *Pp 34-49*

## CHAPTER 5 REVOLUTION WILL HAPPEN (BUT ELSEWHERE) 1946-1950

Disappointment follows the war. He travels to Greece but the revolutionary moment has passed and he realises that Trotsky's prediction of a wave of European revolutions after the war will not happen. Dawning awareness of the extent and significance of the colonial revolution. Disagreements with Natalia Sedova (Trotsky's widow), Cornelius Castoriadis and others over the nature of the Soviet bloc. Understands the significance of the Yugoslav split with Moscow but underestimates the strength of the recovery of European capitalism. *Pp 50-67*

## CHAPTER 6 MOHAMMED MUST GO TO THE MOUNTAIN 1951-1954

Pablo becomes convinced that World War III will break out between, on the one hand, the colonial revolutionaries, Communist Parties and the Soviet bloc, and on the other, an imperialist coalition led by Washington. To overcome their isolation he proposes the Trotskyists needed to 'enter' major workers parties in each country but 'orthodox' Trotskyists in France, then US and Britain, denounce Pablo and split away. . The reach of the Fourth International extends into Latin America. Pablo slowly revises his apocalyptic prognoses. With the death of Stalin he anticipates the rapid breakdown of the worst of the 'communist' dictatorships. First contacts with the Algerian rebels. Reconciles with Natalia Sedova. His signature concern with 'autogestion' or self-managed socialism now appears. *Pp 68-82*

## CHAPTER 7 THE ALGERIAN REVOLUTION 1954-1962

At the outbreak of the Algerian war/revolution in November 1954 Pablo meets FLN emissaries, promises support and with a small team sets up a secret printery, forges ID cards and passports, provides transport and hideouts, and ferries suitcases stuffed with money to Switzerland. Sponsors Free Algeria committees. Welcomes the Hungarian uprising as harbinger of a genuinely democratic socialism. Attempts to introduce feminist and youth concerns into the Fourth International and advocates a bolder 'entrist' approach. *Pp 83-98*

## CHAPTER 8 THE ARMS FACTORY IN MOROCCO 1958-60

With the Algerians facing defeat and the French secret police assassinating their arms dealers, Pablo establishes a secret factory in Morocco to manufacture French Army-issue submachine guns. Conflicts in the Fourth International leadership break out over 'entrism' and Algeria – exacerbated by the presence of an outspoken Elly. Pablo and Sal Santen arrested in Amsterdam on charges of forging passports and French francs, and buying and exporting arms-making machinery. Pablo's supporters initiate a vigorous international campaign to free Pablo and Santen. It involves Sartre, de Beauvoir, Isaac Deutscher, Natalia Sedova, Latin American cultural figures, and an array of British Labour MPs, but Mandel, Frank and Maitan hang back. *Pp 99-115*

## CHAPTER 9 THE TRIAL OF PABLO AND SAL SANTEN 1960-1961

Pablo and Santen are eventually brought to trial and use proceedings to denounce French colonialism and champion the Algerian cause. A distinguished array of European intellectuals and politicians appear as defence witnesses. The week-long trial is complete with demonstrations inside and outside the court. Guilty verdicts but only a 15-month sentence. Prior to the trial and with Pablo facing a long stretch in prison, the remaining leaders of the Fourth International jockey to take over the leadership. *Pp 116-123*

## CHAPTER 10 PRISON WRITINGS 1960-1961

Behind bars Pablo writes essays on the liberation of women, dialectics in Plato, crime and punishment, and the 'revolutionary' late Freud. The liberation of women essay anticipates a mass women's movement for the total liberation of women (sexual and cultural as well as economic) and insists that for revolutionaries 'the personal is political'. Reads Marx's *Grundisse*, reshapes his view of the evolution of capitalism. Sketches out the revolutionary Marxist response to the Cuban and Algerian revolutions – insisting on the relevance of classical 4th and 5th century Athens. *Pp 124-138*

## CHAPTER OUTLINES

### CHAPTER 11 **JOINING THE WRETCHED OF THE EARTH 1961-1963**

After his release from prison in September 1961 he is granted political asylum in Morocco. The provisional Algerian government in Tunisia commissions him to write a report on agrarian reform. Algeria wins independence in July 1962. Pablo travels through Algeria to settle in Algiers in September. Meets Ben Bella and Boumediene, the leaders of independent Algeria. Summons his closest supporters to Algiers to join him. Differences, both personal and political, confirmed with the new leaders of the Fourth International. *Pp 139-157*

### CHAPTER 12 **PABLO'S WAGER: ATHENS IN ALGIERS 1963-1965**

Now settled in Algiers as advisor to Ben Bella (his first ever paid employment) and the FLN Left. Writes the new self-management decrees of March 1963 systematising the workers' takeover of farms and factories abandoned by their European owners in the wake of independence. Drafts agrarian reform legislation and new direct democracy structures but Ben Bella equivocates. Algiers becomes the 'Mecca for revolutionaries', including briefly Che Guevara. Domestically, conflict between the secular, democratic socialists and the Islamic, state-socialist, army coalition intensifies. An army coup overthrows Ben Bella and the coup leader denounces Pablo who manages to escape to Switzerland. *Pp 158-180*

### CHAPTER 13 **PARALLEL DEFEATS (AND ROSA) 1964-1965**

Escape from Algeria is followed by 'exclusion' from the Fourth International for 'indiscipline' – although the indiscipline amounts to public differences over the majority's critical support for Mao in the Sino-Soviet dispute, Roberto Holden in Angola, the importance of de-Stalinisation and the centrality of 'self-management' to socialism. It is complicated by the bad faith generated during the arrest and imprisonment of Pablo and Santen. Pablo embraces his new political and ideological freedom. *Pp 189-206*

### CHAPTER 14 **'THE GYPSY YEARS' 1965-1967**

Pablo has no fixed address and becomes more cosmopolitan than ever. Campaigns for Vietnam independence including the attempt to raise an 'international brigade', as in Spain in 1936-39. Pablo develops ideas about the new dynamism of advanced capitalism and its revolutionary potential, especially around the possibilities of 'self-management'. The plan to rescue Ben Bella from prison betrayed by Castro. Involved in the resistance to the military junta in Greece. Establishes his first contacts with the new Palestinian liberation movement. *Pp 207-225*

### CHAPTER 15 **PARIS, PRAGUE AND PALESTINE 1968-1971**

Pablo is in Paris for the May events of 1968 – more revolutionary than the Paris Commune of 1871 in his view. Follows developments and visits Czechoslovakia during the 'Prague Spring' and before the Soviet-led invasion to suppress it. These uprisings in the West and East convince him that the central revolutionary aspiration of the era is for a 'self-managed' socialism. Deepens involvement with the Palestinians and warns of the Jordanian attack of 'Black September' 1970. Also visits Cuba. *Pp 226-235*

### CHAPTER 16 **CLOSE ESCAPES AND CHILE 1970-1973**

Organises a number of successful escapes from Algeria. After the victory of Salvador Allende in the Chilean presidential elections, Pablo is invited by members of the Allende government to Chile to consult on the development of workers self-management which is spontaneously spreading in the country. He works to cement an alliance between the Socialist Party left-wing, the Christian Left and the Castroite MIR. Extraordinary times but a bloody denouement. He is temporarily absent from the country promoting his book on Chile when the army coup occurs but Elly is caught there and must escape. Once again fortune favours Elly and Pablo. *Pp 236-252*

## CHAPTER 17 **THE TURN TO EUROPE 1974-1980**

Pablo is in Lisbon after 'the revolution of the carnations' occurs in April 1974. He strikes up a friendship with the left-wing army captains – particularly, Otelo de Carvahlo – and renews links with the representatives of the Angolan and Mozambican independence movements. In Greece in 1974 the colonels are ejected and Greece reverts to parliamentary democracy. Pablo returns to find himself hailed as a legendary Greek revolutionary and the main centre-left dailies in Athens engage him as a regular columnist. Meanwhile his involvement with French politics continues and he elaborates and pursues his ideas for a revolutionary socialist strategy in developed capitalist societies. Incorporates awareness of the ecological crisis. Consolidates his ideas on the bureaucratic regimes as obstacles to socialism (accepts that Natalia Sedova was right 30 years before). Responds to the rise of terrorism in western Europe and the Pol Pot regime in Cambodia. *Pp 253-268*

## CHAPTER 18 **END OF AN ERA 1980s**

Pablo leaves behind many of the old schemas and certainties and defends and refines his Marxism. Embraces new ideas about the revolutionary subject, welcomes Polish Solidarity and Gorbachev, re-evaluates the utopian disposition, further develops his concerns to include the anti-nuclear movements and casts a doubtful eye over the rise of the German Greens. New supporters include (briefly) a young Keir Starmer, now current right-wing leader of the British Labour Party. *Pp 269-288*

## CHAPTER 19 **THE FATE OF FRIENDS AND COMRADES 1980s**

Pablo has for decades been a member of a global community of extraordinary revolutionaries and ex-revolutionaries. As he prepares for his own 'departure', he farewells many friends and comrades of the past 50 years of revolutionary activity, heals broken friendships and expands his circle of close friends and comrades, as well as continuing his involvement in the politics of France, Portugal, Poland, Palestine, Algeria and Greece. *Pp 289-303*

## CHAPTER 20 **THE LAST BATTLE: HOW GREEN IS MY PARTY? 1988-89**

During the 1980s a new cohort of young *pablistes* joins his organisation. Free of many of the shibboleths and loyalties of the past and attracted to Pablo because of his ideological radicalism, these new adherents clash with him over his continued insistence of the centrality of the labour movement and its parties. This conflict with his young supporters in France, Britain, Italy and Germany centres on the significance of the Green parties. Pablo is at his best and worst in this final conflict. *Pp 304-315*

## CHAPTER 21 **A NEW ERA: THE FINAL YEARS 1990-1996**

Continues with his weekly columns, publishing and conference appearances – increasingly peppered with allusions to classical Athens and Greek poets. He has few regrets about the fall of the bureaucratic states of the Eastern bloc but decides that a circling of the wagons of surviving Marxist currents is called for. Reconciles with Ernest Mandel and temporarily rejoins the Fourth International. Accused of being the secret leader of the 17 November terrorist group. Organises an international conference for busting the US sanctions on Iraq and opposes the break-up of Yugoslavia, including support for the Serbs. Nurses Elly who suffers from dementia, and records his final memoirs. An honorary doctorate is bestowed two months before he dies. Has a heart attack during his regular morning coffee with friends on Kolonaki Square in Athens. A quasi-state funeral follows. *Pp 316-335*

## EPILOGUE **A PROPHET OUT OF TIME**

Reflections from various observers on the meaning and significance of Pablo's life, his emancipatory Marxism and key ideas, principally on the new revolutionary subject, the Third World, internationalism, utopianism and imagination, the need for a new *Capital* and the 'self-managed' republic. *Pp 336-343*

Milton Keynes UK
Ingram Content Group UK Ltd.
UKHW020806200224
438156UK00007B/252